THE COMPLETE WORKS OF
CHRISTOPHER MARLOWE

Despite the modern fascination with Marlowe, and in particular with his *Dr. Faustus*, there has been no edition of his works which not only gives them in the original spelling—with full textual apparatus—but also supplies a detailed commentary. The Oxford English Texts *Complete Works of Christopher Marlowe*, edited in three volumes by Roma Gill, supplies the need for a fully annotated scholarly treatment of the works.

The present volume brings together the works which were in some measure translations: *Lucans First Booke*, *All Ovids Elegies*, *Dido Queene of Carthage*, and *Hero and Leander*—three early works with one of the latest; and one play with three non-dramatic pieces. The volume is prefaced with an essay on 'Marlowe and Translation'. Each individual work also has its own introduction, containing both literary and textual comment and explanation. A new theory of the sequence and authority of the early editions underlies the texts of the *Elegies*; and *Hero and Leander* is for the first time presented in a critical edition without the additions of 1598, so that Marlowe's poem can now be properly evaluated.

The English verse of these translations is compared with the Latin and Greek originals, and Marlowe's skill both as a translator and as a poet is discussed; difficult expressions and obscure allusions are fully explained in the commentary.

ROMA GILL is a freelance writer and lecturer; her previous editions include *The Plays of Christopher Marlowe* (Oxford, 1971) and eight texts in the Oxford School Shakespeare Series. She was formerly a General Editor of the New Mermaid Texts (for which she edited three plays), and Reader in English Literature at the University of Sheffield.

THE COMPLETE WORKS
OF
CHRISTOPHER MARLOWE

EDITED BY
ROMA GILL

VOLUME I
All Ovids Elegies, Lucans First Booke,
Dido Queene of Carthage,
Hero and Leander

CLARENDON PRESS · OXFORD
1987

Oxford University Press, Walton Street, Oxford OX2 6DP
Oxford New York Toronto
Delhi Bombay Calcutta Madras Karachi
Petaling Jaya Singapore Hong Kong Tokyo
Nairobi Dar es Salaam Cape Town
Melbourne Auckland

and associated companies in
Beirut Berlin Ibadan Nicosia

Oxford is a trade mark of Oxford University Press

Published in the United States
by Oxford University Press, New York

British Library Cataloguing in Publication Data
Marlowe, Christopher, 1564–1593
The complete works of Christopher Marlowe.
—(Oxford English texts)
Vol. 1: All Ovids elegies, Lucans first
booke, Dido Queene of Carthage, Hero and Leander
I. Title II. Gill, Roma
822'.3 PR2660
ISBN 0–19–811878–3

Library of Congress Cataloging in Publication Data
Marlowe, Christopher, 1564–1593.
The complete works of Christopher Marlowe.
(Oxford English texts)
Includes bibliographical references.
Contents: v. 1. All Ovids elegies. Lucans first
booke. Dido Queene of Carthage. Hero and Leander.
I. Gill, Roma. II. Title.
PR2661.G5 1987 822'.3 86–11354
ISBN 0–19–811878–3 (v. 1)

Set by Eta Services (Typesetters) Ltd, Beccles, Suffolk
Printed in Great Britain
at the University Printing House, Oxford
by David Stanford
Printer to the University

For
F.W.L.
sine quo non

ACKNOWLEDGEMENTS

Tot hominibus tantum debetur. There are the institutions: the University of Sheffield granted me two periods of study-leave to work on this volume; and the final stages of preparation have been made easier with financial assistance from the Leverhulme Trust. Libraries (and library staff) have been generous with their help: I should mention especially the Bodleian Library at Oxford, the University Library at Cambridge, the British Library, and the library of the University of Sheffield. Publishers have been patient—above all Dan Davin of Oxford University Press, who has been a constant comfort ever since he first supplied the impetus and inspiration for the undertaking. It would take too long to list the Sheffield colleagues who have willingly answered the many questions that baffled me: academics from disciplines as varied as classics, biblical studies, space physics, electrical engineering, and computer sciences. But I have been particularly grateful for the scholarship (and time) so freely given by Professor Norman Blake, of the Department of English Language.

My debts to my friends are innumerable; I know that they will not expect (or even wish) to be mentioned by name, and so I give my 'thanks to all at once, and to each one'—except that I record exceptional gratitude, for exceptional friendship, to Mrs Sandra Stork.

And I must also make reference to the skills of members of the medical profession, singling out Dr D. J. K. White, but thinking mainly of Dr F. Winston Leigh, to whom a grateful patient now dedicates her book.

R.G.

CONTENTS

LIST OF FIGURES

INTRODUCTION

Marlowe and the Art of Translation[1]

THERE are four major works in this first volume of Marlowe's
*opera: All Ovids Elegies; Lucans First Booke; Dido Queene of
Carthage;* and *Hero and Leander.* Three early pieces are joined
with the late poem *Hero and Leander;* and three non-dramatic ones
are printed together with the play of *Dido.* Linked by neither time
nor form, the works find their common denominator in the fact
that all are translations from a classical language into English. But
the translations are not all of the same kind. In the preface to a
collection of Ovid's *Epistles* by divers hands, the poet Dryden,
meditating on the art of translation, recognized three separate
methods, which he termed 'metaphrase', 'paraphrase', and 'imitation'.[2] This division serves admirably to distinguish Marlowe's
translations from each other. 'First, that of metaphrase, or turning
an author word by word, and line by line, from one language into
another.' This, of course, is the technique we learned at school
when we began to study a foreign language, and it was
immediately adequate for the first simple sentences that we
translated. But Ovid's *Amores* are far from simple, and Marlowe
must have learned—very quickly—the truth that Dryden was later
to articulate: 'Tis almost impossible to translate verbally, and well,
at the same time.' Two lines from Elegy III. v illustrate the
shortcomings of the metaphrastic method. Ovid's lover recalls the
amorous adventures of various river-deities, including Alpheus,
whose love for the nymph Arethusa caused him to flow through
many distant lands:

> quid? non Alpheon diversis currere terris
> virginis Arcadiae certus adegit amor.

---

[1] The substance of this introduction is taken from a paper read to the First International
Conference of the Marlowe Society of America (Sheffield, 1983); it was subsequently
published in *A Poet and a Filthy Play-maker: Essays on Christopher Marlowe*, edited by
Kenneth Friedenreich, Roma Gill, and Constance Kuriyama (New York, 1986).

[2] 'Preface to the Translation of Ovid's *Epistles* (1680)', in *Essays of John Dryden*, ed. W.
P. Ker (Oxford, 1926), i. 237.

Marlowe returns word for word, in almost the order of Ovid's inflected language:

> What? not *Alpheus* in strange lands to runne,
> Th'*Arcadian* Virgins constant love hath wunne?   (29–30)

Such infelicities are not uncommon; but they should not be allowed to diminish the magnitude of Marlowe's achievement in this translation of the *Amores*, or its implications for his personal development and for his contribution to the tradition of English poetry.

For Marlowe himself, the *Elegies* (in both form and substance) led to *Hero and Leander*, with its triumphant mastery of verse which is both erotic and satiric. For subsequent English poets, the *Elegies* introduced a new tone—a declared attitude to sexual love that was very far from the idealized lyricism of Petrarch. And the rhymed pentameter couplet, in which Marlowe rendered the Latin elegiac metre, gave impetus to later poets such as John Donne when they extended the range of the elegiac genre in English literature.[3]

However, one must admit that the technique of metaphrase is hopelessly inadequate for the *Amores*, in which the most accomplished of the Latin lyric poets is at his brilliant best with this inflected language. And it is not only linguistic craftsmanship that makes the elegiac Ovid an unsuitable companion for Marlowe at what appears to be a very early stage in his career: the Roman poet has a sophistication which is still foreign to the English writer—although it seems to have become native to the author by the time he wrote *Hero and Leander*. The Earl of Roscommon (when translation had become a finer art) could offer this advice to a novice:

> Examine how your Humour is inclin'd,
> And which the Ruling Passion of your Mind;
> Then seek a Poet who *your* way do's bend,
> And Chuse an Author as you chuse a friend:
> United by this Sympathetic Bond,
> You grow Familiar, Intimate and Fond;
> Your Thoughts, your Words, your Stiles, your Souls agree,
> No longer his Interpreter, but He.[4]

---

[3] See my essay '*Musa Iocosa Mea*: thoughts on the *Elegies*', in *John Donne: Essays in Celebration*, ed. A. J. Smith (London, 1972), pp. 47–72.

[4] *An Essay on Translated Verse* (1684); cited in Charles Tomlinson, Introduction to *The Oxford Book of Verse in English Translation* (1980), p. xii.

Marcus Annaeus Lucanus seems to have been such a 'friend' for Marlowe, whose metaphrastic rendering of *Lucans First Booke* recognizes in the Roman poem a grim relevance to the Elizabethan age. Marlowe responds to Lucan's formal rhetoric with a dramatic vigour that surely adumbrates the much-praised 'mighty line'[5] which develops into *Tamburlaine the Great*.

Certainly, metaphrase is now mastered; and in the writing of *Dido Queene of Carthage* Marlowe essays what Dryden described as the second kind of translation:

The second way is that of paraphrase, or translation with latitude, where the author is kept in view by the translator, so as never to be lost, but his words are not so strictly followed as his sense; and that too is admitted to be amplified, but not altered.

The story of Dido and Aeneas occupies Book IV of the *Aeneid*, but Marlowe—moving now with greater ease and confidence in his Latin text—picks up and transposes details from the first two books to serve his dramatic intentions. With considerable 'latitude' he turns the epic narrative into dramatic action: Anna and Iarbus are developed into substantial characters, and Marlowe invents the sub-plot (with its ludicrous climax) of Anna's love for her sister's rejected suitor. But except for this interpolation, Marlowe is true to his original: Virgil is always 'kept in view'.

Virgil's Aeneas is described by the epithet *pius*, and by nothing else. Marlowe creates a character capable of provoking contradictory responses from twentieth-century critics, who see him variously as Elizabethan hero or medieval villain, a man of high visionary instincts—or gross moral turpitude. Reactions to Dido are simpler. The problem here for Virgil's translator was of a different kind from that posed by the characterization of Aeneas; there was less scope for the dramatist's own inventiveness and—for that very reason—there was a greater challenge. Although Aeneas is indeed the protagonist of the epic poem, he is ousted from this position for the duration of Book IV of the *Aeneid*, where Virgil 'creates within an epic of grand historical scope the intimate tragedy of a woman in love'.[6] Marlowe reacts to Virgil's challenge with amazing confidence, creating (in Act III, scene iv, for instance) a broken verse form whose movement enacts the

[5] The famous phrase is that of Ben Jonson.
[6] Reuben A. Brower, *Hero and Saint: Shakespeare and the Graeco-Roman Heroic Tradition* (Oxford and New York, 1971), 48.

narrative poet's simple description: *incipit effari, mediaque in voce resistit* (iv. 76). Yet there are a few moments when he appears to be defeated. The parting of Dido and Aeneas, when the hero obeys the divine injunction to sail away from Carthage in search of a new world, is conducted almost entirely in the original Latin—so that as Dido attempts to dissuade her lover, Aeneas replies to her lamentations with the dignity of

> *Desine meque tuis incendere teque querelis.*
> *Italiam non sponte sequor.*   (v. i. 139–40)

To my mind, however, this is not evasion: the remarkable patterning of the first of these lines is possible only in an inflected language; and this is followed by the simplicity of one of the most famous half-lines in world literature. For such poetry, there is no translation; and Marlowe is brave to resist any impulse to tamper with it. Furthermore, since *Dido Queene of Carthage* translates epic into drama, there is no need for translation when the epic poem itself becomes dramatic.

After the 'paraphrase' of Virgil in *Dido Queene of Carthage*, Marlowe abandoned translation for a few years to write his plays for the public theatre. When he returned to the art—perhaps when the theatres were closed during the plague months of 1592–3—it was to attempt what Dryden recognized as the third kind of translation: 'imitation'.

> I take imitation of an author . . . to be an endeavour of a later poet to write like one who has written before him, on the same subject; that is, not to translate his words, or to be confined to his sense, but only to set him as a pattern, and to write as he supposes that author would have done, had he lived in our age and in our country.

Marlowe's *Hero and Leander* can be considered as a translation of the Greek poem on the same subject by Musaeus only if 'translation' is used in Dryden's sense of 'imitation'. Marlowe's reference to his predecessor (or 'pattern') is significant:

> Amorous *Leander*, beautifull and yoong,
> (Whose tragedie divine *Musaeus* soong).   (51–2)

Musaeus sang the *tragedy* of the two lovers; but it was 'a diviner Muse than he, Kit Marlowe'[7] who sang their *comedy*.

---

[7] *Nashe's Lenten Stuffe* (1599); McKerrow, iii. 195.

Marlowe's *Hero and Leander* is almost twice as long as Musaeus' poem. Its simple story is laid out in formal rhetorical schemes, and is richly embroidered with classical allusions—the work, one could say, of another *grammatikos*. It is also comic—and the comedy of idea is underlined and reinforced by the form of the verse: the rhymed couplets that Marlowe had experimented with in his early translation of Ovid's *Amores*. There are undertones of ironic pathos in the gentle reminders of the lovers' well-known tragic ending, but Marlowe leaves his two characters when their love has reached its climax—so that the poem ends with a glorious fulfilment which is the apotheosis of comedy. It does not need the extra lines—more than 1300 of them—which George Chapman added to the 818 lines of the first quarto publication in order to bring the lovers to their deaths and make the poem conform to the narrative of Musaeus. Dryden's third kind of translation, 'imitation' of the original author, permits—and even encourages—freedom of the sort exercised by Marlowe.

References and Quotations

EDITIONS OF MARLOWE'S WORKS

Each section of this volume carries its own bibliography, but the major editions of Marlowe's works, cited by the name of the editor, are listed here to avoid unnecessary repetition:

Bowers   *The Complete Works of Christopher Marlowe*, ed. Fredson Bowers (Cambridge, 1974).

Bullen   *The Works of Christopher Marlowe*, ed. A. H. Bullen (London, 1885).

Cunningham   *The Works of Christopher Marlowe*, ed. F. Cunningham (London, 1870).

Maclure   *The Poems of Christopher Marlowe*, ed. Millar Maclure (London, 1968).

Martin   *Marlowe's Poems*, ed. L. C. Martin (London, 1931).

Robinson   *The Works of Christopher Marlowe*, ed. G. Robinson (London, 1826).

Tucker Brooke   *The Works of Christopher Marlowe*, ed. C. F. Tucker Brooke (Oxford, 1910).

The present edition is used for the works contained in this volume. Quotations from *Dr Faustus* are taken from the Parallel Texts Edition prepared by W. W. Greg (Oxford, 1960; reprinted 1968). For Marlowe's other plays, the edition used is that of Fredson Bowers (Cambridge, 1974).

Quotations from the works of authors frequently cited throughout this volume are taken from the following editions:

Nashe   *The Works of Thomas Nashe*, ed. R. B. McKerrow
            (Oxford, 1904), with corrections and supplementary notes
            by F. P. Wilson (Oxford, 1958; reprinted 1966); referred
            to in the text as McKerrow.
Ovid   *Ovid's Metamorphoses*, trans. Arthur Golding (1567), ed.
            John Frederick Nims (New York, 1965).
Shakespeare The Riverside Edition, ed. G. Blakemore Evans *et al.*
            (Boston, 1974).

ALL OVIDS ELEGIES

General Introduction

FROM time to time in the *Amores* Ovid comments on the kind of poetry he is writing, and on the basic unit of his verse, a couplet consisting of a hexameter followed by a pentameter:

Let my first verse be sixe, my last five feete. (I. i. 31)

For English readers to feel the effect of this couplet, Coleridge described and enacted it:

In the hexameter rises the fountain's silvery column;
In the pentameter aye falling in melody back.
('The Ovidian Elegiac Metre described and exemplified')

The Roman poets met the challenge of the couplet in different ways. For all its apparent artificiality, in the hands of Propertius it became an instrument of sincerity, helping to create an impression of immediacy and deep feeling. For Ovid, however, it was yet another device for exhibiting his superb technical skill. The poems of the *Amores* are highly polished and sophisticated, probably representing what in the poet's view were the best of his works in this kind. He speaks at the outset of a selection:

We which were *Ovids* five bookes now are three,
For these before the rest preferreth he. (I. i. 1–2)

The brilliance of technique and the subtlety of idea and expression, unmistakable enough in the Latin, are not easily discerned through Marlowe's translations. English poetry knew no such measure as the Latin elegiac couplet, and Marlowe's first self-imposed task was to find an acceptable substitute. He chose the heroic couplet, itself not very widely used in the 1580s; as a result of his efforts in the *Elegies*, it became the accepted form for writing such non-lyrical love poems. But the effect of the English couplet could never be that of the Latin. Acutely self-aware, the Roman poets provide enough observations on their poetry for us to appreciate the effect they sought and to measure Marlowe's achievement against it. The Latin movement is a delicate one. Propertius speaks of his book that sounds so soft upon the tongue:

meus . . . mollis in ore liber (II. i. 2). Domitius Marsus in his funeral elegy on Tibullus laments that there will be none now to croon the soft songs of love: *ne foret aut elegis molles qui fleret amores*. And Ovid's strongest weapons as a lover are, paradoxically, the *blanditias elegosque levis* with their *lenia verba*:

> Toyes, and light Elegies my darts I tooke,
> Quickly soft words hard dores wide open strooke. (II. i. 21–2)

The elegy is always compared with martial poetry and with the epic. Ovid tells us that he was in fact preparing to write of military exploits in appropriate verse: 'With Muse upreard I meant to sing of Armes' (I. i. 5), when Love came upon him and, by docking his second line of one metrical foot, forced him to write love poetry. Propertius loyally explains that, if indeed he had the gift for writing heroic poetry, he would use it in praise of Caesar; but since this gift has been denied, he must instead tell of lovers' struggles on their narrow beds: *nos contra angusto versantes proelia lecto* (II. i. 45). From comments like these one begins to think of the Roman elegy and its couplet as very delicate creations; experience of the poems themselves shows the great variety of which the form is capable, and how it is suited to the inflected language. The English couplet, on the other hand, was a comparatively clumsy vehicle when Marlowe was using it for the *Elegies*; and its demands for rhyme led Marlowe into some very odd convolutions of meaning and syntax: in his translation of III. ii. 29–30, for example:

> Swift *Atalantas* flying legges like these,
> Wish in his hands graspt did *Hippomenes*.

Neither the delicacy of the Roman poets in general, nor the verbal dexterity of Ovid in particular, are to be looked for in Marlowe's translations of the *Amores*. Sometimes he reaches after Ovid's skill, but it always eludes him. The Ovidian balance of *multa supercilio vidi vibrante loquentes*, where the pivotal verb separates nouns from adjectival participles, can hardly be reproduced in an uninflected language, although Marlowe does his best with 'I sawe your nodding eye-browes much to speake.' (II. v. 15) He is more successful with the chiastic symmetry of II. iv. 39: *candida me capiet, capiet me flava puella*, which he translates as 'A white wench thralles me, so doth golden yellowe.' By way of compensation for these deficiencies, which are those of the English language as much

as those of the poet, Marlowe's *Elegies* at their best reproduce the
accents of the speaking voice, and set the voice's rhythms
dramatically against those of the couplet, in a manner that looks
forward to Donne. The variety which Ovid achieves by means of
rhetorical devices is equalled in Marlowe's poems by the variety of
conversational tone, since the nuances of the human voice are
infinitely greater than those of even the most highly developed art.

The individual talents of the Roman poets worked upon a mass
of very conventional material, and this is especially noticeable in
their use of legendary events and characters to illustrate their
themes. When, for example, Ovid is confronted by a small stream
which separates him from his mistress (III. v), he addresses it with
reminders of the fabled loves of mortals and rivers. In part this is
delight in the mythical world of gods and nymphs, but in part it is,
as A. W. Allen explains, the Roman poet's establishment of 'a
community of experience with his readers',[1] all of whom would
recognize the fiction and share in the poet's attitude to it. A
translator encounters difficulty here: first, the superficial difficulty
of making sure his readers can identify the references; and then the
more serious problem of·communicating the Roman feelings.
Marlowe is tactful in dealing with the first issue: where Ovid is
circumlocutory, Marlowe is straightforward. Ovid speaks, for
instance, of *vitis . . . repertor*, which Marlowe translates unam-
biguously as '*Bacchus*' (I. iii. 11). It is reasonable to suppose that
most, if not indeed all, of the myths to which Ovid refers would be
familiar to sixteenth-century English readers, and it is also
probable that they would have much the same attitudes towards
them as the Romans, although naturally diluted. But the situation
since then has changed: the amours of Jupiter and the metamorphosis of Philomela are no longer every schoolboy's stock-in-trade,
and it has seemed best to give in the notes a brief, but full, account
of each of the mythological references, thereby ensuring that the
poem as Ovid—and Marlowe—intended it is understood.

Editions of the *Amores* were frequent in the sixteenth century.
They differ considerably from modern texts, and Marlowe's
apparent mistranslations can often be accounted for by the
readings of a contemporary edition. It is not possible to isolate a

---

[1] 'Sunt Qui Propertium Malint', in *Critical Essays on Roman Literature: Elegy and Lyric*,
ed. J. P. Sullivan (1962), 146.

single text as Marlowe's source; those that I have seen are identical, and the Latin text used for these notes, a three-volume edition of *P. Ovidii Nasonis Opera* published by Plantin (Antwerp, 1575) was chosen more or less at random. When it has seemed necessary to record the readings of a modern edition of the *Amores*, that of E. J. Kenney (Oxford, 1961) has been used. Many commentaries on the *Amores* were available to Marlowe, but I cannot see that he made use of any of them; there are several occasions when a commentary would have helped him to make sense of a line with which he had difficulty.[2] For myself, I have occasionally found such a commentary valuable, and have made use of Dominicus' observations in *Publius Ovidii Nasonis Sulmonensis Poetae Opera* (Frankfurt, 1551). I have also referred on occasion to the Latin dictionary available to Marlowe, Thomas Cooper's *Thesaurus Linguae Romane et Britannicae* (1565) in the edition of 1578. These two reference books are referred to in the notes as, respectively, 'Dominicus' and 'Cooper'.

Textual Introduction

For all but ten of the *Elegies* the single source for Marlowe's translation of Ovid's *Amores* is the anonymously printed *ALL OVIDS ELEGIES* (STC 18931) which was probably published early in the seventeenth century.

ALL | OVIDS ELEGIES: | 3. BOOKES | By C. M. | Epigrams by J.D. | [type ornament] | *At Middlebourgh.*

8° A–F⁸ G⁴; not paginated.

Contents: A1 title, verso blank; A2–F3ᵛ text of Marlowe's 48 elegies and the version of 1. xv by B[en] I[onson] concluding 'FINIS'; F4–G4ᵛ text of Davies's 48 epigrams concluding 'FINIS. I.D.'

Three copies survive: those in the Bodleian and Huntington libraries are identical, but the one in the Dyce Collection of the Victoria and Albert Museum has three minor errors of printing (two on outer B and one on inner B), which point to a minimal

---

[2] For further discussion of this, see my 'Snakes Leape by Verse', in *Mermaid Critical Commentaries: Christopher Marlowe*, ed. Brian Morris (London, 1968), 135–50.

proof correction in the other two. The Bodleian copy, Mason AA 207, has been used as copy-text, and is referred to here (and in most other editions) as *Mason*. Of an earlier date than *Mason* are two selections of the poems, *Epigrammes and Elegies* by I.D. and C.M. One of these was almost certainly the book condemned by the Bishop of London and the Archbishop of Canterbury when on 1 June 1599 they ordered the public burning of a group of books which included 'Davyes Epigrams with Marlowes Elegyes'. The list of proscribed books was followed by the injunction 'That noe *Satyres* or *Epigrams* be printed hereafter', which suggests that ecclesiastical displeasure was occasioned by Davies's work rather than Marlowe's. In a Preface to his reprint of one of these texts in 1870, Charles Edmonds asserted that this selection of Marlowe's poems must have preceded the collection, since it bore the advertisement that here were '*CERTAINE*' elegies whilst *Mason* boasted '*ALL*' of them. This easy logic was rejected by Tucker Brooke, editing Marlowe's poems in 1910, whose view was that the text of the collection 'appears to be certainly the best and not improbably the oldest', whereas the two selections 'May equally well be cheap pirated reprints of such portions of the work as would find readiest acceptance among the vulgar'. This opinion of the sequence of texts and the principles of selection became the accepted one, repeated by both Martin and Maclure in their editions of the poems. Yet the selection cannot have been made solely in the interests of pornography. True, Elegy III. vi on temporary impotence is included, but so too is I. xv on the immortality of verse, which would have less appeal to the 'base conceipted witts [who] admire vilde things' (line 35). To me it seems far more likely that *Mason* is the third edition, and that the two selections represent the first two printings. One of these would have made Marlowe's version of I. xv available to Ben Jonson, whose revision was incorporated into *The Poetaster* (1601) and would then have been available for reprinting in *Mason*.

To distinguish the two selections, I am again following the example of other editors of the *Elegies* in using the names of previous owners of the volumes, *Bindley* and *Isham*.

Bindley: EPIGRAMMES | and | ELEGIES. | By. I.D. and | C.M. | [type ornament] | *At Middleborugh*.

8° in fours A⁴ (−A1) B–F⁴ G⁴ (−G4); not paginated.

Contents: A2 title, verso blank: A3–D3ᵛ text of Davies's 48 epigrams concluding 'FINIS. I.D.'; D4 head title 'IGNOTO': text of three poems begins; D4ᵛ text of three poems concludes 'FINIS'; E1 second title, verso blank; E2–G3ᵛ text of Marlowe's ten elegies concluding 'FINIS'.

Second title: CERTAINE | OF OVIDS | ELEGIES. By C Marlow | [type ornament] | *At Middleborugh*

STC 6350: British Museum (A4 missing); Pforzheimer Collection (second title) '*At Midleborugh*'.

Isham: EPIGRAMMES | and ELEGIES. | By I.D. and | C.M. | [type ornament] | *At Middleborough*.

8° in fours: A⁴ (−A1) B–F⁴ (−G4); not paginated.

Contents: A2 title, verso blank; A3–D3ᵛ text of Davies's 48 epigrams concluding 'FINIS. I.D.'; D4 headpiece type ornament; head title 'IGNOTO'; text of three poems begins; D4ᵛ text of three poems concludes 'FINIS'; E1 second title, verso blank; E2–G3ᵛ text of Marlowe's ten elegies concluding 'FINIS.'

Second title: CERTAINE | OF OVIDS | ELEGIES. | By C. Marlow. | [type ornament] | *At Middleborough*.

STC 6350 (wrongly identified with *Bindley*): Huntington Library.

These two books are not identical; their sequence and the reasons for their variants are matters for dispute. Fredson Bowers gives priority to Isham on bibliographical grounds, claiming for instance that the prevalence of full stops in *Bindley* can be explained by the compositor's use in setting up this text of a copy of *Isham* whose commas were damaged. To explain the major substantive variants he postulates an 'editor' who looked over the *Isham* copy and occasionally altered it—always, from an aesthetic viewpoint, for the worse. It seems more likely to me, however, that *Bindley* has the priority, and that its accidentals—the heavy pointing, the mixture of upper- and lower-case letters to begin a line of verse—reflect manuscript practice. In the printing of Davies's *Epigrams* this following of a manuscript is especially clear. On two occasions (xxx. 11 and xxxvi. 3) *Bindley* reads 'with' where the obviously correct reading is *Isham*'s 'which'. A compositor setting from printed copy could hardly have made this mistake twice, yet the most common of all misreadings of secretary hand is to confuse 'with' and 'which' in their usual and near-identical abbreviated forms of 'wᵗʰ' and 'wᶜʰ'. A misreading of a manuscript might also account for *Bindley*'s 'tēder' in Elegy I. iii. 7, which *Isham* corrects to 'slender' (a more accurate rendering of the Latin *tenues*). The scribe's hand is reflected in the abbreviation, and the erroneous *t* could easily have been misread from manuscript but not from printed copy.

The printer of *Isham* did not set up from *Bindley* alone, simply making a few obvious corrections. A manuscript must have been available (but not that from which *Bindley* was printed) to supply the substantive variants. These are perhaps most striking in Elegy II. iv. At line 14 *Mason* reads: 'Me thinkes she would be nimble when shees down', while *Bindley* offers: 'Me thinks she should be quick when she is down', saving the 'nimble' for line 28 and printing 'those nimble hands' where *Mason* has 'those hands'. At line 43 *Bindley* suggests that the mistress may be 'Yellow trest', instead of 'Amber trest', as in *Mason*. *Isham* shares readings with both—the 'Yellow trest' of *Bindley* and 'those hands' of *Mason*. In line 14 *Isham*'s reading is a conflation of the two: 'Me thinkes she should be nimble when shees down.' *Isham* fails to correct a mistake in line 8, and follows *Bindley* in reading 'And driven' where the sense demands *Mason*'s 'Am driven'. Lines 37–40 in *Mason* are omitted in both *Bindley* and *Isham*, perhaps because *Bindley*'s compositor was careless, and *Isham*'s too intent on making his page look like that of his printed copy, although there was plenty of room for the addition.

Consideration of these variants leads me to conjecture that the *Elegies* existed in two forms, the first a draft which was used as copy for *Bindley*, and a more polished revision, the source of *Isham*'s corrections of *Bindley* and the copy for *Mason* (see Figure 1). If this were the case, there could be no question but that Marlowe himself was responsible for the polishing. We need think only of the reading of I. v. 24. *Mason* and *Isham* have: 'I cling'd her naked body, downe she fell', but *Bindley* translates Ovid's *nudam* as 'faire white'. In the two later texts the translation is improved, and the collocation of 'cling'd' and 'naked' is wholly Marlovian: it re-appears in *Hero and Leander-*

> But as her naked feet were whipping out,
> He on the suddaine cling'd her so about. (797–8)

Details of all substantive variants in these ten poems are printed in Appendix A.

For the poems of Davies, *Mason* has its own kind of corruption.

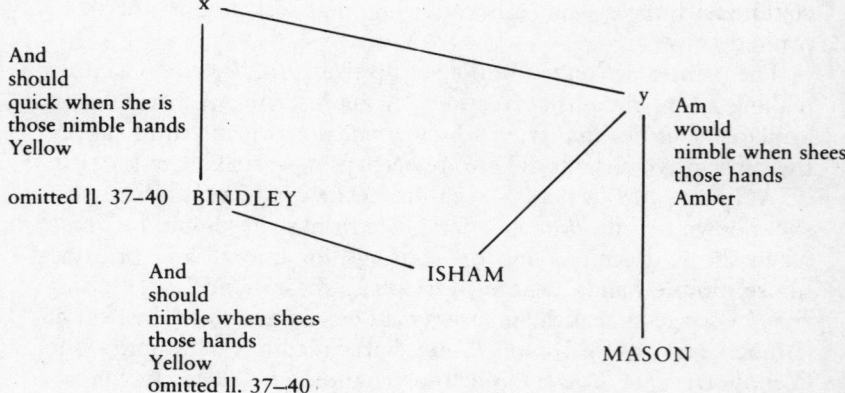

FIG. 1. Elegy II. iv: relationship of *Bindley*, *Isham*, and *Mason*

It is clear that some readings in the *Epigrams* originated when the printer was correcting his copy-text (which for the *Epigrams*, but not the *Elegies*, was Bindley) and were not derived from any manuscript. At xx. 1 he adds the required *s* to make *Bindley*'s 'Geron' possessive; but the metre demands the reading of *Isham* and the manuscripts: 'Geron whose'. At xxiv. 8 he apparently did not know the military term 'brayes' and so altered it to 'baites'. Not surprisingly, he could make no sense of *Bindley*'s 'Nepenthe Hekens drinke with gladnes brings' (xxvi. 3) and so attempted 'Nepenthe Hevens drink most gladnes brings': the manuscripts correctly witness the Homeric fact that '*Nepenthe*' is '*Hellens* drink'. In a few instances the printer seems to have altered a word merely for the sake of refinement: *Bindley*'s 'like' at xiii. 13 becomes 'as', and 'eke' at xiv. 3 becomes 'then'. Aware of this sophistication, one grows suspicious of the printer, and unwilling to take on trust any of his variant readings for the *Elegies*.

The text of *Mason* was prepared with great care. There are a few obvious misspellings (such as 'laug'd' for 'laugh'd' at I. vi. 11); and occasionally the italicizfor of proper names is inconsistent. In this edition I have tried to avoid all but the most essential alterations to Q's punctuation, since this seems to have its own coherent logic, usually pointing to a rhetorical stress. It is probable that these accidentals, and the carefulness to which they bear witness, originate with Marlowe himself. In the *Elegies*, there are some unmistakable confusions of 'my' and 'thy' (at II. i. 1, for instance; and at II. viii. 16); and the same peculiarity is to be seen in *Dido Queen of Carthage* (for example at v. i. 117 and 268). An explanation is to be found in Marlowe's signature, where the *M* is very like the character for *th* in Elizabethan secretary hand.

None of the three editions could have been published before 1594: this *terminus a quo* is supplied by Davies's Epigram 40, *In Afrum*, with its reference to a military victory of that year. Indeed, Epigram 47 speaks of 'the war twixt *France* and *Spaine*'—which was perhaps the fighting of 1595; and the last four epigrams, 45–8, are not to be found in manuscripts dated November 1594 and 1595.

Following the publication of *Mason* were three more seventeenth-century editions of the *Elegies and Epigrammes*; their textual value is slight. The earliest of these is represented by a

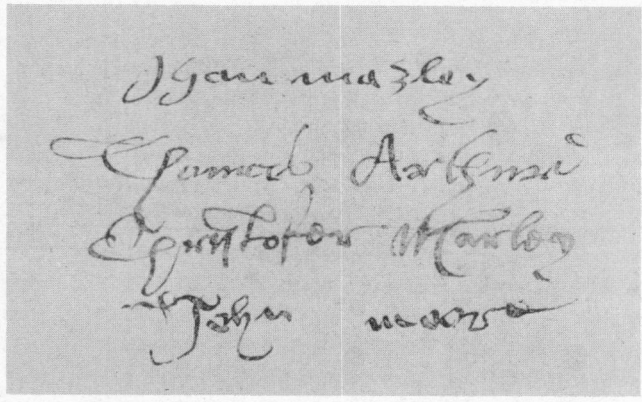

FIG. 2. Marlowe's signature (third line), from the will of Mrs Benchkyn, a neighbour (1585)

single copy in the Bodleian Library, Douce 0.31, which was printed from *Mason* and contains many variants which, though interesting, are without any authority. It has some curiosity value, perhaps, with errors that could more easily arise from a mishearing than a misreading: where in Elegy II. xiii. 23 *Mason* has: 'In white, with incense', *Douce's* rather deaf compositor printed: 'In wives, with incest'. The Bodleian's Malone 368 represents a later edition, of which several copies survive; and Malone 368 served as copy for the latest seventeenth-century edition (Malone 133) of which, again, many copies survive. Unless a reading which corrects a manifest error in *Mason* originates in one of these editions, they are not mentioned in the apparatus criticus.

Fuller discussions of these texts are to be found in Roma Gill and Robert Krueger, 'The Early Editions of Marlowe's *Elegies* and Davies's *Epigrams*: Sequence and Authority', (*The Library*, 5th series, vol. xxvi, no. 3 (1971); 243–9), and in Fredson Bowers 'The Early Editions of Marlowe's *Ovid's Elegies*', (*Studies in Bibliography* xxv (1972); 149–72).

SIGLA

Mason	*All Ovids Elegies* (Bodleian Library Mason AA 207; copy-text)
Bindley	*Epigrammes and Elegies*, by John Davies and Christopher Marlowe (British Library and Pforzheimer Collection)
Isham	*Epigrammes and Elegies*, by John Davies and Christopher Marlowe (Huntington Library)
Douce	*All Ovids Elegies* (Bodleian Library, Douce 0.31)
Mal 368	*All Ovids Elegies* (Bodleian Library, Malone 368)
Mal 133	*All Ovids Elegies* (Bodleian Library, Malone 133)

P. Ovidii Nasonis Amorum
Liber Primus

ELEGIA 1

*Quemadmodum a Cupidine, pro bellis
amores scribere coactus sit*

We which were *Ovids* five bookes now are three,
For these before the rest preferreth he.
If reading five thou plainst of tediousnesse,
Two tane away, thy labour will be lesse.
With Muse upreard I meant to sing of Armes,   5
Choosing a subject fit for fierce alarmes.
Both verses were a like till love (men say)
Began to smile and tooke one foote away.
Rash boy, who gave thee power to change a line?
We are the Muses Prophets, none of thine.   10
What if thy mother take *Dianas* bowe?
Shall *Dian* fanne, when loue begins to glowe.
In wooddie groves ist meete that *Ceres* raigne?
And quiver-bearing *Dian* till the plaine.
Who'le set the faire trest sunne in battell ray   15
While *Mars* doth take the *Aonian* Harpe to play.
Great are thy kingdomes, over strong and large,
Ambitious impe, why seekst thou further charge?
Are all things thine? the Muses *Tempe* thine?
Then scarse can *Phoebus* say, this Harpe is mine.   20
When in this workes first verse I trode aloft,
Love slackt my Muse, and made my numbers soft.
I have no mistresse, nor no favorit,
Being fittest matter for a wanton wit.
Thus I complain'd, but love unlockt his quiver,   25
Tooke out the shaft ordain'de my hart to shiver:
And bent his sinewie bowe upon his knee,
Saying Poet heere's a worke beseeming thee.

5 upreard] *Bindley, Isham*; prepar'd *Mason*   19 *Tempe*] *Bindley, Isham*; *Temple*
Mason   26 shaft ordain'de] ~ , ~ *Mason*

Oh woe is mee, hee never shootes but hits,
I burne, love in my idle bosome sits.   30
Let my first verse be sixe, my last five feete,
Fare-well sterne warre, for blunter Poets meete.
Elegian Muse, that warblest amorous laies,
Girt my shine browe with Sea-banke Mirtle praise.

ELEGIA 2

*Quod primo amore correptus, in triumphum
duci se a Cupidine patiatur.*

What makes my bed seeme hard seeing it is soft?
Or why slips downe the coverlet so oft?
Although the nights be long, I sleepe not tho,
My sides are sore with tumbling too and fro.
Were love the cause, it's like I should descry him,   5
Or lyes he close, and shootes where none can spie him.
'Twas so, hee strooke mee with a slender dart,
'Tis cruell love turmoyles my captive heart.
Yeelding or strugling doe we give him might,
Lets yeeld, a burthen easly borne is light.   10
I saw a brandisht fire encrease in strength,
Which being not shakt, I saw it dye at length.
Young Oxen newly yoakt are beaten more
Then Oxen which have drawne the plough before.
And rough Jades mouthes with stuborne bits are torne, 15
But managde horses heads are lightly borne.
Unwilling lovers, love doth more torment
Then such as in their bondage feele content.
Loe I confesse, I am thy captive I,
And hold my conquer'd hands for thee to tie.   20
What needst thou warre, I sue to thee for grace,
With armes to conquer armelesse men is base.
Yoake *Venus* Doves, put Mirtle on thy haire,
Vulcan will give thee chariots rich and faire.

12 shakt] *Bindley, Isham*; slackt Mason

The people thee applauding thou shalt stand, 25
Guiding the harmeless Pigeons with thy hand.
Yong men, and women shalt thou lead as thrall,
So will thy triumph seeme magnificall.
I lately caught, will have a new made wound,
And captive like be manacled and bound. 30
Good meaning, shame, and such as seeke loves wracke,
Shall follow thee their hands tyed at their backe.
Thee all shall feare, and worship as a King,
Io, triumphing shall thy people sing.
Smooth speeches, feare, and rage shall by thee ride, 35
Which troopes have alwayes beene on *Cupids* side;
Thou with these soldiours conquerest gods and men,
Take these away, where is thine honour then?
Thy mother shall from heaven applaud this showe,
And on their faces heapes of Roses strowe. 40
With beautie of thy wings thy faire haire guilded,
Ride golden love in chariots richly builded.
Unlesse I erre, full many shalt thou burne,
And give wounds infinite at every turne.
In spite of thee forth will thine arrowes flye, 45
A scortching flame burnes all the standers by.
So having conquer'd *Inde* was *Bacchus* hew,
Thee pompous Birds, and him two Tygers drew.
Then seeing I grace thy show in following thee,
Fobeare to hurt thy selfe in spoiling me. 50
Behold thy kinsmans *Caesars* prosperous bands.
Who guards the conquered with his conquering hands.

ELEGIA 3

Ad amicam.

I aske but right: let her that caught me late,
Either love, or cause that I may never hate,
I aske too much, would she but let me love her,
Jove knowes with such like praiers I daily move her.

---

31 meaning, shame] ∼ˬ ∼ *Mason*   52 the] *Dyce*; thee *Mason*

1 her] *Bindley, Isham*; he *Mason*

Accept him that will serve thee all his youth,   5
Accept him that will love with spotlesse truth.
If loftie titles cannot make me thine,
That am descended but of Knightly line,
Soone may you plow the little land I have,
I gladly graunt my parents given, to save.   10
Apollo, *Bacchus* and the Muses may,
And *Cupid* who hath markt me for thy pray;
My spotlesse life, which but to Gods gives place,
Naked simplicitie and modest grace.
I love but one, and her I love, change never,   15
If men have faith, Ile live with thee for ever.
The yeares that fatall destinie shall give
Ile live with thee, and dye, ere thou shall grieve.
Be thou the happy subject of my bookes,
That I may write things worthy thy faire lookes.   20
By verses horned *Io* got her name,
And she to whom in shape of Swanne *Jove* came,
And she that on a fain'd Bull swamme to land,
Griping his false hornes with her virgin hand.
So likewise we will through the world be rung,   25
And with my name shall thing be alwayes sung.

ELEGIA 4

Amicam, qua arte, quibusve nutibus in caena,
praesente viro uti debeat, admonet.

Thy husband to a banquet goes with me,
Pray God it may his latest supper be,
Shall I sit gazing as a bashfull guest,
While others touch the damsell I love best?
Wilt lying under him his bosome clippe;   5
About thy neck shall he at pleasure skippe?
Marveile not, though the faire Bride did incite,
The drunken *Centaures* to a sodaine fight.
I am no halfe horse, nor in woods I dwell,
Yet scarse my hands from thee containe I well.   10

But how thou shouldst behave thy selfe now know;
Nor let the windes away my warnings blowe.
Before thy husband come, though I not see,
What may be done, yet there before him bee.
Lie with him gently, when his limbes he spread, 15
Upon the bed, but on my foote first tread.
View me, my becks, and speaking countenance
Take, and receive each secret amorous glaunce.
Words without voyce shall on my eye browes sit,
Lines thou shalt read in wine by my hand writ. 20
When our lascivious toyes come in thy minde,
Thy Rosie cheekes be to thy thombe inclinde.
If ought of me thou speak'st in inward thought,
Let thy soft finger to thy eare be brought.
When I (my light) do or say ought that please thee, 25
Turne round thy gold-ring, as it were to ease thee.
Strike on the board like them that pray for evill,
When thou doest wish thy husband at the devill.
What wine he fills thee, wisely will him drinke,
Aske thou the boy, what thou enough doest thinke. 30
When thou hast tasted, I will take the cup,
And where thou drinkst, on that part I will sup.
If hee gives thee what first himselfe did tast,
Even in his face his offered Gobbets cast.
Let not thy necke by his vile armes be prest, 35
Nor leane thy soft head on his boistrous brest.
Thy bosomes Roseat buds let him not finger,
Chiefly on thy lips let not his lips linger.
If thou givest kisses, I shall all disclose,
Say they are mine, and hands on thee impose. 40
Yet this Ile see, but if thy gowne ought cover,
Suspitious feare in all my veines will hover,
Mingle not thighes, nor to his legge joyne thine,
Nor thy soft foote with his hard foote combine.
I have been wanton, therefore am perplext, 45
And with mistrust of the like measure vext.
I and my wench oft under clothes did lurke,
When pleasure mov'd us to our sweetest worke.

34 Gobbets] *Dyce*; Goblets *Mason*

Do not thou so, but throw thy mantle hence.
Least I should thinke thee guilty of offence.   50
Entreat thy husband drinke, but do not kisse,
And while he drinkes, to adde more do not misse,
If hee lyes downe with Wine and sleepe opprest,
The thing and place shall counsell us the rest.
When to go homewards we rise all along,   55
Have care to walke in middle of the throng.
There will I finde thee, or be found by thee,
There touch what ever thou canst touch of mee.
Aye me I warne what profits some few howers,
But we must part, when heav'n with black night lowers.   60
At night thy husband clippes thee, I will weepe
And to the dores sight of thy selfe will keepe:
Then will he kisse thee, and not onely kisse
But force thee give him my stolne honey blisse.
Constrain'd against thy will give it the pezant   65
Forbeare sweet wordes, and be your sport unpleasant.
To him I pray it no delight may bring
Or if it do to thee no joy thence spring:
But though this night thy fortune be to trie it
To me to morrow constantly deny it.   70

ELEGIA 5

Corinnae Concubitus.

In summers heate and mid-time of the day
To rest my limbes upon a bed I lay,
One window shut, the other open stood,
Which gave such light, as twincles in a wood,
Like twilight glimps at setting of the Sunne   5
Or night being past, and yet not day begunne.
Such light to shamefast maidens must be showne,
Where they may sport, and seeme to be unknowne.
Then came *Corinna* in a long loose gowne,
Her white neck hid with tresses hanging downe: 10
Resembling fayre *Semiramis* going to bed
Or *Layis* of a thousand wooers sped,

I snacht her gowne: being thin, the harme was small,
Yet striv'd she to be covered there withall.
And striving thus as one that would be cast,   15
Betray'd her selfe, and yeelded at the last.
Starke naked as she stood before mine eye,
Not one wen in her body could I spie.
What armes and shoulders did I touch and see,
How apt her breasts were to be prest by me.   20
How smooth a belly under her wast saw I?
How large a legge, and what a lustie thigh?
To leave the rest all lik'd me passing well,
I cling'd her naked body, downe she fell,
Judge you the rest, being tirde she bad me kisse;   25
Jove send me more such after-noones as this.

ELEGIA 6

Ad Janitorem, ut fores sibi aperiat.

Unworthy porter, bound in chaines full sore
On mooved hookes set ope the churlish dore.
Little I aske, a little entrance make,
The gate halfe ope my bent side in will take.
Long love my body to such use makes slender   5
And to get out doth like apt members render.
He shewes me how unheard to passe the watch,
And guides my feete least stumbling falles they catch.
But in times past I fear'd vaine shades, and night,
Wondring if any walked without light.   10
Love hearing it laugh'd with his tender mother
And smiling sayed, be thou as bold as other.
Forth-with love came, no darke night-flying spright
Nor hands prepar'd to slaughter, me affright.
Thee feare I too much: only thee I flatter,   15
Thy lightning can my life in pieces batter.

25 tirde] *Bindley, Isham*; tride *Mason*

5 makes] *Robinson*; make *Mason*

Why enviest me this hostile denne unbarre
See how the gates with my teares wat'red are.
When thou stood'st naked ready to be beate,
For thee I did thy mistris faire entreate.   20
But what entreates for thee some-times tooke place,
(O mischiefe) now for me obtaine small grace.
Gratis thou maiest be free, give like for like
Night goes away: the dores barre backeward strike.
Strike, so againe hard chaines shall binde thee never,   25
Nor servile water shalt thou drinke for ever.
Heard-hearted *Porter* doest and wilt not heare,
With stiffe oake propt the gate doth still appeare.
Such rampierd gates beseiged Cittyes ayde,
In midst of peace why art of armes afraide?   30
Excludst a lover, how wouldst use a foe?
Strike backe the barre, night fast away doth goe.
With armes or armed men I come not guarded,
I am alone, were furious love discarded.
Although I would, I cannot him cashiere   35
Before I be divided from my geere.
See love with me, wine moderate in my braine,
And on my haires a crowne of flowers remaine.
Who feares these armes? who wil not go to meete them?
Night runnes away; with open entrance greete them.   40
Art carelesse? or ist sleepe forbids thee heare
Giving the windes my words running in thine eare.
Well I remember when I first did hire thee
Watching till after mid-night did not tire thee.
But now perchaunce thy wench with thee doth rest,   45
Ah howe thy lot is above my lot blest:
Though it be so, shut me not out therefore
Night goes away: I pray thee ope the dore.
Erre we? or do the turned hinges sound,
And opening dores with creaking noyse abound?   50
We erre: a strong blast seem'd the gates to ope:
Aie me how high that gale did lift my hope!
If *Boreas* beares *Orithyas* rape in minde
Come breake these deafe dores with thy boysterous wind.
Silent the Cittie is: nights deawie hoast   55
March fast away: the barre strike from the poast.

Or I more sterne then fire or sword will turne,
And with my brand these gorgeous houses burne.
Night, love, and wine to all extreames perswade:
Night shamelesse, wine and love are fearelesse made.　　60
All have I spent: no threats or prayers move thee,
O harder then the dores thou gardest I prove thee.
No pritty wenches keeper maist thou bee:
The carefull prison is more meete for thee.
Now frosty night her flight beginnes to take,　　65
And crowing Cocks poore soules to worke awake.
But thou my crowne from sad haires tane away,
On this hard threshold till the morning lay.
That when my mistresse there beholds thee cast,
She may perceive how we the time did wast:　　70
What ere thou art, farewell, be like me paind,
Carelesse farewell with my falt not distaind.
And farewell cruell posts rough thresholds block,
And dores conjoynd with an hard iron lock.

ELEGIA 7

Ad pacandam amicam, quam verberaverat.

Binde fast my hands, they have deserved chaines,
While rage is absent, take some friend the paynes.
For rage against my wench mov'd my rash arme,
My Mistresse weepes whom my mad hand did harme.
I might have then my parents deare misus'd,　　5
Or holy gods with cruell strokes abus'd.
Why? *Ajax*, maister of the seven-fould shield,
Butcherd the flocks he found in spatious field
And he who on his mother veng'd his sire
Against the destinies durst sharpe darts require.　　10
Could I therefore her comely tresses teare?
Yet was she graced with her ruffled hayre.
So fayre she was, *Atalanta* she resembled,
Before whose bow th'*Arcadian* wild beasts trembled.
Such *Ariadne* was, when she bewayles　　15
Her perjur'd *Theseus* flying vowes and sayles,

So chast *Minerva* did *Cassandra* fall,
Deflowr'd except, within thy Temple wall.
That I was mad, and barbarous all men cried,
She nothing said, pale feare her tongue had tyed.   20
But secretlie her lookes with checks did trounce mee,
Her teares, she silent, guilty did pronounce me.
Would of mine armes, my shoulders had beene scanted,
Better I could part of my selfe have wanted.
To mine owne selfe have I had strength so furious?   25
And to my selfe could I be so injurious?
Slaughter and mischiefs instruments, no better,
Deserved chaines these cursed hands shall fetter,
Punisht I am, if I a *Romaine* beat,
Over my Mistris is my right more great?   30
Tydides left worst signes of villanie,
He first a Goddesse strooke; an other I.
Yet he harm'd lesse, whom I profess'd to love,
I harm'd: a foe did *Diomedes* anger move.
Go now thou Conqueror glorious triumphs raise,   35
Pay vowes to *Jove*, engirt thy hayres with baies,
And let the troupes which shall thy Chariot follow,
Io a strong man conquerd this Wench, hollow.
Let the sad captive formost with lockes spred
On her white necke but for hurt cheekes be led.   40
Meeter it were her lips were blewe with kissing
And on her necke a wantons marke not missing.
But though I like a swelling floud was driven,
And as a pray unto blinde anger given.
Wast not enough the fearefull Wench to chide?   45
Nor thunder in rough threatings haughty pride?
Nor shamefully her coate pull ore her crowne,
Which to her wast her girdle still kept downe.
But cruelly her tresses having rent
My nayles to scratch her lovely cheekes I bent.   50
Sighing she stood, her bloodlesse white lookes shewed
Like marble from the *Parian* Mountaines hewed.
Her halfe dead joynts, and trembling limmes I sawe,
Like *Popler* leaves blowne with a stormy flawe,
Or slender eares, with gentle *Zephire* shaken,   55
Or waters tops with the warme south winde taken.

And downe her cheekes, the trickling teares did flow,
Like water gushing from consuming snowe.
Then first I did perceive I had offended
My bloud, the teares were that from her descended.   60
Before her feete thrice prostrate downe I fell,
My feared hands thrice back she did repell
But doubt thou not (revenge doth griefe appease)
With thy sharpe nayles upon my face to seaze.
Bescratch mine eyes spare not my lockes to breake,   65
(Anger will helpe thy hands though nere so weake.)
And least the sad signes of my crime remaine,
Put in their place thy keembed haires againe.

ELEGIA 8

Exaecratur lenam, quae puellam suam meretricia
arte instituebat.

There is, who ere will knowe a bawde aright
Give eare, there is an old trot *Dipsas* hight.
Her name comes from the thing: she being wise,
Sees not the morne on rosie horses rise.
She magick arts and *Thessale* charmes doth know,   5
And makes large streams back to their fountaines flow,
She knows with gras, with thrids on wrong wheeles spun
And what with Mares ranck humour may be done.
When she will, cloudes the darckned heav'n obscure,
When she will, day shines every where most pure.   10
(If I have faith) I sawe the starres drop bloud,
The purple moone with sanguine visage stood.
Her I suspect among nights spirits to fly,
And her old body in birdes plumes to lie.
Fame saith as I suspect, and in her eyes   15
Two eye-balles shine, and double light thence flies.
Great grand-sires from their antient graves she chides
And with long charmes the solide earth divides.
She drawes chast women to incontinence,
Nor doth her tongue want harmefull eloquence.   20

By chaunce I heard her talke, these words she sayd
While closely hid betwixt two dores I layed.
Mistris thou knowest, thou hast a blest youth pleas'd,
He staide, and on thy lookes his gazes seaz'd.
And why shouldst not please? none thy face exceedes,   25
Aye me, thy body hath no worthy weedes.
As thou art faire, would thou wert fortunate,
Wert thou rich, poore should not be my state.
Th'opposed starre of *Mars* hath done thee harme,
Now *Mars* is gone: *Venus* thy side doth warme.   30
And brings good fortune, a rich lover plants
His love on thee, and can supply thy wants.
Such is his forme as may with thine compare,
Would he not buy thee thou for him shouldst care.
She blusht: red shame becomes white cheekes, but this   35
If feigned, doth well; if true it doth amisse.
When on thy lappe thine eyes thou dost deject,
Each one according to his gifts respect.
Perhaps the *Sabines* rude, when *Tatius* raignde,
To yeeld their love to more then one disdainde.   40
Now *Mars* doth rage abroad without all pitty,
And *Venus* rules in her *Aeneas* Citty.
Faire women play, shee's chast whom none will have,
Or, but for bashfulnesse her selfe would crave.
Shake off these wrinckles that thy front assault,   45
Wrinckles in beauty is a grievous fault.
Penelope in bowes her youths strength tride,
Of horne the bowe was that approv'd their side.
Time flying slides hence closely, and deceaves us,
And with swift horses the swift yeare soone leaves us.   50
Brasse shines with use; good garments would be worne,
Houses not dwelt in, are with filth forlorne.
Beauty not exercisde with age is spent,
Nor one or two men are sufficient.
Many to rob is more sure, and lesse hatefull,   55
From dog-kept flocks come preys to woolves most gratefull.
Behold what gives the Poet but new verses?
And thereof many thousand he rehearses.
The Poets God arayed in robes of gold,
Of his gilt Harpe the well tun'd strings doth hold.   60

Let *Homer* yeeld to such as presents bring
(Trust me) to give, it is a witty thing.
Nor, so thou maist obtaine a wealthy prize,
The vaine name of inferiour slaves despize.
Nor let the armes of antient lives beguile thee, 65
Poore lover with thy gransires I exile thee.
Who seekes, for being faire, a night to have,
What he will give, with greater instance crave.
Make a small price, while thou thy nets doest lay,
Least they should fly, being tane, the tirant play. 70
Dissemble so, as lov'd he may be thought,
And take heed least he gets that love for nought.
Deny him oft, feigne now thy head doth ake:
And *Isis* now will shew what scuse to make.
Receive him soone, least patient use he gaine, 75
Or least his love oft beaten backe should waine.
To beggers shut, to bringers ope thy gate,
Let him within heare bard out lovers prate.
And as first wrongd the wronged some-times banish,
Thy fault with his fault so repuls'd will vanish. 80
But never give a spatious time to ire,
Anger delaide doth oft to hate retire.
And let thine eyes constrained learne to weepe,
That this, or that man may thy cheekes moist keepe.
Nor, if thou couzenst one, dread to for-sweare, 85
"*Venus* to mockt men lendes a sencelesse eare".
Servants fit for thy purpose thou must hire
To teach thy lover, what thy thoughts desire.
Let them aske some-what, many asking little,
Within a while great heapes grow of a tittle. 90
And sister, Nurse, and mother spare him not,
By many hands great wealth is quickly got.
When causes fale thee to require a gift,
By keeping of thy birth make but a shift.
Beware least he unrival'd loves secure, 95
Take strife away, love doth not well endure.
On all the bed mens tumbling let him viewe
And thy neck with lascivious markes made blew.
Chiefly shew him the gifts, which others send:
If he gives nothing, let him from thee wend. 100

When thou hast so much as he gives no more,
Pray him to lend what thou maiest nere restore.
Let thy tongue flatter, while thy minde harme-workes:
Under sweete hony deadly poison lurkes.
If this thou doest to me by long use knowne,   105
Nor let my words be with the windes hence blowne,
Oft thou wilt say, live well, thou wilt pray oft,
That my dead bones may in their grave lie soft.
As thus she spake, my shadow me betraide,
With much a do my hands I scarsely staide.   110
But her bleare eyes, balde scalpes thin hoary flieces
And riveld cheekes I would have puld a pieces.
The gods send thee no house, a poore old age,
Perpetuall thirst, and winters lasting rage.

ELEGIA 9

Ad Atticum, amantem non oportere desidiosum
esse, sicuti nec militem.

All Lovers warre, and *Cupid* hath his tent,
Atticke, all lovers are to warre farre sent.
What age fits *Mars*, wtih *Venus* doth agree
Tis shame for eld in warre or love to be.
What yeares in souldiours Captaines do require   5
Those in their lovers, pretty maydes desire.
Both of them watch: each on the hard earth sleepes:
His Mistris dores this; that this Captaines keepes.
Souldiers must travaile farre: the wench forth send
Her valiant lover followes without end.   10
Mounts, and raine-doubled flouds he passeth over,
And treades the deserts snowy heapes to cover.
Going to sea, *East* windes he doth not chide
Nor to hoist saile attends fit time and tyde.
Who but a souldiour or a lover is bould   15
To suffer storme mixt snowes with nights sharpe cold?
One as a spy doth to his enemies goe
The other eyes his rivall as his foe.

He Citties greate, this thresholds lies before:
This breakes Towne gates, but he his Mistris dore.   20
Oft to invade the sleeping foe tis good
And arm'd to shed unarmed peoples bloud.
So the fierce troupes of *Thracian Rhesus* fell
And Captive horses bad their Lord fare-well.
Sooth Lovers watch till sleepe the hus-band charmes,   25
Who slumbring, they rise up in swelling armes.
The keepers hands and corps-dugard to passe
The souldiours, and poore lovers worke ere was.
Doubtfull is warre and love, the vanquisht rise
And who thou never think'st should fall downe lies.   30
Therefore who ere love sloathfulnesse doth call,
Let him surcease: love tries wit best of all.
Achilles burnd *Briseis* being tane away:
Troianes destroy the *Greeke* wealth, while you may.
Hector to armes went from his wives embraces,   35
And on *Andromache* his helmet laces.
Great *Agamemnon* was, men say amazed,
On *Priams* loose-trest daughter when he gazed.
Mars in the deed the black-smithes net did stable
In heaven was never more notorious fable.   40
My selfe was dull, and faint, to sloth inclinde,
Pleasure, and ease had mollifide my minde.
A faire maides care expeld this sluggishnesse,
And to her tentes wild me my selfe addresse.
Since maist thou see me watch and night warres move: 45
He that will not growe slothfull let him love.

ELEGIA 10

Ad puellam, ne pro amore praemia poscat.

Such as the cause was of two husbands warre,
Whom *Troiane* ships fetcht from *Europa* farre.
Such as was *Leda*, whom the God deluded
In snowe-white plumes of a false swanne included.
Such as *Amimone* through the drie fields strayed   5
When on her head a water pitcher laied.

Such wert thou, and I fear'd the Bull and Eagle
And what ere love made *Jove* should thee invegle.
Now all feare with my mindes hot love abates,
No more this beauty mine eyes captivates.   10
Ask'st why I chaunge? because thou crav'st reward:
This cause hath thee from pleasing me debard.
While thou wert plaine, I lov'd thy minde and face:
Now inward faults thy outward forme disgrace.
Love is a naked boy, his yeares saunce staine   15
And hath no cloathes, but open doth remaine.
Will you for gaine have *Cupid* sell himselfe?
He hath no bosome, where to hide base pelfe.
Love and Loves sonne are with fierce armes to oddes;
To serve for pay beseemes not wanton gods.   20
The whore stands to be bought for each mans mony
And seekes vild wealth by selling of her Cony,
Yet greedy Bauds command she curseth still,
And doth constraind, what you do of good will.
Take from irrationall beasts a president,   25
Tis shame their wits should be more excelent.
The Mare askes not the Horse, the Cowe the Bull
Nor the milde Ewe gifts from the Ramme doth pull.
Only a Woman gets spoiles from a Man,
Farmes out her-self on nights for what she can.   30
And lets what both delight, what both desire,
Making her joy according to her hire.
The sport being such, as both alike sweete try it
Why should one sell it, and the other buy it?
Why should I loose, and thou gaine by the pleasure   35
Which man and woman reape in equall measure?
Knights of the post of perjuries make saile
The unjust Judge for bribes becomes a stale.
Tis shame sould tongues the guilty should defend
Or great wealth from a judgement seate ascend.   40
Tis shame to grow rich by bed merchandize,
Or prostitute thy beauty for bad prize.
Thankes worthely are due for things unbought,
For beds ill hyr'd we are indebted nought.
The hirer payeth al, his rent discharg'd   45
From further duty he rests then inlarg'd.

Faire Dames for-beare rewards for nights to crave
Ill gotten goods good end will never have.
The Sabine gauntlets were too dearely wunne
That unto death did presse the holy Nunne.   50
The sonne slew her, that forth to meete him went,
And a rich neck-lace caus'd that punnishment.
Yet thinke no scorne to aske a wealthy churle
He wants no gifts into thy lap to hurle.
Take clustred grapes from an ore-laden vine,   55
May bounteous lome *Alcinous* fruite resigne.
Let poore men slow their service, faith, and care
All for their Mistrisse, what they have, prepare.
In verse to praise kinde Wenches tis my part,
And whom I like eternize by mine art.   60
Garments do weare, jewells and gold do wast
The fame that verse gives doth for ever last.
To give I love, but to be ask't disdayne
Leave asking, and Ile give what I refraine.

ELEGIA 11

Napen alloquitur, ut paratas tabellas ad
Corinnam perferat.

In skilfull gathering ruffled haires in order,
Nape free-borne whose cunning hath no border
Thy service for nights scapes is knowne commodious
And to give signes dull wit to thee is odious.
Corinna clips me oft by thy perswasion   5
Never to harme me made thy faith evasion.
Receive these lines, them to my Mistrisse carry
Be sedulous, let no stay cause thee tarry.
Nor flint, nor iron, are in thy soft brest
But pure simplicity in thee doth rest.   10
And tis suppos'd Loves bowe hath wounded thee
Defend the ensignes of thy warre in mee.
If, what I do, she askes, say hope for night
The rest my hand doth in my letters write.

Time passeth while I speake, give her my writ   15
But see that forth-with shee peruseth it.
I charge thee marke her eyes and front in reading
By speechlesse lookes we guesse at things succeeding.
Straight being read, will her to write much backe,
I hate faire *Paper* should writte matter lacke.   20
Let her make verses, and some blotted letter,
On the last edge to stay mine eyes the better.
What neede she tyre her hand to hold the quill,
Let this word, come, alone the tables fill.
Then with triumphant laurell will I grace them   25
And in the midst of *Venus* temple place them.
Subscribing that to her I consecrate
My faithfull tables being vile maple late.

ELEGIA 12

Tabellas quas miserat execratur, quod amica
noctem negabat.

Bewaile my chaunce the sad booke is returned,
This day denyall hath my sport adjourned.
Presages are not vaine, when she departed
Nape by stumbling on the threshold started
Going out againe passe forth the dore more wisely   5
And som-what higher beare thy foote precisely.
Hence luck-lesse tables, funerall wood be flying
And thou the waxe stuft full with notes denying.
Which I thinke gather'd from cold hemlocks flower
Wherein bad hony *Corsicke* Bees did power.   10
Yet as if mixt with red leade thou wert ruddy,
That colour rightly did appeare so bloudy.
As evill wood throwne in the high-waies lie,
Be broake with wheeles of chariots passing by.
And him that hew'd you out for needfull uses   15
Ile prove had hands impure with all abuses.
Poore wretches on the tree themselves did strangle
There sat the hang-man for mens neckes to angle.

To hoarse scrich-owles foule shadowes it allowes
Vultures and furies nestled in the boughes.   20
To these my love I foolishly committed
And them with sweete words to my Mistrisse fitted.
More fitly had they wrangling bondes contained
From barbarous lips of some Atturney strained,
Among day bookes and billes they had laine better   25
In which the Merchant wayles his banquerout debter,
Your name approves you made for such like things
The number two no good divining bringes.
Angry, I pray that rotten age you wrackes.
And sluttish white-mould overgrowe the waxe.   30

ELEGIA 13

Ad Aurorem ne properet.

Now ore the sea from her old Love comes she
That drawes the day from heavens cold axletree.
Aurora whither slidest thou? downe againe
And birdes from *Memnon* yearely shal be slaine.
Now in her tender armes I sweetly bide   5
If ever, now well lies she by my side.
The aire is cold, and sleepe is sweetest now
And birdes send forth shrill notes from every bough:
Whither runst thou, that men, and women love not?
Hold in thy rosy horses that they move not.   10
Ere thou rise, starres teach sea-men where to saile
But when thou commest they of their courses faile.
Poore travailers though tierd, rise at thy sight,
And souldiours make them ready to the fight.
The painefull hinde by thee to field is sent,   15
Slowe Oxen early in the yoake are pent.
Thou cousenst boyes of sleepe, and doest betray them
To Pedants that with cruell lashes pay them.
Thou mak'st the surety to the Lawyer runne,
That with one word hath nigh himselfe undone.   20

22 them] then *Mason*

The Lawyer and the client hate thy view,
Both whom thou raisest up to toyle anew.
By thy meanes women of their rest are bard,
Thou setst their labouring hands to spin and card.
All could I beare, but that the wench should rise,   25
None can endure save him with whom none lyes?
How oft wisht I, night would not give thee place,
Nor morning starres shunne thy uprising face.
How oft that either winde would breake thy coach,
Or steeds might fall forc'd with thick clouds approach.   30
Whether goest thou hatefull Nimph? *Memnon* the elfe
Receiv'd his cole-black colour from thy selfe.
Say that thy love with *Cephalus* were not knowne,
Then thinkest thou thy loose life is not showne.
Would *Tithon* might but talke of thee a while,   35
Not one in heaven should be more base and vile.
Thou leavest his bed, because hee's faint through age,
And early mountest thy hatefull carriage.
But heldst thou in thine armes some *Cephalus*,
Then wouldst thou cry, stay night and runne not thus.   40
Doest punish me, because yeares make him waine?
I did not bid thee wed an aged swaine.
The Moone sleepes with *Endymion* every day,
Thou art as faire as she, then kisse and play.
Jove that thou shouldst not hast but waite his leasure, 45
Made two nights one to finish up his pleasure.
I chid no more, she blusht and therefore heard me
Yet lingered not the day, but morning scard me.

ELEGIA 14

Puellam consulatur cui prae nimia cura
comae deciderant.

Leave colouring thy tresses I did cry,
Now hast thou left no haires at all to die.
But what had beene more faire had they beene kept?
Beyond thy robes thy dangling lockes had sweept.

Feardst thou to dresse them being fine and thinne 5
Like to the silke the curious *Seres* spinne,
Or thrids which spiders slender foote drawes out
Fastning her light web some old beame about.
Not black, nor golden were they to our viewe,
Yet although neither mixt of eithers hue, 10
Such as in hilly *Idas* watry plaines,
The Cedar tall spoyld of his barke retaines.
Ad they were apt to curle an hundred waies,
And did to thee no cause of dolour raise.
Nor hath the needle, or the combes teeth reft them, 15
The maide that kembd them ever safely left them.
Oft was she drest before mine eyes, yet never,
Snatching the combe, to beate the wench out drive her.
Oft in the morne her haires not yet digested,
Halfe sleeping on a purple bed she rested, 20
Yet seemely like a *Thracian Bacchinall*
That tyr'd doth rashly on the greene grasse fall.
When they were slender, and like downy mosse,
Thy troubled haires, alas, endur'd great losse.
How patiently hot irons they did take 25
In crooked trammells crispy curles to make.
I cryed, tis sinne, tis sinne, these haires to burne
They well become thee, then to spare them turne.
Farre off be force, no fire to them may reach
Thy very haires will the hot bodkin teach. 30
Lost are the goodly lockes, which from their crowne
Phoebus and *Bacchus* wisht were hanging downe.
Such were they as *Dione* painted stands
All naked holding in her wave-moist hands.
Why doest thy ill kembd tresses losse lament? 35
Why in thy glasse doest looke being discontent?
Bee not to see with wonted eyes inclinde
To please thy selfe, thy selfe put out of minde.
No charmed herbes of any harlot skathd thee,
No faithlesse witch in *Thessale* waters bath'd thee. 4c
No sickness harm'd thee, farre be that a way,
No envious tongue wrought thy thicke lockes decay.

10 neither] *Robinson*; either *Mason*   26 trammells] *Robinson*; ιannells *Mason*
33 *Dione*] *Diana Mason*

By thine owne hand and fault thy hurt doth growe,
Thou mad'st thy head with compound poyson flow.
Now *Germany* shall captive haire-tyers send thee,   45
And vanquisht people curious dressings lend thee.
Which some admiring, O thou oft wilt blush
And say he likes me for my borrowed bush,
Praysing for me some unknowne *Guelder* dame,
But I remember when it was my fame.   50
Alas she almost weepes, and her white cheekes,
Died red with shame to hide from shame she seekes.
She holds, and viewes her old lockes in her lappe
Aye me rare gifts unworthy such a happe.
Cheere up thy selfe, thy losse thou maiest repaire.   55
And be heereafter seene with native haire.

ELEGIA 15

Ad invidos, quod fama poetarum sit perennis.

Envie why carpest thou my time is spent so ill,
And termst my workes fruites of an idle quill.
Or that unlike the line from whence I come,
Warres dustie honours are refus'd being yong.
Nor that I study not the brawling lawes,   5
Nor set my voyce to sale in every cause.
Thy scope is mortall, mine eternall fame,
That all the world may ever chaunt my name.
Homer shall live while *Tenedos* stands and *Ide*,
Or into Sea swift *Simois* doth slide.   10
Ascraeus lives, while grapes with new wine swell,
Or men with crooked Sickles corne downe fell.
The world shall of *Callimachus* ever speake,
His Art excelld, although his witte was weake.
For ever lasts high *Sophocles* proud vaine,   15
With Sunne and Moone, *Aratus* shall remaine.
While bond-men cheate, fathers be hard, bawds whorish,
And strumpets flatter, shall *Menander* flourish.
Rude *Ennius*, and *Plautus* full of witte,
Are both in fames eternall legend writt.   20

What age of *Varroes* name shall not be tolde,
And *Jasons Argos* and the fleece of golde.
Loftie *Lucretius* shall live that howre,
That nature shall dissolve this earthly bower.
Aeneas warre, and *Tityrus* shall be read,   25
While *Rome* of all the conquered world is head.
Till *Cupids* Bowe and fiery Shafts be broken,
Thy verses sweet *Tibullus* shalbe spoken.
And *Gallus* shall be knowne from East to West,
So shall *Licoris* whom he loved best.   30
Therefore when Flint and Iron weare away,
Verse is immortall, and shall nere decay.
To verse let Kings give place, and Kingly showes,
And bankes ore which gold-bearing *Tagus* flowes.
Let base conceipted witts admire vilde things,   35
Faire *Phoebus* lead me to the *Muses* springs.
About my head be quivering mirtle wound,
And in sad lovers heads let me be found.
The living, not the dead can' envy bite.
For after death all men receive their right.   40
Then though death rackes my bones in funerall fire,
Ile live, and as he puls me downe mount higher.

P. Ovidii Nasonis Amorum
Liber Secundus

ELEGIA 1

Quod pro gigantomachia amores scribere
sit coactus.

I *Ovid* Poet of my wantonnesse
Borne at *Peligny* to write more addresse.
So *Cupid* wills, farre hence be the severe
You are unapt my looser lines to heare.
Let Maydes whom hot desire to husbands leade,   5
And rude boyes toucht with unknowne love me reade.
That some youth hurt as I am with loves bowe
His owne flames best aquainted signes may knowe.
And long admiring say by what meanes learnd
Hath this same Poet my sad chaunce discernd?   10
I durst the great celestiall battells tell
Hundred-hand *Gyges*, and had done it well,
With earthes revenge and how *Olimpus* toppe
High *Ossa* bore mount *Pelion* up to proppe.
Jove and *Joves* thunderbolts I had in hand   15
Which for his heaven fell on the *Gyants* band.
My wench her dore shut, *Joves* affares I left
Even *Jove* himselfe out off my wit was reft,
Pardon me *Jove*, thy weapons ayde me nought
Her shut gates greater lightning then thyne brought.   20
Toyes, and light Elegies my darts I tooke
Quickly soft words hard dores wide open strooke.
Verses deduce the horned bloudy moone
And call the sunnes white horses backe at noone.
Snakes leape by verse from caves of broken mountaines   25
And turned streames run back-ward to their fountaines.
Verses ope dores, and lockes put in the poast
Although of oake, to yeeld to verses boast.

---

1 my] *Robinson*; they *Mason*   23 deduce] *Bowers*; reduce *Mason*   24 backe]
Robinson; blacke *Mason*

What helpes it me of fierce *Achill* to sing?
What good to me wil either *Ajax* bring? 30
Or he who war'd and wand'red twenty yeare?
Or wofull *Hector* whom wilde jades did teare?
But when I praise a pretty wenches face
Shee in requitall doth me oft imbrace.
A great reward: *Heroes*, O famous names 35
Farewel, your favour nought my minde inflames.
Wenches apply your faire lookes to my verse
Which golden love doth unto me rehearse.

ELEGIA 2

Ad Bagoum, ut custodiam puellae sibi commissae
laxiorem habeat.

Bagous whose care doth thy Mistrisse bridle
While I speake some fewe, yet fit words be idle.
I sawe the damsell walking yesterday
There where the porch doth *Danaus* fact display.
Shee pleas'd me soone, I sent, and did her woo, 5
Her trembling hand writ back she might not doo.
And asking why, this answeare she redoubled
Because thy care too much thy Mistresse troubled.
Keeper if thou be wise cease hate to cherish,
Beleeve me, whom we feare, we wish to perish. 10
Nor is her husband wise, what needes defence
When un-protected ther is no expence,
But furiously he follow his loves fire
And thinkes her chast whom many doe desire.
Stolne liberty she may by thee obtaine 15
Which giving her, she may give thee againe.
Wilt thou her fault learne, she may make thee tremble,
Feare to be guilty then thou maiest desemble.
Thinke when she reades, her mother letters sent her
Let him goe forth knowne, that unknowne did enter, 20

12 un-protected] *Robinson*; un-protested *Mason*

Let him goe see her though she doe not languish
And then report her sicke and full of anguish.
If long she stayes to thinke the time more short
Lay downe thy forehead in thy lap to snort.
Enquire not what with *Isis* may be done   25
Nor feare least she to th'theater's runne.
Knowing her scapes thine honour shall encrease,
And what lesse labour then to hold thy peace?
Let him please, haunt the house, be kindly usd
Enjoy the wench, let all else be refusd.   30
Vaine causes faine of him, the true to hide
And what she likes, let both hold ratifide.
When most her husband bends the browes and frownes
His fauning wench with her desire he crownes.
But yet sometimes to chide thee let her fall   35
Counterfet teares: and thee lewd hangman call.
Object thou then what she may well excuse,
To staine all faith in truth, by false crimes use.
Of wealth and honour so shall grow thy heape,
Do this and soone thou shalt thy freedome reape.   40
On tell-tales neckes thou seest the linke-knitt chaines,
The filthy prison faithlesse breasts restraines.
Water in waters, and fruite flying touch
Tantalus seekes, his long tongues gaine is such.
While *Junos* watch-man *Io* too much eyde,   45
Him timelesse death tooke, she was deifide.
I sawe ones legges with fetters black and blewe,
By whom the husband his wives incest knewe.
More he deserv'd, to both great harme he fram'd
The man did grieve, the woman was defam'd.   50
Trust me all husbands for such faults are sad
Nor make they any man that heare them glad.
If he loves not, deafe eares thou doest importune,
Or if he loves, thy tale breedes his misfortune.
Nor is it easily prov'd though manifest,   55
She safe by favour of her judge doth rest.
Though himselfe see; heele credit her denyall
Condemne his eyes, and say there is no tryall.
Spying his mistrisse teares, he will lament
And say this blabbe shall suffer punishment.   60

Why fightst gainst oddes? to thee being cast do happe
Sharpe stripes, she sitteth in the judges lappe.
To meete for poyson or vilde facts we crave not,
My hands an unsheath'd shyning weapon have not.
Wee seeke that through thee safely love we may,   65
What can be easier then the thing we pray?

ELEGIA 3

Ad Eunuchum servantem dominam.

Aye me an *Eunuch* keepes my mistrisse chaste,
That cannot *Venus* mutuall pleasure taste.
Who first depriv'd yong boys of their best part,
With selfe same woundes he gave, he ought to smart.
To kinde requests thou wouldst more gentle prove,   5
If ever wench had made luke-warme thy love:
Thou wert not borne to ride, or armes to beare,
Thy hands agree not with the warlike speare.
Men handle those, all manly hopes resigne,
Thy mistrisse enseignes must be likewise thine.   10
Please her, her hate makes others thee abhorre,
If she discardes thee, what use servest thou for?
Good forme there is, yearest apt to play togither,
Unmeete is beauty without use to wither.
Shee may deceive thee, though thou her protect,   15
What two determine never wants effect.
Our prayers move thee to assist our drift,
While thou hast time yet to bestowe that gift.

ELEGIA 4

Quod amet mulieres, cuiuscunque formae sint.

I meane not to defend the scapes of any,
Or justifie my vices being many.
For I confesse, if that might merite favour,
Heere I display my lewd and loose behaviour.

I loathe, yet after that I loathe, I runne,   5
Oh how the burthen irkes, that we should shunne.
I cannot rule my selfe, but where love please,
Am driven like a ship upon rough seas.
No one face likes me best, all faces move,
A hundred reasons make me ever love.   10
If any eye me with a modest looke,
I blush, and by that blushfull glance am tooke.
And she thats coy I like for being no clowne,
Me thinkes she would be nimble when shees downe.
Though her sowre lookes a *Sabines* browe resemble,   15
I thinke sheele do, but deepely can dissemble.
If she be learn'd, then for her skill I crave her,
If not, because shees simple I would have her.
Before *Callimachus* one preferres me farre,
Seeing she likes my bookes why should we jarre?   20
An other railes at me and that I write
Yet would I lie with her if that I might.
Trips she, it likes me well, plods she, what than?
Shee would be nimbler, lying with a man.
And when one sweetely sings, then straight I long   25
To quaver on her lips even in her song.
Or if one touch the Lute with arte and cunning
Who wold not love those hands for their swift running?
And her I like that with a majesty
Folds up her armes and makes lowe curtesy.   30
To leave my selfe, that am in love with all
Some one of these might make the chastest fall.
If she be tall, shees like an *Amazon*,
And therefore filles the bed she lies upon.
If short, she lies the rounder to say troth   35
Both short and long please me, for I love both.
I thinke what one undeckt would be, being drest
Is she attired, then shew her graces best.
A white wench thralles me, so doth golden yellowe
And nut-browne girles in doing have no fellowe.   40
If her white necke be shadoed with blacke haire
Why so was *Ledas*, yet was *Leda* faire.
Amber trest is she, then on the morne thinke I
My love alludes to every history:

A yong wench pleaseth, and an old is good   45
This for her lookes that for her woman-hood.
Nay what is she that any *Roman* loves
But my ambitious ranging minde approves.

ELEGIA 5

Ad amicam corruptam.

No love is deere (quiverd *Cupid* flie)
That my chiefe wish should be so oft to die.
Minding thy fault, with death I wish to revill,
Alas a wench is a perpetuall evill.
No intercepted lines thy deedes display,   5
No gifts given secretly thy crime bewray.
O would my proofes as vaine might be withstood,
Aye me poore soule, why is my cause so good.
He's happy, that his love dares boldly credit,
To whom his wench can say, I never did it.   10
He's cruell, and too much his griefe doth favour
That seekes the conquest by her loose behaviour.
Poore wretch I sawe when thou didst thinke I slumbred,
Not drunke, your faults in the spilt wine I numbred.
I sawe your nodding eye-browes much to speake,   15
Even from your cheekes parte of a voice did breake.
Not silent were thine eyes, the boord with wine
Was scribled, and thy fingers writ a line.
I knew your speech (what do not lovers see?)
And words that seem'd for certaine markes to be.   20
Now many guests were gone, the feast being done,
The youthfull sort to divers pastimes runne.
I sawe you then unlawfull kisses joyne,
(Such with my tongue it likes me to purloyne).
None such the sister gives her brother grave,   25
But such kinde wenches let their lovers have.
Phoebus gave not *Diana* such tis thought,
But *Venus* often to her *Mars* such brought.

13 wretch] *Dyce*; wench *Mason*

What doest, I cryed transportst thou my delight?
My lordly hands Ile throwe upon my right.   30
Such blisse is onely common to us two,
In this sweete good, why hath a third to do?
This, and what grife inforc'd me say I say'd,
A scarlet blush her guilty face arayed.
Even such as by *Aurora* hath the skie,   35
Or maides that their betrothed husbands spie.
Such as a rose mixt with a lilly breedes,
Or when the Moone travailes with charmed steedes.
Or such, as least long yeares should turne the die,
Arachne staynes *Assyrian* ivory.   40
To these, or some of these like was her colour,
By chaunce her beauty never shined fuller.
She viewed the earth: the earth to viewe, beseem'd her
She looked sad: sad, comely I esteem'd her.
Even kembed as they were, her lockes to rend,   45
And scratch her faire soft cheekes I did intend.
Seeing her face, mine upreard armes discended,
With her owne armor was my wench defended.
I that ere-while was fierce, now humbly sue,
Least with worse kisses she should me indue.   50
She laught, and kissed so sweetly as might make
Wrath-kindled *Jove* away his thunder shake.
I grieve least others should such good perceive,
And wish hereby them all unknowne to leave.
Also much better were they then I tell,   55
And ever seemed as some new sweete befell.
Tis ill they pleas'd so much, for in my lips,
Lay her whole tongue hid, mine in hers she dips.
This grieves me not, no joyned kisses spent,
Bewaile I onely, though I them lament.   60
No where can they be taught but in the bed,
I know no maister of so great hire sped.

ELEGIA 6

In mortem psittaci.

The parrat from east *India* to me sent,
Is dead, al fowles her exequies frequent.
Go goodly birdes, striking your breasts bewaile,
And with rough clawes your tender cheekes assaile.
For wofull haires let piece-torne plumes abound,   5
For long shrild trumpets let your notes resound.
Why *Philomele* doest *Tereus* leudnesse mourne?
All wasting years have that complaint out worne.
Thy tunes let this rare birdes sad funerall borrowe,
Itis is great, but auntient cause of sorrowe.   10
All you whose pineons in the cleare aire sore,
But most thou friendly turtle-dove deplore.
Full concord all your lives was you betwixt,
And to the end your constant faith stood fixt.
What *Pylades* did to *Orestes* prove,   15
Such to the parrat was the turtle dove.
But what availde this faith? her rarest hue?
Or voice that howe to change the wilde notes knew?
What helpes it thou wert given to please my wench,
Birdes haples glory death thy life doth quench.   20
Thou with thy quilles mightst make greene *Emeralds* darke
And passe our scarlet of red saffrons marke.
No such voice-feigning bird was on the ground,
Thou spokest thy words so well with stammering sound.
Envy hath rapt thee, no fierce warres thou movedst,   25
Vaine babling speech, and pleasant peace thou lovedst.
Behould how quailes among their battailes live,
Which do perchance old age unto them give.
A little fild thee, and for love of talke,
Thy mouth to taste of many meates did balke.   30
Nuts were thy food, and Poppie causde thee sleepe,
Pure waters moisture thirst away did keepe.
The ravenous vulture lives, the Puttock hovers
Around the aire, the Cadesse raine discovers,

8 out] Tucker Brooke; not *Mason*   10 *Itis* is] Martin; It is as *Mason*

And Crowes survive armes-bearing *Pallas* hate,   35
Whose life nine ages scarce bring out of date.
Dead is that speaking image of mans voice,
The Parrat given me, the farre worlds best choice.
The greedy spirits take the best things first,
Supplying their voide places with the worst.   40
Thersites did *Protesilaus* survive,
And *Hector* dyed his brothers yet alive.
My wenches vowes for thee what should I show,
Which stormie South-windes into sea did blowe?
The seventh day came, none following mightst thou see   45
And the fates distaffe emptie stood to thee,
Yet words in thy benummed palate rung,
Farewell *Corinna* cryed thy dying tongue.
Elisium hath a wood of holme trees black,
Whose earth doth not perpetuall greene-grasse lacke,   50
There good birds rest (if we beleeve things hidden)
Whence uncleane fowles are said to be forbidden.
There harmelesse Swans feed all abroad the river,
There lives the *Phoenix* one alone bird ever,
There *Junoes* bird displayes his gorgious feather,   55
And loving Doves kisse eagerly together.
The Parrat into wood receiv'd with these,
Turnes all the goodly birdes to what she please.
A grave her bones hides, on her corps great grave,
The little stones these little verses have.   60
This tombe approves, I pleasde my mistresse well,
My mouth in speaking did all birds excell.

ELEGIA 7

Amicae se purgat quod ancillam non amet.

Doost me of new crimes alwayes guilty frame?
To over-come, so oft to fight I shame.
If on the Marble Theater I looke,
One among many is to grieve thee tooke.

38 worlds] *Robinson*; words *Mason*

If some faire wench me secretly behold,   5
Thou arguest she doth secret markes unfold.
If I praise any, thy poore haires thou tearest,
If blame, dissembling of my fault thou fearest.
If I looke well, thou thinkest thou doest not move,
If ill, thou saiest I die for others love.   10
Would I were culpable of some offence,
They that deserve paine, beare't with patience.
Now rash accusing, and thy vaine beliefe,
Forbid thine anger to procure my griefe.
Loe how the miserable great eared *Asse*,   15
Duld with much beating slowly forth doth passe.
Behold *Cypassis* wont to dresse thy head,
Is charg'd to violate her mistresse bed.
The Gods from this sinne rid me of suspition,
To like a base wench of despisd condition.   20
With *Venus* game who will a servant grace?
Or any back made rough with stripes imbrace?
Adde she was diligent thy locks to braide,
And for her skill to thee a gratefull maide.
Should I sollicit her that is so just?   25
To take repulse, and cause her shew my lust:
I sweare by Venus, and the wingd boyes bowe,
My selfe unguilty of this crime I know.

ELEGIA 8

Ad Cypassim ancillam Corinnae.

Cypassis that a thousand wayes trimst haire,
Worthy to keembe none but a Goddesse faire,
Our pleasant scapes shew thee no clowne to be,
Apt to thy mistrisse, but more apt to me.
Who that our bodies were comprest bewrayde?   5
Whence knowes *Corinna* that with thee I playde?
Yet blusht I not, nor usde I any saying,
That might be urg'd to witnesse our false playing.
What if a man with bond-women offend,
To prove him foolish did I ere contend?   10

Achilles burnt with face of captive *Briseis*,
Great *Agamemnon* lov'd his servant *Chriseis*.
Greater then these my selfe I not esteeme,
What graced Kings, in me no shame I deeme.
But when on thee her angry eyes did rush,   15
In both thy cheekes she did perceive thee blush,
But being present, might that worke the best,
By *Venus* Deity how did I protest.
Thou Goddesse doest command a warme South-blast,
My false oathes in *Carpathian* seas to cast.   20
For which good turne my sweete reward repay,
Let me lie with thee browne *Cypasse* to day.
Ungrate why feignest new feares? and doest refuse;
Well maiest thou one thing for thy Mistresse use.
If thou deniest foole, Ile our deeds expresse,   25
And as a traitour mine owne fault confesse.
Telling thy mistresse, where I was with thee,
How oft, and by what meanes we did agree.

ELEGIA 9

Ad Cupidinem.

O *Cupid* that doest never cease my smart,
O boy that lyest so slothefull in my heart.
Why me that alwayes was thy souldiour found,
Does harme, and in thy tents why doest me wound?
Why burnes thy brand, why strikes thy bow thy friends?   5
More glory by thy vanquisht foes assends.
Did not *Pelides* whom his Speare did grieve,
Being requirde, with speedy helpe relieve?
Hunters leave taken beasts, pursue the chase,
And then things found do ever further pace.   10
We people wholy given thee, feel thine armes,
Thy dull hand stayes thy striving enemies harmes.

-----

16 thy] *Dyce*; my *Mason*   20 false] *Tucker Brooke*; selfe *Mason*

Doest joy to have thy hooked Arrowes shaked,
In naked bones? love hath my bones left naked.
So many men and maidens without love,   15
Hence with great laude thou maiest a triumph move.
Rome if her strength the huge world had not fild,
With strawie cabins now her courts should build.
The weary souldiour hath the conquerd fields,
His sword layed by, safe, though rude places yeelds.   20
The Docke inharbours ships drawne from the flouds,
Horse freed from service range abroad the woods.
And time is was for me to live in quiet,
That have so oft serv'd pretty wenches dyet.
Yet should I curse a God, if he but said,   25
Live without love, so sweete ill is a maide.
For when my loathing it of heate deprives me,
I know not whether my mindes whirle-wind drives me.
Even as a head-strong courser beares away,
His rider vainely striving him to stay,   30
Or as a sodaine gale thrustes into sea,
The haven touching barcke now nere the lea,
So wavering *Cupid* bringes me backe amaine.
And purple love resumes his dartes againe.
Strike boy, I offer thee my naked brest,   35
Heere thou hast strength, here thy right hand doth rest.
Here of themselves thy shafts come, as if shot,
Better then I, their quiver knowes them not.
Haples is he that all the night lies quiet
And slumbring, thinkes himselfe much blessed by it.   40
Foole, what is sleepe but image of cold death,
Long shalt thou rest when Fates expire thy breath.
But me let crafty damsells words deceive,
Great joyes by hope I inly shall conceive.
Now let her flatter me, now chide me hard,   45
Let me enjoy her oft, oft be debard.
Cupid by thee, *Mars* in great doubt doth trample,
And thy step-father fights by thy example.
Light art thou, and more windie then thy winges,
Joyes with uncertaine faith thou takest and brings.   50

32 haven] *Mal 368*; heaven *Mason*

Yet love, if thou with thy faire mother heare,
Within my brest no desert empire beare.
Subdue the wandring wenches to thy raigne,
So of both people shalt thou homage gaine.

ELEGIA 10

Ad Graecinum quod eodem tempore duas amet.

Graecinus (well I wot) thou touldst me once,
I could not be in love with two at once.
By thee deceived, by thee surpriz'd am I
For now I love two women equally.
Both are well favor'd, both rich in aray,   5
Which is the loveliest it is hard to say.
This seemes the fairest, so doth that to me,
And this doth please me most, and so doth she.
Even as a boate, tost by contrary winde,
So with this love, and that, wavers my minde.   10
Venus, why doublest thou my endlesse smart?
Was not one wench enough to grieve my hart?
Why addst thou stars to heaven, leaves to greene woods
And to the vast deepe sea fresh water flouds?
Yet this is better farre then lie alone,   15
Let such as be mine enemies have none.
Yea let my foes sleepe in an empty bed,
And in the midst their bodies largely spread.
But may soft love rowse up my drowsie eyes,
And from my mistris bosome let me rise.   20
Let one wench cloy me with sweete loves delight
If one can doote, if not, two every night.
Though I am slender, I have store of pith
Nor want I strength but weight to presse her with.
Pleasure addes fuell to my lust-full fire   25
I pay them home with that they most desire.
Oft have I spent the night in wantonnesse,
And in the morne beene lively nere the lesse.

Hee's happy who loves mutuall skirmish slayes,
And to the Gods for that death *Ovid* prayes.   30
Let souldiours chase their enemies amaine,
And with their bloud eternall honour gaine.
Let Marchants seeke wealth with perjured lips;
And being wrackt carowse the sea tir'd with their ships.
But when I dye, would I might droupe with doing,   35
And in the midst thereof, set my soule going,
That at my funeralls some may weeping crye,
Even as he led his life, so did he dye.

ELEGIA 11

Ad amicam navigantem.

The lofty Pine from high mount *Pelion* raught
Ill waies by rough seas wondring waves first taught,
Which rashly twixt the sharpe rocks in the deepe,
Caried the famous golden-fleeced sheepe.
O would that no Oares might in seas have suncke,   5
The *Argos* wrackt had deadly waters drunke.
Loe country Gods, and known bed to forsake,
Corinna meanes, and dangerous wayes to take.
For thee the East and West winds make me pale,
With Icy *Boreas*, and the Southerne gale: 10
Thou shalt admire no woods or Citties there,
The unjust seas all blewish do sppeare.
The Ocean hath no painted stones or shelles,
The sucking shore with their aboundance swels.
Maides on the shore, with marble white feete tread,   15
So farre 'tis safe, but to go farther dread.
Let others tell how winds fierce battailes wage,
How *Scyllaes* and *Caribdis* waters rage.
And with what rockes the feard *Cerannia* threat,
In what gulfe either *Syrtes* have their seate.   20

29 slayes] *Bindley, Isham*; layes *Mason*

7 known] *Robinson*; know *Mason*

Let others tell this, and what each one speakes
Beleeve, no tempest the beleever wreakes.
Too late you looke back, when with anchors weighd,
The crooked Barque hath her swift sailes displayd.
The carefull ship-man now feares angry gusts,   25
And with the waters sees death neere him thrusts,
But if that *Triton* tosse the troubled floud,
In all thy face will be no crimsen bloud.
Then wilt thou *Laedas* noble twinne-starres pray,
And he is happy whom the earth holds, say,   30
It is more safe to sleepe, to read a booke,
The *Thracian* Harpe with cunning to have strooke,
But if my words with winged stormes hence slip,
Yet *Galatea* favour thou her ship.
The losse of such a wench much blame will gather,   35
Both to the Sea-nimphes, and the Sea-nimphes father.
Go, minding to returne with prosperous winde,
Whose blast may hether strongly be inclinde,
Let *Nereus* bend the waves unto this shore,
Hether the windes blowe, here the spring-tide rore.   40
Request milde *Zephires* helpe for thy availe,
And with thy hand assist thy swelling saile.
I from the shore thy knowne ship first will see,
And say it brings her that preserveth me;
Ile clip and kisse thee with all contentation,   45
For thy returne shall fall the vowd oblation,
And in the forme of beds weele strowe soft sand,
Each little hill shall for a table stand:
There wine being fild, thou many things shalt tell,
How almost wrackt thy ship in maine seas fell.   50
And hasting to me, neither darkesome night,
Nor violent South-windes did thee ought affright.
Ile thinke all true, though it be feigned matter.
Mine owne desires why should my selfe not flatter?
Let the bright day-starre cause in heaven this day be,   55
To bring that happy time so soone as may be.

ELEGIA 12
Exultat, quod amica potitus sit.

About my temples go triumphant bayes,
Conquer'd *Corinna* in my bosome layes.
She whom her husband, guard, and gate as foes,
Least Arts should winne her firmely did inclose,
That victory doth chiefely triumph merit,   5
Which without bloud-shed doth the pray inherit.
No little ditched townes, no lowlie walles,
But to my share a captive damsell falles.
When *Troy* by ten yeares battle tumbled downe,
With the *Atrides* many gainde renowne.   10
But I no partner of my glory brooke,
Nor can an other say his helpe I tooke.
I guide and souldiour wunne the field and weare her,
I was both horse-man, foote-man, standard bearer.
Nor in my act hath fortune mingled chance,   15
O care-got triumph hetherwards advance.
Nor is my warres cause new, but for a Queene
Europe, and *Asia* in firme peace had beene.
The *Laphithes*, and the *Centaures* for a woman,
To cruell armes their drunken selves did summon.   20
A woman forc'd the *Troyanes* new to enter
Warres, just *Latinus*, in thy kingdomes center:
A woman against late-built *Rome* did send
The *Sabine* Fathers, who sharpe warres intend.
I saw how Bulls for a white Heifer strive,   25
Shee looking on them did more courage give.
And me with many, but yet me without murther,
Cupid commands to move his ensignes further.

ELEGIA 13
Ad Isidem, ut parientem Corinnam iuvet.

While rashly her wombes burthen she casts out,
Wearie *Corinna* hath her life in doubt.
She secretly with me such harme attempted,
Angry I was, but feare my wrath exempted.

But she conceiv'd of me, or I am sure   5
I oft have done, what might as much procure.
Thou that frequents *Canopus* pleasant fields,
Memphis, and *Pharos* that sweete date trees yeelds,
And where swift *Nile* in his large channell slipping,
By seaven hugh mouthes into the sea is skipping,   10
By fear'd *Anubis* visage I thee pray,
So in thy Temples shall *Osiris* stay,
And the dull snake about thy offrings creepe,
And in thy pompe hornd *Apis* with thee keepe.
Turne thy lookes hether, and in one spare twaine,   15
Thou givest my mistris life, she mine againe.
Shee oft hath serv'd thee upon certaine dayes,
Where the *French* rout engirt themselves with Bayes.
On labouring women thou doest pitty take,
Whose bodies with their heavy burthens ake.   20
My wench *Lucina*, I intreat thee favour,
Worthy she is, thou shouldst in mercy save her.
In white, with incense Ile thine Altars greete,
My selfe will bring vowed gifts before thy feete,
Subscribing *Naso* with *Corinna* sav'd: 25
Do but deserve gifts with this title grav'd.
But if in no great feare I may advize thee,
To have this skirmish fought, let it suffice thee.

ELEGIA 14

In amicam, quod abortivum ipsa fecerit.

What helpes it Woman to be free from warre?
Nor being arm'd fierce troupes to follow farre?
If without battell selfe-wrought wounds annoy them,
And their owne privie weapon'd hands destroy them.
Who unborne infants first to slay invented,   5
Deserv'd thereby with death to be tormented.

<hr />

10 skipping] *Dyce*; slipping *Mason*

Because thy belly should rough wrinckles lacke,
Wilt thou thy wombe-inclosed off-spring wracke?
Had ancient Mothers this vile custome cherisht,
All humaine kinde by their default had perisht.
Or stones, our stockes originall should be hurld,
Againe by some in this unpeopled world.
Who should have Priams wealthy substance wonne,
If watry *Thetis* had her childe fordone?
In swelling wombe her twinnes had *Ilia* kilde?
He had not beene that conquering *Rome* did build.
Had *Venus* spoilde her bellies *Troyane* fruite,
The earth of *Caesars* had beene destitute.
Thou also, that wert borne faire, hadst decayed,
If such a worke thy mother had assayed.
My self that better dye with loving may
Had seene, my mother killing me, no day.
Why takest increasing grapes from Vine-trees full?
With cruell hand why doest greene Apples pull?
Fruites ripe will fall, let springing things increase,
Life is no light price of a small surcease:
Why with hid irons are your bowels torne?
And why dire poison give you babes unborne?
At *Colchis* stain'd with childrens bloud men raile,
And mother-murthered *Itis* they bewaile,
Both unkinde parents, but for causes sad,
Their wedlocks pledges veng'd their husbands bad.
What *Tereus*, what *Jason* you provokes,
To plague your bodies with such harmefull strokes?
Armenian Tygers never did so ill,
Nor dares the Lyonesse her young whelpes kill.
But tender Damsels do it, though with paine,
Oft dyes she that her paunch-wrapt child hath slaine.
Shee dyes, and with loose haires to grave is sent,
And who ere see her, worthily lament.
But in the ayre let these words come to nought,
And my presages of no weight be thought.
Forgive her gratious Gods this one delict,
And on the next fault punishment inflict.

10

15

20

25

30

35

40

11 Or] *Dyce*; On *Mason*   22 no] *Dyce*; to *Mason*   30 they] *Robinson*; thee *Mason*

ELEGIA 15

Ad annulum, quem dono amicae dedit.

Thou ring that shalt my faire girles finger binde,
Wherein is seene the givers loving minde:
Be welcome to her, gladly let her take thee,
And her small joynts incircling round hoope make thee.
Fit her so well, as she is fit for me: 5
And of just compasse for her knuckles bee.
Blest ring thou in my mistris hand shalt lye,
My selfe poore wretch mine owne gifts now envie.
O would that sodainly into my gift,
I could my selfe by secret Magicke shift. 10
Then would I wish thee touch my mistris pappe,
And hide thy left hand underneath her lappe.
I would get off though straight, and sticking fast,
And in her bosome strangely fall at last.
Then I, that I may seale her privy leaves, 15
Least to the waxe the hold-fast drye gemme cleaves,
Would first my beautious wenches moist lips touch,
Onely Ile signe nought, that may grieve me much.
I would not out, might I in one place hit,
But in lesse compasse her small fingers knit. 20
My life, that I will shame thee never feare,
Or be a loade thou shouldst refuse to beare.
Weare me, when warmest showers thy members wash,
And through the gemme let thy lost waters pash.
But seeing thee, I thinke my thing will swell, 25
And even the ring performe a mans part well.
Vaine things why wish I? go small gift from hand,
Let her my faith with thee given understand.

22 be] *Robinson*; by *Mason*

ELEGIA 16

Ad amicam, ut ad rura sua veniat.

Sulmo, *Pelignies* third part me containes,
A small, but wholesome soyle with watrie veynes.
Although the sunne to rive the earth incline,
And the *Icarian* froward Dog-starre shine,
Pelignian fields with liqued rivers flowe,   5
And on the soft ground fertile greene grasse growe.
With corne the earth abounds, with vines much more,
And some few pastures *Pallas* Olives bore.
And by the rising herbes, where cleare springs slide,
A grassie turffe the moistened earth doth hide.   10
But absent is my fire, lyes ile tell none,
My heate is heere, what moves my heate is gone.
Pollux and *Castor*, might I stand betwixt,
In heaven without thee would I not be fixt.
Upon the cold earth pensive let them lay,   15
That meane to travaile some long irkesome way.
Or els will maidens, yong-mens mates, to go
If they determine to persever so.
Then on the rough *Alpes* should I tread aloft,
My hard way with my mistrisse would seeme soft.   20
With her I durst the *Lybian* Syrtes breake through,
And raging Seas in boistrous South-winds plough.
No barking Dogs that *Syllaes* intrailes beare,
Nor thy gulfes crooked *Malea*, would I feare.
No flowing waves with drowned ships forth poured,   25
By cloyed *Charibdis*, and againe devoured.
But if sterne *Neptunes* windie powre prevaile,
And waters force, force helping Gods to faile,
With thy white armes upon my shoulders seaze,
So sweete a burthen I will beare with eaze.   30
The youth oft swimming to his *Hero* kinde,
Had then swum over, but the way was blinde,
But without thee, although vine-planted ground
Conteines me, though the streames in fields surround,

5 with] *Mal 368*; which *Mason*

Though *Hindes* in brookes the running waters bring,   35
And coole gales shake the tall trees leavy spring,
Healthfull *Peligny* I esteeme nought worth,
Nor do I like the country of my birth.
Sythia, Cilicia, Brittaine are as good,
And rockes dyed crimson with *Prometheus* bloud.   40
Elmes love the Vines, the Vines with Elmes abide,
Why doth my mistresse from me oft devide?
Thou swearest, devision should not twixt us rise,
By me, and by my starres, thy radiant eyes.
Maides words more vaine and light then falling leaves,   45
Which as it seemes, hence winde and sea bereaves.
If any godly care of me thou hast,
Adde deeds unto thy promises at last.
And with swift Naggs drawing thy little Coach,
(Their reines let loose) right soone my house approach.   50
But when she comes, you swelling mounts sinck downe,
And falling vallies be the smooth-wayes crowne.

ELEGIA 17

Quod Corinnae soli sit serviturus.

To serve a wench if any thinke it shame,
He being Judge, I am convinc'd of blame.
Let me be slandered, while my fire she hides,
That *Paphos*, and the floud-beate *Cithera* guides.
Would I had beene my mistresse gentle prey,   5
Since some faire one I should of force obey.
Beauty gives heart, *Corinnas* lookes excell,
Aye me why is it knowne to her so well?
But by her glasse disdainefull pride she learnes,
Nor she her selfe but first trim'd up discernes.   10
Not though thy face in all things make thee raigne,
(O face most cunning mine eyes to detaine)
Thou oughtst therefore to scorne me for thy mate,
Small things with greater may be copulate.
Love-snarde *Calpyso* is supposde to pray,   15
A mortall nimphes refusing Lord to stay.

Who doubts, with *Pelius*, *Thetis* did consort,
Egeria with just *Numa* had good sport,
Venus with *Vulcan*, though smiths tooles laide by,
With his stumpe-foote he halts ill-favouredly.   20
This kinde of verse is not alike, yet fit,
With shorter numbers the heroicke sit.
And thou my light accept me how so ever,
Lay in the mid bed, there be my law giver.
My stay no crime, my flight no joy shall breede,   25
Nor of our love to be asham'd we need,
For great revenews I good verses have,
And many by me to get glory crave.
I know a wench reports her selfe *Corinne*,
What would not she give that faire name to winne?   30
But sundry flouds in one banke never go,
Eurotas cold, and poplar-bearing *Po*.
Nor in my bookes shall one but thou be writ,
Thou doest alone give matter to my wit.

ELEGIA 18

Ad Macrum, quod de amoribus scribat.

To tragick verse while thou *Achilles* trainst,
And new sworne souldiours maiden armes retainst,
Wee *Macer* sit in *Venus* slothfull shade,
And tender love hath great things hatefull made.
Often at length, my wench depart, I bid,   5
Shee in my lap sits still as earst she did.
I sayd it irkes me, halfe to weping framed,
Aye me she cries, to love, why art a shamed?
Then wreathes about my necke her winding armes,
And thousand kisses gives, that worke my harmes: 10
I yeeld, and back my wit from battells bring,
Domesticke acts, and mine owne warres to sing.
Yet tragedies, and scepters fild my lines,
But though I apt were for such high deseignes,
Love laughed at my cloak, and buskines painted,   15
And rule so soone with private hands acquainted.

My Mistris deity also drewe me fro it,
And love triumpheth ore his buskind Poet.
What lawfull is, or we professe loves art,
(Alas my precepts turne my selfe to smart)   20
We write, or what *Penelope* sends *Ulysses*,
Or *Phillis* teares that her *Demophoon* misses,
What thanklesse *Jason*, *Macareus*, and *Paris*,
Phedra, and *Hipolite* may read, my care is,
And what poore *Dido* with her drawne sword sharpe,   25
Doth say, with her that lov'd the *Aonian* harpe.
As soone as from strange lands *Sabinus* came,
And writings did from diverse places frame,
White-cheekt *Penelope* knewe *Ulisses* signe
The stepdame read *Hyppolitus* lustlesse line.   30
Eneas to *Elisa* answere gives,
And *Phillis* hath to reade; if now she lives.
Jasons sad letter doth *Hipsipile* greete,
Sappho her vowed harpe laies at *Phoebus* feete.
Nor of thee *Macer* that resoundst forth armes,   35
Is golden love hid in *Mars* mid-alarmes.
There *Paris* is, and *Helens* crymes record,
With *Laodameia* mate to her dead Lord.
Unlesse I erre to these thou more incline,
Then warres, and from thy tents wilt come to mine.   40

ELEGIA 19

Ad rivalem, cui uxor curae non erat.

Foole if to keepe thy wife thou hast no neede,
Keepe her for me, my more desire to breede.
Wee skorne things lawfull, stolne sweetes we affect,
Cruell is he, that loves whom none protect.
Let us both lovers hope, and feare a like,   5
And may repulse place for our wishes strike.
What should I do with fortune that nere failes me?
Nothing I love, that at all times availes me.
Wily *Corinna* sawe this blemish in me,
And craftily knowes by what meanes to winne me.   10

Ah often, that her hale head aked, she lying,
Wild me, whose slowe feete sought delay be flying.
Ah oft how much she might she feignd offence;
And doing wrong made shew of innocence.
So having vext she nourisht my warme fire,   15
And was againe most apt to my desire.
To please me, what faire termes and sweet words ha's shee,
Great gods what kisses, and how many gave she?
Thou also that late tookest mine eyes away,
Oft couzen me, oft being wooed say nay.   20
And on thy threshold let me lie dispred,
Suffring much cold by hoary nights frost bred.
So shall my love continue many yeares,
This doth delight me this my courage cheares.
Fat love, and too much fulsome me annoyes,   25
Even as sweete meate a glutted stomacke cloyes.
In brazen tower had not *Danae* dwelt,
A mothers joy by *Jove* she had not felt.
While *Juno Io* keepes when hornes she wore,
Jove liked her better then he did before.   30
Who covets lawfull things takes leaves from woods,
And drinkes stolne waters in surrownding floudes.
Her lover let her mocke, that long will raigne,
Aye me, let not my warnings cause my paine.
What ever haps, by suffrance harme is done,   35
What flies, I followe, what followes me I shunne.
But thou of thy faire damsell too secure,
Beginne to shut thy house at evening sure.
Search at the dore who knocks oft in the darke,
In nights deepe silence why the ban-dogges barke.   40
Whether the subtile maide lines bringes and carries,
Why she alone in empty bed oft tarries.
Let this care some-times bite thee to the quick,
That to deceits it may me forward pricke.
To steale sands from the shore he loves alife,   45
That can effect a foolish wittalls wife.
Now I forewarne, unlesse to keepe her stronger,
Thou doest beginne, she shall be mine no longer.
Long have I borne much, hoping time would beate thee
To guard her well, that well I might entreate thee.   50

Thou suffrest what no husband can endure,
But of my love it will an end procure.
Shall I poore soule be never interdicted?
Nor never with nights sharpe revenge afflicted?
In sleeping shall I fearelesse drawe my breath?   55
Wilt nothing do, why I should wish thy death?
Can I but loath a husband growne a baude?
By thy default thou does our joyes defraude.
Some other seeke that may in patience strive with thee,
To pleasure me, for-bid me to corive with thee.   60

P. Ovidii Nasonis Amorum
Liber tertius.

ELEGIA 1

*Deliberatio poetae, utrum elegos pergat scribere
an potius tragedias.*

An old wood, stands uncut of long yeares space,
Tis credible some god head haunts the place.
In midst thereof a stone-pav'd sacred spring,
Where round about small birdes most sweetely sing.
Heere while I walke hid close in shadie grove,   5
To finde, what worke my muse might move, I strove.
Elegia came with haires perfumed sweete,
And one, I thinke, was longer, of her feete.
A decent forme, thinne robe, a lovers looke,
By her footes blemish greater grace she tooke.   10
Then with huge steps came violent *Tragedie*,
Sterne was her front, her cloake on ground did lie.
Her left hand held abroad a regal scepter,
The *Lydian* buskin in fit paces kept her.
And first she sayd, when will thy love be spent?   15
O Poet carelesse of thy argument.
Wine-bibbing banquets tell thy naughtinesse,
Each crosse waies corner doth as much expresse.
Oft some points at the prophet passing by,
And this is he whom fierce love burnes, they cry.   2.
A laughing stocke thou art to all the citty,
While without shame thou singst thy lewdnesse ditty.
Tis time to move grave things in lofty stile,
Long hast thou loyterd, greater workes compile.
The subject hides thy wit, mens acts resound,   25
This thou wilt say to be a worthy ground.
Thy muse hath played what may milde girles content,
And by those numbers is thy first youth spent.

2 god head] *Robinson*; good head *Mason*   12 cloake] *Dyce*; looke *Mason*
14 buskin in fit] *Robinson*; buskin fit *Mason*   15 she] *Dyce*; he *Mason*

Now give the *Roman* Tragedie a name,
To fill my lawes thy wanton spirit frame.   30
This saied, she mov'd her buskins gaily varnisht,
And seaven times shooke her head with thicke locks garnisht.
The other smilde, (I wot) with wanton eyes,
Erre I? or mirtle in her right hand lies.
With lofty wordes stout *Tragedie* (she sayd)   35
Why treadst me downe? art thou aye gravely plaied?
Thou deignst unequall lines should thee rehearse,
Thou fightst against me using mine owne verse.
Thy lofty stile with mine I not compare,
Small doores unfitting for large houses are.   40
Light am I, and with me, my care, light love,
Not stronger am I, then the thing I move.
Venus without me should be rusticall,
This goddesse company doth to me befall.
What gate thy stately words cannot unlocke,   45
My flatt'ring speeches soone wide open knocke.
And I deserve more then thou canst in verity,
By suffring much not borne by thy severity.
By me *Corinna* learnes, cousening her guard,
To get the dore with little noise unbard.   50
And slipt from bed cloth'd in a loose night-gowne,
To move her feete unheard in setting downe.
Ah howe oft on hard doores hung I engrav'd,
From no mans reading fearing to be sav'd.
But till the keeper went forth, I forget not   55
The maide to hide me in her bosome let not.
What gift with me was on her birth day sent,
But cruelly by her was drown'd and rent.
First of thy minde the happy seedes I knewe,
Thou hast my gift, which she would from thee sue.   60
She left; I say'd, you both I must beseech,
To empty aire may go my fearefull speech.
With scepters, and high buskins th'one would dresse me,
So through the world shold bright renown expresse me.
The other gives my love a conquering name,   65
Come therefore, and to long verse shorter frame.

32 times] *Mal 368*; time *Mason*   52 setting] *Dyce*; sitting *Mason*   55 keeper]
Robinson; keepes *Mason*

Graunt *Tragedie* thy Poet times least tittle,
Thy labour ever lasts, she askes but little.
She gave me leave, soft loves in time make hast
Some greater worke will urge me on at last.   70

ELEGIA 2

Ad amicam cursum equorum spectantem.

I sit not here the noble horse to see,
Yet whom thou favourst, pray may conquerour be.
To sit, and talke with thee I hether came,
That thou maiest know with love thou mak'st me flame.
Thou views the course, I thee: let either heed,   5
What please them, and their eyes let either feede.
What horse-driver thou favourst most is best,
Because on him thy care doth hap to rest.
Such chaunce let me have: I would bravely runne,
On swift steedes mounted till the race were done.   10
Now would I slacke the reines, now lash their hide,
With wheeles bent inward now the ring-turne ride.
If running if I see thee, I shall stay,
And from my hands the reines will slip away.
Ah *Pelops* from his coach was almost feld,   15
Hippodameias lookes while he beheld.
Yet he attain'd by her support to have her,
Let us all conquer by our mistris favour.
In vaine why flyest backe? force conjoynes us now:
The places lawes this benefit allowe.   20
But spare my wench thou at her right hand seated,
By thy sides touching ill she is entreated.
And sit thou rounder, that behind us see,
For shame presse not her backe with thy hard knee.
But on the ground thy cloathes too loosely lie,   25
Gather them up, or lift them loe will I.
Envious garments so good legges to hide,
The more thou look'st, the more the gowne envide.
Swift *Atalantas* flying legges like these,
Wish in his hands graspt did *Hippomenes*.   30

Coate-tuckt *Dianas* legges are painted like them,
When strong wilde beasts, she stronger hunts to strike them.
Ere these were seene, I burnt: what will these do?
Flames into flame, flouds thou powrest seas into.
By these I judge, delight me may the rest,   35
Which lie hid under her thinne veile supprest.
Yet in the meane time wilt small windes bestowe,
That from thy fanne, mov'd by my hand may blow?
Or is my heate, of minde, not of the skie?
Ist womens love my captive brest doth frie?   40
While thus I speake, blacke dust her white robes ray:
Foule dust, from her faire body, go away.
Now comes the pompe; themselves let all men cheere:
The shout is nigh; the golden pompe comes heere.
First victory is brought with large spred wing,   45
Goddesse come here, make my love conquering.
Applaud you *Neptune*, that dare trust his wave,
The sea I use not: me my earth must have.
Souldiour applaud thy *Mars*: no warres we move,
Peace pleaseth me, and in mid peace is love.   50
With *Augures Phoebus*, *Phoebe* with hunters standes,
To thee *Minerva* turne the craftes-mens hands.
Ceres and *Bacchus* Country-men adore,
Champions pleace *Pollux*, *Castor* loves horsemen more.
Thee gentle *Venus*, and the boy that flies,   55
We praise: great goddesse ayde my enterprize.
Let my new mistris graunt to be beloved,
She beckt, and prosperous signes gave as she moved.
What Venus promisd, promise thou we pray,
Greater then her, by her leave th'art, Ile say.   60
The Gods, and their rich pompe witnesse with me,
For evermore thou shalt my mistris be.
Thy legges hang downe: thou maiest, if that be best,
Or while thy tiptoes on the foote-stoole rest.
Now greater spectacles the *Praetor* sends,   65
Fower chariot-horses from the lists even ends.
I see whom thou affectest: he shall subdue,
The horses seeme, as thy desire they knewe.

Alas he runnes too farre about the ring,
What doest? thy wagon in lesse compasse bring. 70
What doest unhappy? her good wishes fade,
Let with strong hand the reine to bend be made.
One slowe we favour, *Romans* him revoke:
And each give signes by casting up his cloake.
They call him backe, least their gownes tosse thy haire, 75
To hide thee in my bosome straight repaire.
But now againe the barriers open lye;
And forthe the gay troupes on swift horses flie.
At least now conquer, and out-runne the rest:
My mistris wish confirme with my request 80
My mistris hath her wish, my wish remaine:
He holdes the palme: my palme is yet to gaine.
She smilde, and with quicke eyes behight some grace:
Pay it not heere, but in an other place.

ELEGIA 3

De amica, quae periuraverat.

What, are there Gods? her selfe she hath forswore,
And yet remaines the face she had before.
How long her lockes were, ere her oath she tooke:
So long they be, since she her faith forsooke.
Faire white with rose red was before commixt: 5
Now shine her lookes pure white and red betwixt.
Her foote was small: her footes forme is most fit:
Comely tall was she, comely tall shee's yet.
Sharpe eyes she had: radiant like starres they be,
By which she perjurd oft hath lyed to me. 10
Insooth th'eternall powers graunt maides society
Falsely to sweare, their beauty hath some deity.
By her eyes I remember late she swore,
And by mine eys, and mine were pained sore.
Say gods: if she unpunisht you deceive, 15
For others faults, why do I losse receive?
But did you not so envy *Cepheus* Daughter,
For her ill-beautious Mother judgd to slaughter.

Tis not enough, she shakes your record off,
And unrevengd mockt Gods with me doth scoffe.   20
But by my paine to purge her perjuries,
Couzend, I am the couzeners sacrifice.
God is a name, no substance, feard in vaine,
And doth the world in fond beliefe deteine.
Or if there be a God, he loves fine wenches,   25
And all things too much in their sole power drenches.
Mars girts his deadly sword on for my harme:
Pallas launce strikes me with unconquerd arme.
At me *Apollo* bends his pliant bowe:
At me *Joves* right-hand lightning hath to throwe.   30
The wronged Gods dread faire ones to offend,
And feare those, that to feare them least intend.
Who now will care the Altars to perfume?
Tut, men should not their courage so consume.
Jove throwes downe woods, and Castles with his fire: 35
But bids his darts from perjurd girles retire.
Poore *Semele* among so many burn'd;
Her owne request to her owne torment turnd.
But when her lover came, had she drawne backe,
The fathers thigh should unborne *Bacchus* lacke.   40
Why grieve I? and of heaven reproches pen?
The Gods have eyes, and brests as well as men.
Were I a God, I should give women leave,
With lying lips my God-head to deceave,
My selfe would sweare, the wenches true did sweare,   45
And I would be none of the Gods severe.
But yet their gift more moderately use,
Or in mine eyes good wench no paine transfuse.

ELEGIA 4

Ad virum servantem conjugem.

Rude man, 'tis vaine, thy damsell to commend
To keepers trust: their wits should them defend.
Who, without feare, is chaste: is chast in sooth,
Who, because meanes want, doeth not she doth.

Though thou her body guard, her minde is staind: 5
Nor, least she will, can any be restrainde.
Nor canst by watching keepe her minde from sinne.
All being shut our, th'adulterer is within.
Who may offend, sinnes least; power to do ill,
The fainting seedes of naughtinesse doth kill. 10
Forbeare to kindle vice by prohibition,
Sooner shall kindnesse gaine thy wills fruition.
I saw a horse against the bitte stiffe-neckt,
Like lightning go, his strugling mouth being checkt.
When he perceivd the reines let slacke, he stayde, 15
And on his loose mane the loose bridle laide.
How to attaine, what is denyed, we thinke,
Even as the sicke desire forbidden drinke.
Argus had either way an hundred eyes,
Yet by deceit love did them all surprize. 20
In stone, and Yron walles *Danae* shut,
Came forth a mother, though a maide there put.
Penelope, though no watch look'd unto her,
Was not defilde by any gallant wooer.
What's kept, we covet more: the care makes theft: 25
Few love, what others have unguarded left.
Nor doth her face please, but her husbands love;
I know not, what men thinke should thee so move.
She is not chaste, that's kept but a deare whore:
Thy feare is, then her body, valued more. 30
Although thou chafe, stolne pleasure is sweet play,
She pleaseth best, I feare, if any say.
A free-borne wench no right 'tis up to locke:
So use we women of strange nations stocke.
Because the keeper may come say, I did it, 35
She must be honest to thy servants credit.
He is too clownish, whom a lewd wife grieves,
And this townes well knowne customes not beleeves,
Where *Mars* his sonnes not without fault did breed,
Remus and *Romulus*, *Ilias* twinne-borne seed. 40
Cannot a faire one, if not chast, please thee?
Never can these by any meanes agree.
Kindly thy mistris use, if thou be wise.
Looke gently, and rough husbands lawes despise.

Honour what friends thy wife gives, sheele give many: 45
Least labour so shall winne great grace of any.
So shalt thou go with youths to feast together,
And see at home much, that thou nere broughtst thether.

ELEGIA 5

Ad amnem, dum iter faceret ad amicam.

Floud with reede-growne slime bankes, till I be past
Thy waters stay: I to my mistris hast.
Thou hast no bridge, nor boate with ropes to throw,
That may transport me without oares to rowe.
Thee I have pass'd, and knew thy streame none such,   5
When thy waves brim did scarse my anckles touch.
With snow thaw'd from the next hill now thou rushest,
And in thy foule deepe waters thicke thou gushest.
What helpes my hast: what to have tane small rest?
What day and night to travaile in her quest?   10
If standing here I can be no meanes get,
My foote upon the further banke to set.
Now wish I those wings noble *Perseus* had,
Bearing the head with dreadfull Adders clad,
Now wish the chariot, whence corne seedes were found,   15
First to be throwne upon the untill'd ground.
I speake old Poets wonderfull inventions,
Nere was, nor shall be, what my verse mentions.
Rather thou large banke over-flowing river,
Slide in thy bounds, so shalt thou runne for ever.   20
(Trust me) land-streame thou shalt no envie lack,
If I a lover bee by thee held back.
Great flouds ought to assist young men in love,
Great flouds the force of it do often prove.

---

1 reede] *Dyce*; redde *Mason*   8 gushest] *Tucker Brooke*; rushest *Mason*
14 Adders] *Dyce*; Arrowes *Mason*   15 seedes] *Tucker Brooke*; fields *Mason*

In mid *Bithynia* 'tis said *Inachus*, 25
Grew pale, and in cold foords hot lecherous.
Troy had not yet beene ten years siege out-stander,
When nimph-*Neaera* rapt thy lookes *Scamander*.
What? not *Alpheus* in strange lands to runne,
Th'*Arcadian* Virgins constant love hath wunne? 30
And *Crusa* unto *Zanthus* first affide,
They say *Peneus* neere *Phthias* towne did hide.
What should I name *Aesope*, that *Thebe* lov'd,
Thebe who Mother of five Daughters prov'd?
If *Achelous*, I aske where thy hornes stand, 35
Thou saiest broke with *Alcides* angry hand.
Not *Calydon*, nor *Aetolia* did please:
One *Deianira* was more worth then these.
Rich *Nile* by seaven mouthes to the vast sea flowing,
Who so well keepes his waters head from knowing, 40
Is by *Evadne* thought to take such flame,
As his deepe whirle-pooles could not quench the same.
Drye *Enipeus*, *Tyro* to embrace,
Flye backe his streame chargd, the streame chargd, gave place, 45
Nor passe I thee, who hollow rocks downe tumbling,
In *Tiburs* field with watry fome art rumbling,
Whom *Ilia* pleasd, though in her lookes griefe reveld,
Her cheekes were scratcht, her goodly haires discheveld.
She wailing *Mars* sinne, and her uncles crime,
Strayd bare-foote through sole places on a time. 50
Her, from his swift waves, the bold floud perceav'd,
And from the mid foord his hoarse voice upheav'd,
Saying why sadly treadst my banckes upon,
Ilia, sprung from *Idaean Laomedon*?
Where's thy attire? why wand'rest heere alone? 55
To stay thy tresses white veyle hast thou none?
Why weepst? and spoilst with teares thy watry eyes?
And fiercely knockst thy brest that open lyes?
His heart consists of flint, and hardest steele,
That seeing thy teares can any joy then feele. 60
Feare not: to thee our Court stands open wide,
There shalt be lov'd: *Ilia* lay feare aside.

---

44 his streame] *Robinson*; his shame *Mason*

Thou ore a hundreth Nimphes, or more shalt raigne:
For five score Nimphes, or more our flouds conteine.
Nor *Romane* stocke scorne me so much (I crave)   65
Gifts then my promise greater thou shalt have.
This said he: shee her modest eyes held downe,
Her wofull bosome a warme shower did drowne.
Thrice she prepar'd to flie, thrice she did stay,
By feare depriv'd of strength to runne away.   70
Yet rending with enraged thumbe her tresses,
Her trembling mouth these unmeete sounds expresses.
O would in my fore-fathers tombe deepe layde,
My bones had beene, while yet I was a maide.
Why being a vestall am I wooed to wed,   75
Deflowr'd and stained in unlawfull bed?
Why stay I? men point at me for a whore,
Shame, that should make me blush, I have no more.
This said: her coate hood-winckt her fearefull eyes,
And into water desperately she flies.   80
Tis said the slippery streame held up her brest,
And kindly gave her, what she liked best.
And I beleeve some wench thou hast affected:
But woods and groves keepe your faults undetected.
While thus I speake, the waters more abounded: 85
And from the channell all abroad surrounded.
Mad streame, why doest our mutuall joyes deferre?
Clowne, from my journey why doest me deterre?
How wouldst thou flowe wert thou a noble floud?
If thy great fame in every region stood.   90
Thou hast no name, but com'st from snowy mountaines;
No certaine house thou hast, nor any fountaines.
Thy springs are nought but raine and melted snowe:
Which wealth, cold winter doth on thee bestowe.
Either th'art muddy in mid winter tide: 95
Or full of dust doest on the drye earth slide.
What thirstie traveller ever drunke of thee?
Who sayd with greatefull voyce perpetuall bee?
Harmefull to beasts, and to the fields thou proves:
Perchance these others, me mine owne losse mooves.   100
To this I fondly loves of flouds told plainly:
I shame so great names to have usde so vainly:

I know not what expecting, I ere while
Nam'd *Achelaus*, *Inachus*, and *Nile*,
But for thy merits I wish thee, white streame, 105
Drye winters aye, and sunnes in heate extreame.

ELEGIA 6

Quod ab amica receptus, cum ea coire non
potuit, conqueritur.

Either she was foule, or her attire was bad,
Or she was not the wench I wisht t'have had.
Idly I lay with her, as if I lov'd not,
And like a burthen griev'd the bed that mov'd not.
Though both of us perform'd our true intent, 5
Yet could I not cast anckor where I meant.
She on my necke her Ivory armes did throwe.
Her armes farre whiter then the *Sythian* snow.
And eagerly she kist me with her tongue,
And under mine her wanton thigh she flung. 10
Yea, and she soothd me up, and calld me sir,
And usde all speech that might provoke, and stirre.
Yet like as if cold Hemlock I had drunke,
It mocked me, hung downe the head, and sunke.
Like a dull Cipher, or rude block I lay, 15
Or shade, or body was I who can say?
What will my age do? age I cannot shunne,
When in my prime my force is spent and done.
I blush, that being youthfull, hot, and lustie,
I prove neither youth nor man, but old and rustie. 20
Pure rose she, like a Nunne to sacrifice,
Or one that with her tender brother lyes.
Yet boorded I the golden *Chie* twise,
And *Libas*, and the white cheekt *Pitho* thrice.
Corinna crav'd it in a summers night, 25
And nine sweete bowts we had before day-light.

104 *Nile*] Robinson; *Ile* Mason

What wast my limbs through some *Thessalian* charmes?
May spells, and drugges do silly soules such harmes?
With virgin waxe hath some imbast my joynts?
And pierc'd my liver with sharpe needles points?   30
Charmes change corne to grasse and make it die.
By charmes are running springs and fountaines dry.
By charmes mast drops from oakes, from vines grapes fal
And fruite from trees when ther's no winde at all.
Why might not then my sinewes be inchaunted?   35
And I grow faint as with some spirit haunted.
To this adde shame: shame to performe it quailde me
And was the second cause why vigour failde me.
My idle thoughts delighted her no more,
Then did the robe or garment which she wore.   40
Yet might her touch make youthful *Pylius* fire
And *Tithon* livelier then his yeares require.
Even her I had, and she had me in vaine,
What might I crave more, if I aske againe?
I thinke the great gods griev'd they had bestow'd,   45
The benefit: which lewdly I for-slow'd.
I wish to be receiv'd in, in I get me,
To kisse, I kisse: to lie with her she let me.
Why was I blest? why made King to refuse it?
Chuffe-like had I not gold and could not use it?   50
So in a spring thrives he that told so much,
And lookes upon the fruits he cannot touch.
Hath any rose so from a fresh yong maide,
As she might straight have gone to church and praide?
Well I beleeve, she kist not as she should,   55
Nor us'd the sleight and cunning which she could,
Huge oakes, hard adamants might she have moved,
And with sweet words cause deafe rocks to have loved.
Worthy she was to move both gods and men,
But neither was I man nor lived then.   60
Can deafe eares take delight when *Phemius* sings?
Or *Thamiras* in curious painted things.
What sweete thought is there but I had the same?
And one gave place still as another came.

58 loved] *Bindley, Isham*; moned *Mason*

Yet not-withstanding like one dead it lay, 65
Drouping more then a rose puld yester-day.
Now when he should not jette, he boults upright,
And craves his taske, and seekes to be at fight.
Lie downe with shame, and see thou stirre no more,
Seeing thou wouldst deceive me as before. 70
Thou cousenest me: by thee surpriz'd am I,
And bide sore losse with endlesse infamy.
Nay more the wench did not disdaine a whit,
To take it in her hand, and play with it.
But when she sawe it would be no meanes stand, 75
But still droupt downe, regarding not her hand.
Why mockst thou me she cryed? or being ill
Who bad thee lie downe heere against thy will?
Either th'art witcht with bloud of frogs newe dead
Or jaded camst thou from some others bed. 80
With that her loose gowne on, from me she cast her,
In skipping out her naked feete much grac'd her.
And least her maide should know of this disgrace,
To cover it, spilt water on the place.

ELEGIA 7

Quod ab amica non recipiatur, dolet.

What man will now take liberall arts in hand,
Or thinke soft verse in any stead to stand.
Wit was some-times more pretious then gold,
Now poverty great barbarisme we hold.
When our bookes did my mistris faire content, 5
I might not go, whether my papers went.
She prais'd me, yet the gate shutt fast upon her,
I heere and there go witty with dishonour.
See a rich chuffe whose wounds great wealth inferr'd,
For bloudshed knighted, before me preferr'd. 10
Foole canst thou him in thy white armes embrace?
Foole canst thou lie in his enfolding space?
Knowest not his head a helme was wont to beare,
This side that serves thee, a sharpe sword did weare.

His left hand whereon gold doth ill alight,
A target bore: bloud sprinckled was his right.
Canst touch that hand wherewith some one lie dead?
Ah whether is thy brests soft nature fled?
Behold the signes of antient fight, his skarres,
What ere he hath his body gaind in warres.   20
Perhaps he'ele tell howe oft he slewe a man,
Confessing this, why doest thou touch him than?
I the pure priest of *Phoebus* and the muses,
At thy deafe dores in verse sing my abuses,
Not what we slouthfull knowe, let wise men learne,   25
But follow trembling campes, and battailes sterne,
And for a good verse drawe the first dart forth,
Homer without this shall be nothing worth.
Jove being admonisht gold had soveraigne power,
To winne the maide came in a golden shewer.   30
Till then, rough was her father, she severe,
The posts of brasse, the walles of iron were.
But when in gifts the wise adulterer came,
She held her lap ope to receive the same.
Yet when old *Saturne* heavens rule possest,   35
All gaine in darknesse the deepe earth supprest.
Gold, silver, irons heavy weight, and brasse,
In hell were harboured, here was found no masse.
But better things it gave, corne without ploughes,
Apples, and hony in oakes hollow boughes.   40
With strong plough shares no man the earth did cleave,
The ditcher no markes on the ground did leave.
Nor hanging oares the troubled seas did sweepe,
Men kept the shoare, and sailde not into deepe.
Against thy selfe, mans nature, thou wert cunning,   45
And to thine owne losse was thy wit swift running.
Why gird'st thy citties with a towred wall?
Why letst discordant hands to armour fall?
What doest with seas? with th'earth thou wert content,
Why seek'st not heav'n the third realme to frequent?   50
Heaven thou affects, with *Romulus*, temples brave
Bacchus, *Alcides*, and now *Caesar* have.

Gold from the earth in steade of fruits we pluck,
Souldiours by bloud to be inricht have lucke.
Courts shut the poore out; wealth gives estimation   55
Thence growes the Judge, and knight of reputation.
All, they possesse: they governe fieldes, and lawes,
They manadge peace, and rawe warres bloudy jawes,
Onely our loves let not such rich churles gaine,
Tis well, if some wench for the poore remaine.   60
Now, *Sabine*-like, though chast she seemes to live,
One her commands, who many things can give.
For me, she doth keeper, and husband feare,
If I should give, both would the house forbeare.
If of scornd lovers god be venger just,   65
O let him change goods so ill got to dust.

ELEGIA 8

Tibulli mortem deflet.

If *Thetis*, and the morne their sonnes did waile,
And envious fates great goddesses assaile,
Sad *Elegia* thy wofull haires unbinde:
Ah now a name too true thou hast, I finde.
Tibullus, thy workes Poet, and thy fame,   5
Burnes his dead body in the funerall flame.
Loe *Cupid* brings his quiver spoyled quite
His broken bowe, his fire-brand without light.
How piteously with drouping wings he stands,
And knocks his bare brest with selfe-angry hands.   10
The locks spred on his necke receive his teares,
And shaking sobbes his mouth for speeches beares.
So at *Aeneas* buriall men report,
Faire-fac'd *Julus*, he went forth thy court.
And *Venus* grieves, *Tibullus* life being spent,   15
As when the wilde boare *Adons* groine had rent.

---

62 he] *Dyce*; she *Mason*

2 goddesses] *Dyce*; goodesses *Mason*

The gods care we are cald, and men of piety,
And some there be that thinke we have a deity.
Outrageous death profanes all holy things
And on all creatures obscure darcknesse brings.   20
To *Thracian Orpheus* what did parents good?
Or songs amazing wilde beasts of the wood.
Where *Linus* by his father Phoebus layed
To sing with his unequald harpe is sayed.
See *Homer* from whose fountaine ever fild,   25
Pierian deawe to Poets is distild.
Him the last day in black *Averne* hath drownd,
Verses alone are with continuance crown'd.
The worke of Poets lasts *Troyes* labours fame,
And that slowe webbe nights fals-hood did unframe.   30
So *Nemesis*, so *Delia* famous are,
The one his first love, th'other his new care,
What profit to us hath our pure life bred?
What to have laine alone in empty bed?
When bad fates take good men, I am forbod,   35
By secreat thoughts to thinke there is a god.
Live godly, thou shalt die, though honour heaven,
Yet shall thy life be forcibly bereaven.
Trust in good verse, *Tibullus* feeles deaths paines,
Scarse rests of all what a small urne conteines.   40
Thee sacred Poet could sad flames destroy?
Nor feared they thy body to annoy?
The holy gods gilt temples they might fire,
That durst to so great wickednesse aspire.
Eryx bright *Empresse* turnd her lookes aside,   45
And some, that she refrain'd teares, have deni'd.
Yet better ist, then if *Corcyras* Ile
Had thee unknowne interr'd in ground most vile.
Thy dying eyes here did thy mother close,
Nor did thy ashes her last offrings lose.   50
Part of her sorrowe heere thy sister bearing,
Comes forth her unkeembd locks a sunder tearing.
Nemesis and thy first wench joyne their kisses
With thine, nor this last fire their presence misses.
Delia departing, happier lov'd she saith,   55
Was I: thou liv'dst, while thou esteemdst my faith.

Nemesis answeares, what's my losse to thee?
His fainting hand in death engrasped mee.
If ought remaines of us but name, and spirit,
Tibullus doth *Elysiums* joy inherit.   60
Their youthfull browes with Ivie girt to meete him,
With *Calvus* learnd *Catullus* comes and greete him.
And thou, if falsely charged to wrong thy friend,
Gallus that carst not bloud, and life to spend.
With these thy soule walkes, soules if death release,   65
The godly, sweete *Tibullus* doth increase.
Thy bones I pray may in the urne safe rest,
And may th'earths weight thy ashes nought molest.

ELEGIA 9

Ad Cererem, conquerens quod eius sacris cum amica
concumbere non permittatur.

Come were the times of *Ceres* sacrifize,
In emptie bed alone my mistris lies.
Golden-hair'd *Ceres* crownd with eares of corne,
Why are our pleasures by thy meanes forborne?
Thee, goddesse, bountifull all nations judge,   5
Nor lesse at mans prosperity any grudge.
Rude husband-men bak'd not their corne before,
Nor on the earth was knowne the name of floore.
On mast of oakes, first oracles, men fed,
This was their meate, the soft grasse was their bed.   10
First *Ceres* taught the seede in fields to swell,
And ripe-earde corne with sharpe-edg'd sithes to fell.
She first constraind bulles necks to beare the yoake,
And untild ground with crooked plough-shares broake.
Who thinkes her to be glad at lovers smart,   15
And worshipt by their paine, and lying apart?
Nor is she, though she loves the fertile fields
A clowne, nor no love from her warme brest yeelds.
Be witnesse *Crete* (nor *Crete* doth all things feigne)
Crete proud that *Jove* her nourcery maintaine.

There, he who rules the worlds starre-spangled towers,
A little boy druncke teate-distilling showers.
Faith to the witnesse *Joves* praise doth apply,
Ceres, I thinke, no knowne fault will deny.
The goddesse sawe *Iasion* on *Candyan Ide*,   25
With strong hand striking wild-beasts brist'led hyde.
She sawe, and as her marrowe tooke the flame,
Was divers waies distract with love, and shame.
Love conquer'd shame, the furrowes dry were burnd,
And corne with least part of it selfe returnd.   30
When well-toss'd mattocks did the ground prepare,
Being fit broken with the crooked share,
And seedes were equally in large fields cast,
The plough-mans hopes were frustrate at the last.
The graine-rich goddesse in high woods did stray,   35
Her long haires eare-wrought garland fell away.
Onely was Crete fruitfull that plenteous yeare,
Where *Ceres* went each place was harvest there.
Ida the seate of groves did sing with corne,
Which by the wild boare in the woods was shorne.   40
Law-giving *Minos* did such yeares desire;
And wisht the goddesse long might feele loves fire.
Ceres what sports to thee so grievous were,
As in thy sacrifize we them forbeare?
Why am I sad, when *Proserpine* is found,   45
And *Juno* like with *Dis* raignes under ground?
Festivall dayes aske *Venus*, songs, and wine,
These gifts are meete to please the powers divine.

ELEGIA 10

Ad amicam, a cuius amore discedere non potest.

Long have I borne much, mad thy faults me make:
Dishonest love my wearied brest forsake,
Now have I freed my selfe, and fled the chaine,
And what I have borne, shame to beare againe.
We vanquish, and tread tam'd love under feete,   5
Victorious wreathes at length my Temples greete.

Suffer, and harden: good growes by this griefe,
Oft bitter juice brings to the sicke reliefe.
I have sustainde so often thrust from the dore,
To lay my body on the hard moist floore.   10
I know not whom thou lewdly didst imbrace,
When I to watch supplyed a servants place.
I saw when forth a tyred lover went,
His side past service, and his courage spent.
Yet this lesse, then if he had seene me,   15
May that shame fall mine enemies chance to be.
When have not I fixt to thy side close layed?
I have thy husband, guard, and fellow plaied.
The people by my company she pleasd,
My love was cause that more mens love she seazd.   20
What should I tell her vaine tongues filthy lyes,
And to my losse God-wronging perjuries?
What secret becks in banquets with her youths,
With privy signes, and talke dissembling truths?
Hearing her to be sicke, I thether ranne,   25
But with my rivall sicke she was not than.
These hardned me, with what I keepe obscure,
Some other seeke, who will these things endure,
Now my ship in the wished haven crownd,
With joy heares *Neptunes* swelling waters sound.   30
Leave thy once powerfull words, and flatteries,
I am not as I was before, unwise.
Now love, and hate my light brest each way move;
But victory, I thinke will hap to love.
Ile hate, if I can; if not, love gainst my will: 35
Bulles hate the yoake, yet what they hate have still.
I flie her lust, but follow beauties creature;
I loath her manners, love her bodies feature.
Nor with thee, nor without thee can I live,
And doubt to which desire the palme to give.   40
Or lesse faire, or lesse lewd would thou mightst bee,
Beauty with lewdnesse doth right ill agree.
Her deeds gaine hate, her face entreateth love:
Ah, she doth more worth then her vices prove.
Spare me, O by our fellow bed, by all   45
The Gods who by thee to be perjurde fall,

And by thy face to me a powre divine,
And by thine eyes whose radiance burnes out mine.
What ere thou art mine art thou: choose this course,
Wilt have me willing, or to love by force?   50
Rather Ile hoist up saile, and use the winde,
That I may love yet, though against my minde.

ELEGIA 11

Dolet amicam suam ita suis carminibus innotuisse
ut rivales multos sibi pararit.

What day was that, which all sad haps to bring,
White birdes to lovers did not alwayes sing.
Or is I thinke my wish against the starres?
Or shall I plaine some God against me warres?
Who mine was cald, whom I lov'd more then any,   5
I feare with me is common now to many.
Erre I? or by my bookes is she so knowne?
'Tis so: by my witte her abuse is growne.
And justly: for her praise why did I tell?
The wench by my fault is set forth to sell.   10
The bawde I play, lovers to her I guide:
Her gate by my hands is set open wide.
'Tis doubtfull whether verse availe, or harme,
Against my good they were an envious charme.
When *Thebes*, when *Troy*, when *Caesar* should be writ,   15
Alone *Corinna* moves my wanton wit.
With Muse oppos'd would I my lines had done,
And *Phoebus* had forsooke my worke begun.
Nor, as use will not Poets record heare,
Would I my words would any credit beare.   20
Scylla by us her fathers rich haire steales,
And *Scyllaes* wombe mad raging dogs conceales.
Wee cause feete flie, wee mingle haires with snakes,
Victorious *Perseus* wingd steedes back takes.

7 bookes] *Dyce*; lookes *Mason*

Our verse great *Tityus* a huge space out-spreads, 25
And gives the viper curled Dogge three heads.
We make *Enceladus* use a thousand armes,
And men inthralled by Mermaids singing charmes.
The East winds in *Ulisses* baggs we shut,
And blabbing *Tantalus* in mid-waters put. 30
Niobe flint, *Callist* we make a Beare,
Bird-changed *Progne* doth her *Itys* teare.
Jove turnes himselfe into a Swanne, or gold,
Or his Bulles hornes *Europas* hand doth hold.
Proteus what should I name? teeth, *Thebes* first seed? 35
Oxen in whose mouthes burning flames did breede?
Heav'n starre *Electra* that bewaild her sisters?
The ships, whose God-head in the sea now glisters?
The Sunne turnd backe from *Atreus* cursed table?
And sweet toucht harpe that to move stones was able? 40
Poets large power is boundlesse, and immense,
Nor have their words true histories pretence,
And my wench ought to have seem'd falsely praisd.
Now your credulity harme to me hath raisd.

ELEGIA 12

De Junonis festo.

When fruite fild *Tuscia* should a wife give me,
We toucht the walles, *Camillus* wonne by thee.
The Priests to *Juno* did prepare chaste feasts,
With famous pageants, and their home-bred beasts.
To know their rites, well recompenc'd my stay, 5
Though thether leades a rough steepe hilly way.
There stands an old wood with thick trees darke clouded,
Who sees it graunts some deity there is shrowded.
An Altar takes mens incense, and oblation,
An Altar made after the ancient fashion. 10
Here when the Pipe with solemne tunes doth sound,
The annuall pompe goes on the covered ground.
White Heifers by glad people forth are led,
Which with the grasse of *Tuscane* fields are fed.

And calves from whose feard front no threatning flyes,   15
And little Piggs base Hog-sties sacrifice,
And Rams with hornes their hard heads wreathed back.
Onely the Goddesse hated Goate did lack,
By whom disclosd, she in the high woods tooke,
Is said to have attempted flight forsooke.   20
Now is the goat brought through the boyes with darts,
And give to him that the first wound imparts.
Where *Juno* comes, each youth, and pretty maide,
Shew large wayes with their garments there displayed.
Jewels, and gold their Virgin tresses crowne,   25
And stately robes to their gilt feete hang downe.
As is the use, the Nunnes in white veyles clad,
Upon their heads the holy mysteries had.
When the chiefe pompe comes, lowd the people hollow,
And she her vestall virgin Priests doth follow.   30
Such was the *Greeke* pompe, *Agamemnon* dead,
Which fact, and country wealth *Halesus* fled.
And having wandred now through sea and land,
Built walles high towred with a prosperous hand.
He to th'*Hetrurians Junoes* feast commended,   35
Let me, and them by it be aye be-friended.

ELEGIA 13

Ad amicam, si peccatura est, ut non occulte peccet.

Seeing thou art faire, I barre not thy false playing,
But let not me poore soule know of thy straying.
Nor do I give thee counsell to live chaste,
But that thou wouldst dissemble, when 'tis paste.
She hath not trod awry, that doth deny it.   5
Such as confesse have lost their good names by it.
What madnesse ist to tell nights pranckes by day?
And hidden secrets openly to bewray?
The strumpet with the stranger will not doo,
Before the roome be cleere, and dore put too.   10

Will you make ship-wrack of your honest name?
And let the world be witnesse of the same.
Be more advisde, walke as a puritan,
And I shall think you chaste, do what you can.
Slip still, onely deny it, when 'tis done,   15
And before folke immodest speeches shunne.
The bed is for lascivious toyings meete,
There use all tricks, and tread shame under feete.
When you are up, and drest, be sage and grave,
And in the bed hide all the faults you have.   20
Be not asham'de to strip you being there,
And mingle thighes yours ever mine to beare.
There in your Rosie lips my tongue in-tombe,
Practise a thousand sports when there you come.
Forbeare no wanton words you there would speake,   25
And with your pastime let the bed-stead creake.
But with your robes put on an honest face,
And blush, and seeme as you were full of grace.
Deceive all, let me erre, and thinke I am right,
And like a Wittall think thee voide of slight.   30
Why see I lines so oft receiv'd, and given?
This bed and that by tumbling made uneven?
Like one start up your haire tost and displac'd,
And with a wantons tooth your neck new rac'd.
Graunt this, that what you doe I may not see,   35
If you weigh not ill speeches, yet weigh mee.
My soule fleetes, when I thinke what you have done,
And thorough every veine doth cold bloud runne.
Then thee whom I must love, I hate in vaine,
And would be dead, but dead with thee remaine.   40
Ile not sift much, but holde thee soone excusde,
Say but thou wert injuriously accusde.
Though while the deed be dooing you be tooke,
And I see when you ope the two leav'd booke,
Sweare I was blinde, deny, if you be wise,   45
And I will trust your words more then mine eyes.
From him that yeelds the palme is quickly got,
Teach but your tongue to say, I did it not,
And being justifide by two words thinke,
The cause acquits you not, but I that winke.   50

ELEGIA 14

Ad Venerem, quod elegis finem imponat.

Tender loves Mother a new Poet get,
This last end to my *Elegies* is set,
Which I *Pelignis* foster-child have framde,
(Nor am I by such wanton toyes defamde).
Heire of an ancient house, if helpe that can,   5
Not onely by warres rage made Gentleman.
In *Virgil Mantua* joyes: in *Catul Verone*,
Of me *Pelignis* nation boasts alone,
Whom liberty to honest armes compeld,
When carefull *Rome* in doubt their prowesse held.   10
And some guest viewing watry *Sulmoes* walles,
Where little ground to be inclosed befalles,
How such a Poet could you bring forth, sayes,
How small so ere, Ile you for greatest praise.
Both loves to whom my heart long time did yeeld,   15
Your golden ensignes plucke out of my field,
Horned *Bacchus* graver furie doth distill,
A greater ground with great horse is to till.
Weake Elegies, delightfull Muse farewell;
A worke, that after my death, heere shall dwell.   20

FINIS

16 plucke] *Dyce*; pluckt *Mason*

LUCANS FIRST BOOKE

General Introduction

PHARSALIA, the usual title for Lucan's long narrative poem, is in fact a misnomer, since it describes only the events of Book VII. The ten books should rightly be given the title which appears in the manuscripts: *De Bello Civili*. Lucan's intention was to recount the conflict between Julius Caesar and the Roman Senate—a conflict that started with the momentous crossing of the Rubicon in 49 BC, and came to a climax five years later when Caesar was assassinated on the ides of March. The abrupt ending of the poem, however, has persuaded classical scholars that the poet did not fulfil his intentions, and that some was left unwritten when Lucan died at the age of twenty-six.

Marlowe translated only the first of the ten books, the one describing the gathering storm of Caesar 'musters men for *Roome*', the terrifying phenomena of a macrocosm which reflects turmoil within the little world of men, the panic of the Roman citizens, and the apocalyptic vision of a Roman matron who foresees the battles of the civil war—Pharsalia, Thapsus, Munda, and Philippi.

For Lucan, however, narrative seems to have been of secondary importance. His education, like that of all Roman youths of his age and status, had been directed to a single object: the acquisition of rhetorical skill. In this poem he demonstrates the success of his teachers. But the brilliance of formal rhetoric is not easily transmitted from one language to another, and to aid his understanding of the Roman's sense, Marlowe relied heavily upon the commentary of Sulpitius—so heavily, indeed, that at times the words he translates are not the poet's elaborations, but the scholar's plain annotations.[1] Examples are easily found. To describe the hysterical phophetess at the end of Book I, Lucan supplies a simile which seems less striking for its originality than for its phrasing: the Roman matron ran through the city streets *qualis vertice Pindi | Edonis Ogygio decurrit plena Lyeo*. Marlowe

---

[1] The standard edition (of text plus commentary) was *M. Annei Lucani, de Bello Civili, libri decem. Cum Scholijs, integris quidem Ioannis Sulpitij Verulani, certis autem locis etiam Omniboni, Una cum Annotationibus quibusdam adiectis Jacobi Micylli* (Frankfurt, 1551). For conveneince, this is referred to as 'Sulpitius'; see also my essay 'Marlowe, Lucan, and Sulpitius', *RES*, NS xxiv (November 1973): 401–13.

arrived at his simpler line with the help of Sulpitius, who explained that Edon was a mountain in Thrace sacred to Bacchus, and that *Edonis* was to be understood as a priest of Bacchus— *Maenas*. But the gloss on *Plena Lyeo Og*, while identifying Ogyges as a king of Thebes, shows a certain delicacy with its interpretation: *Corrupta furore Bacchi*. Marlowe says exactly what is meant: 'As *Maenas* full of wine on *Pindus* raves' (line 674).

Sulpitius is helpful in elucidating Lucan's favourite trope, the figure *metonymia*, which Peacham defines as the device used 'when of thinges that be nigh together, wee put one name for another'.[2] The poem opens with this figure: *Bella per Emathios plus quam civilia campos*. The commentary explains that Emathia was a region of Macedonia adjacent to Thessaly, and that *Pharsalia Thessaliae oppidum fuit . . . . In huius agro sive campo suprema pugna inter Caesarem & Pompeium commissa fuit*; and Marlowe translates *per Emathios . . . campos* as 'on Thessalian playnes' (line 1).

Whereas Marlowe's translations of Ovid's *Amores* are marred by occasional infelicities of expression, and clumsy random guesses at the sense of the Latin originals, this is not the case with *Lucans First Booke*. Here the work of translation is surprisingly careful, respecting not only the poet's lines, but also the annotations of the scholiasts. It would not, I think, be unreasonable to suggest for this work a date early in Marlowe's writing career, perhaps while he was still at Cambridge, where he would have had easy access through his college library to the necessary kind of scholarly edition (text plus commentary) of Lucan's poem.

An early date, with a *terminus ad quem* of 1587, would also prompt an answer to the question of *why* Marlowe chose to translate Lucan's poem. It is easy to see why a young man would be attracted to the *Amores*, because of both the amatory subject-matter, and the poet's dexterity in manipulating his language. In this latter respect Ovid is certainly 'a poet's poet'. But Quintilian made an acute assessment of his near-contemporary when he praised *De Bello Civili* for its fire and energy (*ardens et concitatus*), but added that the author was a fitter model for the orator than for the poet (*magis oratoribus quam poetis imitandus*).[3]

I would hazard a guess, however, that it was the subject rather than the style which drew Marlowe to the first book of *De Bello*

<hr />

[2] Thomas Peacham, *The Garden of Eloquence* (1577), C2.
[3] Quintilian, *Institutio Orationibus*, X. 1. 90.

Civili at a time when he was apparently working for Walsingham's secret service. Perhaps it would be idealistic to ascribe the motivation for both activities (translation and espionage) to youthful, fervent patriotism; equally, perhaps, it would be cynical to attribute it solely to a smart opportunism which saw hopes of preferment in the presentation of a work whose translation was academically laudable and whose content was politically sound.

Some of the best writing in *Lucans First Booke* speaks directly to Elizabethans, warning of the horror of civil war. In the recorded history of mankind such wars have happened; and they could easily happen again:

> That now the walles of houses halfe rear'd totter,
> That rampiers fallen down, huge heapes of stone
> Lye in our townes, that houses are abandon'd,
> And few live that behold their ancient seats
>
> .   .   .   .
>
> . . . no forraine foe could so afflict us,
> These plagues arise from wreake of civill power.   (lines 24 ff.)

The words have a grim topicality for the decade which experienced the Babington Conspiracy, the execution of a queen who rivalled their own monarch's claim to the throne, and the threat of the Spanish Armada. Nor was Marlowe alone in his literary appeal to the hearts and consciences of his countrymen: this was also the period of Thomas Lodge's play *The Wounds of Civil War*, and of Shakespeare's *Henry VI* trilogy.

In Marlowe's poem, the Centurion promises to wage civil war at all costs, even if Caesar's command is to 'Intombe my sword within my brothers bowels; | Or fathers throate' (lines 377–8). The words may be compared with the stage direction, more eloquent than the explanatory speeches, of the Folio text of *3 Henry VI*: *Enter a Sonne that hath kill'd his Father, at one doore: and a Father that hath kill'd his Sonne at another doore*. For Shakespeare and for the authors of *Gorboduc*, this indicates the greatest of all disorders in nature, when

> One kinsman shall bereave anothers life,
> The father shall unwitting slay the sonne,
> The sonne shall slay the sire and know it not.
>
> (*Gorboduc*, v. ii. 212–14)

Introducing a collection of verse in English translation, Charles Tomlinson observed that Ezra Pound's *Cathay* poems represented 'a confrontation deepened by history between the personal and a text in a language distanced in time and place'. He compares Pound, in respect of the experience which became the *Cathay* poems, with Gavin Douglas, who completed his translation of the *Aeneid* in 1513, the year which brought the culmination of the troubles of Scotland in the Battle of Flodden. For Douglas in his time, and for Pound at the time of the First World War, the translations were, says Tomlinson, 'a story of the man and the moment'.[4] Marlowe's name, along with the title of *Lucans First Booke*, belongs here too.

Textual introduction

There is only one early edition of Marlowe's translation of *Lucans First Booke*, and this (STC 17415) was published in 1600 by Thomas Thorpe:

LVCANS | FIRST BOOKE | TRANSLATED LINE | FOR LINE, BY CHR. | MARLOVV. | [device: McKerrow, no. 119] | *AT LONDON*, | Printed by P. Short, and are to be sold by Walter | Burre at the Signe of the Flower de Luce in | Paules Churchyard, 1600.

This edition, described by Fredson Bowers as 'a quarto-form octavo' (i.e. it was printed as a quarto, but from cut double sheets) collates A² B–D⁴ E² (E² is missing and presumed blank). It survives in four copies, which give evidence of minor proof correction. The British Library, Huntington, and Folger texts have a corrected inner forme of B; and in the Bodleian and British Library copies a turned *n* on D2 (inner D) has been corrected. Outer B is corrected in the Bodleian, British Library, and Folger copies. All but one of these alterations are of obvious details (such as turned letters), but on B1ᵛ the Bodleian text reads 'plume bearing' where the other three have 'flame bearing' (line 48), the correct translation of Lucan's *flammigeros*.

The earliest reference to the work is the entry in the *Stationers' Register*: on 28 September 1593 John Wolf claimed his right to 'a

---

4   *The Oxford Book of Verse in English Translation*, ed. Charles Tomlinson (1980), p. xiii.

booke *intituled* LUCANS *firste booke of the famous Civill warr betwixt*
POMPEY *and* CESAR England by CHRISTOPHER
MARLOW'. This is immediately followed by Wolf's entry for
Hero and Leander, but he appears to have published neither poem.
Edward Blount obtained possession of *Hero and Leander*, which he
published in 1598 before transferring his right in the copy to Paul
Linley, who in turn (on 26 June 1600) transferred the rights of
both *Hero and Leander* and *Lucans First Booke* to John Flasket.
That year Flasket reprinted Linley's 1598 edition of *Hero and
Leander*, and on the title-page advertised that this work would be
accompanied by 'the first book of Lucan *translated line for line* by
the same Author'. It has proved impossible to verify this claim. Of
the four surviving copies, two (British Library and Folger) appear
as books in their own right; the other two (Bodleian and
Huntington) are indeed bound with *Hero and Leander*, but the
binding is modern, and there is no evidence from watermarks or
the remains of stabbing that the works were originally joined.

A possible explanation for this confusion is that Flasket
originally intended to print only Marlowe's 818 lines of *Hero and
Leander*, and thought by the addition of the *Lucan* to make a more
substantial volume, comparable to Linley's 1598 Quarto, whose
title-page boasts that it was '*finished by* George Chapman', and
which contains the latter's 1300 lines, to which Flasket could not at
first perhaps obtain the rights. But when these became available,
he may have decided to discard the *Lucan*. The manuscript
somehow (without record of the transactions involved) reached the
hands of Thomas Thorpe, the publisher (some years later) of
Shakespeare's *Sonnets*.

In the dedicatory epistle to *Lucans First Booke* Thorpe
addresses Edward Blount in something of the ambiguous manner
with which, in 1609, he speaks to 'Mr W. H.'. His reference to
Blount's 'old right' in the poem suggests that Blount may have
acquired the *Lucan* along with *Hero and Leander*. The tone of the
epistle might be one of jocular friendliness or, as Greg was inclined
to think, of 'bitter sarcasm'.[5] If Greg is correct, it is difficult to
explain Thorpe's possession of *Lucans First Booke*, and perhaps a
little surprising to find Blount amicably transferring to Thorpe the
copyright of *Sejanus* in 1605, surely one of the 'manie more

---

[5] W. W. Greg, 'The Copyright of *Hero and Leander*', *The Library*, xxiv (1934), 170.

succeeding offices' that Thorpe anticipates in the epistle. It seems to me more satisfactory to accept the initial impression of friendly banter and to think that Blount, perhaps with the intention of helping a younger colleague in the publishing business, had given him *Lucans First Booke* in some unregistered transaction.

Fredson Bowers has analyzed the printing of the 'quarto-form octavo'[6] which was published by Thorpe, who seems not to have owned a printing-house himself, but to have jobbed out his work to different printers—in this case, to P. Short. Variations in spelling (especially of the word *Rome*) suggest that two compositors were engaged on the job. Bowers also believes that their copy might have been holograph, and that the printed text may, consequently, reflect some of Marlowe's own spelling and punctuation.

Copy-text for the present edition is Thorpe's 1600 quarto: the four surviving copies have been collated, together with all available modern editions. Editorial intervention is minimal, although I have been consistent in italicizing geographical names (including the different spellings of *Rome*, which the Q compositors are consistent in printing in roman type).

SIGLA

B Bodleian Library copy
F Folger Shakespeare Library copy
H Huntington Library copy
L British Library copy
Q Quarto 1600 (all copies)

[6] In *The Complete Works of Christopher Marlowe* (Cambridge, 1973), ii. 275–8.

Blount: *I purpose to be blunt with you, & out of my dulnesse to encounter you with a* Dedication *in the memory of that pure Elementall wit* Chr. Marlow; *whose ghoast or* Genius *is to be seene walke the* Churchyard *in (at the least) three or foure sheets. Me thinks you should presently looke wilde now, and growe humorously frantique upon the tast of it. Well, least you should, let mee tell you. This spirit was sometime a familiar of your own,* Lucans first booke *translated; which (in regard of your old right in it) I have rais'd in the circle of your Patronage. But stay now* Edward *(if I mistake not) you are to accommodate your selfe with some fewe instructions, touching the property of a Patron, that you are not yet possest of; and to study them for your better grace as our Gallants do fashions. First you must be proud and thinke you have merit inough in you, though you are ne're so emptie; then when I bring you the booke take physicke, and keepe state, assigne me a time by your man to come againe, and afore the day be sure to have chang'd your lodging; in the meane time sleepe little, and sweat with the invention of some pittiful dry jest or two which you may happen to utter, with some little (or not at al) marking of your friends when you have found a place for them to come in at: or if by chance something has dropt from you worth the taking up weary all that come to you with the often repetition of it; Censure scornefully inough, and somewhat like a travailer; commend nothing least you discredit your (that which you would seeme to have) judgement. These things if you can mould your selfe to them* Ned *I make no question but they will not become you. One speciall vertue in our Patrons of these daies I have promist my selfe you shall fit excellently, which is to give nothing; Yes, thy love I will challenge as my peculiar Object both in this, and (I hope) manie more succeeding offices: Farewell, I affect not the world should measure my thoughts to thee by a scale of this Nature: Leave to thinke good of me when I fall from thee.*

Thine in all rites of perfect friendship,
THOM. THORPE.

The First Booke of Lucan
Translated into English

Wars worse then civill on *Thessalian* playnes,
And outrage strangling law & people strong,
We sing, whose conquering swords their own breasts launcht,
Armies alied, the kingdoms league uprooted,
Th'affrighted worlds force bent on publique spoile,　　　　5
Trumpets, and drums like deadly threatning other,
Eagles alike displaide, darts answering darts.
Romans, what madnes, what huge lust of warre
Hath made *Barbarians* drunke with *latin* bloud?
Now *Babilon*, (proud through our spoile) should stoop,　　　　10
While slaughtred *Crassus* ghost walks unreveng'd,
Will ye wadge war, for which you shall not triumph?
　　Ay me, O what a world of land and sea,
Might they have won whom civil broiles have slaine,
As far as *Titan* springs where night dims heaven,　　　　15
I to the *Torrid Zone* where midday burnes,
And where stiffe winter whom no spring resolves,
Fetters the *Euxin* sea, with chaines of yce:
Scythia and wilde *Armenia* had bin yoakt,
And they of *Nilus* mouth (if there live any.)　　　　20
Roome if thou take delight in impious warre,
First conquer all the earth, then turne thy force
Against thy selfe: as yet thou wants not foes.
　　That now the walles of houses halfe rear'd totter,
That rampiers fallen down, huge heapes of stone　　　　25
Lye in our townes, that houses are abandon'd,
And few live that behold their ancient seats;
Italy many yeares hath lyen until'd,
And choakt with thorns, that greedy earth wants hinds
Fierce *Pirhus*, neither thou nor *Hanniball*　　　　30
Art cause, no forraine foe could so afflict us,
These plagues arise from wreake of civill power.
But if for *Nero* (then unborne) the fates
Would find no other meanes, (and gods not sleightly

Purchase immortal thrones; nor *Jove* joide heaven   35
Untill the cruel Giants war was done.)
We plaine not heavens, but gladly beare these evils
For *Neros* sake: *Pharsalia* grone with slaughter;
And *Carthage* soules be glutted with our blouds;
At *Munda* let the dreadfull battailes joyne;   40
Adde *Caesar*, to these illes *Perusian* famine;
The *Mutin* toyles; the fleet at *Leuca* suncke;
And cruel field, nere burning *Aetna* fought:
　　Yet *Room* is much bound to these civil armes,
　　Which made thee Emperor, thee (seeing thou being old   45
　　Must shine a star) shal heaven (whom thou lovest,)
　　Receive with shouts; where thou wilt raigne as King,
　　Or mount the sunnes flame bearing charriot,
　　And with bright restles fire compasse the earth,
　　Undaunted though her former guide be chang'd;   50
　　Nature, and every power shal give thee place,
　　What God it please thee be, or where to sway:
But neither chuse the north t'erect thy seat;
Nor yet the adverse reking southerne pole,
Whence thou shouldst view thy *Roome* with squinting beams; 55
If any one part of vast heaven thou swayest,
The burdened axes with thy force will bend;
The midst is best; that place is pure, and bright,
There *Caesar* may'st thou shine and no cloud dim thee;
Then men from war shal bide in league, and ease,   60
Peace through the world from *Janus Phane* shal flie,
And boult the brazen gates with barres of Iron.
Thou *Caesar* at this instant art my God,
Thee if I invocate, I shall not need
To crave *Apolles* ayde, or *Bacchus* helpe;   65
Thy power inspires the *Muze* that sings this war.
　　The causes first I purpose to unfould
　　Of these garboiles, whence springs a long discourse,
　　And what made madding people shake off peace.
The fates are envious, high seats quickly perish,   70
Under great burdens fals are ever greevous;
Roome was so great it could not beare it selfe:

So when this worlds compounded union breakes,
Time ends and to old *Chaos* all things turne;
Confused stars shal meete, celestiall fire   75
Fleete on the flouds, the earth shoulder the sea,
Affording it no shoare, and *Phoebe's* waine,
Chace *Phoebus* and inrag'd affect his place,
And strive to shine by day, and ful of strife
Disolve the engins of the broken world.   80
    All great things crush themselves, such end the gods,
    Allot the height of honor, men so strong
    By land, and sea, no forreine force could ruine:
    O *Roome* thy selfe art cause of all these evils,
    Thy selfe thus shivered out to three mens shares,   85
    Dire league of partners in a kingdome last not.
O faintly joyn'd friends with ambition blind,
Why joine you force to share the world betwixt you?
While th'earth the sea, and ayre the earth sustaines;
While *Titan* strives against the worlds swift course;   90
Or *Cynthia* nights Queene waights upon the day;
Shall never faith be found in fellow kings.
Dominion cannot suffer partnership;
This need no forraine proofe, nor far fet story:
Roomes infant walles were steept in brothers bloud;   95
Nor then was land, or sea, to breed such hate,
A towne with one poore church set them at oddes.
    Caesars, and *Pompeys* jarring love soone ended,
    T'was peace against their wils, betwixt them both
    Stept *Crassus* in, even as the slender *Isthmos*,   100
    Betwixt the *Aegean* and the *Ionian* sea,
    Keepes each from other, but being worne away
    They both burst out, and each incounter other:
    So when as *Crassus* wretched death who stayd them,
    Had fild *Assirian Carras* wals with bloud,   105
    His losse made way for *Roman* outrages.
Parthians y'afflict us more then ye suppose,
Being conquered, we are plaugde with civil war,
Swords share our Empire, fortune that made *Roome*
Governe the earth, the sea, the world it selfe,   110
Would not admit two Lords: for *Julia*
Snatcht hence by cruel fates with ominous howles,

Bare downe to hell her sonne the pledge of peace,
And all bands of that death presaging aliance.
   Julia, had heaven given thee longer life 115
   Thou hadst restrainde thy headstrong husbands rage,
   Yea and thy father to, and swords thrown down,
   Made all shake hands as once the *Sabines* did;
   Thy death broake amity and trainde to war,
   These Captaines emulous of each others glory. 120
Thou feard'st (great *Pompey*) that late deeds would dim
Olde triumphs, and that *Caesars* conquering *France*,
Would dash the wreath thou wearst for Pirats wracke.
Thee wars use stirde, and thoughts that alwaies scorn'd
A second place; *Pompey* could bide no equall, 125
Nor *Caesar* no superior, which of both
Had justest cause unlawful tis to judge:
Each side had great partakers; *Caesars* cause,
The gods abetted; *Cato* likt the other;
Both differ'd much, *Pompey* was strooke in yeares, 130
And by long rest forgot to manage armes,
And being popular sought by liberal gifts,
To gaine the light unstable commons love,
And joyed to heare his *Theaters* applause;
He liv'd secure boasting his former deeds, 135
And thought his name sufficient to uphold him,
Like to a tall oake in a fruitfull field,
Bearing old spoiles and conquerors monuments,
Who though his root be weake, and his owne waight
Keepe him within the ground, his armes al bare, 140
His body (not his boughs) send forth a shade;
Though every blast it nod, and seeme to fal,
When all the woods about stand bolt up-right,
Yet he alone is held in reverence.
   Caesars renowne for war was lesse, he restles, 145
   Shaming to strive but where he did subdue,
   When yre, or hope provokt, heady, & bould,
   At al times charging home, & making havock;
   Urging his fortune, trusting in the gods,
   Destroying what withstood his proud desires, 150
   And glad when bloud, & ruine made him way:
   So thunder which the wind teares from the cloudes,

With cracke of riven ayre and hideous sound,
Filling the world, leapes out and throwes forth fire,
Affrights poore fearefull men, and blasts their eyes   155
With overthwarting flames, and raging shoots
Alongst the ayre and not resisting it
Falls, and returnes, and shivers where it lights.
Such humors stirde them up; but this warrs seed,
Was even the same that wrack's all great dominions.   160
When fortune made us lords of all, wealth flowed,
And then we grew licencious and rude,
The soldiours pray, and rapine brought in ryot,
Men tooke delight in Jewels, houses, plate,
And scorn'd old sparing diet, and ware robes   165
Too light for women; Poverty (who hatcht
Roomes greatest wittes) was loath'd, and al the world
Ransackt for golde, which breeds the world decay;
And then large limits had their butting lands,
The ground which *Curius* and *Camillus* till'd,   170
Was stretcht unto the fields of hinds unknowne;
Againe, this people could not brooke calme peace,
Them freedome without war might not suffice,
Quarrels were rife, greedy desire stil poore
Did vild deeds, then t'was worth the price of bloud,   175
And deem'd renowne to spoile their native towne,
Force mastered right, the strongest govern'd all,
Hence came it that th'edicts were overrul'd,
That lawes were broake, *Tribunes* with *Consuls* strove,
Sale made of offices, and peoples voices,   180
Bought by themselves & solde, and every yeare
Frauds and corruption in the field of *Mars*;
Hence interest and devouring usury sprang,
Faiths breach, & hence came war to most men welcom.
Now *Caesar* overpast the snowy *Alpes*,   185
His mind was troubled, and he aim'd at war,
And comming to the foord of *Rubicon*,
At night in dreadful vision fearefull *Roome*,
Mourning appear'd, whose hoary hayres were torne,
And on her Turret-bearing head disperst,   190
And armes all naked, who with broken sighes,
And staring, thus bespoke, what mean'st thou *Caesar*?

Whether goes my standarde? *Romans* if ye be,
And beare true harts, stay heare: this spectacle
Stroake *Caesars* hart with feare, his hayre stoode up,   195
And faintnes numm'd his steps there on the brincke:
He thus cride out: Thou thunderer that guardst
Roomes mighty walles built on *Tarpeian* rocke,
Ye gods of *Phrigia* and *Júlus* line,
Quirinus rites and *Latian Jove* advanc'd,   200
On *Alba* hill, ô *Vestall* flames, ô *Roome*,
My thoughts sole *goddes*, aide mine enterprise,
I hate thee not, to thee my conquests stoope,
Caesar is thine, so please it thee, thy soldier;
He, he afflicts *Roome* that made me *Roomes* foe.   205
This said, he laying aside all lets of war,
Approcht the swelling streame with drum and ensigne,
Like to a Lyon of scortcht desart *Affricke*,
Who seeing hunters pauseth till fell wrath
And kingly rage increase, then having whiskt   210
His taile athwart his backe, and crest heav'd up,
With jawes wide open ghastly roaring out;
(Albeit the *Moores* light Javelin or his speare
Sticks in his side) yet runs upon the hunter.
　　In summer time the purple *Rubicon*,   215
　Which issues from a small spring is but shallow,
　And creepes along the vales deviding just
　　The bounds of *Italy*, from *Cisalpin Fraunce*;
　But now the winters wrath and wat'ry moone,
　Being three daies old inforst the floud to swell,   220
　And frozen *Alpes* thaw'd with resolving winds.
The thunder hov'd horse in a crooked line,
To scape the violence of the streame first waded,
Which being broke the foot had easie passage.
　　As soone as *Caesar* got unto the banke   225
　　And bounds of *Italy*; here, here (saith he)
An end of peace; here end polluted lawes;
Hence leagues, and covenants; Fortune thee I follow,
Warre and the destinies shall trie my cause.
　　This said, the restles generall through the darke   230
　　(Swifter then bullets throwne from Spanish slinges,
　　Or darts which *Parthians* backward shoot) marcht on

And then (when *Lucifer* did shine alone,
And some dim stars) he *Arriminum* enter'd:
Day rose and viewde these tumultes of the war;   235
Whether the gods, or blustring south were cause
I know not, but the cloudy ayre did frown;
The soldiours having won the market place,
There spred the colours, with confused noise
Of trumpets clange, shril cornets, whistling fifes;   240
The people started; young men left their beds;
And snatcht armes neer their household gods hung up
Such as peace yeelds; wormeaten leatherne targets,
Through which the wood peer'd, headles darts, olde swords
With ugly teeth of blacke rust fouly scarr'd: 245
But seeing white Eagles, & *Roomes* flags wel known,
And lofty *Caesar* in the thickest throng,
They shooke for feare, & cold benumm'd their lims,
And muttering much, thus to themselves complain'd.
O wals unfortunate too neere to *France*,   250
Predestinate to ruine; all lands else
Have stable peace, here wars rage first begins,
We bide the first brunt, safer might we dwel,
Under the frosty beare, or parching East,
Wagons or tents, then in this frontire towne,   255
We first sustain'd the uproares of the *Gaules*,
And furious *Cymbrians* and of *Carthage* moores,
As oft as *Roome* was sackt, here gan the spoile:
Thus sighing whispered they, and none durst speake
And shew their feare, or griefe: but as the fields   260
When birds are silent thorough winters rage;
Or sea far from the land, so all were whist.
Now light had quite dissolv'd the mysty night,
And *Caesars* mind unsetled musing stood;
But gods and fortune prickt him to this war,   265
Infringing all excuse of modest shame,
And laboring to approve his quarrell good.
The angry Senate urging *Grachus* deeds,
From doubtfull *Roome* wrongly expel'd the *Tribunes*,
That crost them; both which now approacht the camp,   270

263 night] *Robinson*; might *Q*

And with them *Curio*; sometime *Tribune* too,
One that was feed for *Caesar*, and whose tongue
Could tune the people to the Nobles mind:
Caesar (said he) while eloquence prevail'd,
And I might pleade, and draw the Commons minds   275
To favour thee, against the Senats will,
Five yeeres I lengthned thy commaund in *France*:
But law being put to silence by the wars;
We from our houses driven, most willingly
Suffered exile: let thy sword bring us home.   280
Now while their part is weake, and feares, march hence,
"Where men are ready, lingering ever hurts":
In ten yeares wonst thou *France*; *Roome* may be won
With farre lesse toile, and yet the honors more;
Few battailes fought with prosperous successe   285
May bring her downe, and with her all the world;
Nor shalt thou triumph when thou comst to *Roome*;
Nor capitall be adorn'd with sacred bayes:
Envy denies all, with thy bloud must thou
Abie thy conquest past: the sonne decrees   290
To expel the father; share the world thou canst not;
Injoy it all thou maiest: thus *Curio* spake,
And therewith *Caesar* prone ennough to warre,
Was so incenst as are *Eleius* steedes
With clamors: who though lockt and chaind in stalls,   295
Souse downe the wals, and make a passage forth:
Straight summon'd he his severall companies
Unto the standard: his grave looke appeasd
The wrastling tumult, and right hand made silence:
And thus he spake; you that with me have borne   300
A thousand brunts, and tride me ful ten yeeres,
See how they quit our bloudshed in the North;
Our friends death; and our wounds; our wintering
Under the *Alpes*; *Roome* rageth now in armes
As if the *Carthage Hannibal* were neere;   305
Cornets of horse are mustered for the field;
Woods turn'd to ships; both land and sea against us:
Had forraine wars ill thriv'd; or wrathful *France*
Pursu'd us hither, how were we bestead
When comming conqueror *Roome* afflicts me thus?   310

Let come their leader whom long peace hath quail'd;
Raw soldiours lately prest; and troupes of gownes;
Brabbling *Marcellus*; *Cato* whom fooles reverence;
Must *Pompeis* followers with strangers ayde,
(Whom from his youth he bribde) needs make him king?   315
And shal he triumph long before his time,
And having once got head still shal he raigne?
What should I talke of mens corne reapt by force,
And by him kept of purpose for a dearth,
Who sees not warre sit by the quivering Judge;   320
And sentence given in rings of naked swords,
And lawes assailde, and arm'd men in the *Senate*;
Twas his troupe hem'd in *Milo* being accusde;
And now least age might waine his state, he casts
For civill warre, wherein through use he's known   325
To exceed his maister, that arch-traitor *Sylla*.
 A brood of barbarous *Tygars* having lapt
  The bloud of many a heard, whilst with their dams
  They kennel'd in *Hircania* evermore
   Wil rage and pray: so *Pompey* thou having lickt   330
   Warme goare from *Syllas* sword art yet athirst,
  Jawes flesht with bloud continue murderous.
Speake, when shall this thy long usurpt power end?
What end of mischiefe? *Sylla* teaching thee,
At last learne wretch to leave thy monarchy;   335
What, now *Scicillian* Pirats are supprest,
And jaded king of *Pontus* poisoned slaine,
Must *Pompey* as his last foe plume on me,
Because at his commaund I wound not up
My conquering Eagles? say I merit nought,   340
Yet for long service done, reward these men,
And so they triumph, be't with whom ye wil.
Whether now shal these olde bloudles soules repaire?
What seates for their deserts? what store of ground
For servitors to till? what *Colonies*   345
To rest their bones? say *Pompey*, are these worse
Then Pirats of *Sycillia*? they had houses:
Spread, spread these flags that ten years space have conquer'd,

Lets use our tried force, they that now thwart right
In wars wil yeeld to wrong: the gods are with us,   350
Neither spoile, nor kingdom seeke we by these armes,
But *Roome* at thraldoms feet to rid from tyrants.
 This spoke none answer'd but a murmuring buz
Th'unstable people made: their houshold gods
And love to *Room* (thogh slaughter steeld their harts   355
And minds were prone) restrain'd them; but wars love
And *Caesars* awe dasht all: then *Lalius*
The chiefe *Centurion* crown'd with Oaken leaves,
For saving of a *Romaine* Citizen,
 Stept forth, and cryde, chiefe leader of *Rooms* force,   360
So be I may be bold to speake a truth:
We grieve at this thy patience and delay,
What doubtst thou us? even nowe when youthfull bloud
Pricks forth our lively bodies, and strong armes
Can mainly throw the dart; wilt thou indure   365
These purple groomes? that *Senates* tyranny?
Is conquest got by civill war so hainous?
Well, leade us then to *Syrtes* desart shoare;
Or *Scythia*; or hot *Libiaes* thirsty sands.
This hand that all behind us might be quail'd,   370
Hath with thee past the swelling Ocean;
And swept the foming brest of *Articks Rhene*,
Love over-rules my will, I must obay thee,
Caesar, he whom I heare thy trumpets charge
I hould no *Romaine*; by these ten blest ensignes   375
And all thy several triumphs, shouldst thou bid me
Intombe my sword within my brothers bowels;
Or fathers throate; or womens groning wombe;
This hand (albeit unwilling) should performe it;
Or rob the gods; or sacred temples fire: 380
These troupes should soone pull down the church of *Jove*;
If to incampe on *Thuscan Tybers* streames,
Ile bouldly quarter out the fields of *Rome*;
What wals thou wilt be leaveld with the ground,
These hands shall thrust the ram, and make them flie,   385
Albeit the Citty thou wouldst have so ra'st
Be *Roome* it selfe. Here every band applauded,
And with their hands held up, all joyntly cryde

They'ill follow where he please: the showts rent heaven,
As when against pine bearing *Ossa's* rocks,   390
Beates *Thracian Boreas*; or when trees bowe down,
And rustling swing up as the wind fets breath.
When *Caesar* saw his army proane to war,
And fates so bent, least sloth and long delay
Might crosse him, he withdrew his troupes from *France*,   395
And in all quarters musters men for *Roome*.
    They by *Lemannus* nooke forsooke their tents;
They whom the *Lingones* foild with painted speares,
Under the rockes by crooked *Vogesus*;
And many came from shallow *Isara*,   400
Who running long, fals in a greater floud,
And ere he sees the sea looseth his name;
The yellow *Ruthens* left their garrisons;
Mild *Atax* glad it beares not Roman boats;
And frontier *Varus* that the campe is farre,   ·   405
Sent aide; so did *Alcides* port, whose seas
Eate hollow rocks, and where the north-west wind,
Nor *Zephir* rules not, but the north alone,
Turmoiles the coast, and enterance forbids;
And others came from that uncertaine shore,   410
Which is nor sea, nor land, but oft times both,
And changeth as the Ocean ebbes and flowes:
Whether the sea roul'd alwaies from that point,
Whence the wind blowes stil forced to and fro;
Or that the wandring maine follow the moone?   415
Or flaming *Titan* (feeding on the deepe,)
Puls them aloft, and makes the surge kisse heaven,
Philosophers looke you, for unto me
Thou cause what ere thou be whom God assignes
This great effect, art hid. They came that dwell   420
By *Nemes* fields, and bankes of *Satirus*,
Where *Tarbels* winding shoares imbrace the sea,
The *Santons* that rejoyce in *Caesars* love,
Those of *Bituriges* and light *Axon* pikes;
And they of *Rhene* and *Leuca*, cunning darters,   425
And *Sequana* that well could manage steeds;

The *Belgians* apt to governe *Brittish* cars;
Th'*Averni* too, which bouldly faine themselves
The Romanes brethren, sprung of *Ilian* race;
The stubborne *Nervians* staind with *Cottas* bloud;   430
And *Vangions* who like those of *Sarmata*,
Were open slops: and fierce *Batavians*,
Whome trumpets clang incites, and those that dwel
By *Cyngas* streame, and where swift *Rhodanus*
Drives *Araris* to sea; They neere the hils,   435
Under whose hoary rocks *Gebenna* hangs;
And *Trevier*; thou being glad that wars are past thee;
And you late shorne *Ligurians*, who were wont
In large spread heire to exceed the rest of *France*;
And where to *Hesus*, and fell *Mercury*   440
They offer humane flesh, and where *Jove* seemes
Bloudy like *Dian*, whom the *Scythians* serve;
And you French *Bardi*, whose immortal pens
Renowne the valiant soules slaine in your wars,
Sit safe at home and chaunt sweet *Poesie*,   445
And *Druides* you now in peace renew
Your barbarous customes, and sinister rites,
In unfeld woods, and sacred groves you dwell,
And only gods & heavenly powers you know,
Or only know you nothing. For you hold   450
That soules passe not to silent *Erebus*
Or *Plutoes* bloodles kingdom, but else where
Resume a body: so (if truth you sing)
Death brings long life. Doubtles these northren men
Whom death the greatest of all feares affright not,   455
Are blest by such sweet error, this makes them
Run on the swords point and desire to die,
And shame to spare life which being lost is wonne;
You likewise that repulst the *Caicke* foe,
March towards *Roome*; and you fierce men of *Rhene*   460
Leaving your countrey open to the spoile.
These being come, their huge power made him bould
To mannage greater deeds; the bordering townes
He garrison'd; and *Italy* he fild with soldiours.

Vaine fame increast true feare, and did invade   465
The peoples minds, and laide before their eies
Slaughter to come, and swiftly bringing newes
Of present war, made many lies and tales,
One sweares his troupes of daring horsemen fought
Upon *Mevanias* plaine, where Buls are graz'd;   470
Other that *Caesars* barbarous bands were spread
Along *Nar* floud that into *Tiber* fals,
And that his owne ten ensignes, and the rest
Marcht not intirely, and yet hide the ground,
And that he's much chang'd, looking wild and big,   475
And far more barbarous then the French (his vassals)
And that he lags behind with them of purpose,
Borne twixt the *Alpes* & *Rhene*, which he hath brought
From out their Northren parts, and that *Roome*
He looking on by these men should be sackt.   480
Thus in his fright did each man strengthen Fame,
And without ground, fear'd, what themselves had faind:
Nor were the Commons only strooke to heart
With this vaine terror; but the Court, the Senate;
The fathers selves leapt from their seats; and flying   485
Left hateful warre decreed to both the *Consuls*.
Then with their feare, and danger al distract,
Their sway of fleight carries the heady rout
That in chain'd troupes breake forth at every port;
You would have thought their houses had bin fierd   490
Or dropping-ripe, ready to fall with Ruine,
So rusht the inconsiderate multitude
Thorough the Citty hurried headlong on,
As if, the only hope (that did remaine
To their afflictions) were t'abandon *Roome*.   495
Looke how when stormy *Auster* from the breach
Of *Libian Syrtes*, roules a monstrous wave,
Which makes the maine saile fal with hideous sound;
The Pilot from the helme leapes in the sea;
And Marriners, albeit the keele be sound   500
Shipwracke themselves: even so the Citty left,
All rise in armes; nor could the bed-rid parents
Keep back their sons, or womens teares their husbands;
They stai'd not either to pray or sacrifice,

Their household gods restrain them not, none lingered,   505
As loath to leave *Roome* whom they held so deere,
Th'irrevocable people flie in troupes.
    O gods that easie grant men great estates,
    But hardly grace to keepe them: *Roome* that flowes
    With Citizens and Captives, and would hould   510
    The world (were it together) is by cowards
    Left as a pray now *Caesar* doth approach:
    When Romans are besieg'd by forraine foes,
    With slender trench they escape night stratagems,
    And suddaine rampire raisde of turfe snatcht up   515
    Would make them sleepe securely in their tents.
    Thou *Roome* at name of warre runst from thy selfe,
    And wilt not trust thy Citty walls one night:
    Wel might these feare, when *Pompey* fear'd and fled.
    Now evermore least some one hope might ease   520
    The Commons jangling minds, apparent signes arose,
    Strange sights appear'd, the angry threatning gods
    Fill'd both the earth and seas with prodegies;
    Great store of strange and unknown stars were seene
    Wandering about the North, and rings of fire   525
    Flie in the ayre, and dreadfull bearded stars,
    And Commets that presage the fal of kingdoms.
The flattering skie gliter'd in often flames,
And sundry fiery meteors blaz'd in heaven:
Now spearlike, long; now like a spreading torch: 530
Lightning in silence, stole forth without clouds,
And from the northren climat snatching fier
Blasted the Capitoll: The lesser stars
Which wont to run their course through empty night
At noone day mustered; *Phoebe* having fild   535
Her meeting hornes to match her brothers light,
Strooke with th'earths suddaine shadow waxed pale,
Titan himselfe throand in the midst of heaven,
His burning chariot plung'd in sable cloudes,
And whelm'd the world in darknesse, making men   540
Dispaire of day; as did *Thiestes* towne;
(*Mycenae*) *Phoebus* flying through the East:

510 Captives] *Dyce*; Captaines *Q*

Fierce *Mulciber* unbarred *Aetna*'s gate,
Which flamed not on high; but headlong pitcht
Her burning head on bending *Hespery*.　　　　　545
Cole-blacke *Charibdis* whirl'd a sea of bloud;
Fierce Mastives hould; the vestall fires went out,
The flame in *Alba* consecrate to *Jove*,
Parted in twaine; and with a double point
Rose like the *Theban* brothers funerall fire;　　　550
The earth went off hir hinges; And the *Alpes*
Shooke the old snow from off their trembling laps.
The Ocean swell'd, as high as Spanish *Calpe*;
Or *Atlas* head, their saints and houshold gods
Sweate teares to shew the travailes of their citty.　　555
Crownes fell from holy statues, ominous birds
Defil'd the day, and wilde beastes were seene,
Leaving the woods lodge in the streetes of *Rome*.
Cattell were seene that muttered humane speech:
Prodigious birthes with more and ugly jointes　　　560
Then nature gives, whose sight appauls the mother,
And dismall Prophesies were spread abroad:
And they whom fierce *Bellonaes* fury moves
To wound their armes, sing vengeance, *Sibils* priests,
Curling their bloudy lockes, howle dreadfull things,　565
Soules quiet and appeas'd sigh'd from their graves,
Clashing of armes was heard, in untrod woods
Shrill voices schright, and ghoasts incounter men.
Those that inhabited the suburbe fieldes
Fled, fowle *Erinnis* stalkt about the wals,　　　570
Shaking her snakie haire and crooked pine
With flaming toppe, much like that hellish fiend
Which made the sterne *Lycurgus* wound his thigh,
Or fierce *Agave* mad; or like *Megaera*
That scar'd *Alcides*, when by *Junoes* taske　　　575
He had before lookt *Pluto* in the face.
Trumpets were heard to sound; and with what noise
An armed battaile joines, such and more strange
Blacke night brought forth in secret: *Sylla's* ghost
Was seene to walke, singing sad Oracles,　　　　580

And *Marius* head above cold *Tav'ron* peering
(His grave broke open) did affright the Boores.
To these ostents (as their old custome was)
They call th'*Etrurian Augures*, amongst whom
The gravest, *Aruns*, dwelt in forsaken *Leuca   *or Luna
Well skild in *Pyromancy*; one that knew   586
The hearts of beasts, and flight of wandring foules;
First he commands such monsters *Nature* hatcht
Against her kind (the barren Mules loth'd issue)
To be cut forth and cast in dismall fiers: 590
Then, that the trembling Citizens should walke
About the City; then the sacred priests
That with divine lustration purg'd the wals,
And went the round, in, and without the towne.
Next, an inferiour troupe, in tuckt up vestures;   595
After the *Gabine* manner: then the Nunnes
And their vaild Matron, who alone might view
Minervas statue; then, they that keepe, and read
Sybillas secret works, and wash their saint
In *Almo's* floud: Next learned *Augures* follow;   600
Apolloes southsayers; and *Joves* feasting priests;
The skipping *Salii* with shields like wedges;
And *Flamins* last, with networke wollen vailes.
While these thus in and out had circled *Roome*,
Looke what the lightning blasted, *Aruns* takes   605
And it inters with murmurs dolorous,
And cals the place *Bidentall*, on the Altar
He laies a ne're-yoakt Bull, and powers downe wine,
Then crams salt levin on his crooked knife;
The beast long struggled, as being like to prove   610
An aukward sacrifice, but by the hornes
The quick priest pull'd him on his knees & slew him:
No vaine sprung out but from the yawning gash,
In steed of red bloud wallowed venemous gore,
These direful signes made *Aruns* stand amaz'd,   615
And searching farther for the gods displeasure,
The very cullor scard him; a dead blacknesse
Ranne through the bloud, that turn'd it all to gelly,

599 wash] *Dyce*; washt *Q*

And stain'd the bowels with darke lothsome spots,
The liver swell'd with filth: and every vaine   620
Did threaten horror from the host of *Caesar*;
A small thin skinne contain'd the vital parts,
The heart stird not, and from the gaping liver
Squis'd matter; through the cal the intralls pearde,
And which (aie me) ever pretendeth ill,   625
At that bunch where the liver is, appear'd
A knob of flesh, whereof one halfe did looke
Dead, and discoulour'd; th'other leane and thinne.
By these he seeing what myschiefes must ensue,
Cride out, O gods! I tremble to unfould   630
What you intend, great *Jove* is now displeas'd,
And in the brest of this slaine Bull are crept,
Th'infernall powers. My feare transcends my words
Yet more will happen then I can unfold;
Turne all to good, be *Augury* vaine, and *Tages*   635
Th'arts master falce. Thus in ambiguous tearmes,
Involving all, did *Aruns* darkly sing.
But *Figulus* more seene in heavenly mysteries,
Whose like *Aegiptian Memphis* never had
For skill in stars, and tune-full planeting   640
   In this sort spake. The worlds swift course is lawlesse
And casuall; all the starres at randome radge:
Or if *Fate* rule them, *Rome* thy Cittizens
Are neere some plague: what mischiefe shall insue?
Shall townes be swallowed? shall the thickned aire,   645
Become intemperate? shall the earth be barraine?
Shall water be conjeal'd and turn'd to ice?
O Gods what death prepare ye? with what plague
Meane ye to radge? the death of many men
Meetes in one period. If cold noysome *Saturne*   650
Were now exalted, and with blew beames shinde,
Then *Gaynimede* would renew *Deucalions* flood,
And in the fleeting sea the earth be drencht.
O *Phoebus* shouldst thou with thy rayes now sing
The fell *Nemean* beast, th'earth would be fired,   655
And heaven tormented with thy chafing heate,
But thy fiers hurt not; *Mars*, 'tis thou enflam'st

The threatning Scorpion with the burning taile
And fier'st his cleyes. Why art thou thus enrag'd?
Kind *Jupiter* hath low declin'd himselfe; 660
Venus is faint; swift *Hermes* retrograde;
Mars onely rules the heaven: why doe the Planets
Alter their course; and vainly dim their vertue?
Sword-girt *Orions* side glisters too bright.
Wars radge draws neare; & to the swords strong hand, 665
Let all Lawes yeeld, sinne beare the name of vertue,
Many a yeare these furious broiles let last,
Why should we wish the gods should ever end them?
War onely gives us peace, ô *Rome* continue
The course of mischiefe, and stretch out the date 670
Of slaughter; onely civill broiles make peace.
These sad presages were enough to scarre
The quivering *Romans*, but worse things affright them,
As *Maenas* full of wine on *Pindus* raves,
So runnes a Matron through th'amazed streetes, 675
Disclosing *Phoebus* furie in this sort:
Pean whither am I halde? where shall I fall,
Thus borne aloft? I see *Pangeus* hill,
With hoarie toppe, and under *Hemus* mount
Philippi plaines; *Phoebus* what radge is this? 680
Why grapples *Rome*, and makes war, having no foes?
Whither turne I now? thou lead'st me toward th'east,
Where *Nile* augmenteth the *Pelusian* sea:
This headlesse trunke that lies on *Nylus* sande
I know, now throughout the aire I flie, 685
To doubtfull *Sirtes* and drie *Affricke*, where
A fury leades the *Emathian* bandes, from thence
To the pine bearing hils, hence to the mounts
Pirene, and so backe to *Rome* againe.
Se impious warre defiles the Senat house, 690
New factions rise; now through the world againe
I goe; ô *Phoebus* shew me *Neptunes* shore,
And other Regions, I have seene *Philippi*:
This said being tir'd with fury she sunke downe.

FINIS

677–8 fall, . . . aloft?] *Dyce*; ~? . . . ~, *Q*

DIDO QUEENE OF CARTHAGE

THE
Tragedie of Dido
Queene of Carthage:
Played by the Children of her
Maiesties Chappell.

Written by Christopher Marlowe, and
Thomas Nash. Gent.

Actors

Iupiter.	*Ascanius.*
Ganimed.	*Dido.*
Venus.	*Anna.*
Cupid.	*Achates.*
Iuno.	*Ilioneus.*
Mercurie, or	*Iarbas.*
Hermes.	*Cloanthes.*
Æneas.	*Sergestus.*

AT LONDON,
Printed, by the Widdowe *Orwin,* for *Thomas Woodcocke,* and
are to be solde at his shop, in Paules Church-yeard, at
the signe of the blacke Beare. 1594.

FIG. 3. Title-page of *Dido Queene of Carthage* (1594)

General Introduction

THE title-page of *Dido Queene of Carthage* (Figure 3) claims that the tragedy was '*Played by the Children of her Majesties Chappell*'. This fact gives no assistance in dating the play, however, since there is no trace of any London performance by the Chapel Children between 1584 and 1600. It appears that they were prohibited from acting in the Royal Chapel in 1576, whereupon they moved to the Blackfriars' monastery until that closed in 1583 or 1584. In 1600 they appear again in London, performing at the new Blackfriars' playhouse. During the 16 or 17 years of exile from the capital, the company 'flitted in a shadowy way across the provinces . . . playing seldom and at long intervals.[1] But the statement on the title-page is a valuable guide for the critical assessment of the play, insisting that it must be discussed in the context of entertainments designed to be performed by children in 'private' playhouses, and not by adult companies in the public theatres.

In all the plays written for children during the sixteenth century, the emphasis is on artifice. Boys with unbroken voices took the parts of the great figures from classical mythology ('Hercules and his load too', as Rosencrantz tells Hamlet). The list of dramatis personae for Peele's *Arraignment of Paris* (acted by the Chapel Children in 1584) is an Olympian roll-call, descending from Saturn and Jupiter through Pallas and Venus to the Muses, and adding the shepherds of contemporary pastoral in Hobbinol and Diggon. Verisimilitude was not to be looked for in the characters, a fact which is underlined by Peele's flourishing couplets. Imitation of life, however, was to be found in the costumes, sound effects, and scenery in which these plays went gorgeous. An unknown moralist gave the puritan viewpoint (which was what may have led to the banning of dramatic performances in the Royal Chapel) when he bewailed the example set by the highest in the land: 'Plaies will neuer be supprest, while her maiesties vnfledged minions flaunt it in silkes and sattens. They

---

[1] H. N. Hillebrand, *The Child Actors* (Urbana, Illinois, 1926), 104.

had as well be at their Popish seruice, in the deuils garments.'[2] Her
Majesty, on the other hand, was well pleased with a performance
of Richard Edwardes's *Palamon and Arcyte* at Oxford in 1566: 'At
ye crie of ye houndes in ye Quadrant uppon ye trayne of a foxe in y^e
huntinge of Theseus, when ye boyes in ye wyndowes cried nowe,
nowe, excellent saide ye Queene those boyes are readie to leape out
at windowes to followe ye houndes.'[3]

Even here, though, the imitation was always ready to draw
attention to itself *qua* imitation, expecting applause for the
excellence of its craftsmanship in equalling, or if possible
outdoing, nature. In 1583 a performance was given at Oxford of
William Gager's Latin play about Dido. The performance was in
honour of a visit to the university by Albertus Alasco, Prince
Palatine of Siradia, in Poland, and perhaps Gager thought the
subject appropriate. His play had no influence whatsoever upon
Marlowe's tragedy, but it is tempting to fancy that the production
details might have been comparable. On the twelfth of June,
Alasco

personaly was present with his traine in the hall . . . at the setting out of a
verie statelie tragedie, named *Dido*, wherin the Queene's banket (with
Eneas narration of the destruction of Troie) was livelie described in a
marchpaine patterne; there was also a goodlie sight of hunters with full
crie of a kennel of hounds, Mercurie and Iris descending and ascending
from and to an high place, the tempest wherein it hailed small confects,
rained rose-water, and snew an artificial kind of snew, all strange,
marvellous, and abundant.[4]

Marlowe responds to the call for spectacle by having his characters
comment on their costumes and locality. Venus describes her
disguise in Act I, scene i, when she appears dressed for hunting
according to 'the use for Turen maides' (lines 204 ff.), and no
doubt Dido's hunting-dress in Act III, scene iii, is a variant of
this. Although Dido has 'layd aside' her 'princely robes' with their
'glittering pompe' (lines 3–4), she carries a golden bow, and her

[2] 'The Children of the Chapel Stript and Whipt'. This pamphlet is now lost, but
extracts are quoted by Hazlitt-Warton in his *History of English Poetry* (London, 1871), 127,
and I am quoting such from E. K. Chambers, *The Elizabethan Stage* (Oxford, 1923), ii. 34.

[3] Thomas Neale, *A Brief Rehearsall Of all such things as were done In the University of
Oxford During the Queen's Majesty's Abode There* (Harleian MS 7033, fos. 150–3), cited in F.
S. Boas, *University Drama in the Tudor Age* (Oxford, 1914), 103.

[4] John Nicholls, *The Progresses, and Public Processions, of Queen Elizabeth* (1788), ii. 203.

costume, '*Dianas* shrowdes' (line 4), must have been appropriately sumptuous, the more especially because this hunting scene would have been in direct competition with its analogues in other children's plays such as Wager's *Dido* and Edwardes's *Palamon and Arcyte*. When Iarbus first approaches the shipwrecked Trojans, he is hailed as 'this brave Lord' (I. ii. 1), and he clearly bestows some of his own finery upon them since Aeneas is amazed at their appearance:

> Like *Illioneus* speakes this Noble man,
> But *Illioneus* goes not in such robes.   (II. i. 47–8)

A greater transformation awaits Aeneas. Dido's response when she is introduced to him is immediately prompted by his appearance:

> Warlike *Aeneas*, and in these base robes?
> Goe fetch the garment which *Sicheus* ware.   (II. i. 79–80)

The play's action flows with unusual grace from Olympus to the Carthaginian sea-shore, thence to the city walls, into the banqueting hall prepared for Dido's ceremonious feast, and out again into the extramural woods where Aeneas shot the deer when the Trojans first came on land. A 'discovery' space is called for; when '*the Curtaines draw*' at the beginning of Act I, it represents the throne-room on Olympus; later it becomes the 'grove' with 'greene brakes' where Venus hides Ascanius (II. i. 316–17), as well as the cave in which Dido and Aeneas take refuge from the storm in Act III, scene iv.[5]

The easy movement of characters from one location to another is, of course, characteristic of Elizabethan drama, and it was facilitated on the public stages by the absence (for the most part) of a permanent set. *Dido*, however, requires a set which would divide the stage into two, or even three, acting areas. With the help of a property tree, Marlowe translates Virgil's line *mater media sese tulit obvia silva* (i. 314), and Venus indicates that she has left the home of the gods and is waiting for her son's arrival on the Carthaginian shore: 'Here in this bush disguised will I stand' (I. i. 139). More solid structures are essential at the beginning of Act II if Aeneas and Achates are to be saved from embarrassment. Virgil's Trojans are moved to tears by the exquisite sculpture on the walls of Dido's

---

[5] Unless we follow Oliver in his edition of *Dido Queene of Carthage* (London, 1968), and postulate three separate 'discovery' places.

temple of Juno, but the actors must rhapsodize in a vacuum unless the stage carpenter has given more concrete interpretation to the dramatist's hints. Aeneas recognizes that 'These should be Carthage walles' (II. i. 1); then he and Achates share a fantasy:

> Me thinkes that towne there should be *Troy*, yon *Idas* hill,
> There *Zanthus* streame, because here's *Priamus*.   (II. i. 7–8)

Achates gives him pause: 'saving ayre |Is nothing here, and what is this but stone?' (II. i. 13–14). The situation at best is delicate, the pathetic verging on the ludicrous, and only a convincing 'stone' could save it. Since Marlowe is hardly likely to jeopardize his Trojans' stature at this point in the play, I think we must postulate a stage equipped to evoke, and not destroy, an elevated mood.

The banquet carried in by Dido's servants (II. i. 71) could perhaps be more substantial than the usual sweetmeats; in production, the meaning of the word might be extended to include the furniture which would transform the stage from 'Carthage walles' (where the characters stand at line 62) into the 'hall' in which they find themselves at line 70. At the end of the scene, the solemn palace dissolves as Venus hides Ascanius in the 'cooling shades' (line 334) where he will be discovered by Juno in Act III, scene i.

This description of scene and setting is not intended as a guide to the staging, at any time, of *Dido Queene of Carthage*, but merely to stress the play's emphasis on spectacle—an emphasis less readily achieved in the public theatres than in the 'private' indoor houses used by the children's companies in London and (it may be assumed) adapted for them on provincial tours.

The surface gloss of production details is not the only difference between children's plays and adult drama. Inherent in the words and actions of the former are distinctions more profound and more subtle—so subtle, indeed, that they could apparently be ignored by the adult companies who adopted the children's plays into their own repertoire, perhaps excusing their theft with the counter-charge of two-way traffic made by 'Harry Cundale' in the Induction to *The Malcontent*: 'Why not Maleuole in folio with vs, as Ieronimo in Decimo sexto with them?' (A4). The ease with which such changes were made, especially after 1600 (when the Children of the Chapel began to play at the new Blackfriars') can lead to the neglect, or misinterpretation, of those features that characterize the genre to which *Dido* belongs.

However much their natural gifts might be enhanced by rigorous training and elaborate presentation, the child actors were nevertheless restricted by their greatest asset—their youth. Schoolmaster playwrights accommodated themselves accordingly, writing speeches for recitation rather than scenes for acting, until the sixteenth century produced a professional dramatist for the children's companies in John Lyly. The title-page of Lyly's *Sixe Court Comedies* (1632) described him as 'Witie, Comicall, *Facetiously-Quicke and* unparalleld', and claimed that the plays were 'Often presented and Acted *before Queene* ELIZABETH'. They ask for practised elocution, but little emotion, and the characters are rightly described by Hillebrand as 'animated marionettes, endowed with beautiful speeches but no action'.[6] In *Dido*, however, it almost seems as though Marlowe anticipated such criticism, and forestalled it.

Virgil, in the twelve books of the *Aeneid*, gave context and consequence of his hero's desertion of Dido, setting it *sub specie aeternitatis*. Marlowe had no such scope, and in his presentation of the all-controlling gods he replaces Virgilian high seriousness with deflationary satire. His gods wield their power with the uneasy confidence of children, and Marlowe exploits to the full the comedy of a situation in which children act the parts of gods, who themselves usurp the irresponsibility of childhood. The comedy is sustained throughout the central scenes of the play, whenever Cupid masquerades as Ascanius. It militates against the preparation for a tragic catastrophe, creating indecision in the audience—an uncertainty whether to laugh or cry—which focuses on Dido and Aeneas. These characters are not autonomous: they are the gods' playthings, subject to the apparently arbitrary whims of their morally inferior puppet-masters. Yet they cannot be dismissed along with Lyly's creations as 'marionettes'. The strings that manipulate Dido are very evident, but her struggles to maintain control over her own emotions and over Aeneas show a magnanimity—the same 'greatness of Spirit' that marks Virgil's Dido[7]—which triumphs in her suicide, and ultimately sets her free from the power of the gods. Aeneas is less successful dramatically, partly because his role is more circumscribed than

---

[6] *The Child Actors*, p. 264.
[7] In *Hero and Saint* Reuben A. Brower said of Virgil's Dido: 'in dying she attains not holiness, but greatness of spirit' (Oxford and New York, 1971), 102.

Dido's: he must obey the gods—love at their will, and depart at their command. Whereas Dido's most impassioned utterances (in Act V, scene i) express the emotions she is presently experiencing, Aeneas speaks heroically only when he is recounting past events at the fall of Troy (II. i. 121–288). Yet even Aeneas defies the gods before he capitulates, asserting his existence as an individual and not a mere puppet.

Marlowe's play subsists on the tension between opposites. Eternal and temporal, human and divine, comedy and tragedy are mutually opposed, and underlying these pairs is the contrast between the actual and the apparent which is made manifest in the child actors and their sophisticated, adult presentation.

The play was published in 1594, and on 8 January 1597/8 the Lord Chamberlaine's Men 'fyrst played dido at night', after Henslowe had laid out 29s. 'for co*p*ʳ lace for the littel boye & for a valle for the boye A geanste the playe of dido & eneus'.[8] This may not have been Marlowe's play, although it was the Lord Chamberlaine's company for which he usually wrote. The style suggests that the play is an early work—perhaps *c.* 1585, by which time Marlowe had probably completed his translations of Lucan and Ovid. Comparison with these translations shows a surprising advance in technique. Marlowe is familiar with his material, and moves freely about Books I, II, and IV of the *Aeneid*, picking up details and transposing them with dramatic intent, as well as finding the story for his main plot. He develops the characters of Anna and Iarbus, and he invents the sub-plot of Anna's unrequited love for her sister's suitor. The triple suicide at the end of the play is, unhappily, of Marlowe's construction. Virgil's Dido dies with tragic dignity, but this is lost in the present play when Iarbus rushes to follow her example, and Anna too joins in the act.[9]

Marlowe ignored other English translations of the *Aeneid* that would have been available in print to him, and he seems to have had no need of a commentary on the Latin, such as the one he used when translating Lucan.

---

[8] *Henslowe's Diary*, ed. R. A. Foakes and R. T. Rickert (Cambridge, 1971), 86.
[9] I discuss the relationship between the *Aeneid* and Marlowe's play in 'Marlowe's Virgil: *Dido Queene of Carthage*', *RES*, xxviii. 110 (May 1977), 141–55.

Textual Introduction

Three copies of the 1594 Quarto of *The Tragedy of Dido Queene of Carthage* survive; these are in the possession of the Folger, Huntington, and Bodleian libraries. The Bodleian copy (Malone 133) has been used as the copy-text. The three copies are invariant, and collate A–F⁴, G². Thomas Woodcock, for whom the Widow Orwin printed the book, died in April 1594, so it is reasonable to suppose that the printing was at least begun by the time of his death. There is no entry in the Stationers' Register for this quarto, but there are entries on 9 February 1596, when Woodcock's widow transferred her right to Paul Linley, and on 26 June 1600, when Linley yielded his right to John Flasket. Despite these transactions, no early editions other than Q1 (1594) have been traced. In the eighteenth century Bishop Tanner claimed to have seen a copy of the play to which was prefixed an elegy on Marlowe written by Nashe. The elegy supposedly referred to four of Marlowe's other tragedies, and to one which featured the Duke of Guise: *ubi quatuor ejus tragiarum mentionem facit, nec non at alterius* de duce Guisio.[10] Such a text has never been found, and it seems unlikely that it ever existed. The Bishop may have had some vague recollection of the Prologue to *Dr Faustus*, with its listing of other dramatic ventures.

Although the title-page credits Thomas Nashe with part-authorship, it has never been seriously entertained that he was a collaborator in this play. George Hibbard speaks with authority in his study of Nashe's work: 'An examination of the play leads to the conclusion that Nashe's share in it can have amounted to little or nothing.'[11] Almost all the parallels of phrase and reference which link Nashe's works with *Dido* occur in Act I, scene i, and indeed their number is surprisingly high. But on each occasion the phrasing is undoubtedly Marlowe's. If there is any significance in these parallels, it is for the student of Nashe. The Quarto is remarkably free from error, carefully punctuated (with heavy use of commas and colons), and adequately equipped with stage directions, although these are not of such a kind as to suggest

---

[10] *Bibliotheca Britannica-Hibernica* (1748), 512.
[11] *Thomas Nashe* (London, 1962), 96.

prompt-book for printer's copy. A transcript is the obvious answer to the question of the nature of the printer's copy, and it seems to me very possible that Nashe could have acted as scribe, copying diligently, but introducing intermittently some of his own spelling peculiarities—'hoysing' (IV. iv. 15), for example, and 'emperiall' (IV. iv. 34)—and consistently, but typically, ignoring the possessive apostrophe.[12] Nashe was Marlowe's contemporary at Cambridge, and their names are linked by Robert Greene in his *A Groats-worth of witte* (1592): after lecturing to Marlowe, the 'famous gracer of Tragedians', he goes on to say: 'With thee I ioyne yong *Iuvenall*, that *byting Satyrist*' (fo. F1ʳ). It is usually inferred that Nashe is intended here. Nashe himself speaks familiarly of 'Kit Marloe' in his attack on Gabriel Harvey in *Have With You To Saffron-Waldon* (1596), and turned Harvey's attacks on Marlowe back on their author with the observation: 'How he hath handled *Greene* and *Marloe* since their deaths, those that read his Bookes may iudge'.[13] A proper sense of the duty owed to a recently deceased friend might have prompted Nashe to appoint himself literary executor, and secure for at least one of Marlowe's works the permanence of print.

The only major textual problem posed by *Dido Queene of Carthage* is that of Act IV, scene ii. Dido dismisses Iarbus at the end of the previous scene, and he leaves the stage, only to return immediately, prepared to make sacrifice to the gods. The awkwardness here cannot be removed, even by accepting Oliver's assertion that there were scene divisions and perhaps intermissions in the 'private' playhouses.[14] Iarbus' speech is often meaningless and repetitious. He speaks of the neglect of religious duties, so that Jove's 'emptie Altars have enlarg'd our illes' (line 3), and accuses Dido of having scorned his 'loves and royall marriage rites' (line 16). He declares that Aeneas, having seduced Dido, 'is straight way fled' (line 18), and yet immediately beseeches Jove to 'warne him to his ships' (line 21). Within five lines, Jove is twice called 'gloomie' (lines 2 and 6), and Iarbus' surprising (in view of his stated attitude) reference to Anna's 'alluring eyes' (line 50) anticipates the use, far more appropriately, of the same phrase in v.

---

[12] See McKerrow, iv. 295.

[13] *Have With You to Saffron Walden*, in *The Works of Thomas Nashe*, ed. R. B. McKerrow, iii. 132.

[14] Oliver, p. xxx.

iii. 35. Jingling rhymes—'downe' | 'towne', 'bed' | 'fled', 'vaine' | 'paine', and 'flint' | 'stint'—trivialize the scene still further.

Another difficulty is the repetition of Dido's hysteria in Act V, scene i. After Aeneas has left her, Dido visualizes his progress to the shore, and fantasizes his return:

> By this is he got to the water side,
> And, see the Sailers take him by the hand,
> But he shrinkes backe, and now remembring me,
> Returns amaine: welcome, welcome my love:
> But wheres *Aeneas*? ah hees gone hees gone.   (188–92)

When Anna confirms her fears, Dido imagines another shipwreck, from which Aeneas escapes to safety:

> Now is he come on shoare safe without hurt:
> But see, *Achates* wils him put to sea,
> And all the Sailers merrie make for joy,
> But he remembring me, shrinkes backe againe:
> See where he comes, welcome, welcome my love.   (257–61)

Perhaps one of these passages should ·have been cancelled, but there is now no authority for cancellation, especially since both are needed to prompt Anna's comments on her sister's madness: 'What meanes my sister thus to rave and crye?' (line 193), and 'Ah sister, leave these idle fantasies' (line 262).

The substitution of Cupid for Ascanius is more of a problem in the play than it is in the poem. Virgil makes it clear that the change-over was for one night only—*noctem non amplius unam* (I. 683)—and this is represented by the play's Act III, scene i. Q recognizes Cupid's role here, and again in the invented Act IV, scene v. In the intervening hunting scene, Act III, scene iii, however, Cupid seems to have been forgotten, and the Ascanius who speaks the lines translated from the Latin sounds like a little boy again. Yet the reversion to Ascanius must be maintained, since Hermes at v. i. 40 tells how he has brought Ascanius 'from *Ida* where he slept', and Aeneas realizes that Dido has 'daylie' nursed Cupid in her arms (v. i. 45). In order to distinguish between the real Ascanius and his substitute, I have given *Cupid* as the prefix for all the Cupid-as-Ascanius speeches.

REFERENCES

Q   *The Tragedie of Dido Queene of Carthage* (1594)

Tucker Brooke   *The Tragedy of Dido Queen of Carthage*, ed. C. F. Tucker Brooke (London, 1930)

Oliver   *Dido Queen of Carthage*, ed. H. J. Oliver (London, 1968)

Virgil   *Aeneid*, ed. and trans. H. Rushton Fairclough (Loeb revised edition, London and Cambridge, Mass., 1974)

G. L. Brook   *The Language of Shakespeare* (1976)

Deighton   *The Old Dramatists: Conjectural Readings on the Texts*, by Karl Deighton (London, 1896)

     The Massacre at Paris . . . With Prefatory Remarks, Notes, Critical and Explanatory, by W. Oxberry (London, 1818)

Grosart   *The Complete Works of Thomas Nashe*, ed. A. B. Grosart (London, 1885)

Broughton MS   Manuscript notes made by James Broughton in his copy of Robinson's *Marlowe*; the copy is now in the British Library, 11771, bbb 6.

Sonnino   *A Handbook to Sixteenth-Century Rhetoric*, by Lee A. Sonnino (London, 1968)

THE TRAGEDIE
QUEEN OF *CA*

[Actus 1. Sce

Here the Curtaines draw, there is dis
GANIMED upon his knee, and M

JUPITER. Come gentle *Ganimed* and play with me,
  I love thee well, say *Juno* what she will.
GANIMED. I am much better for your worthless love,
  That will not shield me from her shrewish blowes:
  To day when as I fild into your cups,   5
  And held the cloath of pleasance whiles you dranke,
  She reacht me such a rap for that I spilde,
  As made the bloud run downe about mine eares.
JUPITER. What? dares she strike the darling of my thoughts?
  By *Saturnes* soule, and this earth threatning haire,   10
  That shaken thrise, makes Natures buildings quake,
  I vow, if she but once frowne on thee more,
  To hang her meteor like twixt heaven and earth,
  And bind her hand and foote with golden cordes,
  As once I did for harming *Hercules*.   15
GANIMED. Might I but see that pretie sport a foote,
  O how would I with *Helens* brother laugh,
  And bring the Gods to wonder at the game:
  Sweet *Jupiter*, if ere I pleasde thine eye,
  Or seemed faire walde in with Egles wings,   20
  Grace my immortall beautie with this boone,
  And I will spend my time in thy bright armes.
JUPITER. What ist sweet wagge I should deny thy youth?
  Whose face reflects such pleasure to mine eyes,
  As I exhal'd with thy fire darting beames,   25
  Have oft driven backe the horses of the night,
  When as they would have hal'd thee from my sight:
  Sit on my knee, and call for thy content,

10 haire] *Dyce*; aire *Q*

proud Fate, and cut the thred of time,
not all the Gods at thy commaund,
heaven and earth the bounds of thy delight? 30
ulcan shall daunce to make thee laughing sport,
And my nine Daughters sing when thou art sad,
From *Junos* bird Ile pluck her spotted pride,
To make thee fannes wherewith to coole thy face, 35
And *Venus* Swannes shall shed their silver downe,
To sweeten out the slumbers of thy bed:
Hermes no more shall shew the world his wings,
If that thy fancie in his feathers dwell,
But as this one Ile teare them all from him, 40
Doe thou but say their colour pleaseth me:
Hold here my little love these linked gems,
My *Juno* ware upon her marriage day,
Put thou about thy necke my owne sweet heart,
And tricke thy armes and shoulders with my theft. 45
GANIMED. I would have a jewell for mine eare,
And a fine brouch to put in my hat,
And then Ile hugge with you an hundred times.
JUPITER. And shall have *Ganimed*, if thou wilt be my love.

Enter VENUS.

VENUS. I this is it, you can sit toying there, 50
And playing with that female wanton boy,
Whiles my *Aeneas* wanders on the Seas,
And rests a pray to every billowes pride.
Juno, false *Juno* in her Chariots pompe,
Drawne through the heavens by Steedes of *Boreas* brood, 55
Made *Hebe* to direct her ayrie wheeles
Into the windie countrie of the clowdes,
Where finding *Aeolus* intrencht with stormes,
And guarded with a thousand grislie ghosts,
She humbly did beseech him for our bane, 60
And charg'd him drowne my sonne with all his traine.
Then gan the windes breake ope their brazen doores,
And all *Aeolia* to be up in armes:
Poore *Troy* must now be sackt upon the Sea,
And *Neptunes* waves be envious men of warre, 65

Epeus horse to *Aetnas* hill transformed,
Prepared stands to wracke their woodden walles,
And *Aeolus* like *Agamemnon* sounds
The surges, his fierce souldiers to the spoyle:
See how the night *Ulysses*-like comes forth,   70
And intercepts the day as *Dolon* erst:
Ay me! the Starres supprisde like *Rhesus* Steedes,
Are drawne by darknes forth *Astraeus* tents.
What shall I doe to save thee my sweet boy?
When as the waves doe threat our Chrystall world,   75
And *Proteus* raising hils of flouds on high,
Entends ere long to sport him in the skie.
False *Jupiter*, rewardst thou vertue so?
What? is not pietie exempt from woe?
Then dye *Aeneas* in thine innocence,   80
Since that religion hath no recompence.
JUPITER. Content thee *Cytherea* in thy care,
Since thy *Aeneas* wandring fate is firme,
Whose wearie lims shall shortly make repose,
In those faire walles I promist him of yore: 85
But first in bloud must his good fortune bud,
Before he be the Lord of *Turnus* towne,
Or force her smile that hetherto hath frownd:
Three winters shall he with the Rutiles warre,
And in the end subdue them with his sword,   90
And full three Sommers likewise shall he waste,
In mannaging those fierce barbarian mindes:
Which once performd, poore *Troy* so long supprest,
From forth her ashes shall advance her head,
And flourish once againe that erst was dead: 95
But bright *Ascanius* beauties better worke,
Who with the Sunne devides one radiant shape,
Shall build his throne amidst those starrie towers,
That earth-borne *Atlas* groning underprops:
No bounds but heaven shall bound his Emperie,   100
Whose azured gates enchased with his name,
Shall make the morning hast her gray uprise,
To feede her eyes with his engraven fame.
Thus in stoute *Hectors* race three hundred yeares,
The Romane Scepter royall shall remaine,   105

Till that a Princesse priest conceav'd by *Mars*,
Shall yeeld to dignitie a dubble birth,
Who will eternish *Troy* in their attempts.
VENUS. How may I credite these thy flattering termes,
When yet both sea and sands beset their ships,   110
And *Phoebus* as in Stygian pooles, refraines
To taint his tresses in the Tyrrhen maine?
JUPITER. I will take order for that presently:
Hermes awake, and haste to *Neptunes* realme,
Whereas the Wind-god warring now with Fate,   115
Besiege the ofspring of our kingly loynes,
Charge him from me to turne his stormie powers,
And fetter them in *Vulcans* sturdie brasse,
That durst thus proudly wrong our kinsmans peace.
Venus farewell, thy sonne shall be our care: 120
Come *Ganimed*, we must about this geare.
          Exeunt JUPITER *cum* GANIMED.
VENUS. Disquiet Seas lay downe your swelling lookes,
And court *Aeneas* with your calmie cheere,
Whose beautious burden well might make you proude,
Had not the heavens conceav'd with hel-borne clowdes,   125
Vaild his resplendant glorie from your view.
For my sake pitie him *Oceanus*,
That erst-while issued from thy watrie loynes,
And had my being from thy bubling froth:
Triton I know hath fild his trumpe with *Troy*,   130
And therefore will take pitie on his toyle,
And call both *Thetis* and *Cimodoce*,
To succour him in this extremitie.

Enter AENEAS *with* ASCANIUS, *with one or two more.*

What? doe I see my sonne now come on shoare:
Venus, how art thou compast with content,   135
The while thine eyes attract their sought for joyes:
Great *Jupiter*, still honourd maist thou be,
The while thine eyes attract their sought for joyes:
Great *Jupiter*, still honourd maist thou be,
For this so friendly ayde in time of neede.
Here in this bush disguised will I stand,

Whiles my *Aeneas* spends himselfe in plaints,   140
And heaven and earth with his unrest acquaints.

AENEAS. You sonnes of care, companions of my course,
   Priams misfortune followes us by sea,
   And *Helens* rape doth haunt mee at the heeles.
   How many dangers have we over past?   145
   Both barking *Scilla*, and the sounding Rocks,
   The *Cyclops* shelves, and grim *Ceranias* seate
   Have you oregone, and yet remaine alive?
   Pluck up your hearts, since fate still rests our friend,
   And chaunging heavens may those good daies returne,   150
   Which *Pergama* did vaunt in all her pride.

ACHATES. Brave Prince of *Troy*, thou onely art our God,
   That by thy vertues freest us from annoy,
   And makes our hopes survive to coming joyes:
   Doe thou but smile, and clowdie heaven will cleare,   155
   Whose night and day descendeth from thy browes:
   Though we be now in extreame miserie,
   And rest the map of weatherbeaten woe:
   Yet shall the aged Sunne shed forth his haire,
   To make us live unto our former heate,   160
   And every beast the forrest doth send forth,
   Bequeath her young ones to our scanted foode.

ASCANIUS. Father I faint, good father give me meate.

AENEAS. Alas sweet boy, thou must be still a while,
   Till we have fire to dresse the meate we kild: 165
   Gentle *Achates*, reach the Tinder boxe,
   That we may make a fire to warme us with,
   And rost our new found victuals on this shoare.

VENUS. See what strange arts necessitie findes out,
   How neere my sweet *Aeneas* art thou driven?   170

AENEAS. Hold, take this candle and goe light a fire,
   You shall have leaves and windfall bowes enow
   Neere to these woods, to rost your meate withall:
   Ascanius, goe and drie thy drenched lims,
   Whiles I with my *Achates* roave abroad,   175
   To know what coast the winde hath driven us on,
   Or whether men or beasts inhabite it.

144 mee] *this ed.* thee *Q*   154 coming] *Dyce;* cunning *Q*   159 haire] *Broughton MS;* aire *Q*

ACHATES. The ayre is pleasant, and the soyle most fit
  For Cities, and societies supports:
  Yet much I marvell that I cannot finde,   180
  No steps of men imprinted in the earth.
VENUS. Now is the time for me to play my part:
  Hoe yong men, saw you as you came
  Any of all my Sisters wandring here?
  Having a quiver girded to her side,   185
  And cloathed in a spotted Leopards skin.
AENEAS. I neither saw nor heard of any such:
  But what may I faire Virgin call your name?
  Whose lookes set forth no mortall forme to view,
  Nor speech bewraies ought humaine in thy birth,   190
  Thou art a Goddesse that delud'st our eyes,
  And shrowdes thy beautie in this borrowd shape:
  But whether thou the Sunnes bright Sister be,
  Or one of chast *Dianas* fellow Nimphs,
  Live happie in the height of all content,   195
  And lighten our extreames with this one boone,
  As to instruct us under what good heaven
  We breathe as now, and what this world is calde,
  On which by tempests furie we are cast,
  Tell us, O tell us that are ignorant,   200
  And this right hand shall make thy Altars crack
  With mountaine heapes of milke white Sacrifize.
VENUS. Such honour, stranger, doe I not affect:
  It is the use for Turen maides to weare
  Their bowe and quiver in this modest sort,   205
  And suite themselves in purple for the nonce,
  That they may trip more lightly ore the lawndes,
  And overtake the tusked Bore in chase.
  But for the land whereof thou doest enquire,
  It is the Punick kingdome rich and strong,   210
  Adjoyning on *Agenors* stately towne,
  The kingly seate of Southerne *Libia*,
  Whereas Sidonian *Dido* rules as Queene.
  But what are you that aske of me these things?
  Whence may you come, or whither will you goe?   215
AENEAS. Of *Troy* am I, *Aeneas* is my name,
  Who driven by warre from forth my native world,
  Put sailes to seeke out *Italy*:

And my divine descent from sceptred *Jove*.
With twise twelve Phrigian ships I plowed the deepe,   220
And made that way my mother *Venus* led:
But of them all scarce seven doe anchor safe,
And they so wrackt and weltred by the waves,
As every tide tilts their oken sides:
And all of them unburdened of their loade,   225
Are ballassed with billowes watrie weight.
But haples I, God wot, poore and unknowne,
Doe trace these Libian deserts all despisde,
Exild forth *Europe* and wide *Asia* both,
And have not any coverture but heaven.   230
VENUS. Fortune hath favord thee what ere thou be,
In sending thee unto this curteous Coast:
A Gods name on and hast thee to the Court,
Where *Dido* will receive ye with her smiles:
And for thy ships which thou supposest lost,   235
Not one of them hath perisht in the storme,
But are arived safe not farre from hence:
And so I leave thee to thy fortunes lot,
Wishing good lucke unto thy wandring steps.   *Exit.*
AENEAS. *Achates*, tis my mother that is fled,   240
I know her by the movings of her feete:
Stay gentle *Venus*, flye not from thy sonne,
Too cruell, why wilt thou forsake me thus?
Or in these shades deceiv'st mine eye so oft?
Why talke we not together hand in hand?   245
And tell our griefes in more familiar termes:
But thou art gone and leav'st me here alone,
To dull the ayre with my discoursive moane.

Exeunt.

[Actus 1. Scena 2.]

Enter [IARBUS, *with*] ILLIONEUS, [SERGUSTUS,] *and*
CLOANTHUS.

ILLIONEUS. Follow ye Troians, follow this brave Lord,
And plaine to hime the summe of your distresse.
IARBUS. Why, what are you, or wherefore doe you sewe?

ILLIONEUS. Wretches of *Troy*, envied of the windes,
 That crave such favour at your honors feete,   5
 As poore distressed miserie may pleade:
 Save, save, O save our ships from cruell fire,
 That doe complaine the wounds of thousand waves,
 And spare our lives whom every spite pursues.
 We come not we to wrong your Libian Gods,   10
 Or steale your houshold lares from their shrines:
 Our hands are not prepar'd to lawles spoyle,
 Nor armed to offend in any kind:
 Such force is farre from our unweaponed thoughts,
 Whose fading weale of victorie forsooke,   15
 Forbids all hope to harbour neere our hearts.
IARBUS. But tell me Troians, Troians if you be,
 Unto what fruitfull quarters were ye bound,
 Before that *Boreas* buckled with your sailes?
CLOANTHUS. There is a place *Hesperia* term'd by us, 20
 An ancient Empire, famoused for armes,
 And fertile in faire *Ceres* furrowed wealth,
 Which now we call *Italia* of his name,
 That in such peace long time did rule the same:
 Thither made we,   25
 When suddenly gloomie *Orion* rose,
 And led our ships into the shallow sands,
 Whereas the Southerne winde with brackish breath,
 Disperst them all amongst the wrackfull Rockes:
 From thence a fewe of us escapt to land,   30
 The rest we feare are foulded in the flouds.
IARBUS. Brave men at armes, abandon fruitles feares,
 Since Carthage knowes to entertaine distresse.
SERGESTUS. I but the barbarous sort doe threat our ships,
 And will not let us lodge upon the sands: 35
 In multitudes they swarme unto the shoare,
 And from the first earth interdict our feete.
IARBUS. My selfe will see they shall not trouble ye,
 Your men and you shall banquet in our Court,
 And every Troian be as welcome here,   40
 As *Jupiter* to sillie Baucis house:

41 *Baucis*] Oxberry; *Vausis* Q

Come in with me, Ile bring you to my Queene,
Who shall confirme my words with further deedes.
SERGESTUS. Thankes gentle Lord for such unlookt for grace.
Might we but once more see *Aeneas* face,   45
Then would we hope to quite such friendly turnes,
As shall surpasse the wonder of our speech.   [*Exeunt.*]

Actus 2. [Scena 1.]

Enter AENEAS, ACHATES, *and* ASCANIUS.

AENEAS. Where am I now? these should be Carthage walles.

ACHATES. Why stands my sweete *Aeneas* thus amazde?

AENEAS. O my *Achates*, Theban *Niobe*,
　　Who for her sonnes death wept out life and breath,
　　And drie with griefe was turnd into a stone,　　　　　　5
　　Had not such passions in her head as I.
　　Me thinkes that towne there should be *Troy*, yon *Idas* hill,
　　There *Zanthus* streame, because here's *Priamus*,
　　And when I know it is not, then I dye.

ACHATES. And in this humor is *Achates* to,　　　　　　10
　　I cannot choose but fall upon my knees,
　　And kisse his hand: O where is *Hecuba*,
　　Here she was wont to sit, but saving ayre
　　Is nothing here, and what is this but stone?

AENEAS. O yet this stone doth make *Aeneas* weepe,　　　　15
　　And would my prayers (as *Pigmalions* did)
　　Could give it life, that under his conduct
　　We might saile backe to *Troy*, and be revengde
　　On these hard harted Grecians, which rejoyce
　　That nothing now is left of *Priamus*:　　　　　　20
　　O *Priamus* is left and this is he,
　　Come, come abourd, pursue the hatefull Greekes.

ACHATES. What meanes *Aeneas*?

AENEAS. *Achates* though mine eyes say this is stone,
　　Yet thinkes my minde that this is *Priamus*:　　　　25
　　And when my grieved heart sighes and sayes no,
　　Then would it leape out to give *Priam* life:
　　O were I not at all so thou mightst be.
　　Achates, see King *Priam* wags his hand,
　　He is alive, *Troy* is not overcome.　　　　　　30

ACHATES. Thy mind *Aeneas* that would have it so
　　Deludes thy eye sight, *Priamus* is dead.

AENEAS. Ah *Troy* is sackt, and *Priamus* is dead,
　　And why should poore *Aeneas* be alive?

ASCANIUS. Sweete father leave to weepe, this is not he:　　35
　　For were it *Priam* he would smile on me.

ACHATES. *Aeneas* see here come the Citizens,
   Leave to lament lest they laugh at our feares.

        Enter CLOANTHUS, SERGESTUS, ILLIONEUS

AENEAS. Lords of this towne, or whatsoever stile
   Belongs unto your name, vouchsafe of ruth   40
   To tell us who inhabits this faire towne,
   What kind of people, and who governes them:
   For we are strangers driven on this shore,
   And scarcely know within what Clime we are.
ILLIONEUS. I heare *Aeneas* voyce, but see him not,   45
   For none of these can be our Generall.
ACHATES. Like *Illioneus* speakes this Noble man,
   But *Illioneus* goes not in such robes.
SERGESTUS. You are *Achates*, or I deciv'd.
ACHATES. *Aeneas* see *Sergestus*, or his ghost.   50
ILLIONEUS. He names *Aeneas*, let us kisse his feete.
CLOANTHUS. It is our Captaine, see *Ascanius*.
SERGESTUS. Live long *Aeneas* and *Ascanius*.
AENEAS. *Achates*, speake, for I am overjoyed.
ACHATES. O *Illioneus*, art thou yet alive?   55
ILLIONEUS. Blest be the time I see *Achates* face.
CLOANTHUS. Why turnes *Aeneas* from his trustie friends?
AENEAS. *Sergestus*, *Illioneus* and the rest,
   Your sight amazde me, O what destinies
   Have brought my sweete companions in such plight?   60
   O tell me, for I long to be resolv'd.
ILLIONEUS. Lovely *Aeneas*, these are Carthage walles,
   And here Queene *Dido* weares th'imperiall Crowne,
   Who for *Troyes* sake hath entertaind us all,
   And clad us in these wealthie robes we weare.   65
   Oft hath she askt us under whom we serv'd,
   And when we told her she would weepe for griefe,
   Thinking the sea had swallowed up thy ships,
   And now she sees thee how will she rejoyce?
SERGESTUS. See where her servitors passe through the hall   70
   Bearing a banket, *Dido* is not farre.
ILLIONEUS. Looke where she comes: *Aeneas* view her well.
AENEAS. Well may I view her, but she sees not me.

    51 names] *Oxberry*; means *Q*   72 view] *Oxberry*; viewd *Q*

Enter DIDO [*with* ANNA *and* LARBUS] *and her traine.*

DIDO. What stranger art thou that doest eye me thus?

AENEAS. Sometime I was a Troian, mightie Queene: 75
   But *Troy* is not, what shall I say I am?

ILLIONEUS. Renowmed *Dido*, tis our Generall:
   Warlike *Aeneas.*

DIDO. Warlike *Aeneas*, and in these base robes?
   Goe fetch the garment which *Sicheus* ware: 80
   Brave Prince, welcome to Carthage and to me,
   Both happie that *Aeneas* is our guest:
   Sit in this chaire and banquet with a Queene,
   Aeneas is *Aeneas*, were he clad
   In weedes as bad as ever *Irus* ware.   85

AENEAS. This is no seate for one thats comfortles,
   May it please your grace to let *Aeneas* waite:
   For though my birth be great, my fortunes meane,
   Too meane to be companion to a Queene.

DIDO. Thy fortune may be greater then thy birth,   90
   Sit downe *Aeneas*, sit in *Didos* place,
   And if this be thy sonne as I suppose,
   Here let him sit, be merrie lovely child.

AENEAS. This place beseemes me not, O pardon me.

DIDO. Ile have it so, *Aeneas* be content.   95

ASCANIUS. Madame, you shall be my mother.

DIDO. And so I will sweete child: be merrie man,
   Heres to thy better fortune and good starres.

AENEAS. In all humilitie I thanke your grace.

DIDO. Remember who thou art, speake like thy selfe,   100
   Humilitie belongs to common groomes.

AENEAS. And who so miserable as *Aeneas* is?

DIDO. Lyes it in *Didos* hands to make thee blest,
   Then be assured thou art not miserable.

AENEAS. O *Priamus*, O *Troy*, oh *Hecuba*!   105

DIDO. May I entreate thee to discourse at large,
   And truely to how *Troy* was overcome:
   For many tales goe of that Cities fall,
   And scarcely doe agree upon one poynt:
   Some say *Antenor* did betray the towne,   110
   Others report twas *Sinons* perjurie:

But all in this that *Troy* is overcome,
And *Priam* dead, yet how we heare no newes.
AENEAS. A wofull tale bids *Dido* to unfould,
   Whose memorie like pale deaths stony mace,   115
   Beates forth my senses from this troubled soule,
   And makes *Aeneas* sinke at *Didos* feete.
DIDO. What faints *Aeneas* to remember *Troy?*
   In whose defence he fought so valiantly:
   Looke up and speake.   120
AENEAS. Then speake *Aeneas* with *Achilles* tongue,
   And *Dido* and you Carthaginian Peeres
   Heare me, but yet with *Mirmidons* harsh eares,
   Daily inur'd to broyles and Massacres,
   Lest you be mov'd too much with my sad tale.   125
   The Grecian souldiers tired with ten yeares warre,
   Began to crye, let us unto our ships,
   Troy is invincible, why stay we here?
   With whose outcryes *Atrides* being apal'd,
   Summoned the Captaines to his princely tent,   130
   Who looking on the scarres we Troians gave,
   Seeing the number of their men decreast,
   And the remainder weake and out of heart,
   Gave up their voyces to dislodge the Campe,
   And so in troopes all marcht to *Tenedos*:   135
   Where when they came, *Ulysses* on the sand
   Assayd with honey words to turne them backe:
   And as he spoke to further his entent
   The windes did drive huge billowes to the shoare,
   And heaven was darkned with tempestuous clowdes: 140
   Then he alleag'd the Gods would have them stay,
   And prophecied *Troy* should be overcome:
   And therewithall he calde false *Sinon* forth,
   A man compact of craft and perjurie,
   Whose ticing tongue was made of *Hermes* pipe,   145
   To force an hundred watchfull eyes to sleepe:
   And him *Epeus* having made the horse,
   With sacrificing wreathes upon his head,
   Ulysses sent to our unhappie towne:
   Who groveling in the mire of *Zanthus* bankes,   150
   His bands bound at his backe, and both his eyes

Turnd up to heaven as one resolv'd to dye,
Our Phrigian shepherds haled within the gates,
And brought unto the Court of *Priamus*:
To whom he used action so pitifull,   155
Lookes so remorcefull, vowes so forcible,
As therewithall the old man overcome,
Kist him, imbrast him, and unloosde his bands,
And then, O *Dido*, pardon me.

DIDO. Nay leave not here, resolve me of the rest.   160
AENEAS. O th'inchaunting words of that base slave,
Made him to thinke *Epeus* pine-tree Horse
A sacrifize t'appease *Minervas* wrath:
The rather for that one *Laocoon*
Breaking a speare upon his hollow breast,   165
Was with two winged Serpents stung to death.
Whereat agast, we were commanded straight
With reverence to draw it into *Troy*.
In which unhappie worke was I employd,
These hands did helpe to hale it to the gates,   170
Through which it could not enter twas so huge.
O had it never entred, *Troy* had stood.
But *Priamus* impatient of delay,
Inforst a wide breach in that rampierd wall,
Which thousand battering Rams could never pierce,   175
And so came in this fatall instrument:
At whose accursed feete as overjoyed,
We banquetted till overcome with wine,
Some surfetted, and others soundly slept.
Which *Sinon* viewing, causde the Greekish spyes   180
To hast to *Tenedos* and tell the Campe:
Then he unlockt the Horse, and suddenly
From out his entrailes, *Neoptolemus*
Setting his speare upon the ground, leapt forth,
And after him a thousand Grecians more,   185
In whose sterne faces shin'd the quenchles fire,
That after burnt the pride of *Asia*.
By this the Campe was come unto the walles,
And through the breach did march into the streetes,

153 shepherds] *Oxberry*; shepherd *Q*

Where meeting with the rest, kill kill they cryed.   190
Frighted with this confused noyse, I rose,
And looking from a turret, might behold
Yong infant swimming in their parents bloud,
Headles carkasses piled up in heapes,
Virgins halfe dead dragged by their golden haire,   195
And with maine force flung on a ring of pikes,
Old men with swords thrust through their aged sides,
Kneeling for mercie to a Greekish lad,
Who with steele Pol-axes dasht out their braines.
Then buckled I mine armour, drew my sword,   200
And thinking to goe downe, came *Hectors* ghost
With ashie visage, blewish sulphure eyes,
His armes torne from his shoulders, and his breast
Furrowd with wounds, and that which made me weepe,
Thongs at his heeles, by which *Achilles* horse   205
Drew him in triumph through the Greekish Campe,
Burst from the earth, crying, *Aeneas* flye,
Troy is a fire, the Grecians have the towne.
DIDO. O *Hector* who weepes not to heare thy name?
AENEAS. Yet flung I forth, and desperate of my life,   210
Ran in the thickest throngs, and with this sword
Sent many of their savadge ghosts to hell.
At last came *Pirrhus* fell and full of ire,
His harnesse dropping bloud, and on his speare
The mangled head of *Priams* yongest sonne,   215
And after him his band of Mirmidons,
With balles of wilde fire in their murdering pawes,
Which made the funerall flame that burnt faire *Troy*:
All which hemd me about, crying, this is he.
DIDO. Ah, how could poore *Aeneas* scape their hands?   220
AENEAS. My mother *Venus* jealous of my health,
Convaid me from their crooked nets and bands:
So I escapt the furious *Pirrhus* wrath:
Who then ran to the pallace of the King,
And at *Joves* Altar finding *Priamus*,   225
About whose withered necke hung *Hecuba*,
Foulding his hand in hers, and joyntly both
Beating their breasts and falling on the ground,
He with his faulchions poynt raisde up at once,

And with *Megeras* eyes stared in their face,   230
Threatning a thousand deaths at every glaunce.
To whom the aged King thus trembling spoke:
Achilles sonne, remember what I was,
Father of fiftie sonnes, but they are slaine,
Lord of my fortune, but my fortune turnd,   235
King of this Citie, but my *Troy* is fired,
And now am neither father, Lord, nor King:
Yet who so wretched but desires to live?
O let me live, great *Neoptolemus*.
Not mov'd at all, but smiling at his teares,   240
This butcher whil'st his hands were yet held up,
Treading upon his breast, strooke off his hands.

DIDO. O end *Aeneas*, I can heare no more.

AENEAS. At which the franticke Queene leapt on his face,
And in his eyelids hanging by the nayles,   245
A little while prolong'd her husbands life:
At last the souldiers puld her by the heeles,
And swong her howling in the emptie ayre,
Which sent an eccho to the wounded King:
Whereat he lifted up his bedred lims,   250
And would have grappeld with *Achilles* sonne,
Forgetting both his want of strength and hands,
Which he disdaining whiskt his sword about,
And with the wind thereof the King fell downe:
Then from the navell to the throat at once,   255
He ript old *Priam*: at whose latter gaspe
Joves marble statue gan to bend the brow,
As lothing *Pirrhus* for this wicked act:
Yet he undaunted tooke his fathers flagge,
And dipt it in the old Kings chill cold bloud,   260
And then in triumph ran into the streetes,
Through which he could not passe for slaughtred men:
So leaning on his sword he stood stone still,
Viewing the fire wherewith rich *Ilion* burnt.
By this I got my father on my backe,   265
This young boy in mine armes, and by the hand
Led faire *Creusa* my beloved wife,
When thou *Achates* with thy sword mad'st way,

254 wind] *qy* Collier; wound *Q*

And we were round inviron'd with the Greekes:
O there I lost my wife: and had not we   270
Fought manfully, I had not told this tale:
Yet manhood would not serve, of force we fled,
And as we went unto our ships, thou knowest
We sawe *Cassandra* sprauling in the streetes,
Whom *Ajax* ravisht in *Dianas* Fawne,   275
Her cheekes swolne with sighes, her haire all rent,
Whom I tooke up to beare unto our ships:
But suddenly the Grecians followed us,
And I alas, was forst to let her lye.
Then we got to our ships, and being abourd,   280
Polixena cryed out, *Aeneas* stay,
The Greekes pursue me, stay and take me in.
Moved with her voyce, I lept into the sea,
Thinking to beare her on my backe abourd:
For all our ships were launcht into the deepe,   285
And as I swomme, she standing on the shoare,
Was by the cruell Mirmidons surprizd,
And after by that *Pirrhus* sacrifizde.
DIDO. I dye with melting ruth, *Aeneas* leave.
ANNA. O what became of aged *Hecuba*?   290
IARBUS. How got *Aeneas* to the fleete againe?
DIDO. But how scapt *Helen*, she that causde this warre?
AENEAS. *Achates* speake, sorrow hath tired me quite.
ACHATES. What happened to the Queene we cannot shewe,
We heare they led her captive into Greece.   295
As for *Aeneas* he swomme quickly backe,
And *Helena* betraied *Diiphobus*
Her Lover, after *Alexander* dyed,
And so was reconcil'd to *Menelaus*.
DIDO. O had that ticing strumpet nere been borne: 300
Troian, thy ruthfull tale hath made me sad:
Come let us thinke upon some pleasing sport,
To rid me from these melancholly thoughts.   *Exeunt omnes.*

Enter VENUS [*with* CUPID] *at another doore, and takes*
ASCANIUS *by the sleeve.*

VENUS. Faire child stay thou with *Didos* waiting maide,
Ile give thee Sugar-almonds, sweete Conserves,   305

A silver girdle, and a golden purse,
And this yong Prince shall be thy playfellow.
ASCANIUS. Are you Queene *Didos* sonne?
CUPID. I, and my mother gave me this fine bow.
ASCANIUS. Shall I have such a quiver and bow?   310
VENUS. Such bow, such quiver, and such golden shafts,
Will *Dido* give to sweete *Ascanius*:
For *Didos* sake I take thee in my armes,
And sticke these spangled feathers in thy hat,
Eate Comfites in mine armes, and I will sing.   315
Now is he fast asleepe, and in this grove
Amongst greene brakes Ile lay *Ascanius*,
And strewe him with sweete smelling Violets,
Blushing Roses, purple *Hyacinthe*:
These milke white Doves shall be his Centronels: 320
Who if that any seeke to doe him hurt,
Will quickly flye to *Cithereas* fist.
Now *Cupid* turne thee to *Ascanius* shape,
And goe to *Dido*, who in stead of him
Will set thee on her lap and play with thee: 325
Then touch her white breast with this arrow head,
That she may dote upon *Aeneas* love:
And by that meanes repaire his broken ships,
Victuall his Souldiers, give him wealthie gifts,
And he at last depart to *Italy*,   330
Or els in *Carthage* make his kingly throne.
CUPID. I will faire mother, and so play my part,
As every touch shall wound Queene *Didos* heart.   [*Exit.*]
VENUS. Sleepe my sweete nephew in these cooling shades,
Free from the murmure of these running streames,   335
The crye of beasts, the ratling of the windes,
Or whisking of these leaves, all shall be still,
And nothing interrupt thy quiet sleepe,
Till I returne and take thee hence againe.   *Exit.*

Actus 3. Scena 1.

CUPID. Now *Cupid* cause the Carthaginian Queene,
To be inamourd of thy brothers lookes,
Convey this golden arrowe in thy sleeve,
Lest she imagine thou art *Venus* sonne:
And when she strokes thee softly on the head,   5
Then shall I touch her breast and conquer her.

Enter IARBUS, ANNA, *and* DIDO.

IARBUS. How long faire *Dido* shall I pine for thee?
Tis not enough that thou doest graunt me love,
But that I may enjoy what I desire:
That love is childish which consists in words.   10
DIDO. *Iarbus*, know that thou of all my wooers
(And yet have I had many mightier Kings)
Hast had the greatest favours I could give:
I feare me *Dido* hath been counted light,
In being too familiar with *Iarbus*:   15
Albeit the Gods doe know no wanton thought
Had ever residence in *Didos* breast.
IARBUS. But *Dido* is the favour I request.
DIDO. Feare not *Iarbus*, *Dido* may be thine.
ANNA. Looke sister how *Aeneas* little sonne   20
Playes with your garments and imbraceth you.
CUPID. No *Dido* will not take me in her armes,
I shall not be her sonne, she loves me not.
DIDO. Weepe not sweet boy, thou shalt be *Didos* sonne,
Sit in my lap and let me heare thee sing.   25
No more my child, now talke another while,
And tell me where learnst thou this pretie song?
CUPID. My cosin *Helen* taught it me in *Troy*.
DIDO. How lovely is *Ascanius* when he smiles?
CUPID. Will *Dido* let me hang about her necke?   30
DIDO. I wagge, and give thee leave to kisse her to.
CUPID. What will you give me? now Ile have this Fanne.
DIDO. Take it *Ascanius*, for thy fathers sake.

IARBUS. Come *Dido*, leave *Ascanius*, let us walke.

DIDO. Goe thou away, *Ascanius* shall stay.   35

IARBUS. Ungentle Queene, is this thy love to me?

DIDO. O stay *Iarbus*, and Ile goe with thee.

CUPID. And if my mother goe, Ile follow her.

DIDO. Why staiest thou here? thou art no love of mine.

IARBUS. *Iarbus* dye, seeing she abandons thee.   40

DIDO. No, live *Iarbus*, what hast thou deserv'd,
   That I should say thou art no love of mine?
   Something thou hast deserv'd, Away I say,
   Depart from *Carthage*, come not in my sight.

IARBUS. Am I not King of rich *Getulia*?   45

DIDO. *Iarbus* pardon me, and stay a while.

CUPID. Mother, looke here.

DIDO. What telst thou me of rich *Getulia*?
   Am not I Queene of *Libia*? then depart.

IARBUS. I goe to feed the humour of my Love,   50
   Yet not from *Carthage* for a thousand worlds.

DIDO. *Iarbus*.

IARBUS. Doth *Dido* call me backe?

DIDO. No, but I charge thee never looke on me.

IARBUS. Then pull out both mine eyes, or let me dye.   55
                                        Exit IARBUS.

ANNA. Wherefore doth *Dido* bid *Iarbus* goe?

DIDO. Because his lothsome sight offends mind eye,
   And in my thoughts is shrin'd another love:
   O *Anna*, didst thou know how sweet love were,
   Full soone wouldst thou abjure this single life.   60

ANNA. Poore soule I know too well the sower of love,
   O that *Iarbus* could but fancie me.

DIDO. Is not *Aeneas* faire and beautifull?

ANNA. Yes, and *Iarbus* foule and favourles.

DIDO. Is he not eloquent in all his speech?   65

ANNA. Yes, and *Iarbus* rude and rusticall.

DIDO. Name not *Iarbus*, but sweete *Anna* say,
   Is not *Aeneas* worthie *Didos.* love?

ANNA. O sister, were you Empresse of the world,
   Aeneas well deserves to be your love,   70

58 love *Dyce*; Ioue *Q*

So lovely is he that where ere he goes,
The people swarme to gaze him in the face.
DIDO. But tell them none shall gaze on him but I,
Lest their grosse eye-beames taint my lovers cheekes:
Anna, good sister *Anna* goe for him,   75
Lest with these sweete thoughts I melt cleane away.
ANNA. Then sister youle abjure *Iarbus* love?
DIDO. Yet must I heare that lothsome name againe?
Runne for *Aeneas*, or Ile flye to him.   *Exit* ANNA.
CUPID. You shall not hurt my father when he comes.   80
DIDO. No, for thy sake Ile love thy father well.
O dull conceipted *Dido*, that till now
Didst never thinke *Aeneas* beautifull:
But now for quittance of this oversight,
Ile make me bracelets of his golden haire,   85
His glistering eyes shall be my looking glasse,
His lips an altar, where Ile offer up
As many kisses as the Sea hath sands,
In stead of musicke I will heare him speake,
His lookes shall be my only Librarie,   90
And thou *Aeneas*, *Didos* treasurie,
In whose faire bosome I will locke more wealth,
Then twentie thousand Indiaes can affoord:
O here he comes, love, love, give *Dido* leave
To be more modest then her thoughts admit,   95
Lest I be made a wonder to the world.
Achates, how doth *Carthage* please your Lord?
ACHATES. That will *Aeneas* shewe your majestie.
DIDO. *Aeneas*, art thou there?
AENEAS. I understand your highnesse sent for me.   100
DIDO. No, but now thou art here, tell me in sooth
In what might *Dido* highly pleasure thee.
AENEAS. So much have I receiv'd at *Didos* hands,
As without blushing I can aske no more:
Yet Queene of *Affricke*, are my ships unrigd,   105
My Sailes all rent in sunder with the winde,
My Oares broken, and my Tackling lost,
Yea all my Navie split with Rockes and Shelfes:
Nor Sterne nor Anchor have our maimed Fleete,
Our Masts the furious windes strooke over bourd: 110

Which piteous wants if *Dido* will supplie,
We will account her author of our lives.
DIDO. *Aeneas*, Ile repaire thy Troian ships,
Conditionally that thou wilt stay with me,
And let *Achates* saile to *Italy*:   115
Ile give thee tackling made of riveld gold,
Wound on the barkes of odoriferous trees,
Oares of massie Ivorie full of holes,
Through which the water shall delight to play:
Thy Anchors shall be hewed from Christall Rockes,   120
Which if thou lose shall shine above the waves:
The Masts whereon thy swelling sailes shall hang,
Hollow Pyramides of silver plate:
The sailes of foulded Lawne, where shall be wrought
The warres of *Troy*, but not *Troyes* overthrow: 125
For ballace, emptie *Didos* treasurie,
Take what ye will, but leave *Aeneas* here.
Achates, thou shalt be so meanly clad,
As Seaborne Nymphes shall swarme about thy ships,
And wanton Mermaides court thee with sweete songs,   130
Flinging in favours of more soveraigne worth,
Then *Thetis* hangs about *Apolloes* necke,
So that *Aeneas* may but stay with me.
AENEAS. Wherefore would *Dido* have *Aeneas* stay?
DIDO. To warre against my bordering enemies: 135
Aeneas, thinke not *Dido* is in love:
For if that any man could conquer me,
I had been wedded ere *Aeneas* came:
See where the pictures of my suiters hang,
And are not these as faire as faire may be?   140
ACHATES. I saw this man at *Troy* ere *Troy* was sackt.
AENEAS. I this in *Greece* when *Paris* stole faire *Helen*.
ILLIONEUS. This man and I were at *Olympus* games.
SERGESTUS. I know this face, he is a Persian borne,
I traveld with him to *Aetolia*.   145
CLOANTHUS. And I in *Athens* with this gentleman,
Unlesse I be deceiv'd disputed once.
DIDO. But speake *Aeneas*, know you none of these?
AENEAS. No Madame, but it seemes that these are Kings.
DIDO. All these and others which I never sawe,   150

Have been most urgent suiters for my love,
Some came in person, others sent their Legats:
Yet none obtained me, I am free from all,
And yet God knowes intangled unto one.
This was an Orator, and thought by words   155
To compasse me, but yet he was deceiv'd:
And this a Spartan Courtier vaine and wilde,
But his fantastick humours pleasde not me:
This was *Alcion*, a Musition,
But playd he nere so sweet, I let him goe: 160
This was the wealthie King of *Thessaly*,
But I had gold enough and cast him off:
This *Meleagers* sonne, a warlike Prince,
But weapons gree not with my tender yeares:
The rest are such as all the world well knowes,   165
Yet how I sweare by heaven and him I love,
I was as farre from love, as they from hate.
AENEAS. O happie shall he be whom *Dido* loves.
DIDO. Then never say that thou art miserable,
Because it may be thou shalt be my love: 170
Yet boast not of it, for I love thee not,
And yet I hate thee not: O if I speake
I shall betray my selfe: *Aeneas* speake,
We two will goe a hunting in the woods,
But not so much for thee, thou art but one,   175
As for *Achates*, and his followers.   *Exeunt.*

[Actus 3. Scena 2.]

Enter JUNO *to* ASCANIUS *asleepe.*

JUNO. Here lyes my hate, *Aeneas* cursed brat,
The boy wherein false destinie delights,
The heire of furie, the favourite of face,
That ugly impe that shall outweare my wrath,
And wrong my deitie with high disgrace: 5
But I will take another order now,
And race th'eternall Register of time:

Troy shall no more call him her second hope,
Nor *Venus* triumph in his tender youth:
For here in spight of heaven Ile murder him,   10
And feede infection with his left out life:
Say *Paris*, now shall *Venus* have the ball?
Say vengeance, now shall her *Ascanius* dye.
O no God wot, I cannot watch my time,
Nor quit good turnes with double fee downe told: 15
Tut, I am simple without minde to hurt,
And have no gall at all to grieve my foes:
But lustfull *Jove* and his adulterous child,
Shall finde it written on confusions front,
That onely *Juno* rules in *Rhamnuse* towne.   20

Enter VENUS.

VENUS. What should this meane? my Doves are back returnd,
Who warne me of such daunger prest at hand,
To harme my sweete *Ascanius* lovely life.
Juno, my mortall foe, what make you here?
Avaunt old witch and trouble not my wits.   25

JUNO. Fie *Venus*, that such causeles words of wrath,
Should ere defile so faire a mouth as thine:
Are not we both sprong of celestiall rase,
And banquet as two Sisters with the Gods?
Why is it then displeasure should disjoyne,   30
Whom kindred and acquaintance counites.

VENUS. Out hatefull hag, thou wouldst have slaine my sonne,
Had not my Doves discov'rd thy entent:
But I will teare thy eyes fro forth thy head,
And feast the birds with their bloud-shotten balles,   35
If thou but lay thy fingers on my boy.

JUNO. Is this then all the thankes that I shall have,
For saving him from Snakes and Serpents stings,
That would have kild him sleeping as he lay?
What though I was offended with thy sonne,   40
And wrought him mickle woe on sea and land,
When for the hate of Troian *Ganimed*,
That was advanced by my *Hebes* shame,

16 minde] *Dyce*; made *Q*

And *Paris* judgement of the heavenly ball,
I mustred all the windes unto his wracke,   45
And urg'd each Element to his annoy:
Yet now I doe repent me of his ruth,
And wish that I had never wronged him so:
Bootles I sawe it was to warre with fate,
That hath so many unresisted friends: 50
Wherefore I chaungd my counsell with the time,
And planted love where envie erst had sprong.

VENUS. Sister of *Jove*, if that thy love be such,
As these thy protestations doe paint forth,
We two as friends one fortune will devide: 55
Cupid shall lay his arrowes in thy lap,
And to a Scepter chaunge his golden shafts,
Fancie and modestie shall live as mates,
And thy faire peacockes by my pigeons pearch:
Love my *Aeneas*, and desire is thine,   60
The day, the night, my Swannes, my sweetes are thine.

JUNO. More then melodious are these words to me,
That overcloy my soule with their content:
Venus, sweete *Venus*, how may I deserve
Such amourous favours at thy beautious hand?   65
But that thou maist more easilie perceive,
How highly I doe prize this amitie,
Harke to a motion of eternall league,
Which I will make in quittance of thy love:
Thy sonne thou knowest with *Dido* now remaines,   70
And feedes his eyes with favours of her Court,
She likewise in admyring spends her time,
And cannot talke nor thinke of ought but him:
Why should not they then joyne in marriage,
And bring forth mightie Kings to Carthage towne,   75
Whom casualtie of sea hath made such friends?
And *Venus*, let there be a match confirmd
Betwixt these two, whose loves are so alike,
And both our Deities conjoyned in one,
Shall chaine felicitie unto their throne.   80

VENUS. Well could I like this reconcilements meanes,

51 chaunged] *Dyce*; chaunge *Q*

But much I feare my sonne will nere consent,
Whose armed soule alreadie on the sea,
Darts forth her light to *Lavinias* shoare.
JUNO. Faire Queene of love, I will devorce these doubts, 85
And finde the way to wearie such fond thoughts:
This day they both a hunting forth will ride
Into these woods, adjoyning to these walles,
When in the midst of all their gamesome sports,
Ile make the Clowdes dissolve their watrie workes, 90
And drench *Silvanus* dwellings with their shewers,
Then in one Cave the Queene and he shall meete,
And interchangeably discourse their thoughts,
Whose short conclusion will seale up their hearts,
Unto the purpose which we now propound. 95
VENUS. Sister, I see you savour of my wiles,
Be it as you will have for this once,
Meane time, *Ascanius* shall be my charge,
Whom I will beare to *Ida* in mine armes,
And couch him in *Adonis* purple downe.   *Exeunt.*

[Actus 3. Scena 3.]

Enter DIDO, AENEAS, ANNA, IARBUS, ACHATES, [*with* CUPID
dressed as ASCANIUS], *and followers.*

DIDO. *Aeneas*, thinke not but I honor thee,
That thus in person goe with thee to hunt:
My princely robes thou seest are layd aside,
Whose glittering pompe *Dianas* shrowdes supplies,
All fellowes now disposde alike to sporte, 5
The woods are wide, and we have store of game:
Faire Troian, hold my golden bowe awhile,
Untill I gird my quiver to my side:
Lords goe before, we two must talke alone.
IARBUS. Ungentle, can she wrong *Iarbus* so? 10
Ile dye before a stranger have that grace:
We two will talke alone, what words be these?
DIDO. What makes Iarbus here of all the rest?
We could have gone without your companie.

AENEAS. But love and duetie led him on perhaps, 15
    To presse beyond acceptance to your sight.
IARBUS. Why man of *Troy*, doe I offend thine eyes?
    Or art thou grievde thy betters presse so nye?
DIDO. How now Getulian, are ye growne so brave,
    To challenge us with your comparisons? 20
    Pesant, goe seeke companions like thy selfe,
    And meddle not with any that I love:
    Aeneas, be not movde at what he sayes,
    For otherwhile he will be out of joynt.
IARBUS. Women may wrong by priviledge of love: 25
    But should that man of men (*Dido* except)
    Have taunted me in these opprobrious termes,
    I would have either drunke his dying bloud,
    Or els I would have given my life in gage?
DIDO. Huntsmen, why pitch you not your toyles apace, 30
    And rowse the light foote Deere from forth their laire.
ANNA. Sister, see see *Ascanius* in his pompe,
    Bearing his huntspeare bravely in his hand.
DIDO. Yea little sonne, are you so forward now?
CUPID. I mother, I shall one day be a man, 35
    And better able unto other armes,
    Meane time these wanton weapons serve my warre,
    Which I will breake betwixt a Lyons jawes.
DIDO. What, darest thou looke a Lyon in the face?
CUPID. I, and outface him to, doe what he can.
ANNA. How like his father speaketh he in all? 40
AENEAS. And mought I live to see him sacke rich *Thebes*,
    And loade his speare with Grecian Princes heads,
    Then would I wish me with *Anchises* Tombe,
    And dead to honour that hath brought me up. 45
IARBUS. And might I live to see thee shipt away,
    And hoyst aloft on *Neptunes* hideous hilles,
    Then would I wish me in faire *Didos* armes,
    And dead to scorne that hath pursued me so.
AENEAS. Stoute friend *Achates*, doest thou know this wood? 50
ACHATES. As I remember, here you shot the Deere,
    That sav'd your famisht souldiers lives from death,
    When first you set your foote upon the shoare,
    And here we met faire *Venus* virgine like,
    Bearing her bowe and quiver at her backe. 55

AENEAS. O how these irksome labours now delight,
    And overjoy my thoughts with their escape:
    Who would not undergoe all kind of toyle,
    To be well stor'd with such a winters tale?
DIDO. *Aeneas*, leave these dumpes and lets away,   60
    Some to the mountaines, some unto the soyle,
    You to the vallies, thou unto the house.
                   Exeunt omnes: manet [IARBUS].

IARBUS. I, this it is which wounds me to the death,
    To see a Phrigian far fet on the sea,
    Preferd before a man of majestie: 65
    O love, O hate, O cruell womens hearts,
    That imitate the Moone in every chaunge,
    And like the Planets ever love to raunge:
    What shall I doe thus wronged with disdaine?
    Revenge me on *Aeneas*, or on her: 70
    On her? fond man, that were to warre gainst heaven,
    And with one shaft provoke ten thousand darts:
    This Troians end will be thy envies aime,
    Whose bloud will reconcile thee to content,
    And make love drunken with thy sweete desire: 75
    But *Dido* that now holdeth him so deare,
    Will dye with very tidings of his death:
    But time will discontinue her content,
    And mould her minde unto newe fancies shapes:
    O God of heaven, turne the hand of fate   80
    Unto that happie day of my delight,
    And then, what then? *Iarbus* shall but love:
    So doth he now, though not with equall gaine,
    That resteth in the rivall of thy paine,
    Who nere will cease to soare till he be slaine.   *Exit.*

[Actus 3. Scena 4.]

The storme. Enter AENEAS *and* DIDO *in the Cave
at severall times.*

DIDO. *Aeneas.*
AENEAS. *Dido.*
DIDO. Tell me deare love, how found you out this Cave?

    64 far fet on] *Bowers*; far fet to *Q*

AENEAS. By chance sweete Queene, as *Mars* and *Venus* met.
DIDO. Why, that was in a net, where we are loose,   5
    And yet I am not free, oh would I were.
AENEAS. Why, what is it that *Dido* may desire
    And not obtaine, be it in humaine power?
DIDO. The thing that I will dye before I aske,
    And yet desire to have before I dye.   10
AENEAS. It is not ought *Aeneas* may atchieve?
DIDO. *Aeneas*, No, although his eyes doe pearce.
AENEAS. What, hath *Iarbus* angred her in ought?
    And will she be avenged on his life?
DIDO. Not angred me, except in angring thee.   15
AENEAS. Who then of all so cruell may he be,
    That should detaine thy eye in his defects?
DIDO. The man that I doe eye where ere I am,
    Whose amorous face like *Pean* sparkles fire,
    When as he buts his beames on *Floras* bed,   20
    Prometheus hath put on *Cupids* shape,
    And I must perish in his burning armes:
    Aeneas, O *Aeneas*, quench these flames.
AENEAS. What ailes my Queene, is she falne sicke of late?
DIDO. Not sicke my love, but sicke, I must conceale   25
    The torment, that it bootes me not reveale,
    And yet Ile speake, and yet Ile hold my peace,
    Doe shame her worst, I will disclose my griefe:
    Aeneas, thou art he, what did I say?
    Something it was that now I have forgot.   30
AENEAS. What means faire *Dido* by this doubtfull speech?
DIDO. Nay, nothing, but *Aeneas* loves me not.
AENEAS. *Aeneas* thoughts dare not ascend so high
    As *Didos* heart, which Monarkes might not scale.
DIDO. It was because I sawe no King like thee,   35
    Whose golden Crowne might ballance my content:
    But now that I have found what to effect,
    I followe one that loveth fame for me,
    And rather had seeme faire [to] Sirens eyes,
    Than to the Carthage Queene that dyes for him.   40
AENEAS. If that your majestie can looke so lowe,
    As my despised worths, that shun all praise,

39 faire [to]] *Cunningham*; faire *Q*

With this my hand I give to you my heart,
And vow by all the Gods of Hospitalitie,
By heaven and earth, and my faire brothers bowe,   45
By *Paphos*, *Capys*, and the purple Sea,
From whence my radiant mother did descend,
And by this Sword that saved me from the Greekes,
Never to leave these newe upreared walles,
Whiles *Dido* lives and rules in *Junos* towne,   50
Never to like or love any but her.

DIDO. What more then Delian musicke doe I heare,
That calles my soule from forth his living seate,
To move unto the measures of delight:
Kind clowdes that sent forth such a curteous storme,   55
As made disdaine to flye to fancies lap:
Stoute love in mine armes make thy *Italy*,
Whose Crowne and Kingdome rests at thy commande:
Sicheus, not *Aeneas* be thou calde:
The King of *Carthage*, not *Anchises* sonne: 60
Hold, take these Jewels at thy Lovers hand,
These golden bracelets, and this wedding ring,
Wherewith my husband woo'd me yet a maide,
And be thou king of *Libia*, by my guift.

Exeunt to the Cave.

Actus 4. Scena 1.

Enter ACHATES, [CUPID *as*] ASCANIUS, IARBUS, *and* ANNA.

ACHATES. Did ever men see such a sudden storme?
  Or day so cleere so suddenly orecast?
IARBUS. I thinke some fell Inchantresse dwelleth here,
  That can call them forth when as she please,
  And dive into blacke tempests treasurie,   5
  When as she meanes to maske the world with clowdes.
ANNA. In all my life I never knew the like,
  It haild, it snowde, it lightned all at once.
ACHATES. I thinke it was the divels revelling night,
  There was such hurly burly in the heavens: 10
  Doubtles *Apollos* Axeltree is crackt,
  Or aged *Atlas* shoulder out of joynt,
  The motion was so over violent.
IARBUS. In all this coyle, where have ye left the Queene?
CUPID. Nay, where is my warlike father, can you tell?   15
ANNA. Behold where both of them come forth the Cave.
IARBUS. Come forth the Cave: can heaven endure this sight?
  Iarbus, curse that unrevenging *Jove*,
  Whose flintie darts slept in *Tiphous* den,
  Whiles these adulterors surfetted with sinne: 20
  Nature, why mad'st me not some poysonous beast,
  That with the sharpnes of my edged sting,
  I might have stakte them both unto the earth,
  Whil'st they were sporting in this darksome Cave?
AENEAS. The ayre is cleare, and Southerne windes are whist,   25
  Come *Dido*, let us hasten to the towne,
  Since gloomie *Aeolus* doth cease to frowne.
DIDO. *Achates* and *Ascanius*, well met.
AENEAS. Faire *Anna*, how escapt you from the shower?
ANNA. As others did, by running to the wood.   30
DIDO. But where were you *Iarbus* all this while?
IARBUS. Not with *Aeneas* in the ugly Cave.
DIDO. I see *Aeneas* sticketh in your minde,
  But I will soone put by that stumbling blocke,
  And quell those hopes that thus employ your cares.   *Exeunt.*

[Actus 4. Scena 2.]

Enters IARBUS *to Sacrifize.*

IARBUS. Come servants, come bring forth the Sacrifize,
That I may pacifie that gloomie *Jove*,
Whose emptie Altars have enlarg'd our illes.
Eternall *Jove*, great master of the Clowdes,
Father of gladnesse, and all frollicke thoughts,   5
That with thy gloomie hand corrects the heaven,
When ayrie creatures warre amongst themselves:
Heare, heare, O heare *Iarbus* plaining prayers,
Whose hideous ecchoes make the welkin howle,
And all the woods *Eliza* to resound: 10
The woman that thou wild us entertaine,
Where straying in our borders up and downe,
She crav'd a hide of ground to build a towne,
With whom we did devide both lawes and land,
And all the fruits that plentie els sends forth,   15
Scorning our loves and royall marriage rites,
Yeelds up her beautie to a strangers bed,
Who having wrought her shame, is straight way fled:
Now if thou beest a pitying God of power,
On whom ruth and compassion ever waites,   20
Redresse these wrongs, and warne him to his ships
That now afflicts me with his flattering eyes.

Enter ANNA.

ANNA. How now Iarbus, at your prayers so hard?
IARBUS. I *Anna*, is there ought you would with me?
ANNA. Nay, no such waightie busines of import,   25
But may be slackt untill another time:
Yet if you would partake with me the cause
Of this devotion that detaineth you,
I would be thankfull for such curtesie.
IARBUS. *Anna*, against this Troian doe I pray,   30
Who seekes to rob me of thy Sisters love,
And dive into her heart by coloured lookes.
ANNA. Alas poore King that labours so in vaine,
For her that so delighteth in thy paine:

Be rul'd by me, and seeke some other love,   35
Whose yeelding heart may yeeld thee more reliefe.
IARBUS. Mine eye is fixt where fancie cannot start,
O leave me, leave me to my silent thoughts,
That register the numbers of my ruth,
And I will either move the thoughtles flint,   40
Or drop out both mine eyes in drisling teares,
Before my sorrowes tide have any stint.
ANNA. I will not leave *Iarbus* whom I love,
In this delight of dying pensivenes:
Away with *Dido*, *Anna* be thy song,   45
Anna that doth admire thee more then heaven.
IARBUS. I may nor will list to such loathsome chaunge,
That intercepts the course of my desire:
Servants, come fetch these emptie vessels here,
For I will flye from these alluring eyes,   50
That doe pursue my peace where ere it goes.   *Exit.*
ANNA. *Iarbus* stay, loving *Iarbus* stay,
For I have honey to present thee with:
Hard hearted, wilt not deigne to heare me speake,
Ile follow thee with outcryes nere the lesse,   55
And strewe thy walkes with my discheveld haire.   *Exit.*

[Actus 4. Scena 3.]

Enter AENEAS *alone.*

AENEAS. *Carthage*, my friendly host adue,
Since destinie doth call me from thy shoare:
Hermes this night descending in a dreame,
Hath summond me to fruitfull *Italy*:
Jove wils it so, my mother wils it so: 5
Let my Phenissa graunt, and then I goe:
Graunt she or no, *Aeneas* must away,
Whose golden fortunes clogd with courtly ease,
Cannot ascend to Fames immortall house,
Or banquet in bright honors burnisht hall,   10

Till he hath furrowed *Neptunes* glassie fieldes,
And cut a passage through his toples hilles:
Achates come forth, *Sergestus, Illioneus,*
Cloanthus, haste away, *Aeneas* calles.

Enter ACHATES, CLOANTHUS, SERGESTUS, *and* ILLIONEUS.

ACHATES. What willes our Lord, or wherefore did he call?   15
AENEAS. The dreames (brave mates) that did beset my bed,
    When sleepe but newly had imbrast the night,
    Commaunds me leave these unrenowmed reames,
    Whereas Nobilitie abhors to stay,
    And none but base *Aeneas* will abide: 20
    Abourd, abourd, since Fates doe bid abourd,
    And slice the Sea with sable coloured ships,
    On whom the nimble windes may all day waight,
    And follow them as footemen through the deepe:
    Yet *Dido* casts her eyes like anchors out,   25
    To stay my Fleete from loosing forth the Bay:
    Come backe, come backe, I heare her crye a farre,
    And let me linke thy bodie to my lips,
    That tyed together by the striving tongues,
    We may as one saile into *Italy*.   30
ACHATES. Banish that ticing dame from forth your mouth,
    And follow your foreseeing starres in all;
    This is no life for men at armes to live,
    Where daliance doth consume a Souldiers strength,
    And wanton motions of alluring eyes,   35
    Effeminate our mindes inur'd to warre.
ILLIONEUS. Why, let us build a Citie of our owne,
    And not stand lingering here for amorous lookes:
    Will *Dido* raise old *Priam* forth his grave,
    And build the towne againe the Greekes did burne?   40
    No, no she cares not how we sinke or swimme,
    So she may have *Aeneas* in her armes.
CLOANTHUS. To *Italy*, sweete friends to *Italy*,
    We will not stay a minute longer here.
AENEAS. Troians abourd, and I will follow you,   45
    [*Exeunt* Troians, *manet* AENEAS.]

18 reames] *Dyce*; beames *Q*   28 thy bodie] *Dyce*; my bodie *Q*

I faine would goe, yet beautie calles me backe:
To leave her so and not once say farewell,
Were to transgresse against all lawes of love:
But if I use such ceremonious thankes,
As parting friends accustome on the shoare,   50
Her silver armes will coll me round about,
And teares of pearle, crye stay, *Aeneas*, stay:
Each word she sayes will then containe a Crowne,
And every speech be ended with a kisse:
I may not dure this female drudgerie,   55
To sea *Aeneas*, finde out *Italy*.   *Exit.*

[Actus 4. Scena 4.]

Enter DIDO *and* ANNA.

DIDO. O Anna, runne unto the water side,
They say *Aeneas* men are going abourd,
It may be he will steale away with them:
Stay not to answere me, runne *Anna* runne.   [*Exit* ANNA.]
O foolish Troians that would steale from hence,   5
And not let *Dido* understand their drift:
I would have given *Achates* store of gold,
And *Illioneus* gum and Libian spice,
The common souldiers rich imbrodered coates,
And silver whistles to controule the windes,   10
Which *Circes* sent *Sicheus* when he lived:
Unworthie are they of a Queenes reward:
See where they come, how might I doe to chide?

Enter ANNA, *with* AENEAS, ACHATES, ILLIONEUS, *and*
SERGESTUS.

ANNA. Twas time to runne, *Aeneas* had been gone,
The saile were hoysing up, and he abourd.   15
DIDO. Is this thy love to me?
AENEAS. O princely *Dido*, give me leave to speake,
I went to take my farewell of *Achates*.
DIDO. How haps *Achates* bid me not farewell?
ACHATES. Because I feard your grace would keepe me here. 20

DIDO. To rid thee of that doubt, abourd againe,
  I charge thee put to sea and stay not here.
ACHATES. Then let *Aeneas* goe abourd with us.
DIDO. Get you abourd, *Aeneas* meanes to stay.
AENEAS. The sea is rough, the windes blow to the shoare.   25
DIDO. O false Aeneas, now the sea is rough,
  But when you were abourd twas calme enough,
  Thou and *Achates* ment to saile away.
AENEAS. Hath not the Carthage Queene mine only sonne?
  Thinkes *Dido* I will goe and leave him here?   30
DIDO. *Aeneas* pardon me, for I forgot
  That yong *Ascanius* lay with me this night:
  Love made me jealous, but to make amends,
  Weare the emperiall Crowne of *Libia*,
  Sway thou the Punike Scepter in my steede,   35
  And punish me *Aeneas* for this crime.
AENEAS. This kisse shall be faire *Didos* punishment.
DIDO. O how a Crowne becomes *Aeneas* head!
  Stay here *Aeneas*, and commaund as King.
AENEAS. How vaine am I to weare this Diadem,   40
  And beare this golden Scepter in my hand?
  A Burgonet of steele, and not a Crowne,
  A Sword, and not a Scepter fits *Aeneas*.
DIDO. O keepe them still, and let me gaze my fill:
  Now lookes *Aeneas* like immortall *Jove*,   45
  O where is *Ganimed* to hold his cup,
  And *Mercury* to flye for what he calles?
  Ten thousand *Cupids* hover in the ayre,
  And fanne it in *Aeneas* lovely face,
  O that the Clowdes were here wherein thou fleest,   50
  That thou and I unseene might sport our selves:
  Heavens envious of our joyes is waxen pale,
  And when we whisper, then the starres fall downe,
  To be partakers of our honey talke.
AENEAS. O *Dido*, patronesse of all our lives,   55
  When I leave thee, death be my punishment,
  Swell raging seas, frowne wayward destinies,
  Blow windes, threaten ye Rockes and sandie shelfes,
  This is the harbour that *Aeneas* seekes,
  Lets see what tempests can annoy me now.   60

DIDO. Not all the world can take thee from mine armes,
 Aeneas may commaund as many Moores,
 As in the Sea are little water drops:
 And now to make experience of my love,
 Faire sister *Anna* leade my lover forth,   65
 And seated on my Gennet, let him ride
 As *Didos* husband through the Punicke streetes,
 And will my guard with Mauritanian darts,
 To waite upon him as their soveraigne Lord.
ANNA. What if the Citizens repine threat?   70
DIDO. Those that dislike what *Dido* gives in charge,
 Commaund my guard to slay for their offence:
 Shall vulgar pesants storme at what I doe?
 The ground is mine that gives them sustenance,
 The ayre wherein they breathe, the water, fire, 75
 All that they have, their lands, their goods, their lives,
 And I the Goddesse of all these, commaund
 Aeneas ride as Carthaginian King.
ACHATES. *Aeneas* for his parentage deserves
 As large a kingdome as is *Libia*.   80
AENEAS. I, and unlesse the destinies be false,
 I shall be planted in as rich a land.
DIDO. Speake of no other land, this land is thine,
 Dido is thine, henceforth Ile call thee Lord:
 Doe as I bid thee, sister leade the way,   85
 And from a turret Ile behold my love.
AENEAS. Then here in me shall flourish *Priams* race,
 And thou and I *Achates*, for revenge,
 For *Troy*, for *Priam*, for his fiftie sonnes,
 Our kinsmens lives, and thousand guiltles soules, 90
 Will leade an hoste against the hatefull Greekes,
 And fire proude *Lacedemon* ore their heads.

       Exit [AENEAS *with* Troians].

DIDO. Speakes not *Aeneas* like a Conqueror?
 O blessed tempests that did drive him in,
 O happie sand that made him runne aground: 95
 Henceforth you shall be our *Carthage* Gods:

   90 lives] *Dyce*; loves *Q*

I, but it may be he will leave my love,
And seeke a forraine land calde *Italy*:
O that I had a charme to keepe the windes
Within the closure of a golden ball,   100
Or that the Tyrrhen sea were in mine armes,
That he might suffer shipwracke on my breast,
As oft as he attempts to hoyst up saile:
I must prevent him, wishing will not serve:
Goe, bid my Nurse take yong *Ascanius*,   105
And beare him in the countrey to her house,
Aeneas will not goe without his sonne:
Yet lest he should, for I am full of feare,
Bring me his oares, his tackling, and his sailes:
What if I sinke his ships? O heele frowne: 110
Better he frowne, then I should dye for griefe:
I cannot see him frowne, it may not be:
Armies of foes resolv'd to winne this towne,
Or impious traitors vowde to have my life,
Affright me not, onely *Aeneas* frowne   115
Is that which terrifies poore *Didos* heart:
Not bloudie speares appearing in the ayre,
Presage the downfall of my Emperie,
Nor blazing Commets threatens *Didos* death,
It is *Aeneas* frowne that ends my daies: 120
If he forsake me not, I never dye,
For in his lookes I see eternitie,
And heele make me immortall with a kisse.

Enter a Lord.

[*Lord*.] Your Nurse is gone with yong *Ascanius*,
And heres *Aeneas* tackling, oares and sailes.   125
DIDO. Are these the sailes that in despight of me,
Packt with the windes to beare *Aeneas* hence?
Ile hang ye in the chamber where I lye,
Drive if you can my house to *Italy*:
Ile set the casement open that the windes   130
May enter in, and once againe conspire
Against the life of me poore Carthage Queene:
But though he goe, he stayes in Carthage still,
And let rich Carthage fleete upon the seas,

So I may have *Aeneas* in mine armes.   135
Is this the wood that grew in Carthage plaines,
And would be toyling in the watrie billowes,
To rob their mistresse of her Troian guest?
O cursed tree, hadst thou but wit or sense,
To measure how I prize *Aeneas* love,   140
Thou wouldst have leapt from out the Sailers hands,
And told me that *Aeneas* ment to goe:
And yet I blame thee not, thou are but wood.
The water which our Poets terme a Nimph,
Why did it suffer thee to touch her breast,   145
And shrunke not backe, knowing my love was there?
The water is an Element, no Nimph,
Why should I blame *Aeneas* for his flight?
O *Dido*, blame not him, but breake his oares,
These were the instruments that launcht him forth,   150
Theres not so much as this base tackling too,
But dares to heape up sorrowe to my heart:
Was it not you that hoysed up these sailes?
Why burst you not, and they fell·in the seas?
For this will *Dido* tye ye full of knots,   155
And sheere ye all asunder with her hands:
Now serve to chastize shipboyes for their faults,
Ye shall no more offend the Carthage Queene.
Now let him hang my favours on his masts,
And see if those will serve in steed of sailes: 160
For tackling, let him take the chaines of gold,
Which I bestowd upon his followers:
In steed of oares, let him use his hands,
And swim to *Italy*, Ile keepe these sure:
Come beare them in.   *Exeunt*

[Actus 4. Scena 5.]

Enter the NURSE *with* CUPID *for* ASCANIUS.

NURSE. My Lord *Ascanius*, ye must goe with me.
CUPID. Whither must I goe? Ile stay with my mother.
NURSE. No, thou shalt goe with me unto my house,
    I have an Orchard that hath store of plums,

Browne Almonds, Servises, ripe Figs and Dates, 5
Dewberries, Apples, yellow Orenges,
A garden where are Bee hives full of honey,
Musk-roses, and a thousand sort of flowers,
And in the midst doth run a silver streame,
Where thou shalt see the red gild fishes leape, 10
White Swannes, and many lovely water fowles:
Now speake *Ascanius*, will ye goe or no?

CUPID. Come come Ile goe, how farre hence is your house?

NURSE. But hereby child, we shall get thither straight.

CUPID. Nurse I am wearie, will you carrie me? 15

NURSE. I, so youle dwell with me and call me mother.

CUPID. So youle love me, I care not if I doe.

NURSE. That I might live to see this boy a man,
How pretilie he laughs, goe ye wagge, 20
Youle be a twigger when you come to age.
Say *Dido* what she will I am not old,
Ile be no more a widowe, I am young,
Ile have a husband, or els a lover.

CUPID. A husband and no teeth!

NURSE. O what meane I to have such foolish thoughts! 25
Foolish is love, a toy, O sacred love,
If there be any heaven in earth, tis love:
Especially in women of your yeares.
Blush blush for shame, why shouldst thou thinke of love?
A grave, and not a lover fits thy age: 30
A grave? why, I may live a hundred yeares,
Fourescore is but a girles age, love is sweete:
My vaines are withered, and my sinewes drie,
Why doe I thinke of love now I should dye?

CUPID. Come Nurse.

NURSE. Well, if he come a wooing he shall speede,
O how unwise was I to say him nay! *Exeunt.*

Actus 5. [Scena 1.]

Enter AENEAS *with a paper in his hand, drawing the platforme of the citie, with him* ACHATES, CLOANTHUS, *and* ILLIONEUS.

AENEAS. Triumph, my mates, our travels are at end,
    Here will *Aeneas* build a statelier *Troy*,
    Then that which grim *Atrides* overthrew:
    Carthage shall vaunt her pettie walles no more,
    For I will grace them with a fairer frame   5
    And clad her in a Chrystall liverie,
    Wherein the day may evermore delight:
    From golden *India Ganges* will I fetch,
    Whose wealthie streames may waite upon her towers,
    And triple wise intrench her round about: 10
    The Sunne from Egypt shall rich odors bring,
    Wherewith his burning beames like labouring Bees,
    That loade their thighes with *Hyblas* honeys spoyles,
    Shall here unburden their exhaled sweetes,
    And plant our pleasant suburbes with her fumes.   15
ACHATES. What length or bredth shal this brave towne containe?
AENEAS. Not past foure thousand paces at the most.
ILLIONEUS. But what shall it be calde, *Troy* as before?
AENEAS. That have I not determinde with my selfe.
CLOANTHUS. Let it be term'd *Aenea* by your name.   20
SERGESTUS. Rather *Ascania* by your little sonne.
AENEAS. Nay, I will haue it calde *Anchisaeon*,
    Of my old fathers name.

Enter HERMES *with* ASCANIUS.

HERMES. *Aeneas* stay, *Joves* Herald bids thee stay.
AENEAS. Whom doe I see, *Joves* winged messenger?   25
    Welcome to *Carthage* new erected towne.
HERMES. Why cosin, stand you building Cities here,
    And beautifying the Empire of this Queene,
    While *Italy* is cleane out of thy minde?
    To too forgetfull of thine owne affayres,   30
    Why wilt thou so betray thy sonnes good hap?
    The king of Gods sent me from highest heaven,

To sound this angrie message in thine eares.
Vaine man, what Monarky expectst thou here?
Or with what thought sleepst thou in *Libia* shoare?   35
If that all glorie hath forsaken thee,
And thou despise the praise of such attempts:
Yet thinke upon *Ascanius* prophesie,
And yong *Iulus* more then thousand yeares,
Whom I have brought from *Ida* where he slept,   40
And bore yong *Cupid* unto *Cypresse* Ile.

AENEAS. This was my mother that beguild the Queene,
And made me take my brother for my sonne:
No marvell *Dido* though thou be in love,
That daylie dandlest *Cupid* in thy armes: 45
Welcome sweet child, where hast thou been this long?

ASCANIUS. Eating sweet Comfites with Queene *Didos* maide,
Who ever since hath luld me in her armes.

AENEAS. *Sergestus*, beare him hence unto our ships,
Lest *Dido* spying him keepe him for a pledge.   50

HERMES. Spendst thou thy time about this little boy,
And givest not eare unto the charge I bring?
I tell thee thou must straight to *Italy*,
Or els abide the wrath of frowning *Jove*.

AENEAS. How should I put into the raging deepe,   55
Who have no sailes nor tackling for my ships?
What would the Gods have me *Deucalion* like,
Flote up and downe where ere the billowes drive?
Though she repairde my fleete and gave me ships,
Yet hath she tane away my oares and masts,   60
And left me neither saile nor sterne abourd.

Enter to them IARBUS.

IARBUS. How now *Aeneas*, sad, what meanes these dumpes?

AENEAS. *Iarbus*, I am cleane besides my selfe,
Jove hath heapt on me such a desperate charge,
Which neither art nor reason may atchieve,   65
Nor I devise by what meanes to contrive.

IARBUS. As how I pray, may I entreate you tell.

AENEAS. With speede he bids me saile to *Italy*,
When as I want both rigging for my fleete,
And also furniture for these my men.   70

IARBUS. If that be all, then cleare thy drooping lookes,
  For I will furnish thee with such supplies:
  Let some of those thy followers goe with me,
  And they shall have what thing so ere thou needst.
AENEAS. Thankes good *Iarbus* for thy friendly ayde,   75
  Achates and the rest shall waite on thee,
  Whil'st I rest thankfull for this curtesie.
                            Exit IARBUS *and* AENEAS *traine*.
  Now will I haste unto *Lavinian* shoare,
  And raise a new foundation to old *Troy*,
  Witnes the Gods, and witnes heaven and earth,   80
  How loth I am to leave these *Libian* bounds,
  But that eternall *Jupiter* commands.

       Enter DIDO *and* [*her Traine, to*] AENEAS.

DIDO. I feare I sawe *Aeneas* little sonne,
  Led by *Achates* to the Troian fleete:
  If it be so, his father meanes to flye: 85
  But here he is, now *Dido* trie thy wit.
  Aeneas, wherefore goe thy men abourd?
  Why are thy ships new rigd? or to what end
  Launcht from the haven, lye they in the Rhode?
  Pardon me though I aske, love makes me aske.   90
AENEAS. O pardon me, if I resolve thee why:
  Aeneas will not faine with his deare love,
  I must from hence: this day swift *Mercury*
  When I was laying a platforme for these walles,
  Sent from his father *Jove*, appeard to me,   95
  And in his name rebukt me bitterly,
  For lingering here, neglecting *Italy*.
DIDO. But yet *Aeneas* will not leave his love.
AENEAS. I am commaunded by immortall *Jove*,
  To leave this towne and passe to *Italy*,   100
  And therefore must of force.
DIDO. These words proceed not from *Aeneas* heart.
AENEAS. Not from my heart, for I can hardly goe,
  And yet I may not stay, *Dido* farewell.
DIDO. Farewell: is this the mends for *Didos* love?   105
  Doe Troians use to quit their Lovers thus?

Fare well may *Dido*, so *Aeneas* stay,
I dye, if my *Aeneas* say farewell.
AENEAS. Then let me goe and never say farewell.
DIDO. Let me goe, farewell, I must from hence,   110
These words are poyson to poore *Didos* soule,
O speake like my *Aeneas*, like my love:
Why look'st thou toward the sea? the time hath been
When *Didos* beautie chaind thine eyes to her:
Am I lesse faire then when thou sawest me first?   115
O then *Aeneas*, tis for griefe of thee:
Say thou wilt stay in *Carthage* with thy Queene,
And *Didos* beautie will returne againe:
Aeneas, say, how canst thou take thy leave?
Wilt thou kisse *Dido*? O thy lips have sworne   120
To stay with *Dido*: canst thou take her hand?
Thy hand and mine have plighted mutuall faith,
Therefore unkind *Aeneas*, must thou say,
Then let me goe, and never say farewell?
AENEAS. O Queene of *Carthage*, wert thou ugly blacke,   125
Aeneas could not choose but hold thee deare,
Yet must he not gainsay the Gods behest.
DIDO. The Gods, what Gods be those that seeke my death?
Wherein have I offended *Jupiter*,
That he should take *Aeneas* from mine armes?   130
O no, the Gods wey not what Lovers doe,
It is *Aeneas* calles Aeneas hence,
And wofull *Dido* by these blubbred cheekes,
By this right hand, and by our spousall rites,
Desires *Aeneas* to remaine with her: 135
Si bene quid de te merui, fuit aut tibi quidquam
Dulce meum, miserere domus labentis: & istam
Oro, si quis adhuc precibus locus, exue mentem.
AENEAS. *Desine meque tuis incendere teque querelis,*
Italiam non sponte sequor.   140
DIDO. Hast thou forgot how many neighbour kings
Were up in armes, for making thee my love?
How *Carthage* did rebell, *Iarbus* storme,

---

114 chaind] *Robinson*; chaunged *Q*   117 thy] *Oxberry*; my *Q*   138 *adhuc*]
Oxberry; ad haec *Q*

And all the world calles me a second *Helen*,
For being intangled by a strangers lookes: 145
So thou wouldst prove as true as *Paris* did,
Would, as faire *Troy* was, *Carthage* might be sackt,
And I be calde a second *Helena*.
Had I a sonne by thee, the griefe were lesse,
That I might see *Aeneas* in his face: 150
Now if thou goest, what canst thou leave behind,
But rather will augment then ease my woe?

AENEAS. In vaine my love thou spendst thy fainting breath,
If words might move me I were overcome.

DIDO. And wilt thou not be mov'd with *Didos* words?   155
Thy mother was no Goddesse perjurd man,
Nor *Dardanus* the author of thy stocke:
But thou art sprung from *Scythian Caucasus*,
And Tygers of *Hircania* gave thee sucke:
Ah foolish *Dido* to forbeare this long!   160
Wast thou not wrackt upon this *Libian* shoare,
And cam'st to *Dido* like a Fisher swaine?
Repairde not I thy ships, made thee a King,
And all thy needie followers Noblemen?
O Serpent that came creeping from the shoare,   165
And I for pitie harbord in my bosome,
Wilt thou now slay me with thy venomed sting,
And hisse at *Dido* for preserving thee?
Goe goe and spare not, seeke out *Italy*,
I hope that that which love forbids me doe,   170
The Rockes and Sea-gulfes will performe at large,
And thou shalt perish in the billowes waies,
To whom poore *Dido* doth bequeath revenge,
I traytor, and the waves shall cast thee up,
Where thou and false *Achates* first set foote: 175
Which if it chaunce, Ile give ye buriall,
And weepe upon your liveles carcases,
Though thou nor he will pitie me a whit.
Why star'st thou in my face? if thou wilt stay,
Leape in mine armes, mine armes are open wide: 180
If not, turne from me, and Ile turne from thee:

                                        Exit AENEAS.

For though thou hast the heart to say farewell,
I have not power to stay thee: is he gone?

I but heele come againe, he cannot goe,
He loves me to too well to serve me so: 185
Yet he that in my sight would not relent,
Will, being absent, be obdurate still.
By this is he got to the water side,
And, see the Sailers take him by the hand,
But he shrinkes backe, and now remembring me,   190
Returnes amaine: welcome, welcome my love:
But wheres *Aeneas*? ah hees gone hees gone!

                                        [*Enter* ANNA.]

ANNA. What meanes my sister thus to rave and crye?
DIDO. O *Anna*, my *Aeneas* is abourd,
    And leaving me will saile to *Italy*.   195
    Once didst thou goe, and he came backe againe,
    Now bring him backe, and thou shalt be a Queene,
    And I will live a private life with him.
ANNA. Wicked *Aeneas*.
DIDO. Call him not wicked, sister speake him faire,   200
    And looke upon him with a Mermaides eye,
    Tell him, I never vow'd at *Aulis* gulfe
    The desolation of his native *Troy*,
    Nor sent a thousand ships unto the walles,
    Nor ever violated faith to him: 205
    Request him gently (*Anna*) to returne,
    I crave but this, he stay a tide or two,
    That I may learne to beare it patiently,
    If he depart thus suddenly, I dye:
    Run *Anna*, run, stay not to answere me.   210
ANNA. I goe faire sister, heavens graunt good successe.

                                        Exit ANNA.

                    Enter the NURSE.

NURSE. O *Dido*, your little sonne *Ascanius*
    Is gone! he lay with me last night,
    And in the morning he was stolne from me,
    I thinke some Fairies have beguiled me.   215
DIDO. O cursed hagge and false dissembling wretch!
    That slayest me with thy harsh and hellish tale,
    Thou for some pettie guift hast let him goe,
    And I am thus deluded of my boy:

Away with her to prison presently,   220
Traytoresse too keene and cursed Sorceresse.
NURSE. I know not what you meane by treason, I,
I am as true as any one of yours.
DIDO. Away with her, suffer her not to speake.

Exeunt the NURSE [*with* DIDOS *Traine*].

My sister comes, I like not her sad lookes.   225

Enter ANNA.

ANNA. Before I came, *Aeneas* was abourd,
And spying me, hoyst up the sailes amaine:
But I cried out, *Aeneas*, false *Aeneas* stay.
Then gan he wagge his hand, which yet held up,
Made me suppose he would have heard me speake: 230
Then gan they drive into the Ocean,
Which when I viewd, I cride, *Aeneas* stay,
Dido, faire *Dido* wils *Aeneas* stay:
Yet he whose heart of adamant or flint,
My teares nor plaints could mollifie a whit: 235
Then carelesly I rent my haire for griefe,
Which seene to all, though he beheld me not,
They gan to move him to redresse my ruth,
And stay a while to heare what I could say,
But he clapt under hatches saild away.   240
DIDO. O *Anna*, *Anna*, I will follow him.
ANNA. How can ye goe when he hath all your fleete?
DIDO. Ile frame me wings of waxe like *Icarus*.
And ore his ships will soare unto the Sunne,
That they may melt and I fall in his armes: 245
Or els Ile make a prayer unto the waves,
That I may swim to him like *Tritons* neece:
O *Anna*, fetch *Arions* Harpe,
That I may tice a Dolphin to the shoare,
And ride upon his backe unto my love: 250
Looke sister, looke lovely *Aeneas* ships,
See, see the billowes heave him up to heaven,
And now downe falles the keeles into the deepe:
O sister, sister, take away the Rockes,

221 keene] *Oxberry*; keened *Q*   248 *Arions*] *Dyce*; *Orions Q*

Theile breake his ships, O *Proteus*, *Neptune*, *Jove*,   255
Save, save *Aeneas*, *Didos* leefest love!
Now is he come on shoare safe without hurt:
But see, *Achates* wils him put to sea,
And all the Sailers merrie make for joy,
But he remembring me shrinkes backe againe: 260
See where he comes, welcome, welcome my love.

ANNA. Ah sister, leave these idle fantasies,
Sweet sister cease, remember who you are.

DIDO. *Dido* I am, unlesse I be deceiv'd,
And must I rave thus for a runnagate?   265
Must I make ships for him to saile away?
Nothing can beare me to him but a ship,
And he hath all my fleete, what shall I doe
But dye in furie of this oversight?
I, I must be the murderer of my selfe: 270
No but I am not, yet I will be straight.
Anna be glad, now have I found a meane
To rid me from these thoughts of Lunacie:
Not farre from hence
There is a woman famoused for arts,   275
Daughter unto the Nimphs *Hesperides*,
Who wild me sacrifize his ticing relliques:
Goe *Anna*, bid my servants bring me fire.   *Exit* ANNA.

Enter IARBUS.

IARBUS. How long will *Dido* mourne a strangers flight,
That hath dishonord her and *Carthage* both?   280
How long shall I with griefe consume my daies,
And reape no guerdon for my truest love?

DIDO. *Iarbus*, talke not of *Aeneas*, let him goe,
Lay to thy hands and helpe me make a fire,
That shall consume all that this stranger left,   285
For I entend a private Sacrifize,
To cure my minde that melts for unkind love.

IARBUS. But afterwards will *Dido* graunt me love?

DIDO. I, I, *Iarbus*, after this is done,
None in the world shall have my love but thou: 290

268 my] *Oxberry*; thy *Q*

So, leave me now, let none approach this place. *Exit* IARBUS.
Now *Dido*, with these reliques burne thy selfe,
And make *Aeneas* famous through the world,
For perjurie and slaughter of a Queene:
Here lye the Sword that in the darksome Cave   295
He drew, and swore by to be true to me,
Thou shalt burne first, thy crime is worse then his;
Here lye the garment which I cloath'd him in,
When first he came on shoare, perish thou to:
These letters, lines, and perjurd papers all,   300
Shall burne to cinders in this pretious flame.
And now ye gods that guide the starrie frame,
And order all things at your high dispose,
Graunt, though the traytors land in *Italy*,
They may be still tormented with unrest,   305
And from mine ashes let a Conquerour rise,
That may revenge this treason to a Queene,
By plowing up his Countries with the Sword:
Betwixt this land and that be never league,
Littora littoribus contraria, fluctibus undas   310
Imprecor: arma armis: pugnent ipsique nepotes:
Live false *Aeneas*, truest, *Dido* dyes,
Sic sic juvat ire sub umbras.   [*Exit*]

Enter ANNA.

ANNA. O helpe *Iarbus*, *Dido* in these flames
Hath burnt her selfe, aye me, unhappie me!   315

Enter Iarbus *running*

IARBUS. Cursed *Iarbus*, dye to expiate
The griefe that tires upon thine inward soule.
Dido I come to thee, aye me *Aeneas*.   [*Exit*]
ANNA. What can my teares or cryes prevaile me now?
Dido is dead,   320
Iarbus slaine, *Iarbus* my deare love,
O sweet *Iarbus*, *Annas* sole delight,
What fatall destinie envies me thus,
To see my sweet *Iarbus* slay himselfe?
But *Anna* now shall honor thee in death,   325

And mixe her bloud with thine, this shall I doe,
That Gods and men may pitie this my death,
And rue our ends senceles of life or breath:
Now sweet *Iarbus* stay, I come to thee.   [*Exit*]

FINIS

HERO AND LEANDER

General Introduction

HERO *and Leander* is a truly *rare* achievement—a work that is 'of uncommon excellence or merit' (*OED rare adj.* 6). It belongs to a genre whose popularity was short-lived, perhaps because of the problems of blending and balancing the essential and contradictory components: eroticism and humour, sympathetic tenderness and detached wit. *Termini a quo* and *ad quem* for the genre are provided by Thomas Lodge's *Scillaes Metamorphosis* (1589) and James Shirley's *Narcissus* (1646). In the twentieth century scholars have attempted to burden the English form with the label 'epyllion' (from the Greek ἐπύλλιον, the diminutive of ἔπος), and to claim for it a status analogous to that of the small group of Hellenistic and Roman poems which includes Musaeus' short epic. But these suggested prototypes are so heterogeneous that comparison has not proved helpful, and it would seem that the English poems (which have no common metrical or stanzaic formula) are best—if clumsily—described as narratives of sexual love, ranging in mood (within a single poem) from the sentimental to the satiric.[1] The professor of the *Ars Amatoria* is the dominant influence (*Naso magister erat*), but because the same author's *Metamorphoses* so often inspired the stories, the protagonists are often forced to conclude with Berowne in *Love's Labour's Lost*: 'Our wooing doth not end like an old play: | Jack hath not Jill' (v. ii. 862–3).

The romantic story of Hero and Leander appears to have been wellknown from the time of Augustus Caesar, but only two poets—Ovid and Musaeus—used it as the subject-matter for entire works.[2] Ovid constructed imaginary epistles, the eighteenth and nineteenth of the *Heroides*, to go between the lovers. In the first of these, *Leander Heroni*, he explores the passion and determination with which Leander braved the waters of the

[1] The genre is discussed by William Keach in *Elizabethan Erotic Narratives* (Brighton, 1977), and a selection of the best poems appears in the anthology *Elizabethan Minor Epics*, ed. Elizabeth Story Donno (London, 1963).

[2] Quotations from Ovid and Musaeus (with translations) are taken from the Loeb editions (London and Cambridge, Mass.): *Heroides*, ed. and trans. Grant Showerman (1963); *Hero and Leander*, ed. Thomas Gelzer, trans. Cedric Whitman (1975; reprinted 1978).

Hellespont between Sestos and Abydos. The second, *Hero Leandro*, describes the passive suffering of Hero when, denied the diversions which might distract the mind of a man, she is left alone with nothing to do but love: *superest praeter amare nihil* (line 16). Marlowe's poem shows an occasional debt to the two epistles, such as the reminder in the first line that the Hellespont was 'guiltie of True-loves blood'—which could well be a version of Ovid's *satis amissa locus hic infamis ab Helle est* (*Heroides*, xviii. 141). A greater debt, however, is due to the masterpiece by Musaeus, written during the fifth century AD, which Marlowe seems to have read in the original Greek, finding inspiration in the style as well as the content.[3] Musaeus was one of the writers of the fifth and sixth centuries who were given the title γραμματικός. Thomas Gelzer, in his introduction to the Loeb Edition, describes them as 'scholars and teachers learned in the rhetoric, poetics, and philosophy of their time, and expert in the scholarly interpretation of the classical prose—and verse—authors, in particular of Homer, the orators and the philosophers' (p. 297).

The Greek poem opens with fifteen lines of formal invocation, and then the narrative proceeds sequentially from the festival when the visitor from Abydos encounters the virgin priestess of Aphrodite. Hero at first resists Leander's attempts to seduce her, insisting on her vowed virginity, and thereby permitting the comedy of Leander's argument that 'It is not fitting a virgin attend on Aphrodite' (παρθένον οὐκ ἐπέοικεν ὑποδρήσσειν Ἀφροδίτῃ, line 143). An assignation is made, and the union is quickly consummated. Leander swims the Hellespont regularly, to be warmly received by his bride (quite unlike Marlowe's coy virgin) who is content to live 'maiden by day, by night a wife' (παρθένος ἡματίη, νυχίη γυνή, line 287). The poem climaxes in tragedy on a winter's night: 'Love could not fend off the Fates' (Ἔρως δ' οὐκ ἤρκεσε Μοίρας, line 323), and Leander's struggle with the sea ends when his drowned body lies at the foot of Hero's tower!

> κὰδ δ' Ἡρὼ τέθνηκε σὺν ὀλλυμένῳ παρακοίτῃ,
> ἀλλήλων δ' ἀπόναντο καὶ ἐν πυμάτῳ περ ὀλέθρῳ.   (342–3)

('And Hero lay in death beside her dead husband,
And they had joy of each other even in their last perishing.')

---

[3] See T. W. Baldwin, 'Marlowe's Musaeus', *Journal of English and Germanic Philology*, liv (1955), 478–85.

Marlowe's poem, although it reproduces ideas, lines, and even *o* phrases from the Greek of Musaeus, cannot be called a translation in the strict sense that describes his metaphrastic rendering of *Lucan's First Booke* and his presentation of the Latin *Amores* as English *Elegies*. It would be more proper to call the Greek poem a source, recognizing that it afforded Marlowe much more than a Jamesian *donnée*, but that Marlowe is even less restricted here than in his dramatic paraphrase of *The Aeneid* in *Dido Queene of Carthage*.

More than twice as long as its source, *Hero and Leander* was written when Marlowe was at his most mercurial: fluent and witty in his invention, he also shows himself to have been an Autolycus amongst authors—'a snapper-up of unconsidered trifles'.[4] The poem is rich in allusions. Its simple story is heavily embroidered *o* with the classical mythology that the Elizabethans claimed as their rightful heritage. We can assume that Marlowe's contemporaries would usually recognize the allusions without prompting: 'the yron net, | Which limping *Vulcan* and his *Cyclops* set' (151–2), for example, presents no difficulty of identification. However, 'the engins . . . | Which th'earth from ougly *Chaos* den up-wayd' (449–50) are problematic, and it is tempting to suggest that this detail is of Marlowe's own mythopoeic imagining, like the entire episode (385 ff.) of Mercury's love for the country girl and the dire consequences of her hubris.

Having located the setting of his poem in the manner of Ovid, Marlowe immediately transfers his attention to the description of Hero in Musaeus' poem, and almost seems to enter into competition with the Greek writer. Either portrait could be taken as a model for the rhetorical scheme of *effictio* or *prosographia*, 'When that as well the person of a very man as of a fayned, is by his forme, stature, manners, studyes, dooinges, affections, and such other circumstaunces, serving the purpose, so described, that it may appeare a playne pycture paynted in Tables'.[5] Points of contact between the two portraits are few, although both poets delight in the hyperbolic comparison of Hero with the goddess whom she serves. Even here, however, the differences are more striking than the similarities. Musaeus is serious, crowning his

---

[4] *The Winter's Tale*, iv. iii. 26.
[5] Thomas Peacham, *The Garden of Eloquence* (1577), D2ᵛ.

description of Hero's damasked (διδυμόχροο) radiance with the conclusion that: 'So she far far excelling among women, | Priestess of Cypris, revealed herself Cypris anew'.

> Ὥς ἡ μὲν περςπολλὸν ἀριστεύουσα γυναικῶν.
> Κύπριδος ἀρήτειρα, νέη διεφαίνετο Κύπρις.   (67–8).

Marlowe is less reverent. He begins his description with the amazing claim (from his personal mythopeia) that 'young Apollo courted [Hero] for her haire' (line 6), and proceeds to itemize the sacerdotal vestments, praising the elaborate artifice that imitates, yet exceeds, nature. Hero's footwear is a technological *tour de force*:

> Buskins of shels all silvered, used she,
> And brancht with blushing corall to the knee;
> Where sparrowes pearcht, of hollow pearle and gold,
> Such as the world would woonder to behold;
> Those with sweet water oft her handmaid fils,
> Which as shee went would cherupe through the bils.   (31–6)

Marlowe admires the elaborate luxury, while at the same time revealing its absurdity. Hyperbole topples into comedy at the point where Musaeus is most serious—in the comparison with Venus. Marlowe first offers his own explanation of Cupid's blindness (prefixing it with the pseudo-scholarly 'Some say'—the *aiunt* of mythographers), and then invokes Venus in her least expected role—that of mother:

> Some say, for her the fairest *Cupid* pyn'd,
> And looking in her face, was strooken blind.
> But this is true, so like was one the other,
> As he imagyn'd *Hero* was his mother.   (37–40)

The feminine rhyme of 'other | 'mother' makes the fun secure.

Having exalted Hero as a masterpiece in which the hand of man seems to have excelled that of 'great creating nature',[6] Marlowe turns his attention to Leander, and initiates a second example of the scheme *effictio*, for which Musaeus offers no precedent. The writing here is even more enthusiastic than in the portrait of Hero,

---

[6] *The Winter's Tale*, iv. iv. 87.

ransacking mythology for comparisons, and indulging the senses
in a complex interplay of thought and feeling. The description of
Leander's neck is particularly remarkable:

> Even as delicious meat is to the tast,
> So was his necke in touching, and surpast
> The white of *Pelops* shoulder.   (63–5)

The relevance of the first simile is not immediately obvious: taste
and touch are, after all, different senses. But the connection
becomes clear with the introduction of Pelops, whose celebrated
white shoulder was in fact an ivory prosthesis designed to replace
the human shoulder which had served as meat for the goddess
Ceres.

Once again the admixture of comedy prevents the mythological
richness of the passage from becoming self-indulgent. Following
the respectful allusions to Narcissus and 'wilde *Hippolitus*' (line
77) is the sly acknowledgement of Leander's epicene quality:

> Some swore he was a maid in mans attire,
> For in his lookes were all that men desire.   (83–4)

Hyperbole ends in gentle teasing.

Having established his dramatis personae, 'the qualities and
dispositions of the persons', Marlowe proceeds to establish 'the
time when' and 'the place where'.[7] The time is the great festival of
Venus, the feast anticipated in the medieval Latin lyric *Pervigilium
Veneris*, with its lovely refrain *Cras amet qui nunquam amavit;
quisque amavit cras amet*; Marlowe seems to echo the notion,
although without the Latin's elegant economy:

> Thither resorted many a wandring guest,
> To meet their loves; such as had none at all,
> Came lovers home, from this great festivall.   (94–6)

The lovers meet in the temple of Venus, and in his description of
this, Marlowe seems to have been inspired by Ovid and to have
been in competition with Spenser (see notes to lines 135–56). But
whereas Spenser shows proper Elizabethan respect in describing
the great classical gods, Marlowe takes delight in exposing the
perversity of their heightened sexuality. The overall effect is not
pornographic, however, and for this the verse form is partly

---

[7] See *Love's Labour's Lost*, I. i. 210.

responsible, together with the matter-of-fact tone and language
with which he speaks of the 'gods in sundrie shapes, | Committing
headdie ryots, incest, rapes' (143–4).

The encounter, taking place among the mysteries of Hero's
priestly office, is electrifying. The lovers themselves are shocked to
silence: 'True love is mute, and oft amazed stands' (line 186), but
the charge is felt even by the surrounding air, which 'with sparkes
of living fire was spangled' (line 188). The silence is broken by
Leander—and the awesomeness of the entranced moment is
dispersed by the rhyming of the couplet that introduces his
speech:

> At last, like to a bold sharpe Sophister,
> With chearefull hope thus he accosted her.   (197–8)

In the introductory *effictio* Leander was presented as a delicate
youth whose apparent innocence counterbalanced the elegant
artificiality of Hero; but now the simile adds character. Implicit in
Marlowe's use of 'Sophister'—'At Cambridge, a student in his
second or third year', *OED sb.* 3—is the sense of *sophist, sb.* 3: 'one
who makes use of fallacious arguments; a specious reasoner':
Leander's speech of courtship shows the term to be apt. The
speech is formal, and would serve as a model for what Sir Thomas
Wilson, following Quintilian, called 'An Oration deliberative',
with the explanation that

In this kinde of Oration, wee doe not purpose wholy to praise any bodie,
nor yet to determine any matter in controuersie, but the whole compasse
of this cause is, either to aduise our neighbour to that thing, which wee
thinke most needefull for him, or els to call him backe from that follie,
which hindereth much his estimation.[8]

A comparable speech occupies the same position in Musaeus'
poem, but the arguments of Marlowe's Leander owe a debt to
Ovid and to Aristotle, as well as to his Greek counterpart.

Like Musaeus, Marlowe presents Hero's response to her lover's
courtship with sympathetic amusement: initial embarrassment
makes the girl seek protection in her priestly vocation, but
instinctive attraction leads to unconscious encouragement as
'unawares (*Come thither*) from her slipt' (line 358), and the
assignation is made. But now Marlowe departs from Musaeus,

---

[8] *The Arte of Rhetorique*, by Thomas Wilson (1560), ed. G. H. Mair (London, 1909), 29.

diverting himself with his own invention in the story of Mercury, Cupid, and 'those sterne nymphs' (line 379), the Destinies. A half-line in the Greek might have been the 'germ' for this fable: Leander, threatened by the stormy sea, prays to the gods for help: 'But no one helped him, and Love could not fend off the Fates' (ἀλλά οἱ οὔ τις ἄρηγεν, Ἔρως δ'οὐκ ἤρκεσε Μοίρας, line 323).

The digression does not show Marlowe's writing at its best; although his imagination seems to have been actively engaged in mythopeia, he is sometimes irritatingly clumsy in his use of rhetorical devices (such as the scheme of *alliteratio* in line 449: 'faire feathered feet').

When attention returns to the human personages we find that Hero is still, for a moment, at a comic disadvantage—and, as usual, the comedy is emphasized with a rhyme:

> By this, sad *Hero*, with love unacquainted,
> Viewing *Leanders* face, fell downe and fainted.   (485–6)

But she quickly regains her composure, and in the interlude that follows, it seems that the two have exchanged roles. Leander is no longer the 'bold sharpe Sophister' (line 197), but a 'novice' (line 497), 'rude in love, and raw' (line 545), while Hero's calculated movements suggest an experience in the *ars amatoria* that might be proper for '*Venus* Nun' (line 319).

Taught by Hero and his own instincts, Leander achieves some measure of sexual maturity before the morning enforces the lovers' separation; but he is still essentially adolescent when he returns to his home in Abydos and is unable (or unwilling) to conceal his triumph:

> His secret flame apparently was seene,
> *Leanders* Father knew where hee had beene.   (619–20)

The Leander of Musaeus, by contrast, is adult; and his Hero is neither coy nor tantalizing. Their first intimate meeting moves swiftly to consummation: ὁ δ'αὐτίκα λύσατο μίτρην, | καὶ θεσμῶν ἐπέβησαν ἀριστονόου Κυθερείης (272–3). ('Forthwith he loosed her girdle, | And they entered into the rites of the most wise Cythereia.')

The climax of the Greek poem comes when the winter storms menace Leander's nightly swim across the Hellespont. Musaeus is sternly economical in his description of the battle with the waves and the fruitless prayers to the gods. Marlowe too describes an encounter with the sea, but in his poem the description is almost a parody of the episode he imitates. Marlowe's invention is never more delightfully active than in the account of Leander's swimming. Here the sea is not represented by the angry waves of Musaeus' poem. It is 'kingly *Neptune*' (line 650), referred to also as 'The lustie god' (line 651) in a context which makes *OED*'s sense 4 of *lustie* ('Full of lust or sexual desire; lustful. *Obs.*') particularly appropriate. Neptune is both man and sea, and consequently his attempt to seduce Leander is a strangely complex business. When Neptune's attentions become most overtly sexual, the eroticism is dissolved by the comedy of Leander's naive response: while the naked boy was swimming (we are told) the god would

> dive into the water, and there prie
> Upon his brest, his thighs, and everie lim,
> And up againe, and close beside him swim,
> And talke of love: *Leander* made replie,
> You are deceav'd, I am no woman I.   (672–6)

There can be no doubt that comedy is intended for even the god is amused at the boy's reaction: 'Thereat smilde *Neptune*' (line 677). There follows another digression, this time based on the story of Hylas, which by implication identifies Leander with the boy who was loved by Hercules in classical mythology. 'Ere halfe this tale was done' (line 685), however, Leander abandons Neptune and redoubles his efforts to swim to Sestos, where his reception by Hero is narrated with enjoyment:

> She stayd not for her robes, but straight arose,
> And drunke with gladnesse, to the dore she goes.
> Where seeing a naked man, she scriecht for feare,
> Such sights as this, to tender maids are rare.   (719–22)

As we have come to expect in *Hero and Leander*, tenderness is accompanied by gentle amusement, which comes into focus with the rhyme-word *rare*.

Marlowe's poem now moves towards its own climax. Slowly the poet describes the encounter of the two lovers which leads to the consummation of their love. The passage is splendidly orchestrated. It begins with the human comedy of Leander's appeal to Hero's pity: 'This head was beat with manie a churlish billow, |

And therefore let it rest upon thy pillow' (lines 735–6). A second
movement is the sympathetic presentation of Hero's conflicting
emotions as she half-heartedly tries to ward off Leander's
assaulting hands; then after a brief and 'metaphysical' description
of Hero's breasts, we reach the moment of Leander's triumph,
when he achieves the status of a superman and 'like Theban
Hercules' (line 781) accomplishes his mission.

The poem ends in glorious and harmonious fulfilment—the
apotheosis of comedy. But after Marlowe's last line, Blount (or his
printer, or some unknown 'editor') has appended the words in the
first quarto of 1598 *Desunt Nonnulla*. George Chapman responded
to these words, and took it upon himself to remedy what he clearly
thought was Marlowe's negligence by extending the narrative to
include Musaeus' tragic ending. Q2's poem is consequently more
than twice as long as the poem published in Q1; at the end,
Leander is drowned, and at the sight of the dead body Hero

> . . . fell on her loves bosome, hugg'd it fast,
> And with *Leanders* name she breath'd her last.   (vi. 272–3)

Overcome with pity, Neptune revives the pair in a pseudo-Ovidian
metamorphosis, changing them into 'two sweet birds surnam'd th'
Acanthides, | Which we call Thistle-warps' (vi. 276–7).

Since 1598, editions of *Hero and Leander* have followed the
example of Q2, and have included the 1300 lines added by
Chapman. Only one editor has departed from this practice. In
1972 Louis L. Martz was responsible for a facsimile reprint of Q1,
and in the introduction he expressed a desire (which I now share)
to 'disengage Marlowe's "amorous poem" from the frigid embraces of the "stern Muse" of Chapman'.[9] I can see no
justification for including Chapman's work in a modern edition of
Marlowe's poem. There is no known link between the two writers,
and not even in his dedicatory epistle (addressed to Lady
Walsingham) does Chapman suggest that he is carrying out the
wishes of his late contemporary. The only *raison d'être* for
Chapman's addition is the *Desunt nonnulla* at the end of the Q1
text; and this is probably the conclusion of the publisher, trying to
explain the absence of the expected ending to the story.

Marlowe twice alludes to the familiar catastrophe: the reader is
warned (or reminded) of the inevitability of tragedy when Cupid's

[9] The Folger Facsimiles (New York and Washington, DC, 1972), 1.

plea that Hero and Leander 'might enjoy ech other, and be blest' (line 380) is sternly rejected by the 'Adamantine Destinies' (line 444); and very early in the poem, as he begins his portrait of Leander, Marlowe draws attention to his source:

> Amorous *Leander*, beautifull and yoong,
> (Whose tragedie divine *Musaeus* soong)
> Dwelt at *Abidus*.   (51–3)

But this is poor evidence for the assumption (made by the pedestrian Blount and the opportunist Chapman) that Marlowe intended some tragic peripeteia which would bring his poem into conformity with tradition. Marlowe was never a conformist.

Textual Introduction.

Hero and Leander was printed by Adam Islip for Edward Blunt in 1598:

HERO | AND | LEANDER | *By Christopher Marloe.* | [Device: McKerrow, no. 251] | LONDON, | *Printed by Adam Islip,* | *for Edward Blunt.* | 1598.

The poem had been licensed on 28 September 1593 by John Wolfe (on the same day that he claimed rights in Marlowe's translation of Lucan), but there is no other suggestion of publication before 1598. Moreover, the tone of Blunt's dedicatory epistle would be inappropriate for any but a first edition. This survives in a unique copy, STC No. 17413, in the Folger Shakespeare Library. The text of Marlowe's poem (A4–E3ᵛ) is well printed, the only major confusion arising from the dislocation of ten lines now placed as 775–84. This correction was first made by Tucker Brooke in 1910, with the explanation that, 'owing probably to the displacement of a leaf in Marlowe's lost MS, these lines are given in wrong sequence'. Fredson Bowers accepted the ordering, but queried the explanation, arguing that 'the block of ten lines . . . is too short to suppose that it comprised a foul page of manuscript'. Bowers supposed that the lines were written on a separate slip of paper, additional to the main manuscript, and were inserted by the printer in the wrong place (Bowers, ii. 427–8). Whatever the reason for the error, there is no doubt about the need for correction, and the appropriateness of Tucker Brooke's action.

Blunt's edition (Q1) must have been printed very early in 1598; on 2 March 1597/8 he transferred his rights to Linley, who published another edition in the same year.[10] The title-page gave notice of a poem 'Begun by *Christopher Marloe*; and *finished* by *George Chapman*'. In this edition, Marlowe's 818 lines are divided into two Sestyads, and are accompanied by four more such sections; each of the six sestiads is prefaced by a set of couplets summarizing its 'argument'. This edition, Q2 (STC No. 17414) survives in two copies: one in the British Library, the other in the Huntington Library. It has no authority for Marlowe's work, and is of value to an editor only where it can suggest the sixteenth-century correction for patently misleading accidentals.

Subsequent editions, Q2–10 (published in 1600, 1606, 1609, 1613, 1616, 1617, 1622, 1629, and 1637) testify to the poem's popularity, without adding to the clarity of the text.

Copy-text for the present edition is the quarto (Q1) printed by Islip for Blunt in 1598; this has been collated against the other early quartos as far as Q10 (1637) and all available modern editions.

Editorial intervention has been minimal, even in matters of accidence. Obvious printer's errors (such as 'rhought' for 'thought' at line 336) have been corrected; necessary capitals have been supplied (for the persons referred to as the 'destinies' at line 377); and proper names have been uniformly italicized. But Q1's punctuation has been maintained: the pointing in later quartos can be seen to move gradually in the direction of modern practice, but since these editions have no authority for Marlowe's poem, I see no reason for accepting their modifications except when Q1's accidentals are obviously misleading.

[10] Cf. W. W. Greg, 'The Copyright of "Hero and Leander"', *The Library*, 4th series, xxiv (1944), 165–74.

TO THE RIGHT WORSHIPFULL, SIR THOMAS
WALSINGHAM, KNIGHT

Sir, wee thinke not our selves discharged of the dutie wee owe to our friend, when wee have brought the breathlesse bodie to the earth: for albeit the eye there taketh his ever farwell of that beloved object, yet the impression of the man, that hath beene deare unto us, living an after life in our memory, there putteth us in mind of farther obsequies 5 due unto the deceased. And namely of the performance of whatsoever we may judge shal make to his living credit, and to the effecting of his determinations prevented by the stroke of death. By these meditations (as by an intellectuall will) I suppose my selfe executor to the unhappily deceased author of this Poem, upon whom knowing that in 10 his life time you bestowed many kind favours, entertaining the parts of reckoning and woorth which you found in him, with good countenance and liberall affection: I cannot but see so far into the will of him dead, that whatsoever issue of his brain should chance to come abroad, that the first breath it should take might be the gentle aire of your liking: 15 for since his selfe had ben accustomed therunto, it would proove more agreeable and thriving to his right children, than any other foster countenance whatsoever. At this time seeing that this unfinished Tragedy happens under my hands to be imprinted; of a double duty, the one to your selfe, 20
the other to the deceased, I present the same to your most
favourable allowance, offring my utmost selfe
now and ever to bee readie, At your
Worships disposing:

Edward Blunt.

Hero and Leander

On *Hellespont* guiltie of True-loves blood,
In view and opposit two citties stood,
Seaborderers, disjoin'd by *Neptunes* might:
The one *Abydos*, the other *Sestos* hight.
At *Sestos*, *Hero* dwelt; *Hero* the faire,   5
Whom young *Apollo* courted for her haire,
And offred as a dower his burning throne,
Where she should sit for men to gaze upon.
The outside of her garments were of lawne,
The lining, purple silke, with guilt starres drawne,   10
Her wide sleeves greene, and bordered with a grove,
Where *Venus* in her naked glory strove,
To please the carelesse and disdainfull eies,
Of proud *Adonis* that before her lies.
Her kirtle blew, whereon was many a staine,   15
Made with the blood of wretched Lovers slaine.
Upon her head she ware a myrtle wreath,
From whence her vaile reacht to the ground beneath.
Her vaile was artificiall flowers and leaves,
Whose workmanship both man and beast deceaves.   20
Many would praise the sweet smell as she past,
When t'was the odour which her breath foorth cast.
And there for honie, bees have sought in vaine,
And beat from thence, have lighted there againe.
About her necke hung chaines of peble stone,   25
Which lightned by her necke, like Diamonds shone.
She ware no gloves, for neither sunne nor wind
Would burne or parch her hands, but to her mind,
Or warme or coole them, for they tooke delite
To play upon those hands, they were so white.   30
Buskins of shels all silvered, used she,
And brancht with blushing corall to the knee;
Where sparrowes pearcht, of hollow pearle and gold,
Such as the world would woonder to behold;
Those with sweet water oft her handmaid fils,   35
Which as shee went would cherupe through the bils.

3 Seaborderers] *Q8*; Seaborders *Q1–7*

Some say, for her the fairest *Cupid* pyn'd,
And looking in her face, was strooken blind.
But this is true, so like was one the other,
As he imagyn'd *Hero* was his mother.   40
And oftentimes into her bosome flew,
About her naked necke his bare armes threw.
And laid his childish head upon her brest,
And with still panting rockt, there tooke his rest.
So lovely faire was *Hero*, *Venus* Nun,   45
As nature wept, thinking she was undone;
Because she tooke more from her than she left,
And of such wondrous beautie her bereft:
Therefore in signe her treasure suffred wracke,
Since *Heroes* time, hath halfe the world beene blacke.   50
Amorous *Leander*, beautifull and yoong,
(Whose tragedie divine *Musaeus* soong)
Dwelt at *Abidus*, since him, dwelt there none,
For whom succeeding times make greater mone.
His dangling tresses that were never shorne,   55
Had they beene cut, and unto *Colchos* borne,
Would have allur'd the vent'rous youth of Greece,
To hazard more, than for the golden Fleece.
Faire *Cinthia* wisht, his armes might be her spheare,
Greefe makes her pale, because she mooves not there.   60
His bodie was as straight as *Circes* wand,
Jove might have sipt out *Nectar* from his hand.
Even as delicious meat is to the tast,
So was his necke in touching, and surpast
The white of *Pelops* shoulder, I could tell ye,   65
How smooth his brest was, & how white his bellie,
And whose immortall fingars did imprint,
That heavenly path, with many a curious dint,
That runs along his backe, but my rude pen,
Can hardly blazon foorth the loves of men   70
Much lesse of powerfull gods, let it suffise,
That my slacke muse, sings of *Leanders* eies,
Those orient cheekes and lippes, exceeding his
That leapt into the water for a kis
Of his owne shadow, and despising many,   75
Died ere he could enjoy the love of any,

Had wilde *Hippolitus*, *Leander* seene,
Enamoured of his beautie had he beene,
His presence made the rudest paisant melt,
That in the vast uplandish countrie dwelt,   80
The barbarous *Thratian* soldier moov'd with nought,
Was moov'd with him, and for his favour sought.
Some swore he was a maid in mans attire,
For in his lookes were all that men desire,
A pleasant smiling cheeke, a speaking eye,   85
A brow for Love to banquet roiallye,
And such as knew he was a man would say,
Leander, thou art made for amorous play:
Why art thou not in love, and lov'd of all?
Though thou be faire, yet be not thine owne thrall.   90
    The men of wealthie *Sestos*, everie yeare,
(For his sake whom their goddesse held so deare,
Rose-cheekt *Adonis*) kept a solemne feast,
Thither resorted many a wandring guest,
To meet their loves; such as had none at all,   95
Came lovers home, from this great festivall.
For everie street like to a Firmament
Glistered with breathing stars, who where they went,
Frighted the melancholie earth, which deem'd,
Eternall heaven to burne, for so it seem'd,   100
As if another *Phaeton* had got
The guidance of the sunnes rich chariot.
But far above the loveliest, *Hero* shin'd,
And stole away th'inchaunted gazers mind,
For like Sea-nimphs inveigling harmony,   105
So was her beautie to the standers by.
Not that night-wandring pale and watrie starre,
(When yawning dragons draw her thirling carre,
From *Latmus* mount up to the glomie skie,
Where crown'd with blazing light and majestie,   110
She proudly sits) more over-rules the flood,
Than she the hearts of those that neere her stood.
Even as, when gawdie Nymphs pursue the chace,
Wretched *Ixions* shaggie footed race,

86 Love] *Q6*; love *Q1–5*   103 above] *Q2*; ~, *Q1*   103 loveliest,] *Brydges*;
~∧ *Qq*   107 Not] *Englands Parnassus* (1600); Nor *Qq*

Incent with savage heat, gallop amaine,   115
From steepe Pine-bearing mountains to the plaine:
So ran the people foorth to gaze upon her,
And all that view'd her, were enamour'd on her.
And as in furie of a dreadfull fight,
Their fellowes being slaine or put to flight,   120
Poore soldiers stand with fear of death dead strooken,
So at her presence all surpris'd and tooken,
Await the sentence of her scornefull eies:
He whom she favours lives, the other dies.
There might you see one sigh, another rage,   125
And some (their violent passions to asswage)
Compile sharpe satyrs, but alas too late,
For faithfull love will never turne to hate.
And many seeing great princes were denied,
Pyn'd as they went, and thinking on her died.   130
On this feast day, O cursed day and hower,
Went *Hero* thorow *Sestos*, from her tower
To *Venus* temple, were unhappilye,
As after chaunc'd, they did each other spye.
So faire a church as this, had *Venus* none,   135
The wals were of discoloured *Jasper* stone,
Wherein was Proteus carved, and o'rehead,
A livelie vine of greene sea agget spread;
Where by one hand, light headed *Bacchus* hoong
And with the other, wine from grapes out wroong.   140
Of Christall shining faire, the pavement was,
The towne of *Sestos*, cal'd it *Venus* glasse,
There might you see the gods in sundrie shapes,
Committing headdie ryots, incest, rapes:
For know, that underneath this radiant floure,   145
Was *Danaes* statue in a brazen tower,
Jove, slylie stealing from his sisters bed,
To dallie with *Idalian Ganimed*:
And for his love *Europa*, bellowing loud,
And tumbling with the Rainbow in a cloud,   150
Blood-quaffing *Mars*, heaving the yron net,
Which limping *Vulcan* and his *Cyclops* set:
Love kindling fire, to burne such townes as *Troy*,
Sylvanus weeping for the lovely boy

That now is turn'd into a *Cypres* tree,   155
Under whose shade the Wood-gods love to bee,
And in the midst a silver altar stood,
There *Hero* sacrificing turtles blood,
Vaild to the ground, vailing her eie-lids close,
And modestly they opened as she rose: 160
Thence flew Loves arrow with the golden head,
And thus *Leander* was enamoured.
Stone still he stood, and evermore he gazed,
Till with the fire that from his count'nance blazed,
Relenting *Heroes* gentle heart was strooke,   165
Such force and vertue hath an amorous looke.
      It lies not in our power to love, or hate,
For will in us is over-rul'd by fate.
When two are stript, long ere the course begin,
We wish that one should loose, the other win.   170
And one especiallie doe we affect,
Of two gold Ingots like in each respect,
The reason no man knowes, let it suffise,
What we behold is censur'd by our eies.
Where both deliberat, the love is slight,   175
Who ever lov'd, that lov'd not at first sight?
      He kneel'd, but unto her devoutly praid;
Chast *Hero* to her selfe thus softly said:
Were I the saint hee worships, I would heare him,
And as shee spake those words, came somewhat nere him.   180
He started up, she blusht as one asham'd;
Wherewith *Leander* much more was inflam'd.
He toucht her hand, in touching it she trembled,
Love deepely grounded, hardly is dissembled.
These lovers parled by the touch of hands,   185
True love is mute, and oft amazed stands.
Thus while dum signs their yeelding harts entangled,
The aire with sparkes of living fire was spangled,
And night deepe drencht in mystie *Acheron*,   *A periphrasis*
Heav'd up her head, and halfe the world upon,   190 *of night*
Breath'd darkenesse forth (darke night is *Cupids* day.)
And now begins *Leander* to display
Loves holy fire, with words, with sighs and teares,
Which like sweet musicke entred *Heroes* eares,

And yet at evrie word shee turn'd aside,　　195
And alwaies cut him off as he replide,
At last, like to a bold sharpe Sophister,
With chearefull hope thus he accosted her.
　　Faire creature, let me speake without offence,
I would my rude words had the influence,　　200
To lead thy thoughts, as thy faire lookes doe mine,
Then shouldst thou bee his prisoner who is thine.
Be not unkind and faire, mishapen stuffe
Are of behaviour boisterous and ruffe.
O shun me not, but heare me ere you goe,　　205
God knowes I cannot force love, as you doe.
My words shall be as spotlesse as my youth,
Full of simplicitie and naked truth.
This sacrifice (whose sweet perfume descending,
From *Venus* altar to your footsteps bending)　　210
Doth testifie that you exceed her farre,
To whom you offer, and whose Nunne you are,
Why should you worship her, her you surpasse,
As much as sparkling Diamonds flaring glasse.
A Diamond set in lead his worth retaines,　　215
A heavenly Nimph, belov'd of humane swaines,
Receives no blemish, but oft-times more grace,
Which makes me hope, although I am but base,
Base in respect of thee, divine and pure,
Dutifull service may thy love procure,　　220
And I in dutie will excell all other,
As thou in beautie doest exceed Loves mother.
Nor heaven, nor thou, were made to gaze upon,
As heaven preserves all things, so save thou one.
A stately builded ship, well rig'd and tall,　　225
The Ocean maketh more majesticall:
Why vowest thou then to live in *Sestos* here,
Who on Loves seas more glorious wouldst appeare?
Like untun'd golden strings all women are,
Which long time lie untoucht, will harshly jarre.　　230
Vessels of Brasse oft handled, brightly shine,
What difference betwixt the richest mine
And basest mold, but use? for both not us'de,
Are of like worth. Then treasure is abus'de,

When misers keepe it; being put to lone,   235
In time it will returne us two for one.
Rich robes, themselves and others do adorne,
Neither themselves nor others, if not worne.
Who builds a pallace and rams up the gate,
Shall see it ruinous and desolate.   240
Ah simple *Hero*, learne thy selfe to cherish,
Lone women like to emptie houses perish.
Lesse sinnes the poore rich man that starves himselfe,
In heaping up a masse of drossie pelfe,
Than such as you: his golden earth remains,   245
Which after his disceasse, some other gains.
But this faire jem, sweet in the losse alone,
When you fleet hence, can be bequeath'd to none.
Or if could, downe from th'enameld skie,
All heaven would come to claime this legacie,   250
And with intestine broiles the world destroy,
And quite confound natures sweet harmony.
Well therefore by the gods decreed it is,
We humane creatures should enjoy that blisse.
One is no number, mayds are nothing then,   255
Without the sweet societie of men.
Wilt thou live single still? one shalt thou bee,
Though never-singling *Hymen* couple thee.
Wild savages, that drinke of running springs,
Thinke water farre excels all earthly things: 260
But they that dayly tast neat wine, despise it.
Virginitie, albeit some highly prise it,
Compar'd with marriage, had you tried them both,
Differs as much, as wine and water doth.
Base boullion for the stampes sake we allow,   265
Even so for mens impression do we you.
By which alone, our reverend fathers say,
Women receave perfection everie way.
This idoll which you terme *Virginitie*,
Is neither essence subject to the eie,   270
No, nor to any one exterior sence,
Nor hath it any place of residence,

247 sweet in] *Q8*; ~, *Q1–7*

Nor is't of earth or mold celestiall,
Or capable of any forme at all.
Of that which hath no being, doe not boast,   275
Things that are not at all, are never lost.
Men foolishly doe call it vertuous,
What vertue is it, that is borne with us?
Much lesse can honour bee ascrib'd thereto,
Honour is purchac'd by the deedes wee do.   280
Beleeve me *Hero*, honour is not wone,
Untill some honourable deed be done.
Seeke you for chastitie, immortall fame,
And know that some have wrong'd *Dianas* name?
Whose name is it, if she be false or not,   285
So she be faire, but some vile toongs will blot?
But you are faire (aye me) so wondrous faire,
So yoong, so gentle, and so debonaire,
As *Greece* will thinke, if thus you live alone,
Some one or other keepes you as his owne.   290
Then *Hero* hate me not, nor from me flie,
To follow swiftly blasting infamie.
Perhaps, thy sacred Priesthood makes thee loath,
Tell me, to whom mad'st thou that heedlesse oath?
    To *Venus*, answered shee, and as shee spake,   295
Foorth from those two tralucent cesternes brake,
A streame of liquid pearle, which downe her face
Made milk-white paths, whereon the gods might trace
To *Joves* high court. Hee thus replide: The rites
In which Loves beauteous Empresse most delites,   300
Are banquets, Dorick musicke, midnight-revell,
Plaies, maskes, and all that stern age counteth evill.
Thee as a holy Idiot doth she scorne,
For thou in vowing chastitie, hast sworne
To rob her name and honour, and thereby   305
Commit'st a sinne far worse than perjurie.
Even sacrilege against her Dietie,
Through regular and formall puritie.
To expiat which sinne, kisse and shake hands,
Such sacrifice as this, *Venus* demands.   310
    Thereat she smil'd, and did denie him so,
As put thereby, yet might he hope for mo.

Which makes him quickly re-enforce his speech,
And her in humble manner thus beseech.
    Though neither gods nor men may thee deserve,   315
Yet for her sake whom you have vow'd to serve,
Abandon fruitlesse cold Virginitie,
The gentle queene of Loves sole enemie.
Then shall you most resemble *Venus* Nun,
When *Venus* sweet rites are perform'd and done.   320
Flint-brested *Pallas* joies in single life,
But *Pallas* and your mistresse are at strife,
Love *Hero* then, and be not tirannous,
But heale the heart, that thou hast wounded thus,
Nor staine thy youthfull years with avarice,   325
Faire fooles delight, to be accounted nice.
The richest corne dies, if it be not reapt,
Beautie alone is lost, too warily kept.
These arguments he us'de, and many more,
Wherewith she yeelded, that was woon before.   330
Heroes lookes yeelded, but her words made warre,
Women are woon when they begin to jarre.
Thus having swallow'd *Cupids* golden hooke,
The more she striv'd, the deper was she strooke.
Yet evilly faining anger, strove she still,   335
And would be thought to graunt against her will.
So having paus'd a while, at last she said:
Who taught thee Rhethoricke to deceive a maid?
Aye me, such words as these should I abhor,
And yet I like them for the Orator.   340
    With that *Leander* stoopt, to have imbrac'd her,
But from his spreading armes away she cast her,
And thus bespake him; Gentle youth forbeare
To touch the sacred garments which I weare.
    Upon a rocke, and underneath a hill,   345
Far from the towne (where all is whist and still,
Save that the sea playing on yellow sand,
Sends foorth a ratling murmure to the land,
Whose sound allures the golden *Morpheus*,
In silence of the night to visite us.)   350
My turret stands, and there God knowes I play
With *Venus* swannes and sparrowes all the day,

A dwarfish beldame beares me companie,
That hops about the chamber where I lie,
And spends the night (that might be better spent)   355
In vaine discourse, and apish merriment.
Comt thither; As she spake this, her toong tript,
For unawares (*Come thither*) from her slipt,
And sodainly her former colour chang'd,
And here and there her eies through anger rang'd   360
And like a planet, mooving severall waies,
At one selfe instant, she poore soule assaies,
Loving, not to love at all, and everie part,
Strove to resist the motions of her hart.
And hands so pure, so innocent, nay such,   365
As might have made heaven stoope to have a touch,
Did she uphold to *Venus* and againe,
Vow'd spotlesse chastitie, but all in vaine,
Cupid bears downe her praiers with his wings,
Her vowes above the emptie aire he flings: 370
All deepe enrag'd, his sinowie bow he bent,
And shot a shaft that burning from him went,
Wherewith she strooken, look'd so dolefully,
As made Love sigh, to see his tirannie.
And as she wept, her teares to pearle he turn'd,   375
And wound them on his arme, and for her mourn'd.
Then towards the pallace of the Destinies,
Laden with languishment and griefe he flies.
And to those sterne nymphs humblie made request,
Both might enjoy ech other, and be blest.   380
But with a ghastly dreadfull countenaunce,
Threatning a thousand deaths at everie glaunce,
They answered Love, nor would vouchsafe so much
As one poore word, their hate to him was such.
Harken a while, and I will tell you why: 385
Heavens winged herrald, *Jove-borne Mercury*,
The selfe-same day that he asleepe had layd
Inchaunted *Argus*, spied a countrie mayd,
Whose carelesse haire, in stead of pearle t'adorne it,
Glistered with deaw, as one that seem'd to skorne it;   390
Her breath as fragrant as the morning rose,
Her mind pure, and her toong untaught to glose,

Yet prowd she was, (for loftie pride that dwels
In tow'red courts, is oft in sheapheards cels.)
And too too well the faire vermillion knew,   395
 o And silver tincture of her cheekes, that drew
The love of everie swaine: On her, this god
Enamoured was, and with his snakie rod,
Did charme her nimble feet, and made her stay
The while upon a hillocke downe he lay   400
And sweetly on his pipe began to play,
And with smooth speech, her fancie to assay,
Till in his twining armes he lockt her fast,
And then he woo'd with kisses, and at last,
As sheap-heards do, her on the ground hee layd,   405
And tumbling in the grasse, he often strayd
Beyond the bounds of shame, in being bold
 o To eie those parts, which no eie should behold.
And like an insolent commaunding lover,
Boasting his parentage, would needs discover   410
The way to new *Elisium*: but shee,
 o Whose only dower was her chastitie,
Having striv'ne in vaine, was now about to crie,
And crave the helpe of sheap-heards that were nie.
Herewith he stayd his furie, and began   415
To give her leave to rise, away she ran,
After went *Mercurie*, who us'd such cunning,
As she to heare his tale, left off her running.
 o Maids are not woon by brutish force and might,   ·
 o But speeches full of pleasure and delight.   420
And knowing *Hermes* courted her, was glad
That she such lovelinesse and beautie had
As could provoke his liking, yet was mute,
And neither would denie, nor graunt his sute.
Still vowed he love, she wanting no excuse   425
To feed him with delaies, as women use:
Or thirsting after immortalitie,
All women are ambitious naturallie,
Imposed upon her lover such a taske,
As he ought not performe, nor yet she aske.   430
A draught of flowing *Nectar*, she requested,
Wherewith the king of Gods and men is feasted,

He readie to accomplish what she wil'd,
Stole some from *Hebe* (*Hebe*, *Joves* cup fil'd,)
And gave it to his simple rustike love,   435
Which being knowne (as what is hid from *Jove*)
He inly storm'd, and waxt more furious,
Than for the fire filcht by *Prometheus*;
And thrusts him down from heaven, he wandring here,
In mournfull tearmes, with sad and heavie cheare   440
Complaind to *Cupid*, *Cupid* for his sake,
To be reveng'd on *Jove* did undertake,
And those on whom heaven, earth and hell relies,
I mean the Adamantine Destinies,
He wounds with love, and forst them equallie,   445
○ To dote upon deceitfull *Mercurie*.
They offred him the deadly fatall knife,
That sheares the slender threads of humane life,
At his faire feathered feet, the engins layd,
Which th'earth from ougly *Chaos* den up-wayd: 450
These he regarded not, but did intreat,
That *Jove*, usurper of his fathers seat,
Might presently be banisht into hell,
And aged *Saturne* in *Olympus* dwell.
They granted what he crav'd, and once againe,   455
Saturne and *Ops*, began their golden raigne.
○ Murder, rape, warre, lust and trecherie,
Were with *Jove* clos'd in *Stigian* Emperie.
But long this blessed time continued not,
As soone as he his wished purpose got,   460
He recklesse of his promise, did despise
The love of th'everlasting Destinies.
They seeing it, both *Love* and him abhor'd,
And *Jupiter* unto his place restor'd.
And but that Learning, in despight of Fate,   465
Will mount aloft, and enter heaven gate,
And to the seat of *Jove* it selfe advaunce,
Hermes had slept in hell with Ignoraunce
Yet as a punishment they added this,
○ That he and *Povertie* should alwaies kis.   470

463 *Love*] love *Qq*   468 Ignoraunce] ignoraunce *Qq*

And to this day is everie scholler poore,
Grosse gold, from them runs headlong to the boore.
Likewise the angrie sisters thus deluded,
To venge themselves on *Hermes*, have concluded
That *Midas* brood shall sit in Honors chaire, 475
To which the *Muses* sonnes are only heire:
And fruitfull wits that in aspiring are,
Shall discontent, run into regions farre;
And few great lords in vertuous deeds shall joy,
But be surpris'd with every garish toy. 480
And still inrich the loftie servile clowne,
Who with incroching guile, keepes learning downe.
Then muse not, *Cupids* sute no better sped,
Seeing in their loves, the Fates were injured.
  By this, sad *Hero*, with love unacquainted, 485
Viewing *Leanders* face, fell downe and fainted.
He kist her, and breath'd life into her lips,
Wherewith as one displeas'd, away she trips.
Yet as she went, full often look'd behind,
And many poore excuses did she find, 490
To linger by the way, and once she stayd,
And would have turn'd againe, but was afrayd,
In offring parlie, to be counted light,
So on she goes, and in her idle flight,
Her painted fanne of curled plumes let fall, 495
Thinking to traine *Leander* therewithall.
He being a novice, knew not what she meant,
But stayd, and after her a letter sent.
Which joyfull *Hero* answered in such sort,
As he had hope to scale the beauteous fort, 500
Wherein the liberall Graces lock'd their wealth,
And therefore to her tower he got by stealth.
Wide open stood the doore, hee need not clime,
And she her selfe before the pointed time,
Had spread the boord, with roses strowed the roome, 505
And oft look't out, and mus'd he did not come.
At last he came, O who can tell the greeting,
These greedie lovers had, at their first meeting.
He askt, she gave, and nothing was denied,
Both to each other quickly were affied. 510

Looke how their hands, so were their hearts united,
And what he did, she willingly requited.
(Sweet are the kisses, the imbracements sweet,
When like desires and affections meet,
For from the earth to heaven, is *Cupid* rais'd,   515
Where fancie is in equall ballance pais'd.)
Yet she this rashnesse sodainly repented,
And turn'd aside, and to her selfe lamented.
As if her name and honour had beene wrong'd,
By being possest of him for whom she long'd;   520
I, and shee wisht, albeit not from her hart,
That he would leave her turret and depart.
The mirthfull God of amorous pleasure smil'd,
To see how he this captive Nymph beguil'd.
For hitherto hee did but fan the fire,   525
And kept it downe that it might mount the hier.
Now waxt she jealous, least his love abated,
Fearing, her owne thoughts made her to be hated.
Therefore unto him hastily she goes,
And like light *Salmacis*, her body throes   530
Upon his bosome, where with yeelding eyes,
She offers up her selfe a sacrifice,
To slake his anger, if he were displeas'd,
O what god would not therewith be appeas'd?
Like *Aesops* cocke, this jewell he enjoyed,   535
And as a brother with his sister toyed,
Supposing nothing else was to be done,
Now he her favour and good will had wone.
But know you not that creaturess wanting sence,
By nature have a mutuall appetence,   540
And wanting organs to advance a step,
Mov'd by Loves force, unto ech other lep?
Much more in subjects having intellect,
Some hidden influence breeds like effect.
Albeit *Leander* rude in Love, and raw,   545
Long dallying with *Hero*, nothing saw
That might delight him more, yet he suspected
Some amorous rites or other were neglected.
Therefore unto his bodie, hirs he clung,
She, fearing on the rushes to be flung,   550

Striv'd with redoubled strength, the more she strived,
The more a gentle pleasing heat revived,
Which taught him all that elder lovers know,
And now the same gan so to scorch and glow,
As in plaine termes (yet cunningly) he crav'd it,   555
Love alwaies makes those eloquent that have it.
Shee, with a kind of graunting, put him by it,
And ever as he thought himselfe most nigh it,
Like to the tree of *Tantalus* she fled,
And seeming lavish, sav'de her maydenhead.   560
Ne're king more sought to keepe his diademe,
Than *Hero* this inestimable gemme.
Above our life we love a stedfast friend,
Yet when a token of great worth we send,
We often kisse it, often looke thereon,   565
And stay the messenger that would be gon:
No marvell then, though *Hero* would not yeeld
So soone to part from that she deerely held.
Jewels being lost are found againe, this never,
T''is lost but once, and once lost, lost for ever.   570
   Now had the morne espy'de her lovers steeds,
Whereat she starts, puts on her purple weeds,
And red for anger that he stayd so long,
All headlong throwes her selfe the clouds among,
And now *Leander* fearing to be mist,   575
Imbrast her sodainly, tooke leave, and kist.
Long was he taking leave, and loath to go,
And kist againe, as lovers use to do.
Sad *Hero* wroong him by the hand, and wept,
Saying, let your vowes and promises be kept.   580
Then standing at the doore, she turnd about,
As loath to see *Leander* going out.
And now the sunne that through th' orizon peepes,
As pittying these lovers, downeward creepes.
So that in silence of the cloudie night,   585
Though it was morning, did he take his flight.
But what the secret trustie night conceal'd,
Leanders amorous habit soone reveal'd,
With *Cupids* myrtle was his bonet crownd,
About his armes the purple riband wound,   590

Wherewith she wreath'd her largely spreading heare,
Nor could the youth abstaine, but he must weare
The sacred ring wherewith she was endow'd,
When first religious chastitie she vow'd:
Which made his love through *Sestos* to bee knowne,   595
And thence unto *Abydus* sooner blowne,
Than he could saile, for incorporeal Fame,
Whose waight consists in nothing but her name,
Is swifter than the wind, whose tardie plumes,
Are reeking water, and dull earthlie fumes.   600
Home when he came he seem'd not to be there,
But like exiled aire thrust from his sphere,
Set in a forren place, and straight from thence,
Alcides like, by mightie violence,
He would have chac'd away the swelling maine,   605
That him from her unjustly did detaine,
Like as the sunne in a Dyameter,
Fires and inflames objects remooved farre,
And heateth kindly, shining lat'rally;
So beautie, sweetly quickens when t'is ny,   610
But being separated and remooved,
Burnes where it cherisht, murders where it loved.
Therefore even as an Index to a booke,
So to his mind was yoong *Leanders* looke.
O none but gods have power their love to hide,   615
Affection by the count'nance is describe.
The light of hidden fire it selfe discovers,
And love that is conceal'd, betraies poore lovers.
His secret flame apparantly was seene,
Leanders Father knew where hee had beene,   620
And for the same mildly rebuk't his sonne,
Thinking to quench the sparckles new begonne.
But love resisted once, growes passionate,
And nothing more than counsaile, lovers hate.
For as a hote prowd horse highly disdaines,   625
To have his head control'd, but breakes the raines,
Spits foorth the ringled bit, and with his hoves,
Checkes the submissive ground: so hee that loves,
The more he is restrain'd, the woorse he fares,
What is it now, but mad *Leander* dares?   630

O *Hero*, *Hero*, thus he cry'd full oft,
And then he got him to a rocke aloft.
Where having spy'de her tower, long star'd he on't,
And pray'd the narrow toyling *Hellespont*,
To part in twaine, that hee might come and go,   635
But still the rising billowes answered no.
With that hee stript him to the yv'rie skin,
And crying, Love I come, leapt lively in.
Whereat the saphir visag'd god grew prowd,
And made his capring *Triton* sound alowd,   640
Imagining, that *Ganimed* displeas'd,
Had left the heavens, therefore on him hee seaz'd.
Leander striv'd, the waves about him wound,
And puld him to the bottome, where the ground
Was strewd with pearle, and in low corrall groves,   645
Sweet singing Meremaids, sported with their loves
On heapes of heavie gold, and tooke greate pleasure,
To spurne in carelesse sort, the shipwracke treasure.
For here the stately azure pallace stood,
Where kingly *Neptune*, and his traine abode.   650
The lustie god imbrast him, cald him love,
And swore he never should returne to *Jove*.
But when he knew it was not *Ganimed*,
For under water he was almost dead,
He heav'd him up, and looking on his face,   655
Beat downe the bold waves with his triple mace,
Which mounted up, intending to have kist him,
And fell in drops like teares, because they mist him.
Leander being up, began to swim,
And looking backe, saw *Neptune* follow him.   660
Whereat agast, the poore soule gan to crie,
O let mee visite *Hero* ere I die.
The god put *Helles* bracelet on his arme,
And swore the sea should never doe him harme.
He clapt his plumpe cheekes, and with his tresses playd,   665
And smiling wantonly, his love bewrayd.
He watcht his armes, and as they opend wide,
At every stroke, betwixt them would he slide,
And steale a kisse, and then run out and daunce,
And as he turnd, cast many a lustfull glaunce,   670

And threw him gawdie toies to please his eie,
And dive into the water, and there prie
Upon his brest, his thighs, and everie lim,
And up againe, and close beside him swim,
And talke of love: *Leander* made replie,   675
You are deceav'd, I am no woman I.
Thereat smilde *Neptune*, and then told a tale,
How that a sheapheard sitting in a vale,
Playd with a boy so faire and kind,
As for his love, both earth and heaven pyn'd,   680
That of the cooling river durst not drinke,
Least water-nymphs should pull him from the brinke.
And when hee sported in the fragrant lawnes,
Gote-footed Satyrs, and up-staring Fawnes,
Would steale him thence. Ere halfe this tale was done,   685
Aye me, *Leander* cryde, th'enamoured sunne,
That now should shine on *Thetis* glassie bower,
Descends upon my radiant *Heroes* tower.
O that these tardie armes of mine were wings,
And as he spake, upon the waves he springs.   690
Neptune was angrie that he gave no eare,
And in his heart revenging malice bare:
He flung at him his mace, but as it went,
He cald it in, for love made him repent.
The mace returning backe, his owne hand hit,   695
As meaning to be veng'd for darting it.
When this fresh bleeding wound *Leander* viewd,
His colour went and came, as if he rewd
The greefe which *Neptune* felt. In gentle brests,
Relenting thoughts, remorse and pittie rests.   700
And who have hard hearts, and obdurat minds,
But vicious, harebraind, and illit'rat hinds?
The god seeing him with pittie to be moved,
Thereon concluded that he was beloved.
(Love is too full of faith, too credulous,   705
With follie and false hope deluding us.)
Wherefore *Leanders* fancie to surprize,
To the rich *Ocean* for gifts he flies.
'Tis wisedome to give much, a gift prevailes,
When deepe perswading Oratorie failes.   710

By this *Leander* being nere the land,
Cast downe his wearie feet, and felt the sand.
Breathlesse albeit he were, he rested not,
Till to the solitarie tower he got.
And knockt and cald, at which celestiall noise,   715
The longing heart of *Hero* much more joies
Then nymphs & sheapheards, when the timbrell rings,
Or crooked Dolphin when the sailer sings;
She stayd not for her robes, but straight arose,
And drunke with gladnesse, to the dore she goes.   720
Where seeing a naked man, she scriecht for feare,
Such sights as this, to tender maids are rare.
And ran into the darke her selfe to hide,
Rich jewels in the darke are soonest spide.
Unto her was he led, or rather drawne,   725
By those white limmes, which sparckled through the lawne.
The neerer that he came, the more she fled,
And seeking refuge, slipt into her bed.
Whereon *Leander* sitting, thus began,
Through numming cold, all feeble, faint and wan: 730
     If not for love, yet love for pittie sake,
Me in thy bed and maiden bosome take,
At least vouchsafe these armes some little roome,
Who hoping to imbrace thee, cherely swome.
This head was beat with manie a churlish billow,   735
And therefore let it rest upon thy pillow.
Herewith afrighted *Hero* shrunke away,
And in her luke-warme place *Leander* lay.
Whose lively heat like fire from heaven fet,
Would animate grosse clay, and higher set   740
The drooping thoughts of base declining soules,
Then drerie *Mars*, carowsing *Nectar* boules.
His hands he cast upon her like a snare,
She overcome with shame and sallow feare,
Like chast *Diana*, when *Acteon* spyde her,   745
Being sodainly betraide, dyv'd downe to hide her.
And as her silver body downeward went,
With both her hands she made the bed a tent,
And in her owne mind thought her selfe secure,
O'recast with dim and darksome coverture.   750

And now she lets him whisper in her eare,
Flatter, intreat, promise, protest and sweare,
Yet ever as he greedily assayd
To touch those dainties, she the *Harpey* playd,
And every lim did as a soldier stout,   755
Defend the fort, and keep the foe-man out.
For though the rising yv'rie mount he scal'd,
Which is with azure circling lines empal'd,
Much like a globe, (a globe may I tearme this,
By which love sailes to regions full of blis,)   760
Yet there with *Sysiphus* he toyld in vaine,
Till gentle parlie did the truce obtaine.
Wherein Leander on her quivering brest,
Breathlesse spoke something, and sigh'd out the rest;
Which so prevail'd, as he with small ado,   765
Inclos'd her in his armes and kist her to.
And everie kisse to her was as a charme,
And to *Leander* as a fresh alarme.
So that the truce was broke, and she alas,
(Poore sillie maiden) at his mercie was.   770
Love is not full of pittie (as men say)
But deaffe and cruell, where he meanes to pray.
Even as a bird, which in our hands we wring,
Foorthe plungeth, and oft flutters with her wing,
She trembling strove, this strife of hers (like that   775
Which made the world) another world begat,
Of unknowne joy. Treason was in her thought,
And cunningly to yeeld her selfe she sought.
Seeming not woon, yet woon she was at length,
In such warres women use but halfe their strength.   780
Leander now like Theban *Hercules*,
Entred the orchard of Th'*esperides*,
Whose fruit none rightly can describe, but hee
That puls or shakes it from the golden tree;
And now she wisht this night were never done,   785
And sigh'd to thinke upon th'approching sunne,
For much it greeved her that the bright day light,
Should know the pleasure of this blessed night,

763–74 Wherein ... wing] *Tucker Brooke; in all Qq these lines are printed after the present*
784

And them like *Mars* and *Ericine* displayd,
Both in each others armes chaind as they layd.   790
Againe she knew not how to frame her looke,
Or speake to him who in a moment tooke,
That which so long so charily she kept,
And faine by stealth away she would have crept,
And to some corner secretly have gone,   795
Leaving *Leander* in the bed alone.
But as her naked feet were whipping out,
He on the suddaine cling'd her so about,
That Meremaid-like unto the floor she slid,
One halfe appear'd the other halfe was hid.   800
Thus neere the bed she blushing stood upright,
And from her countenance behold ye might,
A kind of twilight breake, which through the heare,
As from an orient cloud, glymse here and there.
And round about the chamber this false morne,   805
Brought foourth the day before the day was borne.
So *Heroes* ruddie cheeke, *Hero* betrayd,
And her all naked to his sight displayd.
Whence his admiring eyes more pleasure tooke,
Than *Dis*, on heapes of gold fixing his looke.   810
By this *Appollos* golden harpe began,
To sound foorth musicke to the *Ocean*,
Which watchfull *Hesperus* no sooner heard,
But he the days bright-bearing Car prepar'd.
And ran before, as Harbenger of light,   815
And with his flaring beamess mockt ougly night,
Till she o'recome with anguish, shame, and rage,
Dang'd downe to hell her loathsome carriage.

Desunt nonnulla

789 them] *Broughton MS*; then *Qq*   814 days] *Broughton MS*; day *Qq*

MISCELLANEOUS

The Passionate Shepherd

INTRODUCTION

IN his agitation and 'trempling of mind', Sir Hugh Evans tries in the words of a popular song to let his mind stray

> To shallow rivers, to whose falls
> Melodious birds sing madrigals:
> There will we make our peds of roses,
> And a thousand fragrant posies.
> (*Merry Wives of Windsor*, II. iii. 15–18)

The incongruity between the singer and the song is no more comic than that achieved by Marlowe himself when Ithamore, the villainous Turkish slave in *The Jew of Malta*, is moved to parody the strains of pastoral amorousness in his declaration to the prostitute Bellamira

> Thou in those Groves, by *Dis* above,
> Shalt live with me and be my love. (IV. ii. 97–8)

Much later, Izaak Walton's compleat angler heard a milkmaid singing, and recognized 'that smooth song which was made by Kit Marlowe, now at least fifty years ago'. Such testimonies bear witness to the enduring popularity of the lyric, which was first published in the selection of poems—many of them by Shakespeare—printed by W. Jaggard in 1599 with the title *The Passionate Pilgrim*. The poem is unascribed, and consists of only four stanzas. Another anthology, *Englands Helicon*, was published the following year (1600); here the poem has six stanzas, and the writer's name is given as 'Chr. Marlow'. As well as these printed texts, there are manuscript copies—in commonplace books— which supply further evidence of the song's widespread appeal. Its 'invitation' theme is traditional, and has been traced back to Theocritus and Virgil,[1] while its tune provided the accompaniment to several other ballads, and seems to have been among the most pervasive airs of its period.[2]

---

[1] See R. S. Forsythe, '*The Passionate Shepherd*; and English Poetry', *PMLA*, xl (1925), 692–742.

[2] See Frederick W. Sternfeld and Mary Joiner Chan, 'Come live with me and be my love', *Comparative Literature* (published by the University of Oregon), xxii. 2 (1970), 97–187.

Not surprisingly, variant readings abound in the manuscript versions, and in the songs recollected by the Windsor parson and the Staffordshire fisherman. To my mind, such variants testify only to the fallibility of human memory; and even the accretions in Walton's version are more probably due to inventive popular demand than bibliographical discovery. As such, their place is with the history of balladry—and they are not included in the present edition. I have elected to include *both* early printed texts of the poem, however, on the grounds that the shorter version in *The Passionate Pilgrim* might have been an early draft for the poem as it appears fully in *Englands Helicon*—a situation which would be comparable to that which I believe obtained with the ten translations of Ovid's *Amores* which are printed in all three early texts of Marlowe's *Elegies*. The version from *The Passionate Pilgrim* is from the edition preserved in the library of Trinity College, Cambridge (and reproduced in facsimile by Joseph Quincy Adams in the Folger Shakespeare Library Publications, 1939). The text from *Englands Helicon* is that of the British Library copy (c.39.3.48).

From *The Passionate Pilgrim*

Live with me and be my Love,
And we will all the pleasures prove
That hilles and vallies, dales and fields,
And all the craggy mountaines yeeld.

There will we sit upon the Rocks,
And see the Shepheards feed their flocks,
By shallow Rivers, by whose fals
Melodious birds sing Madrigals.

There will I make thee a bed of Roses,
With a thousand fragrant poses,
A cap of flowers, and a Kirtle
Imbrodered all with leaves of Mirtle.

A belt of straw and Yvye buds,
With Corall Clasps and Amber studs,
And if these pleasures may thee move,
Then live with me, and be my Love.

From *Englands Helicon*

The passionate Sheepheard to his love.

Come live with mee, and be my love,
And we will all the pleasures prove,
That Vallies, groves, hills and fieldes,
Woods, or steepie mountaine yeeldes.

And wee will sit upon the Rocks,
Seeing the Sheepheards feede theyr flocks,
By shallow Rivers, to whose falls,
Melodious byrds sing Madrigalls.

And I will make thee beds of Roses,
And a thousand fragrant poesies,
A cap of flowers, and a kirtle,
Imbroydred all with leaves of Mirtle.

A gowne made of the finest wooll,
Which from our pretty Lambes we pull,
Fayre lined slippers for the cold:
With buckles of the purest gold.

A belt of straw, and Ivie buds,
With Corall clasps and Amber studs,
And if these pleasures may thee move,
Come live with mee, and be my love.

The Sheepheards Swaines shall daunce & sing,
For thy delight each May-morning,
If these delights thy minde may move;
Then live with mee, and be my love.

FINIS.   *Chr. Marlow.*

Latin Writings

INTRODUCTION

A SINGLE (but complicated) event in Marlowe's life may be the explanation for two occasional pieces, the first a dedication, in Latin prose, of Thomas Watson's *Amintae Gaudia* (published in 1592); the second an epitaph, in Latin hexameters, for Roger Manwood, a Kentishman with Canterbury connections—including friendship with Archbishop Parker. The event which links the two was a street brawl in 1589 when Marlowe, walking in London's Hog Lane, drew his sword in a fight against Watson's enemy—one William Bradley. Bradley was killed, and both Marlowe and Watson were committed to Newgate Prison. They were acquitted (on grounds of having acted in 'self-defence'); but when Marlowe appeared for the formal hearing of the case, he found that one of the judges on the Bench was Roger Manwood, then Chief Baron of the Exchequer. The latter died in 1592.

The dedicatory epistle, signed 'C.M.', is without serious problems of attribution; it is addressed to Mary, Countess of Pembroke, to whom Marlowe was probably unknown, but who was renowned for the generosity and graciousness of her literary patronage. She was the sister of Sir Philip Sidney, and it was for her that Sidney wrote his prose romance *The Arcadia* (sometimes given the full title of *The Countess of Pembroke's 'Arcadia'*). Her death in 1621 inspired (from William Browne) one of the finest of English poetic epitaphs:

> Underneath this sable Herse
> Lyes the subject of all verse:
> Sydney's sister, Pembroke's Mother:
> Death, ere thou hast slaine another,
> Faire, and Learn'd, and good as she,
> Time shall throw a dart at thee.

The Manwood epitaph has aroused some slight suspicion because it was first discovered and published by the notorious John Payne Collier, who claimed to have seen it in a 1629 copy of *Hero and Leander* which belonged to Richard Heber's library, sold by auction in 1834. The volume subsequently disappeared; but determined research by Mark Eccles has established, beyond all doubt, the authenticity of the lines.[1] For the purposes of the epitaph, Manwood may have been the *honoratissimi viri*, and his academic interests—together with Archbishop Parker he founded Sandwich grammar school—may have extended to some (unrecorded) favours to Marlowe, one of the Archbishop Parker scholars at Cambridge; but before his death he was (in the words of *The Dictionary of National Biography*) 'accused of various malpractices and arraigned before privy council'.

For this edition, fresh translations of the Latin have been made by Angus Hulton, of the University of Sheffield, who commented (in a private letter) that the two Latin passages are 'quite a *tour de force*'.

[1] Mark Eccles, 'Marlowe in Kentish Tradition', *Notes and Queries*, clxix (1935), 20–3, 39–41, 58–60, 134–5.

The Text

ILLUSTRISSIMAE HEROINAE OMNIBUS ET
ANIMI ET CORPORIS DOTIBUS ORNATISSIMAE,
MARIAE PENBROKIAE COMITISSAE

Laurigera stirpe prognata Delia, Sydnaei vatis Apollinei genuina
soror; Alma literarum parens, ad cuius immaculatos amplexus,
confugit virtus, barbariei et ignorantiae impetu violata, ut olim a
Threicio Tyranno Philomela; Poetarum nostri temporis, ingeni-
orumque omnium foelicissime pullulantium, Musa; Dia proles, 5
quae iam rudi calamo, spiritus infundis elati furoris, quibus ipse
misellus, plus mihi videor praestare posse, quam cruda nostra
indoles proferre solet: Dignare Posthumo huic Amyntae, ut tuo
adoptivo filio patrocinari: Eoque magis quod moribundus pater,
illius tutelam humillime tibi legaverat. Et licet illustre nomen 10
tuum non solum apud nos, sed exteras etiam nationes, latius
propagatum est, quam ut unquam possit aeruginosa Temporis
vetustate aboleri, aut mortalium encomiis augeri, (quomodo enim
quicquam possit esse infinito plus?) multorum tamen camaenis,
quasi siderum diademate redimita *Ariadne*, noli hunc purum 15
Phoebi sacerdotem, stellam alteram coronae tuae largientem,
aspernari: sed animi candore, quem sator hominum, atque
deorum, Iupiter, praenobili familiae tuae quasi haereditarium
alligavit, accipe, et tuere. Sic nos, quorum opes tenuissimae,
littorea sunt Myrtus Veneris, Nymphaeque Peneiae virens coma, 20
prima quaque poematis pagina, Te Musarum dominam, in
auxilium invocabimus: tua denique virtus, quae virtutem ipsam,
ipsam quoque aeternitatem superabit.

Honoris tui studiosissimus, C.M.

TO THE MOST ILLUSTRIOUS HEROINE,
ENDOWED WITH ALL GIFTS OF MIND AND BODY,
MARY, COUNTESS OF PEMBROKE.

Delia, born of a laureate line, the sister of Sidney, priest of Apollo; nurturing parent of literature, in whose pure embrace virtue, violated by the assault of barbarism and ignorance, has taken refuge, as once Philomela fled from the Thracian tyrant; inspiring Muse of the poets of our time and of all fruitfully budding talents; 5 divine offspring, who pour into my reed, still rude, the breath of lofty madness, by which poor I seem to myself to be able to achieve more than my crude talent is accustomed to display: deign to be a patroness to this late-born Amyntas, as to an adopted son, the more so because his father, when dying, humbly bequeathed 10 his care to you. And though your illustrious name has been so widely spread abroad, not only in our country, but also among foreign nations, that it can never be abolished by the long corrosion of time or be increased by the praises of mortals (for how can anything be greater than that which is boundless?), neverthe- 15 less, being adorned with many poems as was Ariadne with a diadem of stars, do not despise this poor priest of Phoebus as he bestows another star on your crown: but with that candour of mind which Jupiter, the father of men and gods, attached an inheritance to your noble family, receive him and guard him. Thus 20 we, whose slender resources are the sea-shore myrtle of Venus and the green foliage of the Peneian nymph, will, on every page of our poetry, summon you, as mistress of the Muses, to our aid: and finally your virtue, which exceeds virtue itself, will also exceed eternity itself. 25

Most devoted to your honour, C.M.

IN OBITUM HONORATISSIMI VIRI
ROGERI MANWOOD MILITIS,
QUAESTORII REGINALIS CAPITALIS BARONIS

Noctivagi terror, ganeonis triste flagellum,
Et Jovis Alcides, rigido vulturque latroni
Urna subtegitur. Scelerum gaudete Nepotes.
Insons luctifica sparsis cervice capillis
Plange, fori lumen, venerandae gloria legis   5
Occidit. Heu secum effoetas Acherontis ad oras
Multa abiit virtus. Pro tot virtutibus uni
Livor parce viro: non audacissimus esto
Illius in cineres, cuius tot milia vultus
Mortalium attonuit; sic cum te nuncia Ditis   10
Vulneret exsanguis, foeliciter ossa quiescant
Famaque marmorei superet monumenta sepulchri.

ON THE DEATH OF THE MOST HONOURABLE GENTLEMAN, ROGER MANWOOD, KNIGHT, LORD CHIEF BARON OF THE QUEEN'S EXCHEQUER.

Night-wanderer's terror, glutton's harshest scourge,
Reborn Alcides, vengeance on brigands due,
An urn now covers. Sons of crime, rejoice.
But, guiltless one, with hair spread o'er your neck,
Weep for the forum's light, the court's bright glow   5
Now set: with him to Acheron's waste shores
Great goodness has departed. He, one man,
Shewed many virtues; Envy, spare him now
And be not wanton where his ashes lie,
Whose face astonished thousands. So when Death   10
Strikes his last blow, may your bones gently lie
And fame outlast your marble monument.

COMMENTARY

ELEGIES
BOOK I

Elegy 1

1 We . . . lesse] In modern editions of Ovid, but not in sixteenth-century ones, these lines are often printed separately as a preface to the *Amores*.

5 upreard] At first sight it might seem that *Mason*'s 'prepar'd' is closer to Ovid's *parabam*, but *Mason* is tautologous: 'meant' is the translation of *parabam*, and 'upreard' represents the adjective in *gravi numero*. Line 21 repeats the idea of the exaltedness of the epic Muse, a not uncommon expression echoed by Marston in his Satire IX: 'O how on tiptoes proudly mounts my Muse.'

8 tooke one foote away] See General Introduction.

11 *Dianas bowe*] Ovid has *arma Minervae* here; Minerva was traditionally represented with helmet and shield (but not a bow), and like Diana was vowed to chastity.

16 *Aonian*] Aonia was another name for Boeotia, the location of Mt Helicon, home of the Muses.

19 Muses *Tempe*] *Heliconia tempe*. Ovid uses *tempe*, the name of a vale in Thessaly, with its generalized sense of 'a beautiful valley'; he makes the noun specific with *Heliconia* (=pertaining to the Muses, whose temple was on Mt Helicon). Cf. Drayton, preface to *Poly-Olbion*: 'walk forth into the *Tempe* and Feelds of the Muses.'

26 shaft ordain'de my heart to shiver] Removal of the comma between 'shaft' and 'ordain'de' more accurately conveys the meaning of Ovid's *in exitium spicula facta meum*.

33 *Elegian Muse*, that warblest amorous laies] Marlowe's is a free, but effective, rendering of Ovid's technical description: *Muse per undenos emodulanda pedes*.

34 Girt my shine browe with Sea-banke Mirtle praise] *Cingere littorea flaventia tempora myrto* | *Musa*. In the Latin it is the Muse's brow, not the poet's, that is to be bound with myrtle. For 'shine' as an adjective, cf. Spenser, *Faerie Queen*, IV. iii. 3: 'all in armour shine'. Dedicating Watson's *Amintae Gaudia* (1592) to the Countess of Pembroke, Marlowe described himself as one whose *opes tenuissimae*, *littorea sunt Myrtus Veneris*. Dyce's emendation of 'praise' to 'sprays' has been followed by all succeeding editors except Bowers. But the reading of the early editions makes sense; and it is difficult to see how any confusion of 'praise' and 'sprays' could have arisen for the compositor.

Elegy 2

1 is soft] *Bindley*'s variant, 'is so soft', can probably be accounted for by the

layout of the page: the compositor may have started 'soft', found there was not enough room on the line, and printed the whole word above the line, forgetting to remove the 'so'.

7 'Twas so] *Sic erat*; modern texts, *erit*.

12 shakt] *concutiente*.

16 managde] schooled (*OED v.* 1).

20 for thee to tie] *ad tua vincla*; modern texts, *ad tua iura*.

24 *Vulcan*] Commentators, including Dominicus, say that Mars is meant by Ovid's *vitricus*; but Marlowe could be correct in his identification of Cupid's step-father with the husband of Venus (Mars was his father). Furthermore, as the divine blacksmith, Vulcan would be more likely to present the chariots.

31 Good meaning] *Mens bona*; Martin suggests an analogous usage in *King Lear*, I. ii. 172: 'I am no honest man, if there be any good meaning toward you,' but Ovid's meaning here is rather 'good sense' or 'prudence'.

34 *Io*, triumphing] Tucker Brooke emended here to '*triumphe*', but although this is a better rendering of the Latin, *Io magna voce triumphe*, it cannot be justified.

35 feare] *terrorque*; modern texts, *errorque*.

47 having conquer'd *Inde*] After visiting Greece and the Greek Islands, Bacchus travelled east, through Lebanon and over the Euphrates, to India, taking civilization with him. Other accounts make him an Oriental deity originally.

Elegy 3

13 which but to Gods gives place] *non cessuri nisi dis*; modern texts, *nulli cessura fides*.

21 horned *Io*] To protect his mistress from his wife's jealousy, Jupiter turned Io, the daughter of Inachus, an Argive river-god, into a heifer.

22 she to whom in shape of Swanne *Jove* came] Jupiter disguised himself as a swan for the seduction of Leda, wife of Tyndareus, King of Sparta.

23 she that on a fain'd Bull swamme to land] In the form of a bull, Jupiter abducted Europa, daughter of Agenor, King of Tyre, from her home in Phoenicia, and carried her on his back to Crete.

24 false] *falsa*; modern texts, *vara*.

Elegy 4

7 the faire Bride] Hippodamia, at whose wedding to Pirithous, the Centaurs, drunk, offered violence and so began the battle with the Lapithae, who were led by Hercules and Theseus.

34 Gobbets] *libatos ... cibos*.

35 vile] *indignis*; modern texts, *inpositis*.

62 to the dores sight of thy selfe keepe] Robinson and all succeeding editors read 'selfe [will] keepe'. It seems possible, however, that 'dores' was read as a disyllable in the same way as 'poore' in I. viii. 28.

Elegy 5

11 *Semiramis*] An Assyrian queen of great beauty, whose husband Ninus resigned the crown of Assyria to her under duress; legend attributed to her the building of Babylon.

12 *Layis*] A celebrated courtesan of Corinth in the fourth century BC.

wooers] Justifying his choice of the *Bindley* and *Isham* reading 'lovers', Bowers notes: 'The term "wooers" is properly used in III. iv. 24 for those who sought Penelope; but to seek Lais was to find her. The Latin is *Lais amata viris*, which is closer to "lovers".' Lais was not so easily obtained, however: her price proved prohibitive to such suitors as Demosthenes, although he had visited Corinth for her sake alone. The Latin that Bowers quotes is the modern reading; sixteenth-century texts read *procis* for *viris*, and this word is closer in meaning to 'wooers'.

13 being thin, the harme was small] *nec multum rara nocebat*—i.e. the material was transparent, so from the poet's point of view, it did little harm.

25 being tirde she bad me kisse] The need to find a rhyme for 'this' has led Marlowe to distort the sense of Ovid's *lassi requivimus ambo*.

Elegy 6

10 Wondring if any walked without light] *Mirabar, tenebris siquis iturus erat*; modern texts have *quisquis* for *siquis*.

17 Why enviest me] *ut invideas*; modern texts, *uti videas*.

71 be like me paind] *sentique abeuntis amorem*; modern texts have *honorem* for *amorem*.

Elegy 7

7 *Ajax*] After the death of Achilles, Ajax and Ulysses disputed their claims to the arms of the dead hero; when they were given to Ulysses, Ajax slaughtered a flock of sheep, believing them in his madness to be Agamemnon and Menelaus, the sons of Atreus, who had given preference to Ulysses.

9 he who on his mother veng'd his sire] Orestes, who killed his mother, Clytemnestra, in revenge for her murder of his father, Agamemnon.

13 *Atalanta*] *Schoeneida*. In some legends Atalanta is the daughter of Schoeneus, King of Boeotia, but other versions make her the huntress daughter of Iasos and put her birth in Arcadia. Ovid seems to have conflated the two accounts.

15 *Ariadne*] The daughter of Minos, King of Crete, she fell in love with Theseus, who was imprisoned in the labyrinth to be devoured by the Minotaur. She gave him a reel of thread so that he could find his way out of the maze after slaying the Minotaur. According to his promise, he married her, and carried her to Naxos, but there he abandoned her.

17 *Cassandra*] At the sack of Troy, Cassandra, daughter of Priam and Hecuba, took refuge in the temple of Minerva. Ovid points out that the comparison with Ariadne is not quite just, in that as a suppliant at the altar, Cassandra was wearing sacred headbands (*vittatis ... capillis*), and so could not have had the 'ruffled

hayre' (line 12) of the injured mistress. Marlowe's 'Deflowr'd except' is both a misunderstanding of *vittatis . . . capillis* and a reference to the tradition that on this occasion Cassandra was raped by Ajax.

32 an other I] *alter ego*—not, as Marlowe seems to think, 'I struck another goddess', but 'I am the second to strike a goddess'.

40 white necke] Marlowe seems to be translating *candida colla*, a reading referred to but rejected by Dominicus, who has the usual *candida tota*.

Elegy 8

2 *Dipsas*] Malevole in *The Malcontent* (II. ii) addresses the bawd Maquerelle as 'Dipsas'.

3 Her name comes from the thing] *Ex re nomen habet*—i.e. *dipsas*, a serpent whose bite causes extreme thirst. Marlowe ignores the drunkenness of the bawd, which is stressed in Ovid's *non . . . sobria vidit*; his translation of *sobria* as 'wise' misses the meaning and connotation of the word.

5 *Thessale* charmes] *Aeaeaque carmina*. Ovid is speaking particularly of the enchantress Circe, whose home was the island of Aeaea. Marlowe expands the reference; from early times Thessaly was regarded as the special home of witches, including Jason and Medea: cf. *The Golden Ass* of Apuleius, *passim*, and Juvenal vi. 610.

8 Mares ranck humour] *virus amantis equae*.

28 state] Dyce suggested an emendation to 'estate' for the sake of the extra syllable, but it seems possible that 'poore' in the same line could be disyllabic; cf. I. iv. 62n.

39 the *Sabines* rude] *incultae Sabinae*; modern texts, *inmundae*.

42 her *Aeneas* Citty] Venus was the mother of Aeneas, who led the Trojan remnant to Italy to establish a new settlement, from which came the foundation of Rome.

47 *Penelope*] The wife of Ulysses, who was besieged by suitors during her husband's absence at Troy and his subsequent wanderings. She eventually agreed to marry whichever of the suitors could string her husband's bow and shoot an arrow from it; all failed, except the disguised Ulysses (*Odyssey*, xxi).

51–3 Brasse . . . spent] Cf. *Hero and Leander*, 231ff.

56 dog-kept flocks] Marlowe misread *cānīs*, the plural of the adjective *canus*, agreeing with *lupis*, as *canis*, a noun in the genitive singular belonging to *grege*.

64 The vaine name of inferiour slaves] Marlowe may have been trying to make Ovid's *gypsati crimen inane pedis* intelligible to English readers. Ovid refers to the 'inferiour slaves' who were brought from overseas to be sold in Rome, and whose feet were whitened with chalk to distinguish them from the more highly valued slaves born and bred in Italy. For *crimen* Marlowe clearly read *nomen*, a variant which Dominicus notes, but does not print.

74 *Isis*] A great Egyptian goddess, closely connected with the moon, whose cult spread to Greece and Rome; she symbolized the female generative principle

of nature, and her name is perhaps used here by Ovid as a euphemism for menstruation.

89 many asking little] Sixteenth-century texts, like modern ones, read *multos si pauca rogabunt*, but add a marginal note of the variant reading, which is the one Marlowe translates: *multi si pauca rogabunt*.

97 bed mens] As Bowers points out, *Mason*'s 'beds men' is likely to be a memorial transposition of 'bed mens'. The Latin is singular.

100 If he gives nothing, let him from thee wend] Modern texts reading *si dederit nemo, Sacra roganda Via est* make it clear that if the lovers will not give, the girl must resort to the Sacra Via—the shopping centre. Marlowe might have been confused by the reading of his text; *Si tibi nil dederit*.

Elegy 9

2 *Atticke*] A historical Atticus, Titus Pomponius (109–32 BC), was an intimate friend of Cicero, to whom the latter addressed many of his epistles. He was given this surname because he was held to be the perfect master of Greek letters. If this is the Atticus intended (and no other can be traced), the address can be no more than a conventional device, since he died when Ovid was eleven.

23 *Thracian Rhesus*] Rhesus, King of Thrace, came to the assistance of Priam in the Trojan War after an oracle had declared that Troy would not fall as long as Rhesus' horses drank the waters of the Xanthus and fed upon the Trojan plains. This oracle was known to the Greeks, and two of their best generals, Ulysses and Diomedes, were commissioned to intercept the Thracian troops. They entered Rhesus' camp by night, slew him, and carried away his horses (*Iliad*, x).

27 corps-dugard] *OED* gives earliest use as 1590.

33 *Achilles*] When Briseis was taken away from Achilles by Agamemnon, to whose lot she had fallen in the division of the spoils of Lyrnessus, Achilles sulked, and refused to join in the Trojan War; but the death of his friend Patroclus recalled him to action and revenge (*Iliad*, i).

35 *Hector*] Book VI of the *Iliad* gives a tender picture of Hector at home with his wife, Andromache, before he puts on his helmet and returns to the fight: *et, galeam capiti quae daret, uxor erat*.

37 *Agamemnon*] The Greek leader fell in love with Priam's daughter, Cassandra, who was allotted to him at the fall of Troy. Cassandra is 'loose-trest' now (instead of *vittatis ... capillis* as in 1. vii. 17), because Ovid, as the Latin makes plain, is thinking of her as the inspired prophetess: *Maenadis effusis ... comis*.

39 Mars in the deed the black-smithes net did stable] Vulcan, the blacksmith of the gods and the husband of Venus, trapped his wife and her lover, Mars, in an invisible net, and exposed them to the ridicule of the other gods.

45 watch] *vigilem*; modern texts, *agilem*.

Elegy 10

1 the cause] Helen, wife of Menelaus, abducted by the Trojan Paris, was the cause of the war between the Greeks and the Trojans.

2 from *Europa*] *ab Europa*. Dominicus has *a Graecia, quae est in Europa*; modern texts have *ab Eurota*, referring to the river Eurotas.

3 *Leda*] The wife of Tyndareus, King of Sparta, who was visited by Jupiter in the shape of a swan; she became the mother of Helen of Troy.

5 *Amimone*] A daughter of Danaus, King of Argos, Amymone aided her father in supplying water to his city during a prolonged drought. Neptune saw her at this task, fell in love with her, and carried her away; he raised a fountain in the place where she stood.

7 the Bull and Eagle] Two of Jupiter's amorous disguises. As a bull he carried Europa to Crete; as an eagle he snatched Ganymede to heaven.

15 saunce] *OED* offers this as a variant form of *sans*, whose '*archaic*' use (meaning without) is described as 'chiefly with reminiscence of Shakespeare'.

18 bosome] *sinum*. Marlowe's translation loses the sense of Ovid's joke—that Cupid, being naked, has nowhere to carry his money.

22 Cony] Ovid describes the *meretrix* who *miseras iusso corpore quaerit opes*.

32 Making her joy according to her hire] Marlowe reverses the process Ovid describes: *pretium quanti gaudeat ipsa, facit*.

37 Knights of the post] Nashe's 'Knight of the Post' describes himself as 'a fellowe that will sweare you any thing for twelve pence' (*Pierce Penilesse*, McKerrow, i. 164).

50 the holy Nunne] Tarpeia, daughter of the governor of the citadel of Rome; she promised to open the city gates to the Sabines if they would give her what they wore on their left arms. What she wanted were their bracelets, but the Sabines, as they entered the city, threw her not only their bracelets but also their shields, which crushed her to death.

51 The sonne slew her, that forth to meete him went] A commentary would have helped Marlowe here. Ovid refers to Alcmaeon, who was charged by his father to murder his mother, Eriphyle, who had been bribed with a necklace to betray him by sending him as one of the Seven against Thebes: *Ex quibus exierat, traiecit viscera ferro | Filius.*

56 lome] Martin's emendation of *Mason*'s 'love' is justified by the Latin: *praebeat Alcinoi poma benignus ager*. Alcinous, King of Phaeacia, was renowned for his love of agriculture; he was the father of Nausicaa, and entertained Ulysses during his wanderings.

Elegy 11

2 free-borne] This is Marlowe's not very accurate rendering of *nec ancillas inter habenda*.

10 But] *sed*; modern texts, *nec*.

21 some blotted letter] Marlowe does not translate literally, but gives an English equivalent to Ovid's *littera rasa*.

28 maple] On account of its hardness and firmness, maple was used for writing-tablets.

Elegy 12

10 bad hony] *Melle ... infami*. Martin explains that Corsican honey, made from yew-tree blossoms, was bitter and distasteful.

13 evill wood] *inutile lignum*.

26 banquerout] *OED* offers this as a variant form of *bankrupt*, which Marlowe uses in sense 2, meaning a 'merchant, trader or other person' who has become insolvent. Marlowe's 'merchant' is a translation of Ovid's *avarus*; the situation described is that of Shylock and Antonio.

27 Your name] They were *tabellae duplices*, double tablets, but *duplex* could also mean 'deceitful'; Ovid amplifies this thought in the next line.

Elegy 13

1 her old Love] Tithonus, son of Laomedon, King of Troy. He begged Aurora for the gift of immortality, which she granted for love of his beauty. But he neglected to ask for the continuance of this beauty and his youth, and consequently grew old. In response to his pleas for death, which she could not satisfy, the goddess changed him into a cicada.

4 *Memnon*] The son of Aurora and Tithonus, who became King of Ethiopia. He was killed during the Trojan War, when he came to assist his uncle, Priam, and his mother was so distressed at his death that she asked Jupiter to grant her son such honours as might distinguish him from other mortals. Jupiter consented, and from the funeral pyre issued a flight of birds which fought among themselves so fiercely that half of them were killed and fell into the fire to appease the spirit of Memnon. Every year the birds return to the tomb and repeat the sacrifice. (*Metamorphoses*, xiii. 583–619). In this line *Mason* reads 'from', and Dyce emends to 'for'. On the surface, this seems sensible; but since the birds both arose from the funeral pyre and were sacrificed to Aurora's son, they were in fact both 'from' and 'for' Memnon. The Latin allows for either interpretation.

33 *Cephalus*] Cephalus, husband of Procris. Aurora fell in love with him and abducted him, but he refused to accept her advances, and insisted on returning to his wife. Modern editors of Ovid see these two lines as an interpolation, and exclude them, arguing that Ovid would not have thus anticipated the thought in lines 39–40.

43 The Moone sleepes with *Endymion*] The shepherd Endymion persuaded Jupiter to grant him eternal youth and as much sleep as he wanted. Diana caught sight of him, naked, as he slept on Mt Latmos, and was so taken by his beauty that she came down from heaven every day to share his sleep. Ovid is oblique in his reference to *iuveni ... amato*, but Marlowe is tactfully explicit in this line, which seems to have been remembered by Shakespeare in *The Merchant of Venice*: 'the Moon sleeps with Endymion, And would not be awak'd' (v. i. 108).

46 *Made two nights one*] Jupiter got possession of Alcmena's bed by impersonating her husband, Amphitryon. He greatly prolonged the night which he spent in the procreation of Hercules, who was to be the most famous of mortal heroes.

47 and therefore heard me] *scires audisse*.

48 morning scard me] Marlowe's addition to Ovid.

Elegy 14

6 *Seres*] The Chinese.

26 crooked trammells] *torto ... orbe*. Robinson's emendation, substituting a name for braids or curls for *Mason*'s 'trannels' (pins or bodkins), is a better rendering of the Latin.

33 *Dione*] I cannot believe that Marlowe would have mistaken Ovid's *Dione* for Diana, although it is an error that might be expected of a compositor replacing the unknown by the known. Dione was sometimes said to be the mother of Venus, but the name was also given to Venus herself. Here, as Martin suggested, the Venus Anadyomene of Apelles must have been in Ovid's mind.

40 *Thessale* waters] The inhabitants of Thessaly were notorious for the practice of witchcraft; cf. I. viii. 5n.

49 *Guelder* dame] *Sicambram*. The Sigambri were a German tribe, whom Marlowe saw as coming from Guelderland, a former German duchy of which Guelder was the capital. The fair hair of the German tribes was much admired in Rome.

Elegy 15

In this poem Ovid enrols himself among the great poets, Greek as well as Roman, whose verse, he claims, is immortal, and whose names will never be forgotten. Homer is naturally first, with his story of the Trojan War (the *Iliad*): Tenedos (line 9) was the island opposite Troy where the Greeks hid themselves to persuade the Trojans that they had finished the siege and were going home; the River Simois (line 10) flows into the Xanthus from Mt Ida, the mountain on which Paris exercised his judgement in the beauty contest between the three goddesses which resulted in his carrying off Helen, wife of Menelaus, thereby starting the Trojan War. Ascraeus (line 11) is the name given to Hesiod, who was born at Ascra; a near-contemporary of Homer's, his verse was designed to be of practical use, and gave agricultural instruction. Callimachus (line 13) was the acknowledged leader when it came to Alexandrian poetry, and a major influence on the Roman poets, including Propertius and Ovid himself; Ovid here admits a lack of inspiration in his master's work, but finds it compensated by his technique. Sophocles (line 15) was the great Greek tragedian, while Aratus (line 16) was a Greek poet of the third century BC, especially renowned for a poem on astronomy. The cheating servants, cruel fathers, and lecherous bawds (line 17) are the stock figures of the Greek New Comedy, of whose dramatists Menander (line 18) was called the prince. Turning to the Romans, Ovid first considers Ennius (line 19), one of the earliest Roman poets, author of an eighteen-volume history of the Roman republic written in heroic verse, which he was the first to introduce into Latin poetry; he is commended by Quintilian, who blames much of the roughness of his verse on the age, not the poet. Virgil introduces many lines of Ennius' poetry into his own work. Where Marlowe next mentions Plautus (line 19), Ovid in fact speaks of Accius, another early Roman poet, this time of tragic verse. In his translation of this poem (see below), Ben Jonson retains the name Accius, but Marlowe seems to have confused this writer with M. Accius Plautus, on of the most popular comic dramatists of Rome, who died about 184 BC. Varroe (line 21) was born at Atax in 82 BC. His works have not survived, but he is celebrated for an epic poem on the Argonauts. Lucretius (line 23) (98–55 BC) is famous for his *de rerum natura*, a philosophical poem in six books; in many ways he is the Milton of Roman poetry. Tityrus (line 25) is a shepherd in Virgil's *Eclogues*, and the name is here transferred to the poet himself. In mentioning '*Aeneas* warre' (line 25), Marlowe is thinking of Virgil chiefly as author of the *Aeneid*, but Ben Jonson, in his version, takes notice of Ovid's *segetes* and speaks of 'tillage'—i.e. the *Georgics*. Tibullus (line 28) and Gallus (line 29) are Ovid's contemporaties and, like him, writers of elegiac verse; Licoris (line 30) was to Gallus' poetry what Corinna is to Ovid's.

4 dustie] ('rustie' in *Mason*); Robinson's emendation was justified by the Latin *pulverulenta*, and the misreading is one of the *d/r* confusions in these poems.

34 gold-bearing Tagus] According to the poets (e.g. Ovid, *Metamorphoses*, ii, 251), gold was concealed in the sandy bed of the Tagus (modern Tajo), which flows across Portugal into the Atlantic.

37 quivering mirtle] *metuentem frigora myrtum*; cf. I. i. 34.

41 rackes] 'The meaning here, as sufficiently illustrated in *OED vb.* II. 4 and 5b, seems to be *rake*, for which [Mason's] "racke" is an obsolete rare spelling' (Bowers).

The same poem translated by Ben Jonson

> Envie, why twitst thou me, my Time's spent ill?
> And call'st my verse fruites of an idle quill?
> Or that (unlike the line from whence I sprong)
> Wars dustie honors I pursue not young?
> Or that I studie not the tedious lawes;   5
> And prostitute my voyce in every cause?
> Thy scope is mortal; mine eternall Fame,
> Which through the world shall every chaunt my name.
> *Homer* will live, whil'st *Tenedos* stands, and *Ide*,
> Or to the sea, fleete *Simoïs* doth slide;   10
> And so shall *Hesiod* too, while vines doe beare,
> Or crooked sickles crop the ripened eare.
> *Callimachus*, though in Invention lowe,
> Shall still be sung, since he in Arte doth flowe.
> No losse shall come to *Sophocles* proud vaine,   15
> With Sunne and Moone *Aratus* shall remaine.
> Whil'st Slaves be false, Fathers hard, and Bauds be whorish,
> Whilst Harlots flatter, shall *Menander* florish.
> *Ennius*, though rude, and *Accius* high-reared straine,
> A fresh applause in every age shall gaine.   20
> Of *Varro's* name, what eare shall not be tolde?
> Of *Jasons* Argo? And the *Fleece* of *golde*?

Then, shall *Lucretius* loftie numbers die,
When Earth, and Seas in fire and flames shall frie.
Titirus, Tillage, *Aeney* shall be read,   25
Whil'st *Rome* of all the conquer'd world is head.
Till *Cupids* fires be out, and his bowe broken,
Thy verses (neate *Tibullus*) shall be spoken.
Our *Gallus* shall be known from East to west;
So shall *Licoris*, whom he now loves best.   30
The suffering Plough-share or the flint may weare:
But heavenly *Poësie* no death can feare.
Kings shall give place to it, and Kingly showes,
The bankes ore which gold-bearing *Tagus* flowes.
Kneele hindes to trash: me let bright *Phoebus* swell,   35
With cups full flowing from the *Muses* well.
The frost-drad myrtle shall impale my head,
And of sad lovers Ile be often read.
"Envy the living, not the dead, doth bite.
"For after death all men receive their right.   40
Then when this body falls in funeral fire,
My name shall live, and my best part aspire.

BOOK II

Elegy 1

2 Borne at Peligny] Ovid's birthplace was Sulmo, a town of the Paeligni in
what is now the Abruzzi; as he describes it in II. xvi. 2ff., it is a fertile valley, a
'wholesome soyl with watrie veynes' (*irriguis ora salubris aquis*).

11 the great celestiall battells] Neither Ovid nor, consequently, Marlowe
seems wholly clear about these battles. Gyges (the Latin text prints, erroneously,
Gygen, which leads to confusion with the King of Lydia) was one of the three
Hekatoncheires, the hundred-handed, who were the sons of Uranus and Ge.
They are usually represented as being friendly towards the gods, unlike the other
giants, also children of Uranus and Ge, who rose against Jupiter, and for this
were imprisoned in the earth. The piling of Ossa on Olympus and Pelion on Ossa
was the work of the Aloadai, Otos and Ephialtes, in their rebellion against the
gods.

23 deduce] The manuscript from which *Mason* was printed was subject to $d | r$
confusions: cf. 'dustie'|'rustie' (1. xv. 4). Ovid has *carmina sanguineae deducunt
cornua lunae*; and the notion is referred to by Robert Herrick in 'Charms, that call
down the moon from out her sphere'.

25 Snakes leape by verse from caves of broken mountaines] *Carmine dissiliunt
abruptis faucibus angues.*

29 of fierce *Achill* to sing] Ovid is referring to the *Iliad* and the struggle
between Achilles and Hector which ended with the death of the latter, whose
body was dragged round the walls of Troy by Achilles' horses. A difficulty arises
with the next line's 'either *Ajax*'. Marlowe's text reads *Aiaces alter, et alter*, refer-

ring to Ajax the son of Telamon, who fought with Hector in the Trojan War, and Ajax the son of Oileus (who was surnamed Locrian to distinguish him from the son of Telamon). It was this second Ajax who raped Cassandra in the temple of Minerva at the sack of Troy. Modern editions have *Atrides* for *Aiaces*, making it clear that Agamemnon and Menelaus, the two sons of Atreus, are intended.

Elegy 2

4 *Danaus* fact] Danaus became King of Argos after a quarrel with his brother Aegyptus, whose fifty sons pursued the fifty daughters of Danaus to Argos in order to marry them. Danaus was forced to consent to the marriages, but ordered his daughters to stab their husbands on the wedding night. All but one, Amymone, obeyed him, cf. I. x. 5n. Marlowe uses 'fact' in the sense of *OED* I: 'a thing done or performed'.

30 Enjoy the wench, let all else be refused] *Ille placet dominae: cetera turba iacet*; modern texts, *illa potens; alii, sordida turba, iacent*.

36 Counterfet teares] *lachrymas simulet*; in a modernized text, the Latin would justify placing a comma after 'fall' in the preceding line, ensuring that 'Counterfet' is read as a verb and not an adjective.

44 *Tantalus*] Tantalus was King of either Phrygia or Lydia. He was admitted to the society of the gods, but abused the privilege in ways about which the legends differ. One version explains that he stole the food of the gods and gave it to mortals; in another, which Ovid follows here, he is a tell-tale: Jupiter had been in the habit of confiding his plans to Tantalus, who revealed them to men. For his crime he was punished in Hades by being made to stand waist-deep in water surrounded by trees laden with delicious fruit; whenever he reached out his hand, the fruit evaded him, and whenever he leaned down to drink, the water receded.

45 *Junos* watch-man] Argus. Juno had set him to watch Io, whom Jupiter had changed into a heifer, but Mercury, by the command of Jupiter, lulled him to sleep with his lyre and then killed him. Juno placed his hundred eyes in the tail of the peacock, a bird sacred to her divinity. Some say that after her death, Io was worshipped under the name of Isis.

Elegy 3

3–4 Nashe quotes these lines in *The Unfortunate Traveller* (McKerrow, ii. 238), first in Latin and then, without comment, in Marlowe's translation.

Elegy 4

There are at least three other attractive translations of this poem dating from the late sixteenth and early seventeenth centuries. Sir John Harington and Donne both essayed verse translations, and Marston included a prose version in his play *The Fawn* (III. i).

15 a *Sabines* browe] The Sabines were renowned for the uprightness of their lives—which might give them 'sowre lookes' in a lover's eyes.

19 *Callimachus*] See note to I. xv.

42 *Leda*] The wife of Tyndareus, approached by Jupiter in the form of a swan, and thereby the mother of Helen of Troy.

Elegy 5

13 Poore wretch I sawe] *Ipse miser vidi.*

19 I knew your speech (what do not lovers see?)] *Sermonem agnovi* (*quid non videatur amanti?*); modern texts have *quod non videatur, agentem,* without parentheses.

40 *Arachne*] *Maeonis.* Arachne was the daughter of a dyer, born in Maeonia, a country in Asia Minor. She was skilled in needlework, and challenged Minerva to a competition; when she lost, Arachne hung herself in despair. The goddess turned her into a spider.

Elegy 6

3 goodly birdes] *piae volucres.* Dyce emends 'goodly' (here and at line 58) to 'godly'; but these two instances, plus a third at line 51, suggest that Marlowe intended to translate *pius* as 'good'.

7 *Philomele*] Philomela was raped by her sister's husband, Tereus, who then cut out her tongue and imprisoned her in a lonely castle; in a piece of needlework she sent the news of these happenings to Procne, her sister, who in revenge killed her son Itys (see line 10) and served him as food to her husband. Finally they were all changed into birds: Philomela became a nightingale, Tereus a hoopoe, Procne a swallow, and Itys a sandpiper.

15 *Pylades*] The cousin of Orestes, who assisted him in revenging the death of Agamemnon by murdering Clytemnestra (Orestes' mother) and her lover Aegisthus.

35 *Pallas* hate] In Ovid's *Metamorphoses*, ii. 552ff., the Crow tells why she is hated by Pallas Athene (Minerva). An attempt to ravish Athene by Vulcan resulted in the birth of Erichthonius, whom Pallas tried to smuggle away. The Crow saw what happened, and talked about it.

41 *Thersites*] The most deformed and defamatory of the Greek rank and file during the Trojan War.

Protesilaus] The first of the Greeks to set foot on Trojan soil; an oracle had declared that the man who did this should be the first to die.

Elegy 7

2 To over-come] *Ut vincam.*

Elegy 8

16 she did perceive] *vidit*; modern texts, *vidi.*

24 Well maiest thou one thing for thy Mistresse use] *Est unum e dominis promeruisse satis.*

Elegy 9

4 thy tents] *castris . . . tuis*; modern texts, *meis.*

7 *Pelides*] Achilles, who cured (using the rust from his sword) the wound he had inflicted on Telephus.

20 His sword layed by, safe, though rude places yeelds] *Tutaque, deposito poscitur ense, rudis*. Sixteenth-century texts (in which lines 20 and 22 of the Latin are interchanged) are in part responsible for Marlowe's misunderstanding of this line. Modern texts list the soldier, the racehorse, and the ship, and then go on to refer to the gladiator who at the age of 65, retiring, exchanged his sword for a *rudis*—described in Cooper's *Thesaurus* as 'A roode or yarde that was given to sworde players ... in token that they were set at lybertie .... It is sometimes taken for lybertie from labour.' Marlowe fails to recognize the noun *rudis* and the feminine adjective *tuta* which belongs to it, and he completely mistakes the meaning of *poscitur*.

32 haven touching] *tangentem portus*.

46 Let me enjoy her] *fruar domina*.

48 step-father] Once again, as in 1. ii. 24, Ovid's *vitricus* could refer to either Mars or Vulcan. The former seems the more likely here.

Elegy 10

18 largely] *late*; modern texts, *laxe*.

35 would I might droupe with doing] Montaigne, in his essay 'That to Philosophize, is to learne how to die' (trans. Florio), gives instances of those who died in the act of love, telling how '*Cornelius Gallus* the Praetor, *Tigillinus* Captaine of the Roman watch, *Lodowicke* sonne of *Guido Gonzaga*, Marquis of *Mantua*, end their daies between womens thighs'.

Elegy 11

7 country Gods] *patriosque penates*; modern texts, *sociosque*.

18 *Scyllaes* and *Caribdis* waters] The rocks and whirlpools of the sea between Italy and Sicily.

19 *Cerannia*] The Ceraunia, mountains of Epirus which extend far into the sea, forming a promontory that divides the Ionian from the Adriatic. *Mason*'s '*Cerannia*' is not a misprint involving a turned *n*; the same spelling is found in *Dido Queene of Carthage* 1. i. 147.

20 either *Syrtes*] Two large sandbanks in the Mediterranean on the coast of Africa. They were never stable, being sometimes very high, sometimes very low under water, and therefore most dangerous to navigation.

20 *Laedas* noble twinne-starres] Castor and Pollux, the children of Leda, born at the same time as Helen and Clytemnestra. As a constellation (Gemini) they were thought to have seafarers especially under their protection.

34 *Galatea*] A sea-nymph, the daughter of Nereus.

Elegy 12

10 the *Atrides*] Agamemnon and Menelaus, the sons of Atreus.

17 a Queene] Helen of Troy.

19 a woman] Cf. 1. iv. 7–8n.

21 new] *iterum*; the reference is to the battle of Turnus and Aeneas over Lavinia, daughter of Latinus.

23 A woman] The indefinite article is misleading; it was *women*, rather than *a woman* who caused the Sabines to become the first enemies of the newly established Romans after the Romans had insulted them.

Elegy 13

3 secretly with me] Marlowe has mistaken Ovid's idiom. The Roman poet is angry because Corinna has attempted the abortion without his knowledge: *clam me*.

7–14 Thou] The poet addresses Isis. This Egyptian goddess, with her brother (and husband) Osiris, comprehended all nature and all heathen deities. By the time Ovid was writing, the cult of Isis had spread over the whole empire: '*Canopus*', '*Memphis*', '*Pharos*', and 'swift *Nile*' allude to its Egyptian source, and to certain elements of its ritual. Anubis is the Egyptian Mercury, a man with the head of a dog, who accompanied Osiris on his expedition against India. Osiris was murdered and his body cut in pieces by his brother, Set. Isis collected and buried the mangled remains, while Osiris' soul entered the ox, the beast most useful in the cultivation of the earth, and became the god Apis. It was a good omen that the snake should glide around the temple offerings.

18 engirt] *cingit*; modern texts, *tingit* or *tangit*. Dyce says: 'Here Marlowe has confused *Galli*, the priests of Isis, with *Galli*, Gauls, Frenchmen.'

21 *Lucina*] The divine daughter of Jupiter and Juno; because her mother brought her into the world without pain, she became the goddess of childbearing. Further, Lucina is a cult name of both Juno and Diana, who were also associated with the care of pregnant women. Modern texts of the *Amores* have the emendation *Ilythia*, the Greek equivalent of Lucina.

Elegy 14

11 stones, our stockes original] Deucalion and his wife, Pyrrha, who alone were saved from the flood with which Jupiter had overwhelmed mankind, were instructed to throw behind them the bones of their great mother—the stones of the earth. The stones thrown by Deucalion became men, and those thrown by Pyrrha women.

14 watry *Thetis*] The sea-nymph Thetis was the mother of Achilles, who permitted Priam to ransom and take away the body of his son, Hector, whom Achilles had killed in the Trojan War.

15 *Ilia*] Rhea Silvia, the mother of Romulus and Remus, founders of Rome.

16 He ... that conquering *Rome* did build] Aeneas, the son of Venus, who escaped from Troy and sailed to Italy, making the first settlement there, and founding the race of the caesars.

29 At *Colchis*] Medea fell in love with Jason when he came to Colchis in his

search for the Golden Fleece; later, when he was unfaithful to her, she killed two of her children in their father's presence.

30 *Itis*] He was murdered by Procne, his mother, in revenge for her husband Tereus' treatment of Philomela (cf. II. vi. 7n.).

they bewaile] *queruntur*.

40 worthily lament] *merito clamant*; modern texts have *clamant 'merito'*, their punctuation making it clear that *'merito'* is the exclamation.

Elegy 15

19 I would not out, might I in one place hit] *Si dabor, ut condar loculis, exire negabo*.

24 And through the gemme let thy lost waters pash] *Damnaque sub gemma perfer euntis aquae*.

Elegy 16

1 *Sulmo*] Cf. II. i. 2n.

4 the *Icarian* ... Dog-starre] Icarius' dog was made into a star for discovering his master's body after Icarius had been murdered by peasants to whom he had given wine. Being unaccustomed to it, they thought its effects were poisonous.

8 *Pallas* Olives] Pallas Athene and Poseidon argued over the ownership of Attica, and the assembly of the gods promised to give it to whichever of the two produced the most useful present for mankind. Poseidon created the horse, and Pallas the olive; the gods judged the latter, as an emblem of peace, to be preferable to the former, the emblem of war and bloodshed.

20–3 My hard way ... beare] Ovid lists navigational hazards which he would willingly endure in his mistress's company. The *'Lybian Syrtes'* are the sandbanks off the coast of Africa (cf. II. xi. 20n.); Scylla and Charibdis the rocks and whirlpools between Italy and Sicily (cf. II. xi. 18n.); the former is portrayed as a girl as far as the waist, but below that as a pack of snarling, dog-like monsters. Malea is a promontory to the south-east of Laconia, where the sea is always rough.

31 The youth] Leander; cf. Marlowe's *Hero and Leander*.

40 rockes dyed crimson with *Prometheus* bloud] The mountains of the Caucasus, in Albania, where Prometheus was chained while a vulture fed on his liver, as punishment for having stolen fire from the gods to give to mankind.

Elegy 17

4 the floud-beate *Cithera*] Venus, who was surnamed Cytherea because she rose from the sea near the island of Cythera; she was also worshipped at Paphos, a city of Cyprus.

15 *Calypso*] Calypso was not, as line 16 seems to suggest, a mortal, but an immortal nymph, one of the Oceanides, who loved a mortal, Ulysses. The latter was shipwrecked on her island, Ogygia, and although he stayed with her for seven

years, eventually left her. The error in 'A mortall nimphe' arises from Marlowe's having mistaken a genitive for a nominative: *mortalis amore ... Capta*.

17 *Thetis*] Thetis, one of the sea-deities, was courted by both Jupiter and Neptune, but when it was known that her son would be greater than his father, the gods withdrew their addresses, and Peleus, King of Thessaly, married her. He was the only mortal to marry an immortal; the son who was greater than his father was Achilles.

18 just *Numa*] Numa Pompilius, the second king of Rome, famed as a lawgiver and religious reformer. He encouraged a rumour that he paid frequent visits to the nymph Egeria, so that he could use this immortal's name to give sanction to the laws and institutions which he introduced.

21 This kinde of verse] See General Introduction.

24 in the mid bed] *in medio ... toro*; modern texts, *foro*.

Elegy 18

3 *Macer*] Aemilius Macer, a Latin poet of Verona and friend of Tibullus and Ovid. He seems to have composed some didactic poetry, but in the first two lines of this poem (which Marlowe does not completely understand), Ovid suggests that he is working on an epic describing the events leading up to the wrath of Achilles, prior to those described in the *Iliad*.

8 why] *cur*; modern texts, *iam*.

15 my cloak, and buskines painted] The conventional costume of the tragic Muse, and hence the tragic poet.

21–37 We write ... record] Ovid now gives a partial table of contents of his own poems, the *Heroides*, epistles of legendary heroes and heroines. Penelope sends the first of these to Ulysses, from whom she was separated by the Trojan War. Phyllis, the writer of the second, was deserted by Demophoon despite her kindness to him when he stopped at Thrace on his way home after the War. The sixth epistle is a letter from Hypsipyle to Jason, reproaching him for deserting her as he had deserted Medea; in the eleventh Canace writes to her brother Macareus, who had seduced her and made her pregnant; Oenone, the nymph that Paris abandoned for Helen, complains to him in the fifth poem, while in the fourth Phaedra confesses her incestuous love for her stepson Hippolytus. In the seventh, Dido tries to restrain Aeneas from his divine mission which will mean his leaving her, and the fifteenth poem is addressed by the poetess Sappho ('her that lov'd the *Aonian* harpe') to Phaon, the youth whose coldness caused her to commit suicide.

27 *Sabinus*] The poet Sabinus was Ovid's friend (modern editions make this clear by reading *meus ... Sabinus* instead of *celer ... Sabinus*), who wrote, as the next seven lines indicate, 'replies' to the *Heroides*.

38 *Laodameia*] When her husband Protesilaus was killed in the Trojan War by Hector, she ordered a wooden statue to be made of him, and this was regularly placed in her bed until her father ordered the image to be destroyed; Laodamia threw herself into the flames and was burned with the statue.

Elegy 19

13–14 Ah oft ... innocence] *Ah quoties finxit culpam: quantumque licebat,* | *Insontis speciem praebuit ipsa nocens*; modern texts, *a, quotiens finxit culpam, quantumque licebat* | *insonti, speciem praebuit esse nocens*.

20 Oft couzen me] *Saepe face insidias*; modern texts have *time* for *face*.

27 *Danae*] The daughter of Acrisius and Eurydice, she was locked in a brazen tower when her father heard that her son would put him to death. Jove disguised himself as a shower of gold, entered the tower, and made Danae pregnant with Perseus. Cf. also III. vii. 29–34.

29 *Io*] Because of Juno's jealousy, Jupiter turned his mistress Io into a heifer.

46 effect] *amare*; 'effect' is a variant form of 'affect' (see *OED v.* 2).

BOOK III

Elegy 1

7–10 *Elegia* ... tooke] The personification of Elegy is reminiscent of the first poem of Book I, with its reference to the characteristic metre (hexameter followed by pentameter). Cf. General Introduction.

11–14 *Tragedie*] Ovid makes the customary comparison of the lightness of the elegiac form with the more serious tragic (or epic) mode. '*Tragedie*' is clothed in the '*Lydian buskin*' because the buskin—a thick-soled boot which elevated the tragic performers—was the conventional symbol and attribute of tragedy: *Lydius apta pedum vincla cothurnus erat*. Modern editions of Ovid have *alta* for *apta*. The Lydians were a war-like people from Asia Minor, a more ancient name for the country Maeonia. Plato, however, condemns the 'lax' Lydian mode; and it is generally spoken of as a gentle, even effeminate, form of verse—as in Milton's 'Lap me in soft Lydian airs' (*L'Allegro*).

12 cloake] *palla*.

40 Small doores unfitting for large houses are] *Obruit exiguas regia vestra fores*.

Elegy 2

15 *Pelops*] At Pisa, in Elis, Pelops became one of the suitors of Hippodamia, whose father had promised her to the man who could beat him in a chariot race; the losers were put to death. In modern texts Ovid speaks of the Pisaean spear which almost killed Pelops; Marlowe's text had *axe* for *hasta*.

29 *Atalantas*] Atalanta, daughter of Schoeneus, King of Boeotia, vowed to live in perpetual virginity; and to free herself from her suitors, she proposed to run a race with them. The man who beat her she would marry, but those she overtook she would kill. Hippomenes came armed with three golden apples from the orchard of the Hesperides, which he threw in Atalanta's way to delay her, and so won the race. Marlowe translates Ovid's *Melanion* by the less common Hippomenes (line 30) because he needs the rhyme.

31 Coate-tuckt] *succinctae*.

43 themselves let all men cheere] *linguis animisque favete*; Marlowe makes an identical error in III. xii. 29.

54 pleace] Expressing his dissatisfaction with this obsolete form of 'please', Bower comments: 'the use of "please" in the sense required here is a strained one even though it is close to Ovid's *pugilis ... placet.* One would scarcely know it from the English, but the object of "please" is "Pollux", and thus the word must be taken as "pleased by".' In fact Marlowe has mistaken the present subjunctive form *plācet* ('let him appease') for the indicative *plăcet* ('he pleases'). In the same line, and for the same reason, Bowers emends 'loves' to 'love', emphasizing that the 'horsemen' are the subject of the verb, and 'Castor' the object. The result is perhaps a more correct translation of the Latin, but it is uncomfortable and unidiomatic English.

Elegy 3

17 *Cepheus* Daughter] Andromeda, who was almost sacrificed to a sea monster sent by Neptune to ravage her father's kingdom after her mother, Cassiopeia, had boasted herself fairer than Juno and the Nereides. Andromeda was rescued by Perseus.

37 *Semele*] One of Jupiter's many loves, Semele insisted on seeing the god in all his divine splendour. The sight was too much for mortal eyes, and Semele was consumed with the brightness. At the time she was pregnant with Bacchus, and Jupiter snatched the child from her womb and sewed him in his thigh, carrying him there until it was time for him to be born.

Elegy 4

7 minde] Modern Latin texts, reading *corpus* for the sixteenth-century *mentem*, make it clear that this couplet does not repeat the thought of its predecessor.

19 *Argus*] Juno's watchman; set to guard Io, he was lulled to sleep by Mercury, and killed; cf. II. ii. 45–6 and note.

21 *Danae*] Cf. II. xix. 27n.

23 *Penelope*] The faithful wife of Ulysses.

39 *Mars* his sonnes not without fault did breed] Mars violated the chastity of Rhea Silvia (Ilia), a vestal virgin, who then became the mother of Romulus and Remus, the founders of Rome.

Elegy 5

Modern editions have another poem, beginning *Nox erat*, here; it may not be Ovid's, and is not found in sixteenth-century editions.

1 reede] *arundinibus.*

13 *Perseus*] When he went to kill Medusa (one of the Gorgons who had snakes for hair), Perseus was given winged sandals by Mercury.

14 dreadfull Adders] *Terribili ... angue.*

15 the chariot, whence corne seedes were found] This belonged to Ceres.

While she was searching for her daughter Proserpina, the cultivation of the earth was neglected, and the ground became barren; to make amends, Ceres gave corn seeds to Triptolemus of Eleusis, and sent him in her chariot to broadcast them, with instructions about their cultivation, to the inhabitants of the world. The story is told at the end of *Metamorphoses*, v.

23–54 Great flouds ... *Laomedon*] The poem addressed to the small stream gives Ovid the opportunity to write on the subject of the loves between men and rivers. Inachus (line 25) was a river-god, the son of Oceanus, who gave his name and protection to a river in Argolis; he married a daughter of Oceanus, the nymph Melia. Marlowe's text does not help him here, reading *in media Bithynide* for the modern *in Melie Bithynide*. Scamander (line 28), or Xanthus (the name used by the gods), took part in the Trojan War, fighting with Achilles; the river's association with Neaera (a common name for nymphs, line 28) cannot be traced, however. Alpheus (line 29) was a river of Elis which fell in love with Arethusa when she was bathing in his stream; in human shape he pursued her until she appealed to Diana for help. Diana answered her prayer by turning Arethusa into water and, when Alpheus promptly changed back into a river, carried her underground to the island of Ortygia at Syracuse, where the spring of Arethusa was a noted feature. A scribal error in the transmission of Ovid's text is to be blamed for the confusion in line 31. *Xantho* here seems to have been caught up from *Xanthe* (Marlowe's '*Scamander*') three lines earlier. Modern editions accept the conjecture *Xutho*. Xuthus, the son of Hellen (and grandson of Deucalion) married Creusa, daughter of Erechtheus, King of Athens, but she was stolen from him by Peneus line 32, a river-god of Thessaly, and was carried away to Phthiotis, a district (not a town) of that country. Marlowe's '*Aesope*' (line 33) is Asopus, a river in Boeotia; he is said to have been the father, not the husband, of Thebe (line 34), from whom the Boeotian town of Thebes took its name. Achelous (line 35), the most celebrated of rivers and the largest watercourse in Greece, fought against Hercules ('*Alcides*', line 36) for the hand of Deianira (line 38), daughter of Oeneus, King of Calydon (line 37). Achelous turned himself into a wild bull, but Hercules broke off one of his horns (which was made into the Horn of Plenty). Nothing is known of an Evadne (line 41) in connection with the Nile (line 39); in the Latin she is said to have been a daughter of Asopus. The god Poseidon loved Tyro (line 43), daughter of Salmoneus, and visited her disguised as the Thessalian river Enipeus (line 43). Ovid explains that it was in order to dry himself for Tyro's embraces that the god commanded the river waters to retire. When Ilia (Rhea Silvia, line 47) violated her vow of chastity as a vestal virgin, becoming by Mars (line 49) the mother of Romulus and Remus, she was thrown into the river Anio, a tributary of the Tiber, by the order of her uncle Amulius, and became the wife of the river-god.

44 Fly backe ... place] *cedere iussit aquam; iussa recessit aqua.*

50 sole places] *loca sola.*

82 what she liked best] *socii iura ... tori.*

103 I know not what expecting] *Nescio quem spectans*; for a similar mistranslation cf. III. x. 11.

105 white streame] *non candide torrens.*

Elegy 6

41 *Pylius*] Nestor (of Pylos), said to have lived for three generations of men.

42 *Tithon*] Cf. I. xiii. 1n.

46 for-slow'd] The word is used in *OED* sense 1: 'to be slow or dilatory about; to lose or spoil by sloth ....' At this point Marlowe is translating Ovid's couplet:

> credo etiam magnos, quo sum tam turpiter usus
> numeris oblati paenituisse deos.

51 he that told so much] Tantalus; cf. II. ii. 44n.

61 *Phemius*] Phemius, the minstrel in the *Odyssey*, who sang to Penelope's suitors; some say that he taught Homer, and that the grateful poet immortalized him by introducing his name into the *Odyssey*.

62 *Thamiras*] A musician who challenged the Muses to a contest; when he lost, the Muses deprived him of both his eyesight and his voice.

79 .bloud of frogs newe dead] Sixteenth-century texts read as modern ones, but note a variant of *ranis* for *lanis*, adding *ut de rubetis intelligatur, quarum maximus in magicus usus.*

Elegy 7

1 liberall arts] *ingenuas artes: liberales, quibus ingenui homines institui debent* (Dominicus).

11 Foole] *stulta*; modern texts, here and at line 12, *vita*.

29 *Jove*] Cf. II. xix. 27n.

35 old *Saturne*] Supposed to have been King of Italy during the golden age, Saturn was a very ancient agricultural divinity associated with Ops, and was a personification of the earth's riches.

62 One her commands] *Imperat ut captae.* Dyce's emendation is justified not only by the Latin, but also by the reference in the next line to a 'keeper'; perhaps, as Bowers suggests, the 'she' in line 63 (or in line 61) contaminated *Mason*'s reading.

Elegy 8

1 Thetis, and the morne] Thetis was the mother of Achilles, and Aurora ('the morne') the mother of Memnon (cf. I. xiii. 4n.).

14 *Julus*] The son of Aeneas.

16 *Adons*] Adonis, who was loved by Venus, and who was killed while hunting the wild boar; cf. *Metamorphoses*, x.

21 *Thracian Orpheus*] The son of the Muse Calliope and, according to some poets, of the god Apollo; others say, however, that he had a human father, Oeagrus, King of Thrace, with which country Orpheus was always associated. When he played upon his lyre, the beasts forgot their wildness, and trees and mountains moved to listen to his song.

23 *Linus*] Another son of Apollo, to whom was attributed the invention of

melody and rhythm. He challenged his father to a song contest, but Apollo defeated and killed him. Modernized texts usually have 'laid' for 'layed', but it would make more sense, I think, if 'layed' were regarded as a coinage from *lay* (*OED sb.*⁴). This certainly gives a fairer rendering of the Latin *edidit*—which modern texts replace by the lament of Apollo, *aelinon*.

24 unequald] *invicta*; modern texts, *invita*.

29 The worke of Poets] The particular references here are to the *Iliad*, telling of '*Troyes* labours', and the *Odyssey*, recounting the wanderings of Ulysses for ten years following the fall of Troy. During Ulysses' absence, when he was supposed dead, his wife, Penelope, was besieged with suitors. She agreed to remarry when her tapestry ('that slowe webbe') was finished, but every night she unravelled the day's work.

45 *Eryx* bright Empresse] Venus, called Erycina because of her temple on Mt Eryx in Sicily.

47 *Corcyras* Ile] The modern Corfu, where Tibullus was once ill.

62 *Calvus*] Gaius Licinius Calvus, a lyric and elegiac poet and friend of Catullus.

64 *Gallus*] Cornelius Gallus, the first writer of Roman love elegy. He won the favour of Augustus Caesar, and was appointed to rule over Egypt, but was accused of pillaging the province and conspiring against his benefactor, whereupon he committed suicide.

Elegy 9

9 first oracles] The first temple of Jupiter was said to have been built after the flood, by Deucalion, in the neighbourhood of Dodona; it was surrounded by oak trees which frequently delivered sacred oracles.

10 their bed] *torus*; modern texts, *cibus*.

19 nor *Crete* doth all things feigne] Proverbially, the Cretans were liars—a reputation perhaps derived from their wealth of legends, which included claims that Crete was not only the birthplace, but also the burial place, of Jupiter. St Paul alludes to this reputation in his Epistle to Titus: 'One of themselves, even a prophet of their own, said, The Cretians are always liars' (v. 12).

24 *Ceres*] Ceres fell in love with Iasion in Crete, and lay with him in a ploughed field. As a result of this, Jupiter, who according to some accounts was Iasion's father, killed him with a thunderbolt. Because of Ceres' dalliance in Crete, harvests everywhere else failed.

39 *Ida* ... did sing with corne] *cānebat* ... *Ide*. Never very strong on Latin quantities and metre, Marlowe mistakes *cānebat* ('was white') for *cănebat* ('sang'). However, he has some precedent for the singing conceit in Coverdale's translation of Psalm 65: 14, used in the *Booke of Common Prayer*: 'the valleys also shall stand so thick with corn that they shall laugh and sing.'

41 *Minos*] King of Crete, the son of Jupiter and Europa, who gave good laws to his subjects, and is said to have been rewarded for this after his death with the office of supreme judge in Hades.

42 wisht] *optavit*; some modern texts have the subtler *optasset*.

43 what sports] *secubitus*; Martin suggests that Marlowe's untraced text may have read *concubitus*.

Elegy 10

11 I know not whom] *nescio cui*; for a similar mistranslation of this phrase cf. III. v. 103.

Elegy 11

1–2 What . . . sing] *Quis fuit ille dies, quo tristia semper amanti* | *Omina non albae concinuistis aves?*

7 bookes] *libellis*.

17 With Muse oppos'd] *Adversis . . . musis*.

21–40 by us . . . was able?] Ovid now gathers together the most outrageous of the fictions perpetuated by the Greek and Roman poets. The first Scylla (line 21) was the daughter of Nisus, King of Megara, the prosperity of whose kingdom depended on a purple or red hair on his head. Scylla fell in love with Minos, who was besieging the country, and to make him love her, she cut off her father's hair when he was asleep. The second Scylla was a daughter of Typhon who rejected the addresses of Glaucus, a sea-deity. He applied to the enchantress Circe for love potions, but Circe herself fell in love with the god, and the drugs she gave him changed Scylla, her rival, into a monster with dogs' heads, endlessly barking, about her waist (line 22). The winged feet belonged to Mercury, and the snaky hair to Medusa, one of the Gorgons, who was killed by Perseus (line 24). From the drops of blood falling from Medusa's head came the winged horse Pegasus. The Giant Tityus (line 25) was placed in hell by Jupiter for assaulting Leto; Ulysses describes the sight of the monster, with two vultures always plucking at his liver, in the *Odyssey*, xi. The three-headed dog (line 26), Cerberus, was another denizen of hell, this time a watchful keeper whose job it was to prevent the living from entering the realms of the dead. Enceladus (line 27) was another of the Giants, who was buried by Jupiter under Mt Aetna; whenever he turned, the whole of Sicily shook. The 'Mermaids' with 'singing charmes' are the sirens, sea-nymphs who captivated sailors until they lost control of their ships and were drowned (but cf. note to line 28). When Ulysses (line 29) visited the island of Aeolus, the god of the winds (*Odyssey*, x), he was given a leather bag containing the energies of all the winds. Because he told the secrets of the gods, Tantalus (line 30) was doomed in hell to suffer hunger and thirst while standing waist-high in water (cf. II. ii. 44n.). Niobe (line 31), having boasted herself greater than Leto, mother of Apollo and Diana, was for this presumption turned into a stone fountain, and Callisto (line 31), one of Jupiter's many mistresses, was turned into a bear by the jealous Juno; Jupiter elevated her to a constellation with her son Arcas—the Great and Little Bear. Procne (line 32) became a swallow after she had murdered her son Itys (cf. II. vi. 7n.). Jupiter pursued his amours in many disguises: as a swan (line 33) he approached Leda, as a shower of gold he came to Danae, and as a bull he carried Europa (line 34) to Crete. Proteus (line 35) was a sea-deity, who changed his shape constantly. One account of the building of Thebes (line 35) tells how

Cadmus slew a dragon and sowed its teeth in the earth; armed men sprang from
the teeth, and those who did not kill each other assisted Cadmus in the building of
the city. The oxen of Colchis (line 36), with which Jason ploughed the land before
sowing the dragons' teeth, breathed fire. The Heliades, daughters of the Sun and
Clymene, were so affected by the death of their brother Phaethon, who was killed
while attempting to drive his father's solar chariot, that they were changed into
poplars, weeping precious amber (*electra*) on the banks of the river Po (but cf.
note to line 37). In the *Aeneid*, ix. 112–22, Virgil tells how the ships of Aeneas,
who led the Trojan refugees to Italy, turned into sea-nymphs, the Nereids. When
Atreus (line 39) murdered his brother's children (who were the result of incest
between Thyestes and Atreus' wife), the sun turned back from the scene in horror. Finally Ovid refers to the magical power of poetry, exemplified in the harp
and music of Amphion; those who do not give Cadmus the credit for founding
Thebes give it to this musician, and say that the very stones moved at the sound
of his harp and formed the city walls of their own accord (line 40).

28 Mermaids singing charmes] *Ambiguae . . . virginis ore*; Ovid's allusion seems
to be to the sphinx, failure to answer whose riddles meant instant death to the
inhabitants of Thebes. Marlowe, however, was thinking of the sirens, fabulous
creatures with heads of women (but usually said to have the bodies of birds) who
lured men to destruction with their song.

37 Heav'n starre *Electra* that bewaild her sisters] *Flere genis electra, tuas auriga
sorores*. Marlowe ignores *auriga* altogether, and misconstrues the reference to the
Heliades; instead he recalls Electra, the daughter of Atlas and Pleione, who,
together with her six sisters, was changed into a constellation (the Pleiades) when
they were pursued by Orion.

Elegy 12

1 *Tuscia*] *Phaliscis*, the town Falerii, capital of the Falisci, in Tuscany or
Etruria.

2 *Camillus*] M. Furius Camillus, called a second Romulus, who captured the
town of Falerii in Tuscany (or Etruria) in the fourth century BC.

18 the Goddesse hated Goate] This poem gives the only account of Juno's
betrayal by, and hatred of, the goat.

21 Now] Ovid's *Nunc quoque* means 'even in these days', rather than 'at this
present moment'.

27 the Nunnes in white veyles clad] *sanctae veletae*; modern texts omit *sanctae*.

29 lowd the people hollow] *Ore favent populi*; for a similar mistranslation of
this phrase cf. III. ii. 43n.

32 *Halesus*] The son of Agamemnon and either Clytemnestra or Briseis, he
fled from home when Agamemnon was murdered by his wife and settled in Italy,
where he built the city of Falerii, introducing the worship of Juno to the
Etruscans.

Elegy 13

42 Say but thou wert injuriously accusde] *falsi criminis instar erit*; modern
texts, *falli muneris instar erit*.

44 the two leav'd booke] Marlowe's 'booke' was probably rhyme-attracted by the preceding line's 'tooke'; the expression is more usually that of Nashe's *Unfortunate Traveller*, which describes the rapist who 'used his knee as an yron ramme to beate ope the two leavd gate of her chastitie' (McKerrow, ii. 292). Ovid is less precise: *probra*.

Elegy 14

3 *Pelignis*] Cf. ii. i. 2n.

15 Both loves] Cupid and Venus.

17 Horned Bacchus] Greek tragedy centred on the cult of Dionysus or Bacchus, with its origins in the performances of a group of 'goat-singers' (Τραγωδία means 'goat-song'). Bacchus was often represented graphically with small horns on his forehead.

LUCAN'S FIRST BOOKE
EPISTLE

2 *Elementall*] The general sense: 'Of, or pertaining to the "four elements", earth, air, fire, and water' (*OED* 1, 2) is strictly modified by Thorpe's 'pure', which gives the adjective the power of *OED* 3b: 'In its (hypothetical) pure condition, as opposed to the impure form in which it is actually known'; usually fire is being referred to.

3 Genius] Thorpe puns on two senses of the word: *OED* 2: 'A demon or spiritual being', and *OED* 5: 'Native intellectual power of an exalted type'.

4 the *Churchyard*] St Paul's Churchyard, effective centre of the bookselling trade, where most publishers and booksellers had stalls.

sheets] The pun is with printers' sheets: both parts of *Tamburlaine*, *Dido*, *Edward II*, and *Hero and Leander* had been published by 1600.

5 *humorously*] *OED*'s earliest example of this word being used, as here, to mean 'capriciously', 'peevishly', is 1603.

6 *spirit*] Thorpe's imagery has led him to metaphors from necromancy— which are particularly appropriate in connection with the author of *Dr Faustus*, where the eponymous hero describes a magic circle to conjure up the devil, Mephostophilis.

11 *a Patron*] Thorpe writes of patrons in the traditional manner, which found concise expression in Johnson's *Dictionary*, where *patron* is defined as 'commonly a wretch who supports with insolence, and is paid with flattery'.

14 *physicke*] The noun has a specific sense (*OED* 4b) of 'A cathartic or purge'. If this is the usage intended here, the succeeding lines become capable of scatological innuendo.

21 *often*] *OED* describes this adjectival usage as 'Very common in 16th and 17th c.; but rare after 1688'.

THE TEXT

1 worse then civill] Pompey and Caesar were not merely fellow citizens, but actual kinsmen.

Thessalian playnes] Lucan has *per Emathios... campos*, using 'Emathia' for 'Thessalia' in the rhetorical figure *metonymia*: 'when of things that be nigh together, wee put one name for another' (Peacham, C2). Marlowe was perhaps guided in his translation by Sulpitius, whose commentary told him that Pharsalia was a town of Thessaly: *Pharsalus Thessaliae oppidum fuit .... In huius agro sive campo suprema pugna inter Caesarem & Pompeium commissa fuit.* Emathia was a region of Macedonia, which was adjacent to Thessaly.

2 outrage strangling law] The Latin is *Iusque datum sceleri*, which Duff, translator of the Loeb edition (London and Cambridge, Mass., 1962) gives as 'legality conferred on crime'.

3 We sing] Thus Marlowe translates Lucan's *canimus*, disregarding the fact, pointed out by Sulpitius, that the Roman poet's plural form (instead of the more usual *cano*) was probably dictated by the metre: *Metrice eloquimur.*

launcht] *OED* describes as obsolete the first sense of the verb *launch*, meaning 'pierce' or 'wound'.

4 Armies alied] Lucan's *Cognatasque acies* is not easy to translate concisely, but Sulpitius says that many of the fighters were related to each other (*Multitudines armatorum consanguineas*), and that *Cognati* here has the sense of *qui commune nascendi initium habent, quasi una & communiter nati.*

the kingdoms league] Lucan refers to the first triumvirate, formed by Pompey, Caesar, and Crassus in 60 BC.

5 Th' affrighted ... spoile] Sulpitius seems to have failed Marlowe with the difficult lines *Certatum totis concussi viribus orbis | In commune nefas*, which Duff renders: 'All the forces of the shaken world contended to make mankind guilty.'

6 Trumpets, and drums] Lucan uses the single word *Signa* (meaning 'standards'), but Cooper gives 'trumpets' as a possible meaning, and Sulpitius lists *Tubus, tympana, lituos* as synonyms.

like] Sulpitius introduces the idea of 'alikeness' in his comment on Lucan's *obvia: Contra euntia, & similia.*

7 Eagles alike displaide] The standard of the Roman legion was surmounted by an eagle; this was carried into battle at the forefront of the army. In the war between Caesar and Pompey, each of the opposing sides bore the same standard.

darts] *OED* 1: 'A pointed missile thrown by the hand, a light spear or javelin.' With 'darts' Marlowe offers an acceptable Elizabethan equivalent for Lucan's *pila*, one that is preferable to Dryden's solution when he imitated this line in *The Hind and the Panther*: 'That was but civil war, an equal set, | Where Piles with piles, and Eagles Eagles met' (ii. 160–1). The *pilum* was the special weapon of the Romans.

9 *Barbarians*] Lucan's *Gentibus invisis* is glossed by Sulpitius as *Barbaris, quod odistis.*

10–11 Now ... unreveng'd] Lucan is telling the Romans that this was the time when *superba foret Babylon spolianda tropaeis* (Duff: 'It was your duty to rob proud Babylon of her trophies over Italy'). The editorial commas after 'stoop' and 'unreveng'd' are intended to help achieve Lucan's sense, which Marlowe misses because he neglects to translate the *-que* suffixes in lines 10 and 11. Lucan is horrified that the Romans should engage in civil war at a time when they should be retaliating against Babylon *and* avenging the death of Crassus, who was killed by the Parthians ('Babylon' is Lucan's metonymy for 'Parthia') at Carrhae in 53 BC. In 50 BC the Roman Senate, alarmed by rumours of an approaching Parthian army, decreed that Pompey and Caesar should each contribute a legion of soldiers to fight against the Parthians; Lucan believes that this would have been preferable to civil war.

17 resolves] The verb seems to originate with Sulpitius, whose comment on Lucan's *nescia vere remitti* is *Quae verno tempore non resolvitur*. As synonyms for sense 1 now obsolete of *resolve*, *OED* affords 'melt, dissolve, reduce to a fluid state'.

18 the *Euxin* sea] Lucan's *Scythicum ... pontum* is interpreted by Sulpitius: *sinum Euxinum dicit*.

20 And ... any] Some of the error in Marlowe's translation of *Et gens si qua iacet nascenti conscia Nilo* (Duff: 'and any nation that knows the secret of Nile's cradle') can be explained by reference to Sulpitius: *Et si quis ad Nili ortum, qui ignoratur, habitat*. It is strange, however, that he mistakes both *nascenti* and *ortum*, and Tucker Brooke suggests an emendation of 'mouth' to 'fount' or 'source'.

25–6 huge ... townes] Cf. *Edward II*, III. iii. 30: 'Make Englands civill townes huge heapes of stones.'

30 *Pirhus, ... Hanniball*] These were Rome's most dangerous enemies. Pyrrhus, King of Epirus (who claimed descent from his namesake, the son of Achilles), defeated the Roman armies in 280 BC. Hannibal (called *Poeni* by Lucan) invaded Italy in the third century BC.

32 wreake] *OED sb.* 3: 'Harm, injury; damage. *Obs.*' In the *Ruines of Rome: by Bellay*, Spenser invites the reader's contemplation of Rome:

> Behold what wreake, what ruine, and what wast,
> And how that she, which with her mightie powre
> Tam'd all the world, hath tam'd herselfe at last.

33ff. *Nero*] In this elaborate panegyric of the emperor, Lucan is following a tradition started by Virgil who, in *Georgics*, i. 24ff., prophesied that Julius Caesar would be elevated to join the immortal gods, and to shine as a star in heaven. Ovid, in *Metamorphoses*, xv, describes how this happened: after his death, Venus

> from her Caesars bodye tooke his new expulsed spryght
> The which shee not permitting to resolve to ayer quyght,
> Did place it in the skye among the starres that glister bryght,
> And as shee bare it, shee did feele it gather heavenly myght,
> And for to wexen fyrye. Shee no sooner let it flye,
> But that a goodly shyning starre it up aloft did stye
> And drew a greate way after it bryght beames like burning heare.

the fates] The Parcae, or Destinies, were three sisters who had ultimate power over every human life.

34 sleightly] *OED* records this as a variant spelling of *slightly*; it is used here either with the 'rare' sense (2c): 'With slight exertion or effort', or with the more common sense (3): 'easily, readily'.

35–6 *Jove* . . . done] The Giants were angry when Jupiter defeated the Titans (to whom they were closely related, and with whom they are often confused). They conspired to dethrone Jupiter but were defeated.

35 joide] This transitive use of the verb *joy* is in *OED*'s sense 4a: 'To derive enjoyment from, to possess or use with enjoyment'.

39 *Carthage* soules] Martin and Maclure both ignore the plural noun and gloss 'the shade of the Carthaginian, i.e., Hannibal'. But this is one occasion where *Poeni* is not used as a surname for Hannibal (in contrast to line 30), and Marlowe's translation of Lucan's *Poeni* . . . *manes* was guided by reference to his commentary, where Sulpitius explains: *Hoc est, umbrae Carthaginensium, qui bellis Punicis interiere a Romanis occisi.*

40 At . . . joyne] Marlowe's translation is somewhat awry. Lucan writes: *Ultima funesta concurrant proelia Munda* (Duff: 'Let the last battle be joined at fatal Munda'). The final battle of the civil war was fought at Munda, in Spain, where Caesar defeated Pompey's two sons in 45 BC.

41 *Caesar*] Lucan addresses Nero (to whom Sulpitius gave his full name of Claudius Nero Caesar in the gloss on line 33).

Perusian famine] During the winter of 41–40 BC, Lucius Antonius and Fulvia, the brother and wife of Mark Antony, respectively, were blockaded in Perusia by Octavius Caesar.

42 *Mutin* toyles] The fighting (*OED* toil *sb.* 1, 2) around Mutina in 43 BC, when Octavius defeated Antony.

Leuca] For the sake of his rhythm, Marlowe must accept Lucan's metonymy instead of substituting the familiar 'Actium' for the scene of the sea battle in which Augustus Caesar defeated Antony and Cleopatra.

43 And . . . fought] The reference is to the war in Sicily, which was fought by Agrippa (on behalf of Octavius Caesar) against Sextus Pompeius during 36 BC.

45 made thee Emperor] Lucan's *Quod tibi res acta est* is explicated by Sulpitius: *Quod tu imperium obtines*—which helped Marlowe with his translation.

47 where] The Latin, *seu sceptra tenere,* | *Seu te flammigeros Phoebi conscendere currus*, makes it fairly certain that this is a variant form of whether.

50 Undaunted . . . chang'd] The intrusion of 'her' makes this line awkward. Lucan means that the earth will not be distressed because the sun's chariot has a different driver [i.e. Nero instead of Phoebus]: *Tellurem nihil mutato sole timentem.*

53–8 But . . . best] At this point the panegyric almost overbalances into the ludicrous, with the notion that the deified Nero must be careful to maintain the balance of the universe by settling in the centre: if he were to choose either pole, his weight would cause it to sink down (like a seesaw). Marlowe translates Lucan's *onus* as 'force', perhaps not knowing that 'Weight is a regular attribute of divinity in ancient mythology' (Duff).

54 Nor ... pole] Marlowe is translating Lucan's *Nec polus aversi calidus qua vergitur austri* (Duff: '[n]or where the sultry sky of the opposing South sinks down'). It seems to have been generally thought by the Romans that the climate becomes hotter on the other side of the equator, and that the South Pole is the hottest place on earth.

61 *Janus Phane*] The doors of the temple of Janus were always open in time of war, and closed in peacetime.

62 boult ... Iron] Lucan speaks only of iron gates (*Ferrea ... limina*); Marlowe gets his details from Sulpitius: *Claudat portam aeneam et vectibus ferreis munetam.*

68 garboiles] 'Confusion, disturbance, ... brawl' (*OED*). But the word does not seem to have carried these dismissive, even pejorative, overtones in its earliest usages. Richard Stanyhurst begins his translation of the *Aeneid* (1582) with the words: 'Now manhood and garbroyls I chaunt.' T. J. B. Spencer, however, noted that 'garboyls' was Antony's favourite word for dismissing Fulvia's military and political exploits ('Shakespeare and the Romans', *Shakespeare Survey*, x (1957), 27–38).

77 *Phoebe's* waine] The moon. The adjective was applied to Diana, as well as to her brother, Apollo. The apostrophe for the possessive case is rare in this text (and at this time generally).

80 Disolve the engins of the broken world] Lucan has *totaque discors | Machina divulsi turbabit foedera mundi.* Marlowe seems to have taken the preceding *Phoebus* as the subject of *turbabit*, instead of *Machina* (which he understands as the object of the verb). 'Disolve' was suggested by Sulpitius, who glosses *turbabit foedera* as *Dissolvet ̃concordiam.*

87 faintly joyn'd] Marlowe is attempting to give an equivalent of Lucan's *male concordes*: the triumvirs were joined together for an evil purpose.

89 th'earth ... sustaines] Lucan states an old belief that the earth supports the sea, and the air supports the earth.

95 *Roomes* ... bloud] While Rome was being built, its founders quarrelled; Remus was killed by (or at the instigation of) his brother, Romulus.

97 A towne ... church] Marlowe rejects Lucan's *exiguum ... asylum* (referring to the asylum of Romulus) in favour of the explanation of Sulpitius, who identified Lucan's figure as synecdoche, and interpreted it as *exigua urbs, in qua erat asylum, hoc est, templum sanctissimum.*

100 Stept *Crassus* in] Lucan wrote: *Crassus erat ... medius*, meaning that Crassus, the third member of the triumvirate, stood between Caesar and Pompey. Marlowe perhaps got the notion of intervention from Sulpitius, who glosses *medius* as *Interpositus.·*

the slender *Isthmos*] The isthmus of Corinth.

104 *Crassus* wretched death] Crassus was defeated by the Parthians at Carrhae in 53 BC, and was subsequently murdered by them.

111–14 for *Julia* ... aliance] Julia was Caesar's daughter; she married Pompey, but died after giving birth to a child who lived only a few days. Both the marriage and the child could have been 'pledge[s] of peace' (Lucan's *pignora* is glossed by

Sulpitius: *Hoc est, affinitatem et foetum quem conceperat ex Pompeio*). But the marriage became a threat (Lucan's *diro* ... *omine*, Marlowe's 'death presaging') when it turned to mourning.

118 the *Sabines*] The earliest enemies of Rome, the Sabines eventually became allies.

119 trainde] The verb *train* in the sense of *OED* II. 4 is described as 'archaic'; but it is the most frequent early usage, meaning 'to draw by art or inducement'.

121 late deeds] Lucan's *nova acta*—new (or more recent) deeds.

123 Pirats wracke] In 67 BC Pompey drove the pirates from the Mediterranean, where for many years they had been a serious threat to Rome's naval power.

124 Thee] Lucan now addresses Caesar.

129 *Cato*] The Stoics held their great men (of whom Cato was one) in high esteem, respecting them as much as the gods.

134 his *Theaters* applause] Pompey built the first stone theatre in Rome.

137–8 Like ... monuments] Lucan refers to the custom of offering the trophies of war to the gods by hanging them on trees (the oak was sacred to Jupiter). Marlowe uses 'monuments' in *OED*'s sense 4: 'Anything that by its survival commemorates a person, period, or event'.

142 nod] The sense is that of *OED vb.* 9: 'cause to bend or sway'.

145 *Caesars* ... lesse] Marlowe makes a mistake here, perhaps because (as Martin suggests) he understood *non* ... *tantum* to refer back to Pompey. Lucan writes: *Sed non in Caesare tantum | Nomen erat fama ducis* (Duff: 'But Caesar had more than a mere name and military reputation').

146 Shaming ... subdue] The error here is more understandable, since Lucan's meaning is easily misconstrued: *solusque pudor non vincere bello* (Duff: 'his one disgrace was to conquer without war'). But Sulpitius gave a clear explanation: *Nullo pudore Caesar imprudens tangebatur, nisi dolose aut pacifice victor evaderet*.

149 Urging] The sense is that of *OED* 7a: 'To stimulate to expression or action; to increase or intensify'.

151 glad ... way] *gaudensque viam fecisse ruina*.

156 overthwarting flames] *obliqua* ... *flamma*. The participle is from overthwart: 'To pass or lie athwart or across; to traverse, cross' (*OED*).

157 not] Emendation to 'nought' is improper in an edition using old spelling, since 'not' is an acceptable variant.

159–60 Such ... dominions] Marlowe seems to have been striving for too much economy; by neglecting Lucan's *publica*, he fails to achieve his sense: *Haec ducibus causae; suberant sed publica bellis | Semina, quae populos semper mersere potentes* (Duff: 'Such were the motives of the leaders. But among the people there were hidden causes of war—the causes which have ever brought down ruin upon imperial races').

163 The soldiours ... ryot] *Praedaque et hostiles luxum suasere rapinae* (Duff: 'The spoil taken from the enemy lured men to extravagance').

167 greatest wittes] Lucan speaks of Poverty as the begetter of manhood—*fecunda virorum.* Marlowe's 'wittes' seems to imply intellectual, rather than physical, achievement; but Sulpitius includes examples of both in his comment on Lucan's phrase: *Quae producit multos egregios viros, ut Fabritius, Curios, Quintios, & Attilios.*

167–8 al the world ... decay] *totoque accersitur orbe | Quo gens quaeque perit.* Lucan tells how the Romans brought from every part of the world 'the special bane of each nation' (Duff); Sulpitius, however, recognized a single, universal poison: *Id est, opes,* which is the source for Marlowe's 'golde'.

169 then ... lands] Lucan: *tum longos iungere fines | Agrorum* (Duff: 'Next they stretched wide the boundaries of their lands'). Marlowe uses 'butting' in the sense of 'bounding, boundary' (*OED vbl. sb.*[2] '*Obs.*').

170 *Curius*] Marcus Annius Curius Dentatus conquered the Samnites, the Sabines, and the Lucanians in the third century BC; he was renowned for frugality as well as fortitude.

Camillus] L. Furius Camillus (fourth century BC) was called a second Romulus for his services to Rome.

171 Was ... unknowne] *Longa sub ignotis extendere rura colonis* (Duff: 'grew into vast estates tilled by foreign cultivators'). Sulpitius added *agricolas,* which may have given Marlowe the idea for 'hinds' (*OED sb.*[2] 2: 'A servant; esp. in later use, a farm servant, an agricultural labourer').

175–6 then ... towne] *magnumque decus ferroque petendum, | Plus patria potuisse sua* (Duff: 'to overawe the State was high distinction which justified recourse to the sword').

179 *Tribunes* with *Consuls* strove] Both tribunes and consuls were magistrates, but the former were always elected from the plebeians whereas the consuls (originally) were chosen from the patrician families. According to Duff: 'Order should be represented by the consuls, and progress by the tribunes; but both bodies were equally factious' (note to line 177).

180 voices] The electoral votes of the citizens.

182 the field of *Mars*] The Campus Martius, where elections for magistrates were held.

186 His mind ... war] Lucan's Caesar suffers no anxiety: *Ingentesque animo motus bellumque futurum ... Ceperat* (Duff: 'Caesar ... had conceived in his heart the great rebellion and the coming war'). But sixteenth-century texts place a comma after *motus,* and this may be the cause of Marlowe's misunderstanding.

187 the foord of *Rubicon*] The river Rubicon separated metropolitan Italy from the province of Cisalpine Gaul, Caesar's own province. By crossing this river (in fact a small stream) Caesar became an invader, precipitating war with Pompey and the Roman Senate.

188ff. At night ...] Lucan's personification of the city of Rome as a goddess (*dea Roma*) owes something to Virgil's description (*Aeneid,* vi. 781ff.) of Cybele, the Roman *Magna Mater*, especially in the detail of the 'Turret-bearing head'; both wear mural crowns, representing walls and battlements. Plutarch has another version of Caesar's vision: 'It is said that the night before he passed over this river [the Rubicon] he dreamed a damnable dream: that he carnally knew his mother' (*The Life of Julius Caesar*, trans. Thomas North).

192 *a* [*d*] *stare*] Lucan has no equivalent, but Marlowe gives no translation for the Latin *aadgstare* in the same line.

197–8 Thou thunderer ... rocke] The Latin is *O ... tonans*, this being Jupiter's mightiest appellation: he is generally represented seated on a throne with a thunderbolt in his hand. Sulpitius glosses: *O Jupiter optime maxime, qui in Capitolio coleris*. The temple of Jupiter was on the Capitol, which was originally called the Tarpeian Hill.

199 Ye gods ... line] Caesar invokes the Penates, Phrygian gods whose images had been rescued from Troy by Aeneas, the father of Julus (or Ascanius), from whom Caesar claimed descent. Cf. *Aeneid*, iii. 148–50.

200 *Quirinus* rites] Festivals in honour of Romulus, who was given the sur-name Quirinus (also a surname of Mars) when he was made a god by the Romans.

200–1 *Latian Jove ... Alba* hill] Caesar invokes Jupiter in his aspect of pro-tector of Latium, a country whose capital city of Alba Longa was founded by Caesar's supposed ancestor Ascanius. Marlowe seems to be using 'advanc'd' in the sense (*OED ppl. a.* 4) of 'Raise, elevated (physically)' to translate Lucan's *residens*.

201 *Vestall* flames] The worship of Vesta, goddess of hearth and home, was introduced into Rome from Alba Longa. Fire burned continually in the temple of Vesta.

206 laying ... war] *moras solvit belli* (Duff: 'loosed war from its bonds'); 'lets' is used in its original sense (*OED sb.*¹) of 'Hindrance ... obstruction'.

214 runs upon the hunter] Lucan's phrase, *Per ferrum ... exit* is not easy; Marlowe translates the commentary: *Per ipsam hastam ruit in venatorem*.

215 the purple *Rubicon*] Lucan's adjective is *Puniceus*, and Sulpitius comments that the river took its name of 'Rubicon' from its colour, which was that of the reddish soil through which it ran. *OED* gives 'purple' as one meaning (a. 2) of the adjective *punic*.

221 resolving] From the verb *resolve* in *OED*'s sense I. 1: 'To melt, dissolve, reduce to a liquid or fluid state'.

222–4 The ... passage] Cf. Lucan:

> Primus in obliquum sonipes opponitur amnem
> Excepturus aquas; molli tum cetera rumpit
> Turba vado faciles iam fracti fluminis undas.

(Duff: 'First the cavalry took station slantwise across the stream, to meet its flow; thus the current was broken, and the rest of the army forded the water with ease'.)

229 the destinies] Modern editions of Lucan accept Housman's emendation of this line, and read *Credidimus satis his* ('We have believed in them [agreements]

long enough'). But sixteenth-century editions have the reading of the manuscripts: *Credidimus fatis.*

232 *Parthians*] The Parthians were notorious for feigning flight and then
shooting arrows at the enemy pursuing them; cf. Virgil, *Georgics*, iii. 31: *fiden-
temque fuga Parthum versisque sagittis.*

233 *Lucifer*] Phosphor, or Venus; the morning star.

256 the *Gaules*] Lucan refers to the Senones (Sulpitius explains that these
were Gauls) who fought the Romans in the third and fourth centuries BC.

257 furious *Cymbrians*] Marlowe's edition of Lucan could have had *Cimbrumque furentem* where the modern editions read *Cimbrumque ruentem* (Duff: 'the
onrush of the Cimbrian').

Carthage moores] Lucan has *martem Libyes*, which Sulpitius explains as *Secun-
dum bellum punicum*—i.e. the Second Punic War, when Hannibal crossed the Alps
in 218 BC to launch an attack on Rome.

258 gan] The past tense of *gin*, the aphetic form of *begin*.

262 whist] *OED a.*¹ b: 'Keeping silence in relation to something, saying
nothing about the matter'.

268 urging *Grachus* deeds] The tribunes Tiberius and Caius Gracchus were
popular reformers who incurred the hostility of the Senate and were murdered in
(respectively) 133 and 121 BC. The Senate is now using this as a precedent (*minax
iactatis . . . Gracchis*; Duff: 'boasted of the doom of the Gracchi') for the expulsion
of the tribunes Antony and Q. Cassius.

269 doubtfull] Duff translates Lucan's *ancipiti* as 'distracted'; but Marlowe is
influenced by Sulpitius' gloss *Dubia*.

271ff. *Curio*] For this portrait, Marlowe owes much to Sulpitius. Lucan says
that Curio was once a spokesman for the people (*Vox quondam populi*), but it is
Sulpitius who gives him the official title: *Olim Tribunus.* Sulpitius also explains
that Curio was once a formidable opponent of Caesar's, but that *a Caesare ingenti
mercede corruptus est*; it must have been this, rather than Lucan's vague *venali . . .
lingua*, that was the source of line 272: 'One that was feed [i.e. fee'd] for *Caesar*'.
The 'Five yeeres' of line 277 was also provided by Sulpitius (*quinquennium*);
Lucan does not specify the length of time nor the area of command (Sulpitius has
Gallias).

280 let . . . home] Sulpitius was not helpful here. Lucan writes *tua nos faciet
victoria cives* (Duff: 'your victory will make us citizens again'); and this explains
the *volentes* (Marlowe's 'most willingly') of the previous line. Although they were
driven out of Rome by force (and against their wills), Curio and the two tribunes
are now glad to suffer this exile, because Caesar's victory will restore them to their
status as citizens of Rome.

282 "Where . . . hurts"] The quotation marks in Q suggest that this is some
proverb or maxim. They are not present in editions of Lucan (either of the sixteenth or twentieth centuries), but Sulpitius prefaces his gloss on Lucan's *semper
nocuit differre paratis* with the words *Sententia est.* A 'sentence' of this nature
perhaps underlies the following couplet in Donne's elegy 'To His Mistris Going

to Bed': 'The foe oft-times, having the foe in sight, | Is tir'd with standing, though they never fight.'

286 and ... world] Marlowe has failed to understand the meaning of Lucan's *tibi Roma subegerit orben*, even with the help of Sulpitius: *Roma victa orbis te dominum faciet*. Curio argues that if Caesar wins just two or three battles more, it will be for him [*tibi*] that Rome has conquered the world.

287–8 Nor ... bayes] Lucan's *Nunc* is necessary to make sense of this couplet. Curio warns Caesar that *now*—as things are at present—there will be no triumphal procession, or laurel wreath, when he returns to Rome.

287 shalt thou triumph] Be received with the honour of a formal triumphal procession, the appropriate reception for a returning conqueror (Lucan's *longi ... pompa triumphi*.

288 capitall ... bayes] The laurel wreath with which the conqueror was crowned was subsequently dedicated to Jupiter in the Capitol.

290 Abie] *OED v. arch.* 2: 'To pay the penalty for ... atone for'. Lucan writes: *gentesque subactas | Vix inpune feres* (Duff: 'you will scarce go unpunished for your conquest of foreign nations').

the sonne] Pompey, who by his marriage to Julia (see note to line 111–14) was Caesar's son-in-law.

293 prone] *OED* 7: 'Ready in mind (for some action expressed or implied); eager. *Obs.* or *arch.*'.

294 *Eleius* steedes] The racehorses at Elis for the Olympic games.

296 Souse downe the wals] Lucan describes how the racehorses, excited by the shouting, try to break through the starting-barriers. *OED* quotes this line as an example of *souse v.*² 1b: 'To dash *against*, to knock or cast *down*'.

299 wrastling] A variant form of *wrestling*.

302 bloudshed] (*OED* 3: 'The shedding or parting with one's own blood').

in the North] i.e. in the northern lands of Gaul and Britain.

306 Cornets] *OED cornet sb.*² 4: 'A company of cavalry, so called from the standard [a coronet] carried at its head'.

311 leader] Dyce's emendation of Q's 'leaders' is justified by the Latin *dux*; Sulpitius explains the rest of the line: *Pompeius debilitatus longo ocio*.

312 troupes of gownes] Lucan writes: *partes ... togatae*, which Sulpitius explains as *Viri a militia alieni, pacique*. For *gown sb.* 3, *OED* says the word is 'Used as the name of the flowing outer garment worn by the ancients, esp. the Roman toga. Hence after Roman usage: "The dress of peace".'

313 Brabbling *Marcellus*] There were three consuls of this name (two brothers and a cousin) who all spoke against Caesar in the Senate, and so would have merited the scorn of Lucan's *loquax* (which Marlowe's 'Brabbling' suitably translates).

Cato] Marcus Cato Uticensis, who does not seem to deserve either Lucan's dismissal of him as *nomina vana* or Marlowe's scornful 'whom fooles reverence'.

Although the words are spoken by Caesar, one would expect some foundation in reality (as in the reference to Marcellus).

314 strangers] Marlowe uses the word in its earliest sense, meaning 'foreigners', in accordance with the explanation given by Sulpitius that Pompey's supporters were in fact *Clientes remotissimarum nationum.*

315 (Whom ... bribde)] Lucan says that Pompey gave presents to his supporters over a long period; Marlowe takes the interpretation that this meant 'from his youth' from Sulpitius: *A sua adolescentia.*

316 shal ... time] *Ille reget currus nondum patientibus annis* (Duff: 'Shall Pompey hold the chariot reins before reaching the lawful age'. But once again Marlowe translates Sulpitius: *Ille triumphabit ante legitimos annos.* Pompey claimed the right to an official 'triumph' (see line 287n.) when he was no more than 26 years old; this was granted to him by Sulla for his outstanding achievement in the defeat of Iarbas in Numidia, even though the normal age for the receipt of such an honour was about 30.

317 And ... raigne] Pompey refused to give up his consulship at the proper time.

318–19 What ... dearth] In 57 BC Cicero proposed that Pompey should be put in charge of the world's corn supply; Pompey was later accused of having held back supplies, so that he could take advantage of a time of famine.

320–3 Who ... accusde] The reference is to the trial of Milo in 52 BC, when he was accused of the murder of Clodius. Pompey's soldiers occupied the Forum, to maintain order; but the orator, Cicero, was so intimidated by the soldiers that he forgot most of his argument, and Milo was condemned.

324 waine] In its transitive use, the verb *wane* (meaning 'to diminish') is now said to be obsolete (*OED*).

casts] *OED cast v.* VII. 43: 'To machinate, contrive, devise, scheme'.

326 *Sylla*] Lucius Cornelius Sulla led a civil war against Rome (in which he was joined by Pompey, Caesar, and Crassus), and came to power in 82 BC, when he showed himself to be a dictator and a tyrant.

329 *Hircania*] In literature the Hyrcanian, or Hyrcan, tigers are noted for their ferocity; cf. *Macbeth*, III. iv. 99–100: 'Approach thou like the rugged Russian bear, | The arm'd rhinoceros, or th'Hyrcan tiger.'

332 Jawes flesht] Dyce's emendation is essential for the sense of the line (Lucan has *Altus caesorum pavit cruor armentorum*, referring to the tiger 'who has drunk deep of the blood of slain cattle', Duff). The application of *OED v.* 1. *trans.* is particularly appropriate to Lucan's meaning: 'To reward (a hawk or hound) with a portion of the flesh of the game killed, in order to excite his eagerness in the chase'.

334–5 *Sylla* ... monarchy] *ex hoc iam te, inprobe, regno | Ille tuus saltem doceat descendere Sulla* (Duff: 'but let him learn one lesson at least from his master Sulla—to step down at this stage from his unlawful power'). Maclure suggests that Marlowe might have written 'At least' (not 'At last') as a translation of Lucan's *saltem.*

336 *Scicillian* Pirats] See line 123n.

337 jaded . . . slaine] The king of Pontus was Mithridates who, after a long struggle with Pompey, took poison to kill himself.

338 plume] The verb is used technically in falconry (*OED* 1) to describe how the hawk strips the feathers from its prey. *OED* also records a figurative usage comparable to the present one.

342 And . . . wil] *miles sub quolibet iste triumphet* (Duff: 'and let them triumph, be their leader who he may').

347 they had houses] After Pompey had subdued the pirates, he settled some of them as colonists in Calabria.

357 *Lalius*] The character *Laelius* is almost certainly fictitious, an invention of Lucan's to give dramatic force to his poem. The enthusiastic reception of Caesar's speech is narrated in *De Bellum Civile*, i. 7–8.

358 Oaken leaves] The reference is to the *corona civica*, or *querna corona*, which was the Roman equivalent of a medal for life-saving.

365–6 indure . . . groomes] Lucan's *Degenerem patiere togam* (Duff: 'submit to the disgrace of wearing the toga') is glossed by Sulpitius: *Tolerabis togatos inertes*; and this is the source of Marlowe's line. Marlowe expresses the scorn of Sulpitius with 'groomes' (*OED* groom *sb.* 3: 'A man of inferior position'; the 'purple' is not easy to explain: perhaps Marlowe is attempting oxymoron by coupling 'groomes' with the figurative use of *OED* purple *sb.* 2b, where *the purple* is defined as 'imperial, royal, or consular rank, power, or office'.

Senates tyranny] Lucan's *regnumque Senatus* is glossed by Sulpitius with the single word *Tyrannidem*.

368 *Syrtes*] Two wide gulfs on the north coast of Africa, dangerous to shipping. Sulpitius: *Syrtes duae, maior & minor, sunt in mari quod Africam Aegyptum versus alluit*. Both Lucan and Virgil (*Aeneid*, iv. 41) speak of *inhospita Syrtis*.

369 hot . . . sands] For the Elizabethans, as for the Romans, the Libyan sands were the physical embodiment of vastness; cf. Catullus, vii. 3: *quam magnus numerus Libyssae harena*, and *The Taming of A Shrew* (1594), scene xv: 'This angrie sword . . . hewd thee smaller then the Libian sands.'

370 This hand] Dyce suggested 'band' as a more acceptable translation of Lucan's *manus* in *Haec manus . . . Oceani tumidas remo compescuit undas*. Sulpitius appreciated the possible ambiguity, and commented: *Aut suam dextram ostendit, aut militum multitudinem*. However, emendation is not only unnecessary, but also undesirable: 'This hand' at line 370 makes for an effective form of anaphora with 'This hand' at line 379 and 'These hands' at line 385.

that . . . quail'd] *ut victum post terga relinqueret orbem* (Duff: 'that we might leave a conquered world at our backs'). Sulpitius explains that the reference is to Caesar's conquest of Gaul and Britain.

372 *Articks Rhene*] The northern Rhine.

378 womens groning wombe] Dyce suggested 'groaning woman's womb'; but cf. *Measure for Measure*, II. ii. 15–16: 'What shall be done, sir, with the groaning

Juliet? | She's very near her hour'; and *OED groaning vbl. sb.* 2: 'A lying-in'—as in *Hamlet*, III. ii. 259: 'It would cost you a groaning to take off my edge.'

381 These ... *Jove*] Marlowe's line makes sense—but it is not Lucan's sense! The Latin is *Numina miscebit castrensis flamma monetae* (Duff: 'the furnace of the military mint shall melt down the statues of the deities'). Marlowe might have been somewhat misled by Sulpitius, who wrote: *Numina Monetae. Iunonis Monetae templum*, referring to the fact that *Moneta* was a surname for Juno: the temple of Juno Moneta was the Roman mint.

383 quarter out] Mark out, outline (*OED quarter vb.* 2b. '*Obs.*').

390 *Ossa's*] The unusual (at this time) possessive apostrophe may in fact be marking the omission of an *e* (which would give the form *Ossaes*; *e* following a vowel to form the possessive case is found at line 452: *Plutoes*).

391 *Thracian Boreas*] The north wind. For the Romans, as for the Greeks, 'Thratian' was a conventional epithet for 'northern'.

bowe] Dyce's emendation is sensible, giving action to the line and accurately representing the Latin: *curvato robore pressae | Fit sonus aut rursus redeuntis in aethera silvae.*

396–442 musters men] Catalogues of supporters (such as the one which follows) are an epic convention (Pompey's forces are listed in Book III of the *Pharsalia*). But Marlowe seems to be in some error, giving the impression that the named nations rallied to Caesar's aid—like the troops in arms under Tamburlaine. Lucan, however, says simply that the Roman soldiers who guarded these areas (previously conquered by Caesar) were recalled from their duties. It might be noted that Lucan himself is no very reliable authority on the subject of Caesar's conquests, so that identification is not always easy.

'*Lemannus* nooke' (line 397) is Lake Geneva, and the '*Lingones*' (line 398) the people occupying territory to the west of the Vosges ('*Vogesus*', line 399). '*Isara*' (line 400) is the river Isère. The Ruteni ('*Ruthens*', line 403) were a Gallic tribe living in the neighbourhood of what is now Toulouse. '*Atax*' (line 404) and '*Varus*' (line 405) are the rivers Aude and Var; in Lucan's day the latter formed the boundary between Italy and the *provincia*. Monaco is the name now given to '*Alcides* port' (line 406), deriving from *portus Herculis Monoeci*—the harbour sacred to Hercules the solitary dweller. '*Nemes* fields' (line 421) are the lands of the Németes on the left bank of the Rhine near Speyer. With '*Satirus*' (line 421) Marlowe is following the sixteenth-century reading of *Satyri*; modern editions have *Aturi*, referring to the river Adour which flows through Aquae Tarbellicae, '*Tarbels* winding shoares' (line 422). The '*Bituriges*' (line 424) were a Gallic people whose chief town was the modern Bordeaux. The '*Axon*' (line 424) is now called the Aisne, a river entering the Seine below Paris; and '*Rhene*' (line 425) is of course the Rhine. The peoples of '*Leuca*' (line 425) and '*Sequana*' (line 426) inhabited respectively Gallia Belgica north of the Lingones (line 398), and the modern departments of Jura and Doubs. The '*Averni*' (line 428) were from the Auvergne, and the '*Nervians*' (line 430) from the region which is east Flanders. The '*Vangions*' (line 431) were a Germanic race living around the town of Worms, and the '*Batavians*' (line 432) another Germanic tribe from what is now South Holland. '*Cyngas* streame' line 434) is the river Cines, which flows from the Pyrenees; '*Rhodanus*' (line 434) is the Rhône; and '*Araris*' (line 435) the Saône, a tributary of the Rhône. '*Gebenna*' (line 436) and '*Trevier*' (line 437) are Cevennes and Trier. The '*Ligurians*' (line 438) occupied territory between the Alpes-Maritimes and the valley of the Rhône.

After locating the different tribes geographically, Lucan proceeds to the religious groups, beginning with those who worshipped the Celtic deities Teutates, Hesus, and Taranis. The triad had been introduced into Gaul, and the Romans had tried to identify them with their own gods; Mercury, Mars, and Jupiter (440–2).

398 They ... foild] The Roman soldiers who controlled (*OED, foil v.*[1] 11) the Lingones.

with painted speares] Lucan's *pictis* ... *armis* probably refers to the shields which the Lingones carried, which were ornamented with enamel.

399 Under ... *Vogesus*] Modern editions of Lucan read: *Vosegi curvam* ... *ripam* (Duff: 'the winding bank of the Vosegus [Vosges]'). Marlowe's text, however, would have had the traditional reading, *Vogesi*; Sulpitius explained it as *Vogesus mons*, and further confused matters by offering in the margin, as a variant of *ripam*, the word that Marlowe obviously chose to translate, *rupem*.

401 Who ... floud] Lucan means that the river Isère, after flowing for some distance under its own name, merges into a greater river [the Rhône].

403 yellow] *flavi*—fair-haired.

404–5 Mild ... farre] Atax and Varus (the Aude and the Var) were happy to be free from Roman occupation.

407–8 north-west wind ... the north] Lucan names three winds: Corus, Zephyrus, and Circius. Marlowe uses the one name that would be familiar to his readers (Zephyrus, the west wind), but Sulpitius identifies the others. Circius ('the north') is probably the mistral.

409 enterance forbids] i.e. to '*Alcides* port': *tuta prohibet statione Monoeci*.

410 that uncertaine shore] Lucan is probably referring to the Belgian coast; like many Greek and Roman writers (accustomed to the comparatively tideless Mediterranean), he was fascinated by the action of the tides.

416 (feeding on the deepe)] Lucan alludes to the theory (which formed part of Stoic and other ancient cosmologies) that the sun was nourished by vapours arising from water. Marlowe's pronoun 'them' in line 417 should refer to Lucan's *alentes* ... *undas*; but the translation has lost the structure of the original.

419 God] Lucan has the plural, *superi*.

420 that dwell] Lucan's *Qui tenet* does not refer to the natives of '*Nemes fields*', but to the Roman forces who occupied this and the other named regions.

423 rejoyce in *Caesars* love] Marlowe is mistaken, perhaps because he read *amato* for *amoto*: the '*Santons*' are rejoicing at the departure of their [Roman] enemy: *gaudetque amoto Santonus hoste*, and Lucan now proceeds to list other tribes who shared in their relief.

424 light *Axon* pikes] Many editions have *Suessones* for *Axones*; these were *longisque leves* ... *in armis* (Duff: 'nimble in spite of their long spears').

427 *Brittish* cars] Lucan says that the Belgians were expert drivers of *monstrati*
... *covinni* (war chariots invented by others). A *covinnus* was a British chariot, as
Sulpitius explains in his comment on *Monstrati: A Britanni.*

428–9 Th'*Averni* ... race] The inhabitants of the Auvergne claimed that they,
like the Romans, were descended from the Trojans of ancient Ilium (Troy).

430 The ... bloud] The Nervii persisted in rebelling (*nimiumque rebellis*)
against their Roman conquerors, and in one of their uprisings treacherously
murdered one of Caesar's officers, L. Aurunculeius Cotta.

432 Were open slopes] The trousered dress ('Were' is a variant form of *wear*)
of the Gallic nations would naturally attract the attention of the Roman Lucan.
According to Sulpitius, the *laxis* ... *bracis* were short and tight—*vestes breves &*
strictae, quibus pudenda velantur ab umbilico ad genus, but Cooper translates *bracha*
as 'a breech or sloppe'. The chief characteristic of the Elizabethan 'slops' was
their looseness, or width: they seem to have been the forerunner of the clown's
baggy trousers (see my essay '"Such conceits as clownage keeps in pay"', in *The*
Fool and the Trickster, ed. P. V. A. Williams (Cambridge and Ipswich, 1979), 61).

438 late shorne *Ligurians*] Since they inhabited land which had become
Roman territory (*provincia*), they had adopted the Romans' short hair-style.

440–1 to *Hesus* ... flesh] Sulpitius comments that Hesus was *Asper & saevus*,
quia humanis victimis ... *placabantur*. The same was true of the god Teutates, *Qui*
mortis deus interpretatur. Mercurium hoc nomine Galli appellant'.

441–2 *Jove* ... serve] *Et Taranis Scythicae non mitior ara Dianae.* Sulpitius
identified the god (*Qui Jupiter interpretatur*) whose cruelty was comparable with
that of Scythian Diana: both deities were served with human sacrifice.

443 French *Bardi*] Sulpitius provided the nationality for Lucan's *Bardi:*
poetae, qui lingua Gallica cantores significant.

449–50 And only ... nothing] Lucan is quietly sceptical about the Druids:
their beliefs are very different from those of other peoples, and if the Druids are
right, all other faiths are wrong: *Solis nosse deos et caeli numina vobis | Aut solis*
nescire datum.'

452 *Plutoes* bloodles kingdom] For *Ditis* ... *Pallida regna*, Duff offers 'the
sunless realm of Dis', but Marlowe's version is more in the spirit of Sulpitius,
who (after explaining *Ditis* as *Plutonis*) comments on the use of *Pallida: Ab*
effectu, quae pallorem inducunt.

454 Death brings long life] According to Duff's translation of Lucan, 'death is
but a point in the midst of continuous life' (*vitae | Mors media est*). Marlowe seems
to be more nearly following Sulpitius, who has *Media morte pervenitur ad illam*
vitam aeternam.

461 Leaving ... spoile] When the military forces had all withdrawn to join
Caesar's army, the Roman empire was open to attack by foreign nations: *apertum*
gentibus orbem.

465 Vaine fame] *Vana* ... *fama*: Lucan attaches the conventional epithet
(glossed by Sulpitius as *Inanis*) to *fama* (rumour, report).

473 ten ensignes] Sulpitius first translated the metonymy of Lucan's *omnes*
aquilas into the factual *Decem legiones.*

474 not intirely ... ground] Marlowe seems rather awkward in his rendering
of Lucan's *Agmine non uno, densisque incedere castris* (Duff: 'with many a column
and crowded camps'). As Sulpitius explains, *Agmine non uno* implies that there
were many marching columns (*Pluribus aciebus & exercitibus*), and Marlowe's
'intirely' must be understood in the obsolete sense (*OED* 1) of 'as a whole'.
Maclure says that 'hide the ground' is 'a striking version' of *densisque ... castris*;
however, accuracy requires that 'yet' be understood in the sense (*OED* 1. 1) of 'In
addition ... also ... furthermore'.

476 more ... vassals] The comparison does not derive from Lucan, who says
that Caesar appeared 'more savage than the foes he has conquered' (Duff); and
Sulpitius glosses *victo ... hoste* as *Germanis*.

477–8 And that ... *Rhene*] Lucan reports that Caesar was followed by the
Germanic tribes dwelling between the Rhine and the Elbe: *inter Rhenum populos
Albimque iacentes* (though Marlowe's edition probably had *Alpesque*—the reading
of several manuscripts—for *Albimque*).

480 He looking on] Marlowe seems to understand Lucan's rhetoric better than
either Duff or Sulpitius. The former translates *Romano spectante* as 'under the
eyes of the Romans', in agreement with the commentary's explanation that
Romano signifies *Romanis militibus*. Marlowe, however, correctly interprets the
trope—which Puttenham calls '*Antonomasia*, or the Surnamer', instancing the
appellation 'the great *Vallois*' for 'the French king ... because so is the name of
his house' (*The Arte of English Poesie* (1589), 151).

484 the Court, the Senate] *Curia*.

486 Left ... *Consuls*] Marlowe is perhaps too concise in his translation of
invisaque belli | Consulibus fugiens mandat decreta senatus (Duff: 'and the Senate
fled, deputing to the consuls the dreaded declaration of war').

488 Their sway of fleight] Marlowe uses 'sway' in the sense (*OED* 3) of 'Force
or pressure bearing or inclining its object in one direction or another' to translate
Lucan's *fugae ... impetus.*

489 in chain'd troupes breake forth] 'Forth they rush in long unbroken
columns' is Duff's translation of *serieque haerentia longa | Agmina prorumpunt.*

491 Dropping-ripe ... Ruine] Lucan speaks of houses *iam quatiente
ruina | Nutantes pendere* (Duff: 'swaying and tottering in an earthquake shock').

492 the inconsiderate multitude] Sulpitius glosses Lucan's adjective *lymphata*
as *Furiosa*; 'inconsiderate' has the sense (*OED* 2) of 'acting without deliberation;
thoughtless, imprudent'.

496 *Auster*] The south wind.

breach] The breaking of waves on a coast; *OED* (*sb.* 1. 2) instances *Twelfth
Night*: before you took me from breach of the sea' (11. i. 21).

497 *Libian Syrtes*] Two wide gulfs, dangerous to shipping, on the north coast
of Africa; in stormy weather the south wind drives the sea away from the quick-
sands.

500–1 Marriners ... themselves] Although the ship is undamaged by the
storm, the sailors tear off its timbers for their own support in the water, thereby
wrecking the vessel: *Naufragium sibi quisque facit.*

505 Their houshould gods] The *Lares Familiares*, beneficent spirits who watched over each individual household.

507 Th' irrevocable people flie] In his translation of Lucan's *ruit inrenvocabile volgus*, Marlowe joins the 'clerks and scholers and secretaries' described by Puttenham who

... not content with the usual Normane or Saxon word, would convert the very Latine or Greeke word into vulgar French, as to say innumerable for innombrable, revocable, irrevocable, irradiation, depopulation & such like, which are not naturall Normans nor yet French, but altered Latines, and without any imitation at all: which therefore were long time despised for inkehorne termes, and now be reputed the best & most delicat of any other. (*The Arte of English Poesie*, II. xii.)

509–10 *Roome* ... Captives] Lucan pictures the city full of free citizens and conquered peoples: *Urbem populis victisque frequentem*, and his *victis* seems to justify Dyce's emendation from Q's 'Captaines'.

515 suddaine rampire] Marlowe translates the *subitus* ... *agger* with an obsolete sense of *sudden* (*OED adj.* 5): 'Made, provided, or formed in a short time'.

525 the North] Marlowe takes Lucan's *polum* in its absolute sense of North Pole, rather than with the general meaning of 'the sky'.

527 Commets ... kingdoms] Lucan is the source of the expression whose English phrasing was developed from Marlowe by Shakespeare in *1 Henry VI*: 'Comets, importing change of times and states' (I. i. 2).

528 The flattering skie] Lucan describes the omens in a sky of deceptive clearness—*fallaci* ... *sereno*.

often] This adjectival use (*OED* B) is common in the sixteenth and seventeenth centuries; cf. *As You Like It*, IV. i. 19: 'My often rumination wraps me in a most humorous sadness.'

533 the Capitoll] Lucan refers (and Sulpitius explains the reference) to *Latiare caput*—i.e. Alba Longa, the capital of Latium, with its shrine of Jupiter Latialis.

535–7 *Phoebe* ... pale] Lucan describes an eclipse when the moon was full and was reflecting the sun's light with her whole orb. For 'th'earths suddaine shadow', cf. *Dr Faustus*, A 244: 'Now that the gloomy shadow of the earth'— which in the B Text becomes 'shadow of the night' (line 227).

541–2 as did ... East] Mycenae was plunged into darkness when the sun fled back to its place of rising (*per ortus*) in horror at the sight of Thyestes, who banqueted on his own sons.

543 *Mulciber*]Vulcan, whose forges were under Mt Aetna.

545 bending *Hespery*] Instead of shooting upwards, the volcanic flames swept down to the Italian coast (*Ignis in Hesperium cecidit latus*).

546–7 *Charibdis* ... Mastives] The whirlpool Charibdis, traditionally said to be in the Straits of Messina, was opposite the cave of Scylla—who was commonly pictured as a marine monster with canine attributes.

547 the vestall fires] The perpetual flame on the altar of Vesta, goddess of the home.

548 The flame ... *Jove*] Lucan alludes to the sacrificial fires which signified the end of the *feriae Latinae*, and Sulpitius adds the explanation: *Sacra Latialis Iovis a Latinis populis.*

550 the *Theban* brothers] The bodies of Eteocles and Polynices, sons of Oedipus, were burned on the same funeral pyre, but the flames rose in two separate tongues, a sign that even in death the brothers were not reconciled.

551 The earth ... hinges] Marlowe translates Lucan's *cardine tellus Subsedit* with an expression which antedates *OED*'s earliest (1611) use of the phrase to mean 'out of order; in (or into) disorder'.

552 laps] There is a strong temptation here to accept Dyce's emendation 'tops', as being a more accurate translation of the Latin *iugis nutantibus.*

553 Spanish *Calpe*] Gibraltar (Lucan has *Hesperiam Calpen*, and Sulpitius glosses *Hesperiam* as *Hispaniam*).

554 *Atlas*] Sulpitius has *Atlas mons altissimus*. It was believed that this mountain, running from east to west across Africa, was so high that the heavens rested on top.

556 Crownes ... statues] It is Sulpitius who supplies this detail—*Sponte decidisse ornamenta & coronas deorum*—in explanation of Lucan's statement that the temple offerings fell from their places.

557 and wilde beastes] Martin follows Cunningham's suggestion, reading 'at night wild beasts', in order to regularize the rhythm and accommodate Lucan's *sub nocte.*

563-4 they ... armes] Fanatical worshippers of the war-goddess Bellona gashed their arms in orgiastic ecstasy.

564 *Sibils* priests] The *Galli*, eunuch priests of Cybele, were whirling (Marlowe's 'Curling') their hair in frenzy. The spelling here suggests that Marlowe has confused the Cumaean Sibyl (whose prophecies, the Sibylline books, are referred to in line 562) with Cybele, the Great Mother.

566 quiet and appeas'd] Cooper gives both these words in translating *conpono* (Lucan's *conpositis*).

sigh'd] The emendation (from Q's 'sight') makes for both the sense and an accurate rendering of *gemuerunt.*

570-2 fowle ... toppe] One of the Furies, with the traditional attributes of snakes for hair and a flaming torch.

573 the sterne *Lycurgus*] This was a king of Thrace who attempted to drive the worship of Bacchus from his kingdom; intending to cut down the vines, he cut off his own legs.

574 fierce *Agave*] In a state of Bacchic frenzy Agave, wife of the King of Thebes, killed her own son, Pentheus.

574-6 like *Megaera* ... face] The Fury Megaera was sent by Juno (*iussu Junonis iniquae*) to terrify Hercules after his visit to the underworld, where he had seen its ruler, Dis (*viso iam Dite*). Marlowe accepts the gloss of Sulpitius: *Post visum Plutonem.*

579 *Sylla's* ghost] The dictator L. Cornelius Sulla.

581–2 *Marius* ... open] Gaius Marius had opposed Sulla (according to Sulpitius, the two *bellis civilibus gavisi sunt*); on the orders of Sulla, the body of Marius was disinterred and thrown into the Anio, the river Teverone.

584 th'*Etrurian Augures*] *Tuscos ... vates*. Sulpitius: *Hetrusiae aruspices*. The Etruscans invented the art of the *haruspex*—divination from the entrails of a slaughtered beast.

585 *Leuca] Sixteenth-century editions of Lucan (as well as Sulpitius) give the marginal gloss *Luna*.

586 *Pyromancy*] Lucan says that the soothsayer understood the course of the thunderbolt (*Fulminis ... motus*), and Sulpitius explains this as *Pyromanticus*.

589 the barren ... issue] Lucan does not specify an unnatural beast, but Sulpitius explains that the reference is *propter mulam*.

592 the sacred priests] Lucan appears to be contrasting these, the college of high priests, with the *Turba minor* (Marlowe's 'inferiour troupe' in line 595) from the subordinate religious colleges.

596 the *Gabine* manner] According to this fashion a corner of the toga was thrown over the left shoulder, and brought under the right arm to the breast.

597 vaild Matron] The procession of vestals was led by a *vittata sacerdos*, whom Sulpitius describes as *Maxima Vestalium, velata*.

598 *Minervas* statue] The Palladium.

599 *Sybillas* secret works] Sulpitius makes it clear that the *fata deum secreta carmina* are the *Sibyllinos libros*, the prophecies of the Cumaean Sibyl—whom the next line seems to confuse once again with Cybele (cf. line 564n.).

599–600 wash ... floud] The image of the goddess Cybele was washed annually in the Almo, to restore its original purity in the cleansing waters.

601 *Apolloes* southsayers] The *Titii ... sodales* are identified by Sulpitius: *sacerdotes Apollinis*.

Joves feasting priests] Sulpitius is needed to explain Lucan's *Septemvirque epulis festis*; these were *sacerdotes ... qui in dicendorum faciendorumque epulorum Iovi, & diis reliquis facultatem habebant*.

602 The skipping ... wedges] The *Salii* were dancing priests of Mars; the detail of the shape of their shields came from Sulpitius: *Scuta cuneata specie*.

603 *Flamins* ... vailes] The flamens were priests who performed the sacrifice. Lucan mentions the pointed cap (*apicem*) worn as a mark of office, but Marlowe prefers the detail supplied by Sulpitius: *assiduo filo veletur, quasi filamen*.

607 cals ... *Bidentall*] Modern editions read *Datque locis numen*, which refers to the hallowing of the ground where the lightning-blasted wreckage was interred. One textual variant, however, is *nomen* for *numen*, and Sulpitius adds *Appellat Bidental*, alluding to the ritual slaughter of a young sheep (*bidens*) to sanctify the spot.

609 salt levin] Cooper translates Lucan's word *molas* as 'a cake made of meale

and salt'; 'levin' is a form of *leaven*—and indicates that Marlowe is thinking (correctly) of the meal rather than the finished 'cake'.

614 wallowed] A powerful use of the verb in the sense of 'spouted, gushed' (*OED. v. intr.* 5). Cf. the translation of Seneca's *Agamemnon* by John Studley, in *Tenne Tragedies*, ed. Thomas Newton, 1581:

> heere from the Carkasse dead
> The spouting blood came gushing out: and there the head doth lye
> With wallowing, bobling, mumbling tongue. (Act V)

620–1 every vaine ... *Caesar*] Marlowe manages to convey some sense of Lucan's description of the liver: *venasque minantes* [modern editions, *inaces*] *Hostili de parte videt*. The two main lobes of the liver were called the *pars hostilis* and the *pars familiaris*; here the *pars hostilis* is that of Caesar, and its swollen veins portend conflict.

624 Squis'd ... pearde] The emendation of Q's punctuation allows for the accommodation of Lucan's meaning: *produntque suas omenta latebras*. The verb 'Squis'd' could be a form of either of *OED*'s 'obsolete' verbs *squiss* or *squize*; both have a sense of 'squeezing'. It is Cooper who translates *omentum* as 'The call ... wherein the bowels are lapt'.

635 *Tages*] A grandson of Jupiter, who was the first teacher of augury and divination by haruspication.

637 Involving all] Modern editions of Lucan read *omina ... Involvens*, but sixteenth-century texts have *omnia*. Marlowe's 'Involving' (*OED* 3) is a reasonable rendering of the gloss *Confundens & occultans*.

638 *Figulus*] A neo-Pythagorean sage.

639 *Aegiptian Memphis*] The Egyptian school of astrology.

640 tune-full planeting] Marlowe takes Lucan's *numeris* in the sense of the order or harmony of the spheres—the direction indicated by Sulpitius: *Canonicis spaciis temporum, quibus se astra per gradus movent quadam cum harmonia*. Ben Jonson is perhaps recalling Marlowe's phrase when he writes of 'giving to the World | Again, his first and tunefull plannetting' (*The Sad Shepherd*, III. ii. 31–2).

642 casuall] *OED casual* 1: 'produced by chance ... fortuitous'. Lucan's *incerto ... motu* is glossed *Temerario & fortuito*' by Sulpitius.

647 Shall ... ice] Lucan's soothsayer fears that the waters will all be poisoned (*Omnis an effusis miscebitur unda venenis*).

650 cold ... *Saturne*] Sulpitius justifies Lucan's astrological epithet with the explanation that Saturn is called *frigida, Quia a Sole, in quo totus est calor, est astellag remotissima*.

652 *Gaynimede*] Lucan has the more predictable *Aquarius*, but Marlowe changes the name in accordance with the comment of Sulpitius: *Aquarius signum, in quod finxerunt Ganymedem fuisse conversum, & ex urna aquam emittere*.

Deucalions flood] The inundation whereby Jupiter drowned the whole human race except Deucalion and his wife, Pyrrha.

654 sing] A form of *singe*.

655 The fell *Nemean* beast] The Nemean lion killed by Hercules as one of his twelve labours—*qui postea inter signa relatus est* (Sulpitius)—to become the constellation Leo.

657 thy fiers hurt not] *Hi cessant ignes.* The action described by Lucan took place in winter, when Saturn was not 'exalted' (*Summo . . . caelo*), and the Sun was not in the sign of Leo.

659 cleyes] The claws (*chelas*) of Scorpio; 'cleyes' is a variant of *sb. clee*, itself a form of *claw* (*OED*).

660 Kind] Sulpitius gives *Benignus* for Lucan's *mitis.* Lucan makes the standard distinction between the benign planets, Jupiter and Venus, and those of baleful aspect—cold Saturn and fiery Mars—which at the time were dominant.

661 swift *Hermes* retrograde] *motuque celer Cyllenius haeret.* Sulpitius identifies *Cyllenius* as *Mercurius*, and glosses *haeret* as *Retrogradus est.* Mercury is swiftest of the planets because it is closest to the sun.

664 Sword-girt . . . bright] The constellation Orion is conspicuous for its brilliance; three especially bright stars form the 'side' (*latus*), or belt.

666–7 Let all . . . let last] Lucan uses the simple future tense here (*erit* and *exhibit*); Marlowe's 'Let' and 'let' seem to be used jussively.

669 War onely gives us peace] Lucan's soothsayer is rather less ambiguous: peace will bring a reign of tyranny (*Cum domino pax ista venit*).

674 As . . . raves] With the aid of Sulpitius, Marlowe unravels the allusiveness of Lucan's *Nam qualis vertice Pindi | Edonis Ogygio decurrit plena Lyaeo.* Sulpitius glosses *Edonis* as *Maenas, sacerdos Bacchi*, and explains *plena Lyaeo* as *Corrupta furore Bacchi*, adding for *Ogygio* the more usual *Thebano.* Pindus, in Thrace, was renowned for Bacchanalian revels.

676 Disclosing *Phoebus* furie] *Manifestans Phoebi numen* is the gloss given by Sulpitius.

677 *Pean*] A surname of Apollo.

678–94 see . . . downe] The 'Matron's' vision reveals the battles to come and the civil warfare, along with the deaths of Pompey and Caesar, until the time of the final struggle at Philippi in 42 BC.

678 *Pangeus* hill] The mountain that overlooked Philippi.

680 Philippi plaines] Duff comments (and Sulpitius offers a similar observation) that 'She means Pharsalia; but it is a convention with the Roman poets . . . to speak of Pharsalia and Philippi as fought on the same ground'.

683 *Pelusian*] Pelusium was the city at the mouth of the Nile.

684 This headlesse trunke] The body of Pompey.

686–7 where . . . bandes] Some modern editions have *Enyo* (goddess of war) for *Erinnys*, the Fury who drove the Thessalian armies to fight in Africa.

688 pine bearing hils] The reference is to the Alps. In the Latin there is a textual crux, with the variants *piniferae | nubiferae*; modern editors prefer the latter, but Marlowe's text obviously read *piniferae.*

689 *Pirene*] The Pyrenees.

689–90 back to *Rome* ... Senat House] She foresees Caesar's return to Rome after the battle of Munda, and his assassination in the Roman Senate House.

691 New factions rise] She prophesies continuing struggle after the death of Caesar.

693 I have seene *Philippi*] She has already witnessed the Battle of Pharsalia (see line 68on.), and does not want to see the repetition (between Augustus, Brutus, and Cassius) at Philippi.

DIDO QUEENE OF CARTHAGE

Act I, scene i

0.1 *dandling*] According to *OED*, the verb *dandle* was not known before the sixteenth century; early usage supports the definition 'To move (a child, etc.) lightly up and down in the arms or on the knee'.

2 say ... will] Juno hated Ganymede because he was her rival in Jupiter's affections, and also (as she explains in III. ii. 42–3) because he had displaced her daughter, Hebe, as cupbearer to the gods.

5 when as] *OED* 1: 'At the, or a, time at which'.

fild] *OED fill* 13: 'To pour out'.

6 cloath of pleasance] *OED* defines *pleasance* as 'a fine lawn or gauze'; in the early examples it is the fabric of the ladies' scarves tied round the arms of their jousting knights.

10 *Saturnes* soule] Alliteration, rather than filial piety, seems to be the only explanation for this oath.

earth threatning haire] Ovid in the *Metamorphoses* describes how

Jove standing up aloft and leaning on his yvorie Mace,
Right dreadfully his bushie lockes did thrise or four times shake,
Wherewith he made both Sea and Land and Heaven it self to quake. (i. 204–6)

This allusion is also found in Nashe's *The Unfortunate Traveller*, published in the same year as Marlowe's play: '*Iupiter* is said with the shaking of his haire to make heaven & earth to quake' (McKerrow, ii. 217).

Q's spelling, 'aire' (which appears again at line 159), might seem to be compositorial idiosyncrasy; but the aspirated form is used in the rest of the play, and it would be pedantic to retain a probable error here.

13–15 To hang ... *Hercules*] Jupiter reminds Juno of this punishment in the *Iliad*, xv. 18ff. The lines are translated by Chapman thus:

Forgett'st thou, when I hang'd thee up, how to thy feet I tied
Two anvils, golden manacles on thy false wrists implied,
And let thee mercilessly hang from our refined heaven

.   .   .   .

Nor was my angry spirit calm'd so soon, for those foul seas,
On which, inducing northern flaws, thou shipwrack'dst Hercules.

Apollodorus mentions this story in *The Library*: '... when Hercules had taken Troy and was at sea, Hera sent a storm after him; so Zeus hung her from Olympus' (I. iii. 5).

17 *Helens* brother] Helen had two brothers, Castor and Pollux. Castor was mortal and died in battle, but Pollux persuaded Jupiter to allow him to share his immortality with his brother, so they alternately lived and died each day or (according to other writers) every six months.

20 Egles wings] Ganymede was carried to Olympus by Jupiter's eagle (or by Jupiter himself, in the form of an eagle) when the god was captivated by the boy's beauty.

21 my immortall beautie] Ganymede was invested with immortal youth when he was abducted to Olympus.

25 exhal'd] *OED* defines a rare sense of *exhale v.* 2: 'To draw up, raise (a person) to a higher position', suggesting a comparison with *exalt*, and offering as an example Drayton's reference to those 'whose Minds should be exhal'd and hie'. In conjunction with 'hal'd thee from my sight' (line 27) 'exhal'd' forms one of Marlowe's favourite rhetorical devices, the polyptoton—described by Henry Peacham in *The Garden of Eloquence* (1577) as 'A figure which of the word going before deriveth the word following .... To delight the ear by the derived sound and to move the mind with a consideration of the high affinity and concord of the matter.'

26 horses of the night] An allusion to the line from Ovid's *Amores* (I. xiii. 40) that Marlowe quotes at the climax of *Dr Faustus* (A 1459): *O lente lente curite noctis equi.*

29 cut ... time] Jupiter offers Ganymede the job of Atropos, one of the three Fates, whose function was to determine the deaths of men by cutting the threads of human life.

32 *Vulcan* ... sport] At the end of Book I of the *Iliad* the gods are reduced to helpless laughter as Vulcan, the lame god of fire and blacksmiths, bustles round the hall to serve wine at their feast. Nashe elaborates the line in *Summer's Last Will and Testament* (performed in 1592) with an account of how 'To make the gods merry, the coelestiall clowne *Vulcan* tun'de his polt foote to the measures of *Apolloes* Lute, and daunst a limping Gallyard in *Ioues* starrie hall' (iii. 294).

33 my nine Daughters] The Muses, who were the daughters of Jupiter and Mnemosyne.

34 *Junos* bird] The peacock was sacred to Juno (just as the swan (line 36) was an attribute of Venus).

38 *Hermes* ... wings] The messenger of the gods was traditionally represented with winged sandals.

52 my *Aeneas*] Aeneas was the son of the goddess Venus and the mortal Anchises. Juno hated him for his parentage (Venus was her chief rival), and also because he was a Trojan, or Dardanian, the race sprung from Dardanus, who was the son of Jupiter and another of Juno's rivals, Electra. There was a prophecy, too, that a Trojan race would one day destroy Carthage, which Juno loved even

more dearly than her own birthplace, Samos: *quam Iuno fertur terris magis omnibus unam | posthabita coluisse Samo'* (i. 15–16).

55 *Boreas*] The north wind.

56 Made ... wheeles] The notion of Hebe as Juno's charioteer seems to have originated with Marlowe. Hebe was Juno's daughter, and sometime cupbearer to the gods.

58 *Aeolus*] Power to control the winds was delegated to Aeolus, who ruled from the island fortress of Aeolia (see line 63).

64–73 Poore ... tents] Venus envisages the shipwreck of Aeneas' fleet as a re-enactment of the fall of Troy. The Trojan Horse, designed by Epeus, is paralleled by the destructive rocks off the Sicilian coast ('*Aetnas* hill', line 66), and the god of the winds, Aeolus, plays the part of the Greek leader Agamemnon (line 68).

70–1 See ... erst] Nashe provides a gloss on this in *The Unfortunate Traveller*, describing how '*Vlysses, Nestor, Diomed* went as spies together in the night into the Tents of *Rhaesus*, and intercepted *Dolon*, the spie of the Troians' (McKerrow, ii. 220).

72 *Rhesus* Steedes] The capture of these horses was essential for the destruction of Troy. An oracle prophesied that the city would never be taken as long as Rhesus' horses pastured in Troy and drank the waters of the Xanthus.

73 *Astraeus*] This was the husband of Aurora, and father of the stars.

76 *Proteus*] A sea-god (sometimes said to be the son of Neptune). Oliver suggests that Proteus, rather than Neptune, was chosen for this particular action because in the *Aeneid* (i. 124ff.) Virgil describes Neptune's wrath when he witnessed the storm and its destructiveness.

79 pietie] Marlowe seems to be alluding to that special quality in Aeneas designated by Virgil's adjective *pius* and defined in *OED*'s sense II. 3 of *piety* as 'Faithfulness to the duties naturally owed to parents and relatives'.

82 *Cytherea*] This surname of Venus derives from the name of an island close to the spot where the goddess arose from the sea when she was born.

87 *Turnus*] King of the Rutuli in Italy, Turnus was betrothed to Lavinia, who married Aeneas after he had conquered and killed Turnus.

88 her] i.e. Fortune.

92 mannaging] In its earliest form the verb *manage* (*OED* 1) comes directly from the Italian *maneggiare*—to school or train a horse. Marlowe uses the word in this sense in one of his *Elegies*: And rough Jades mouthes with stuborne bits are torne, | But managde horses heads are lightly borne (1. ii. 15–16).

99 That ... underprops] Atlas was the son of Tapetus (a Titan) and Clymene, daughter of Oceanus; as punishment for his part in the Titans' revolt, Atlas was condemned to support the heavens on his shoulders while he stood on the earth (which may be the meaning of 'earth-borne'). Marlowe's phrase seems to be echoed in Nashe's *Pierce Penilesse* (1592) with the comment on the man who could tolerate no rival, preferring 'like *Atlas* [to] vnder-proppe heauen alone' (McKerrow, i. 184).

100 his Emperie] Virgil's Jupiter is in fact referring not to Ascanius, but to the empire of the Romans (his readers) who were the descendants of Romulus: *nec metas rerum nec tempora pono;* | *imperium sine fine dedi* (i. 278–9).

104–7 Thus ... birth] Marlowe follows Virgil closely in this part of the god's prophecy:

hic iam ter centum totos regnabitur annos
gente sub Hectorea, donec regina sacerdos
marte gravis geminam partu dabit Ilia prolem. (i. 272–4)

104 stoute *Hectors* race] Hector was the most valiant of Priam's sons, and was captain of all the Trojans when the Greeks besieged Troy. Ascanius belonged to his 'race' because his mother, Creusa, was one of Priam's daughters.

106–7 a Princesse priest ... birth] Ilia (sometimes called Rhea Silvia) was the daughter of Numitor, King of Alba. She was a vestal virgin, but after being raped by Mars became the mother of the twin boys Romulus and Remus, who grew up to found Rome. *OED* cites this use of 'conceav'd by' to illustrate sense 1. 3 (*pass ... Obs.*) of *conceive*, meaning 'To be made pregnant'; the usage in line 125 is comparable.

108 eternish] The early form of *eternize*, with the sense (b): 'To make eternally famous, to immortalize'.

attempts] *OED*'s sense 2 of *attempt*, referring to the thing attempted rather than the effort expended.

111–12 And *Phoebus* ... maine] Tucker Brooke explains: 'The sun, who never visits the Styx, seems to show, by reason of the continual storm, a similar unwillingness to shine upon the Mediterranean.' The comparison of sun-rays and the golden 'tresses' of Phoebus Apollo was a commonplace—cf. the reference in Marlowe's translation of Ovid's *Elegies*: 'Who'le set the faire treste sunne in battell ray' (i. i. 15).

116 Besiege] In the sixteenth century, disharmony between verb (here in a plural form) and subject (the singular 'wind-god') is common.

ofspring ... loynes] Like all other princes of Troy, Aeneas was descended from Dardanus, the legendary founder of Troy, who was the son of Jupiter and Electra; unlike the other princes, however, his descent was through Anchises, not Priam.

121 geare] many of the contexts of sense 11c of *OED*'s *gear* (matter, affair, business) indicate the word's deprecatory use. In *Edward II* the word is used by Lightborne as he undertakes the murder of Edward: 'So now must I about this geare' (v. v. 39); and in *The Merchant of Venice* Antonio is either cheered or made impatient by Gratiano's chatter: 'I'll grow a talker for this gear' (i. i. 110).

127–9 For my sake ... froth] Venus similarly urges her oceanic birth in an appeal to the sea-god (on behalf of Ino and her children) in the *Metamorphoses:* 'At least wise if amid the Sea engendred erst I were | Of Froth, as of the which yet still my pleasant name I beare' (iv. 663–4).

130 *Triton* ... *Troy*] An ugly line, whose meaning is unclear. Triton's duty was to recall the winds and waves by blowing on a conch shell. Tucker Brooke suggests that Marlowe sees him here as a 'trumpeter of news'; Oliver offers the

notion of his 'playing a kind of lament for Troy'; and Clifford Leech suggested to Oliver the interpretation (which I favour) that 'Triton has had his fill of blowing up waves and winds against the Trojans'. The sense of being satiated is present in *OED*'s description III. 10b of *fill*.

132 *Thetis* and *Cimodoce*] Both were Nereides, but Thetis (mother of Achilles) is not mentioned when Virgil describes the calming of the Seas in Book I, where *Cymothoe simul et Triton adnixus acuto | detrudunt navis scopulo* (144–5). This reference, however, seems to have justified Dyce's emendation (*Cimothoe*) of Q's *Cimodoae*. The emendation has been accepted by subsequent editors, who have neglected Hurst's *Cimodoce*, the reading adopted here. Marlowe seems to have leapt across the *Aeneid* to Book V, when Neptune again stills the waves at the request of Venus, but this time with the aid of *Thetis . . . Cymodoceque* (825–6). In *The Faerie Queene* Spenser describes the nymph 'that with her least word can asswage | The surging seas, when they do sorest rage, | *Cymodoce*' (IV. xi. 50–2).

136 attract] This word (*OED* 1, 'to draw in, absorb') was popular with Nashe, who, for example, describes the pains of hell in *Christs Teares Over Ierusalem* (1593) as 'A hundred thousande thousande times more than thought can attract, or supposition apprehend' (McKerrow, ii. 168).

139 Here in this bush] The line gives information about the stage's equipment, and also translates the Latin *Cui mater media sese tulit obvia silva* (i. 314).

144 mee] Q's reading, 'thee', is clearly erroneous in its singularity, and Dyce's emendation 'ye' articulates the repeated *vos* of Virgil's Aeneas. I do not agree with Bowers, however, that 'ye' is 'most plausible palaeographically' and must therefore be adopted; 'mee' is equally possible, and this reading is supported by three other obvious instances of confusion between *m* and *th* (IV. iii. 28, V. i. 117, and V. i. 268).

146 barking *Scilla*] Virgil speaks only of *Scyllaeam rabiem*, but Marlowe's adjective is a reminder that Scylla was the dog-like monster on one side of the straits of Messina (who devoured most of the ships that avoided the whirlpool Charybdis on the other side).

147 The *Cyclops* shelves] The rocky coast of Sicily, home of the one-eyed man-eating giants, the Cyclops.

Ceranias seate] Virgil has the usual spelling when his Aeneas, at a later point in the poem, recalls how *Prohevimur pelago vicina Ceraunia iuxta* (iii. 506), but Marlowe opts for the spelling *Cerania* here and *Cerannia* in Elegy II. xi. 19, where he also refers to the Ceraunian mountain range and promontory in Epirus.

151 *Pergama*] The word is more commonly found in the singular form—Pergamum (i.e. the citadel of Troy)—but on occasion both Virgil and Ovid use the plural.

154 coming] Dyce's emendation is frequently accepted, with editorial allusion to the fairly common confusion of 'cunning' and 'coming' in texts of this period. Oliver retains Q's 'cunning', explaining that the 'joyes' will be 'subtle, to be eagerly appreciated because they have to be contrived'; the description seems rather to fit his own definition, which has no support from *OED*. In the play Achates is the speaker, but it seems that Marlowe has given him the words of

Aeneas, who urges his shipwrecked comrades: *durate, et vosmet rebus servate secundis* (i. 207). As a translation of *rebus . . . secundis*, 'coming' is perfectly acceptable.

155 Doe . . . cleare] The ability to control the climate with a smile is attributed also to Tamburlaine, who 'with [his] lookes canst cleare the darkened Sky' (Part 1, III. iii. 122), and 'Whose chearful looks do cleare the clowdy aire' (Part 2, I. iii. 3).

159 the aged Sunne] In *Metamorphoses* Phoebus complains, after the death of Phaethon, that he has lighted the world for too long:

> My lot (quoth he) hath had inough of this unquiet state
> From first beginning of the world. It yrkes me (though too late)
> Of restlesse toyles and thanklesse paines.   (ii. 482–4)

165 the meate we kild] Virgil describes how the exhausted Trojans rested on the shore while their indefatigable leader searched out and killed seven stags for their food.

166 Gentle . . . boxe] Although Ascanius' plea (line 163) is Marlowe's addition, the detail of the fire-making is Virgilian:

> ac primum silici scintillam excudit Achates
> succepitque ignem foliis atque arida circum
> nutrimenta dedit rapuitque in fomite flammam.   (i. 174–6)

170 How . . . driven] This is the only example given in *OED* to illustrate the elliptical use (4a) of *near* where '*To drive (one) near*' means 'to force into some strait or extremity'.

175ff. Whiles . . .] Marlowe follows Virgil closely (i. 305ff.) in describing the encounter of Aeneas and Achates with the goddess on their reconnoitring expedition.

183–6 Hoe . . . skin] Marlowe translates i. 321–3:

> 'heus,' inquit, 'iuvenes, monstrate, mearum
> vidistis si quam hic errantem forte sororum,
> succinctam pharetra et maculosae tegmine lyncis.

189–91 Whose lookes . . . Goddesse] *Aeneid* i. 327–8: *namque haud tibi voltus | mortalis, nec vox hominem sonat; o dea certe!*

192 shrowdes] The preceding verb ('delud'st' in line 191) agrees properly with the subject 'Thou'; but because the English relative pronoun is not fully inflected, there is a not uncommon lack of concord between its antecedent and the present verb. G. L. Brook (p. 66) illustrates this Elizabethan characteristic with an example from *Othello* (IV. i. 125): 'So, so, so, so: they laugh, that winnes'.

193 the Sunnes bright Sister] Diana, the virgin huntress, was sister to Phoebus Apollo, and also—as Phoebe—goddess of the moon (which perhaps accounts here for 'bright').

204 Turen] Venus identifies herself as one of those who followed Dido to Africa from her birthplace Tyre (one of the two major towns of Phoenicia, a country of Asia at the east end of the Mediterranean).

207 lawndes] An early form of *lawn*, designating 'An open space between woods' (*OED* 1).

213 Sidonian *Dido*] Dido also takes a surname from Sidon, the other major town of Phoenicia (see line 204n.).

220 twise twelve ... ships] Virgil's Aeneas has fewer vessels: *bis denis navibus*.

241 I know ... feete] An accurate, if inelegant, rendering of the sense of Virgil's *vera incessu patuit dea* (i. 405). However the deities might disguise their forms, there was no way of concealing their effortless ambulation.

244 shades] *OED* 11. 5b (= *shadow* 6): 'an unreal appearance, something that has only a fleeting existence'.

248 discoursive] *OED* claims this line as an example of *discoursive a. Obs.* 3b, where it is apparently synonymous with 'conversational'.

Act I, scene ii

This scene portrays the encounter in Book I of the *Aeneid* between Dido and the Trojan leaders, watched by Aeneas and Achates from the cloud in which Venus has transported them from the shore. Marlowe is responsible for the division of the lines between Illioneus, Cloanthus, and Sergestus. The first of these (*maximus*) is the spokesman in the Latin.

1 brave] *OED* 2: 'Finely-dressed ... grand'; or more probably (*OED* 3): 'a general epithet of admiration or praise: Worthy, excellent ...'.

11 houshold lares] The *lares familiares* were spirits who watched over house and household; their images were carefully tended in every home.

19 buckled] *OED* (1. 1. 3a) gives the rare sense of 'grappled' (with an adversary); presumably the alliteration appealed to Marlowe.

20–4 There is ... same] Italy was first called *Hesperia*, the western land (*Hesperiam Grai cognomine dicunt*, i. 530), but was later given its modern name in honour of the ruler Italus, an Arcadian prince.

26 gloomie *Orion*] The constellation Orion (Virgil's *nimbosus Orion*, i. 535) was usually associated with storms because of the time of its setting towards the end of June.

41 *Jupiter* ... house] For the generosity with which they entertained Jupiter and Mercury (although they were disguised), Baucis and her husband Philemon became symbols of hospitality. The story was well known; it is not referred to in the *Aeneid*, but the full version is in *Metamorphoses*, viii. 801ff.

sillie] The sense is that of *OED* 3a ('simple, rustic'), or 3b ('humble, lowly').

46 quite] A form of the verb *quit*, with the sense (*OED* 11. 10) of 'repay, reward, requite'.

Act II, scene i

1 Carthage walles] In the poem, Aeneas first sees Carthage from a distance, and then, *mirabile dictu*, he is enveloped in a cloud and transported into the city, where he arrives, unseen, before the temple that Dido is intending to dedicate to

Juno. The carvings on the walls depict the story of Troy: *videt Iliacas ex ordine pugnas | bellaque iam fama totum volgata per orbem* (i. 456–7).

3 *Niobe*] Proud of her seven sons and seven daughters, Niobe boasted herself greater than Latona who had only two children (Apollo and Diana). To punish her for this hubris, her husband and all the children were killed, and Niobe herself was turned into a column of stone (or, in some versions of the myth, a stone fountain).

7 *Idas* hill] Near Troy was Mt Ida, from which the rivers Xanthus and Simois flowed into the Hellespont.

16 as *Pigmalions* did] Moved by the entreaties of Pygmalion, Venus changed the statue he had sculpted into a living woman.

40 of ruth] Used here with its sense (*OED* 1) of 'compassionate, pitiful', *ruth* occurs frequently, with a variety of meanings, in this play.

80 *Sicheus*] Dido's uncle and husband, who was murdered by her brother Pygmalion (not to be confused with the sculptor).

85 *Irus*] The beggar who in Ulysses' absence became one of the suitors of Penelope.

110 *Antenor* did betray the towne] Antenor was a Trojan who argued in favour of returning Helen to the Greeks, and was therefore spared at the fall of Troy. Medieval versions of the story, such as that of Caxton and Lydgate, make him the traitor that Dido has heard him to be (and these also couple Aeneas' name with that of Antenor).

111 *Sinons* perjurie] This is the version preferred by Aeneas (see lines 143ff. below).

112 all in this] i.e. 'all agree in this' (contrasting with the disagreement mentioned in line 109).

115 pale deaths stony mace] Behind this phrase lurks the figure who personified Death in the early drama; he was described by Ralph Willis as an old man 'in blew with a serjeant-at-armes his mace on his shoulder' (*Mount Tabor* (1639), cited by F. P. Wilson, *The English Drama 1485–1585* (1969), 76). The same figure appears at the end of *Hamlet*, where 'this fell sergeant, Death, | Is strict in his arrest' (v. ii. 336–7). The mace is 'stony' in the sense of being 'insensible or unfeeling' (*OED* 5a, for which an example is taken from *The Merchant of Venice*, where Shylock is described as 'A stonie adversary, an inhumane wretch | Uncapable of pitty' (IV. i. 4–5).)

121–3 *Achilles . . . eares*] Achilles was taught rhetoric by Phoenix, who accompanied his pupil to the war against Troy (*Iliad*, ix. 438ff.), where the Myrmidons formed his personal bodyguard. Virgil's Aeneas begins his narrative in Book II with the comment that even a Myrmidon would be moved to tears in the telling of such a story (*quis talia fando | Myrmidonum . . . temperet a lacrimis*), but the antithesis of 'Achilles tongue' and 'Mirmidons . . . eares' is Marlowe's own device.

134 Gave up their voyces] Voted.

135 marcht to Tenedos] Tenedos was in fact an island, but medieval writers may be responsible for Marlowe's error. Caxton, for instance, seems to have

thought it was the seaport for Troy, and tells how Paris and Helen 'abood at the porte of *thenedon* that was but thre myle fro Troye' (*The Recuyell of the Historyes of Troye*, ed. H. O. Sommer (1894), ii. 534).

145 ticing] *OED* comments on the verb *tice*: 'Aphetic form of *atise*, *attice* or *entice*, but found earlier than either of these'.

Hermes pipe] With his flute, Hermes charmed to sleep the hundred-eyed Argus, who had been set by Hera to keep watch on Io.

164 *Laocoon*] Marlowe ignores the horrific details in Virgil's account (ii. 198ff.) of the death of Laocoon who, with his two sons, was strangled in the coils of two serpents which emerged from the sea.

183 *Neoptolemus*] Pyrrhus, the son of Achilles, who was brought to Troy after his father's death; he is now acting in revenge ('with *Megeras* eyes', line 230).

215 The mangled head ... sonne] Virgil says merely that Polites, one of Priam's many sons, was murdered before his father's eyes; Marlowe has added the pathos of 'yongest' and the barbarity of the head carried on the spear.

217 balles of wilde fire] Early forms of hand-grenade, these 'balles' were 'composition[s] of highly inflammable substances, readily ignited and very difficult to extinguish' (*OED* 3).

230 *Megeras* eyes] Megera was one of the three Furies, ministers of the vengeance of the gods.

254 wind] To retain Q's 'wound' at this point might impute clumsiness to Neoptolemus. As Bowers comments: 'Pyrrhus does not make an enraged thrust that goes wide of the mark ... but lightly flirts his sword about.' Shakespeare was possibly recalling this line in *Hamlet* when the First Player recites part of 'Aeneas' tale to Dido':

> Unequal match'd,
> Pyrrhus at Priam drives, in rage strikes wide,
> But with the whiff and wind of his fell sword
> Th'unnerved father falls. (II. ii. 471–4)

There is, however, nothing inherently comic in the idea of an opponent being thrown to the ground by the wind of a sword—such as the massive military broadsword; in *Troilus and Cressida* Troilus is wholly serious when he reproves Hector for his generosity:

> When many times the captive Grecian falls,
> Even in the fan and wind of your fair sword,
> You bid them rise and live. (V. iii. 40–2)

265 By this] i.e. by this time (*OED by* 21b).

274–5 *Cassandra* ... Fawne] A daughter of Priam and Hecuba, who took refuge in the temple of Diana, but was discovered and raped by Ajax. Virgil mentions the attempt to rescue Cassandra (ii. 402ff.), but not her rape. 'Fawne' need not be emended to 'Fane' (= 'temple'), of which it is an accepted variant.

281 *Polixena*] Another daughter of Priam and Hecuba; she was betrothed to Achilles, and Virgil refers to her death on her lover's tomb (iii. 321ff.). The frustrated attempt to rescue her is Marlowe's own invention.

294–5 What ... Greece] Virgil makes no mention of the fate of Hecuba, but classical writers generally agree that when Troy was taken, Hecuba, as one of the captives, fell to the lot of Ulysses and embarked with the conquerors to sail to Greece.

297–9 *Helena ... Menelaus*] Virgil's Aeneas does not learn of this until he visits the underworld in Book VI of the *Aeneid*. Here he meets the shade of Deiphobus (a son of Priam), who recounts (lines 494ff.) his night of passion with Helen, who immediately afterwards betrayed him to Menelaus: *scilicet id magnum sperans fore munus amanti, | et famam exstingui veterum sic posse malorum* (526–7). *Alexander* was another name for Paris.

319 *Hyacinthe*] Q's italics perhaps suggest that the compositor understood this to be a proper noun, the name of the youth metamorphosed after his death into the flower. As a common noun denoting this flower, the word's earliest recorded usage (*OED* 2) is 1578.

320 Centronels] An obsolete form of *sentinels*, for which this is one of only two examples in *OED*.

334 nephew] *OED* 3 shows the seventeenth-century's common usage of this word to mean 'grandson'.

Act III, scene i

45 *Getulia*] The modern Morocco.

74 eye-beames] One of the Renaissance theories about the nature of sight held that it was by extramission, beams from the eye striking the object that was seen. This is the notion that underlies the opening lines of the Duke's sonnet in *Love's Labour's Lost*:

> So sweet a kiss the golden sun gives not
> To those fresh morning drops upon the rose,
> As thy eye-beams, when their fresh rays have smote
> The night of dew that on my cheeks down flows.   (IV. iii. 25–8)

116 riveld] In frequent use during the sixteenth century, *Rivelled* ('wrinkled') usually has the pejorative sense found in the lover's allusion to Dipsas 'riveld cheekes' in Elegy I. viii. 112.

123 Pyramides] A form of *pyramid*; the word could be used loosely (*OED* 3) to denote 'any structure of pyramidal form, such as a spire'.

128 meanly] The word has provoked several emendations: meetly (qy Dyce); seemly (Dyce); manly (qy Brereton); newly (qy Collier). I have followed the examples of McKerrow, Tucker Brooke, Oliver, and Bowers in rejecting these and allowing Q's reading to stand. F. P. Wilson, in his revision of McKerrow's *The Works of Thomas Nashe*, claimed a positive reason for retaining 'meanly' in a comparable situation, first noted by J. C. Maxwell, in Donne's elegy 'The Dreame', where the poet bids farewell to reason and welcomes fantasy because imagination is less extreme than reality: 'She can present joys meaner than you do; | Convenient, and more proportionall.' Similarly, one could adduce the remark made by Agrippina to her would-be suitor as she assures him that 'I think the best manner mean enough for your worthiness' (the story of 'Germanicus and

Agrippina' in *A Petite Pallace of Pettie his Pleasure* (1576; ed. I. Gollancz, 1908), i. 91).

Marlowe's passage might then be taken to mean—in the context of the absurd extravagance which Dido intends for the Trojans—that even the normal attire of Achates will be so sumptuous as to compel the attention of 'Seaborne Nymphes' (line 129) and 'wanton Mermaides' (line 130).

132 *Thetis . . . necke*] Oliver explains: 'The comparison is with the glories of the sun (Apollo) setting in the sea.' There is, however, no mythological account of a relationship between Thetis, one of the minor sea-deities, and Apollo. Marlowe also invokes the glory of such a setting sun in *Dr Faustus*, where Helen is described as 'More lovely then the monarke of the skie | In wanton *Arethusaes* azurde armes' (A1374–5). Here too there is no basis in mythology for a connection between Arethusa and the sun-god.

139ff. The description of Dido's rejected suitors seems to have been developed by Marlowe from two suggestions in Book IV of the *Aeneid*. At the beginning (lines 35–53) Anna encourages her sister's love for Aeneas, reminding her of the many lovers (including Iarbus) she has scorned. Later in the book (lines 529–53), Virgil depicts a tormented Dido (*infelix animi Phoenissa*) pondering the proper course to take in her new-found love.

142 AENEAS] Some editors reassign this line, sharing Dyce's view that the ascription to Aeneas 'is proved to be wrong by the next speech of Dido [line 148]'. Bullen, however, argues for the retention of Q's assignation, with the explanation that in line 148 Dido is 'calling Aeneas' attention to another set of pictures on the opposite side of the stage'. In support of Bullen, Tucker Brooke adds: 'Note the reply of Aeneas [line 149], "It seems that *these* are kings". The men discussed in lines [141–7] do not seem to be kings, and there is no reason for singling out Aeneas as the only member of the company unacquainted with any of Dido's distinguished suitors.'

143 *Olympus*] Dyce and Tucker Brooke both emend to 'Olympia's', and Tucker Brooke explains that 'This is, of course, what the author meant, but it is very possible that he wrote *Olympus*'. The games were held at Olympia, where there was a celebrated temple and statue of Jupiter Olympius, to whom the games were dedicated.

163 This *Meleagers* sonne] Meleager was a famous hero of mythology, who sailed with the Argonauts, and who was also noted for the slaying of the Calydonian boar.

164 *gree*] A common aphetic form of *agree*.

Act III, scene ii

At the end of Act II, scene i, Ascanius was laid to sleep in a 'grove' (line 316)— and was presumably hidden (by curtains?) from the audience's sight for the duration of Act III, scene i. He is now revealed for a scene based chiefly on *Aeneid*, iv. 90ff. But Juno's opening speech has no counterpart in the poem. Virgil does not need to demonstrate Juno's duplicity; it is enough for him to explain Venus's recognition of her rival's intention: *sensit enim simulata mente locutam- , | quo regnum Italiae Libycas averteret oras.* For a proper appreciation of the situation in the play, however, the character must be revealed to the audience, and hence this invented speech. But the writing here seems remarkably clumsy; or else the text is unusually corrupt. Several emendations have been suggested at various times, but it seems to me that most of them only complicate, rather than clarify, the situation.

2 destinie] Tucker Brooke points out that Marlowe 'is fond of this name for the embodiment of human fate'. Among other examples, he cites the use in *Hero and Leander* of the plural 'Destinies' to designate the three Fates of classical mythology (lines 377 and 444), and the translation (Elegy I. iii. 17) of Ovid's *sororum* by the tautologous 'fatall destinie'.

3 The heire of furie, the favourite of the face] This line has provoked a number of queries and emendations. Bowers' version is typical: 'The heire of fame, the favourite of the fates'. Oliver says that 'fame' is preferable to the other suggestions ('the Furies', qy Deighton; 'Troy', Cunningham; 'fancy', qy Brereton), because 'it makes better sense . . . and "furie" is conceivably a compositor's misreading of the word'. But the alteration merely repeats the sense of the preceding line, where Ascanius is described as 'The boy wherein false destinie delights'. Ascanius could, perhaps, be called 'heire of furie' in that he has inherited everything that Troy represented now that the city itself has been destroyed by fury (in mythological terms, by the Furies taking vengeance on the theft of Helen from her Greek husband).

The second half of the line becomes even more repetitious with the substitution of 'fate' (Oliver) or 'the Fates' (Hurst) for Q's 'the face'. Oliver justifies his emendation with the explanation that 'A "c" | "t" confusion is the most likely explanation of Q's "face"; and Q's "the" may be an additional error introduced by the compositor to try to make some sense of what he obviously could not understand.'

7 race] A variant of both *rase* and *erase*, the context seems to demand the sense of *OED* 4: 'To alter (a writing) by erasure'.

11 left out] Hurst's emendation, 'let-out', has been generally accepted by subsequent editors; and Tucker Brooke paraphrases the meaning of this line as: 'And let his lifeless body infect the air'. I can accept the paraphrase, and would compare this line with the comment in *The Massacre at Paris* that the Admiral's corpse cannot be burned because 'his bodye will infect the fire, and the fire the aire, and so we shall be poysoned with him' (scene ix). But in both cases it is the *body* that is the source of infection—the body with the life 'left out'—cf. Iachimo's praise of the sculptor in *Cymbeline*: 'The cutter | Was as another Nature, dumb; outwent her, | Motion and breath left out' (II. iv. 83–5).

18 lustfull *Jove* . . . child] Some accounts of the birth of Venus report her to have been the child of Jupiter and the nymph Dione; she is 'adulterous' in her liaison with Mars.

20 *Juno* . . . *Rhamnuse* towne] The town of Rhamnus in Attica was celebrated for its statue of Nemesis, goddess of vengeance, with whom Juno now identifies herself.

22 prest] *OED* offers the word as '*a* and *adv. Obs.* meaning close at hand'.

43 my *Hebes* shame] Classical mythology seems to be silent about any 'shame'

connected with Juno's daughter, but Marlowe could have found a story of the disgrace and deposition of Hebe in Boccaccio's *Genealogie Deorum Gentilium*, Book IX, chapter ii:

Tandem cum ipse una cum ceteriis diis apud Ethyopes commensaturus ivisset, contigit quod, ministrante eis, Hebes, pocula, perque lubricum minus caute incedente, caderet, et casu, vestimentis amotis omnibus, in casu obscena Superis monstraret, quam ob causam factum est, ut illam ab officio pincernatus Juppiter removeret, et loco eius Ganimedem Laomedontis regis Troie fratrem sustitueret.

(ed. Vincenzo Romano (Bari, 1951), ii. 441)

47 ruth] *OED* 4: 'distress'.

50 unresisted] *OED* affords examples of this word's use in the sense of 'irresistible': cf. *The Rape of Lucrece*, 281–2: 'As corne ore growne by weedes, so heedfull feare | Is almost chok'd by unresisted lust.'

58 Fancie] *OED* 8b: 'Amorous inclination, love', as in the song from *The Merchant of Venice* 'Tell me where is Fancy bred'.

Lavinias shoare] Lavinia was the bride destined for Aeneas; her father was king of Latium, part of Italy.

91 *Silvanus* dwellings] The woods: Silvanus was a rural deity.

93 interchangeably] Glossing this word as 'mutually' and pointing to the next line 'seale up', Tucker Brooke comments: 'This is legal language', and he compares the term used for the indenture in *1 Henry IV* which was 'sealed interchangeably' by the interested parties. Juno here seems to be acting in her role of marriage goddess, the Juno Pronuba who is mentioned by Virgil when he refers to the divine consent approving the lovers as they take shelter in the cave: *prima et Tellus et pronuba Juno | dant signum* (iv. 166).

96 savour of my wiles] *OED* offers this line as its only example of an '*Obs.*, *rare*' sense, 12c, of *savour* meaning 'To have a suspicion of'. This is, I think, unnecessary; the context will happily support the more common meaning, *OED* 4a: 'to show traces of the presence or influence of; to have some of the characteristics of'. Moreover, this accords better with the presentation of the two scheming goddesses in both play and poem: in the *Aeneid* Venus assents to Juno's plans, smiling as she recognizes the deception: *adnuit atque dolis risit Cytherea repertis* (iv. 128).

97 as you will have] Some editors, including Bowers, follow Oxberry's example, and supply 'it' as the object pronoun for 'will have', thus making the line a regular pentameter. Such inference seems unjustified: omission of the object pronoun is common at this time, and metrical irregularity is frequent in this play.

99 *Ida*] Ascanius is taken by Venus (i. 692) *in altos | Idaliae lucos*—the groves sacred to the goddess (as Venus Idalaea) near the town of Idalium in Cyprus. The reference to '*Cypresse* Ile' (v. i. 41) shows that Marlowe is not guilty of confusing the Idalian groves with '*Idas* hill', the mountain near Troy which Aeneas refers to in II. i. 7.

100 *Adonis* purple downe] Probably the purple anemones that Venus caused

to spring from the blood of her beloved Adonis, killed by the boar he was hunting. Shakespeare describes the metamorphosis in *Venus and Adonis*:

> And in his blood that on the ground lay spill'd,
> A purple flow'r sprung up, check'red with white,
> Resembling well his pale cheeks and the blood
> Which in round drops upon their whiteness stood.   (1167–70)

Act III, scene iii

For more comment on the hunting scene and its place in the repertoire of the
children's companies, see General Introduction.

1 thinke not but] G. L. Brook (p. 101) points out that at this time 'but' was
used 'with a negative verb of believing or thinking to express an emphatic
affirmative'. This would seem to be an extension of *OED but* 19.

4 shrowdes] This line is offered as an example of *OED shroud* 1, where both
singular and (especially) plural are used to mean 'clothes, clothing, habiliments'.
In sixteenth-century syntax, such plural nouns can take either a singular or a
plural verb, and are likely to take the former when the subject 'though plural in
form, may be one that can be regarded as singular in meaning' (G. L. Brook, p.
65).

24 out of joynt] This is the figurative use of the phrase, meaning 'Disordered,
perverted, out of order' (*OED* 2b), and 'Said of ... persons in relation to
conduct'. The best-known instance of this usage is, of course, in Hamlet's cry of
despair: 'The time is out of joint; O cursed spite, | That ever I was born to set it
right' (I. v. 188–9).

26 man of men] This is an example cited in illustration of *OED* sense 43c,
where *of* (as used in the Hebraistic 'holy of holies', 'king of kings') denotes '(One)
distinguished out of a number, or out of all, on account of excellence'.

30–1 Huntsmen ... aire] In this formalized hunting, nets (*toils, OED* 1) were
set so as to enclose a space into which the quarry would be driven by huntsmen—
as beaters drive pheasant before the guns—so that the shooters would be almost
certain to make a hit. An extreme form of the ritual is described in a pamphlet of
1591, reporting the Queen's entertainment at Cowdray in August of that year:

On Munday, at eight of the clock in the morning, her Highnes took horse, with all
her traine, and rode into the parke: where was a delicate bowre prepared, under
the which were her Highnesse musicians placed, and a crossebowe by a Nymph,
with a sweet song, delivered to her hands, to shoote at the deere, about some
thirtie in number, put into a paddock, of which number she killed three or four,
and the Countess of Kildare one.

> (Cited by John Nichol, *The Progresses, and Public Processions of Queen Eliza-
> beth* (1788), ii.)

Shakespeare's Princess in *Love's Labour's Lost* deplores this 'sport':

> But come, the bow: now mercy goes to kill,
> And shooting well is then accounted ill.
> Thus will I save my credit in the shoot:
> Not wounding, pity would not let me do't;

> If wounding, then it was to show my skill,
> That more for praise than purpose meant to kill
>
> . . . .
>
> And I for praise alone now seek to spill
> The poor deer's blood, that my heart means no ill.   (IV. i. 24ff.)

42–5 And . . . brought me up] The tortured syntax of these lines seems to have been designed largely as a rhetorical parallel for Iarbus' subsequent speech 'mought' is an old form of *might*.

42–3 And . . . heads] Aeneas, in vengeful ambition for his son, which has no Virgilian authority, seems to visualize Ascanius as a counterpart to Pyrrhus: he will be to the Grecian city of Thebes what the son of Achilles was to Troy. The two famous cities were linked in one of Ovid's *Amores* (*Elegies* III. ix. 15–16) where the poet admits that major topics are neglected in his verse: 'When *Thebes*, when *Troy*, when *Caesar* should be writ, | Alone *Corinna* moves my wanton wit.'

44 with *Anchises* Tombe] Expressing a willingness to be with his father in the ancestral tomb, Aeneas uses the rhetorical figure *ellipsis*, which is defined and fairly criticized by Scaliger as a scheme used 'When in an extreme indication of emotion words fail us, thus giving expression to admiration, love, hate, anger. *Ellipsis* of a word may lead to ineptness of expression' (cited by Sonnino, p. 67).

59 a winters tale] Marlowe uses an Elizabethan idiom to render Virgil's line *forsan et haec olim meminisse iuvabit*. The common substance of 'a winters tale' is described in *Richard II*:

> In winter's tedious nights sit by the fire
> With good old folks, and let them tell thee tales
> Of woeful ages long ago betid.   (V. i. 40–2)

61 the soyle] 'To take soil' was a technical term used in deer-hunting when the animal took refuge in water. At Kenilworth the natural landscape of the chase provided an ideal amenity for this phase of the sport, as R. Laneham appreciated in his account of Queen Elizabeth's hunting there in 1575:

Thear to beholld the swift fleeting of the deer afore, with the stately cariage of his head in his swimmyng, spred (for the quantitee) lyke the sail of a ship; the hounds harroing after, as they had bin a number of ships too the spoyle of a karvell . . . so as the earning of the hounds in continuauns of their crie, the swiftness of the deer, the running of footmen, the galloping of horsez the blasting of hornz, the halloing and hewing of the huntsmen, with the excellent echoz between whiles from the woods and waters in valleiz resounding; moved pastime delectabl in so hy a degree, as, for ony parson to take pleazure by moost senses at onez, in mine opinion, thear can be none ony wey comparable to this; and special in this place, that of nature iz formed so feet for the purpose.

(Cited by John Nichols, *The Progresses, and Public Processions of Queen Elizabeth* (1788), i.)

64 a Phrigian] Troy was indeed in Phrygia, a country of Asia Minor; but Iarbus uses the term contemptuously, as Numanus Remulus insults the Trojans in Book IX of the *Aeneid* when he calls them *vere Phrygiae, neque enim Phryges* (line 617) and refers to their effeminate delights.

far fet on] Q's reading has given rise to a multiplicity of emendations. Oliver accepts Broughton's suggestion that the phrase should be 'forfeit to', and explains that in Iarbus' view Aeneas was 'destined to be—and should have been—drowned at sea'. But although Q's preposition creates some difficulty, the literal sense of 'far fet' (where 'fet' is the past participle of the obsolete verb *fet*, synonymous with *fetch*) gives the more powerful line, especially when it can be supported with the near-proverbial saying of the sixteenth century: 'farre fet and deere bought is good for Ladyes' (cf. Lyly's *Euphues* (1578; ed. Edward Arber, 1868), 93). Dyce emended 'to' to 'o'er'; and Tucker Brooke, in his modernized edition, prints 'far-fet o'the sea', with the gloss 'far-fetched by'.

67 imitate the Moone] A commonplace comparison for Elizabethan fickleness; in *Romeo and Juliet* Romeo is warned to

> swear not by the moon, th'inconstant moon,
> That monthly changes in her circled orb,
> Lest that thy love prove likewise variable.   (II. ii. 109–11)

68 like the Planets] These were the 'erring starres' whose 'double motion' is discussed in *Dr Faustus* (A 664ff.); they were contrasted with the fixed stars in the firmament of the geocentric universe.

Act III, scene iv

4–5 *Mars* and *Venus* . . . in a net] In order to catch Venus in the act of adultery with the god of war, her husband, Vulcan, spread a fine mesh over their couch and called all the gods to witness the trapping of the lovers.

12 his eyes] Aeneas assumes that the 'his' refers to Iarbus, but it is more likely that he himself is intended, since it is his 'amorous face' that 'sparkles fire' in line 19. In this scene punctuation is strictly that of Q. Marlowe has taken the cue for Dido's broken, ambiguous, and sometimes almost meaningless speech from Virgil's description of how the Queen, in the grip of sudden and irresistible passion, *incipit effari, mediaque in voce resistit* (iv. 76).

18 I doe eye where ere I am] The play of homophones makes for comparison with the clause in Shakespeare's Sonnet 104: 'when first your eye I eyed'.

19 *Pean*] The surname, deriving from the word *paean* (meaning 'a hymn') was given to Apollo to denote his function as god of music as well as god of the sun—whose bright appearance naturally 'sparkles fire'.

20 he buts . . . bed] The sun shines on the earth. Flora was the goddess of fertility, and Dido's sun shines with violent sexuality. *OED* cites this line as its (only) example of *butt* 5a: 'To aim a missile'.

21–2 *Prometheus* . . . armes] According to Apollodorus (Books I and II of *The Library*), Prometheus made the first man and woman out of clay, and gave them life with fire which he had stolen from the gods. Dido feels herself to be consumed with love, and fears that she will be destroyed as Semele was when Jupiter revealed himself to her in his full glory (cf. *Dr Faustus*, A 1372–3: 'Brighter art thou then flaming *Iupiter* when he appeard to haplesse *Semele*').

37 effect] A variant form of *affect*.

38 for me] Dido could mean either 'before me' (*OED* I. 3) or 'instead of me' (*OED* II. 5).

44 the Gods of Hospitalitie] The function of protecting the host–guest relationship was shared by all the gods, although Jupiter was particularly concerned here, since he, with Mercury, visited the home of Baucis and Philemon to test the peasants' hospitality (cf. I. ii. 41).

46–7 By *Paphos* ... descend] Aeneas swears by his ancestors, both maternal and paternal. Paphos was the city in Cyprus to which (according to some versions of the myth) Venus came after her birth in the sea. Capys was Aeneas' grandfather, the father of Anchises.

52–4 What ... delight] Dido is not so much indulging in hyperbole as acknowledging a philosophy, albeit in its popularized version. Among Neoplatonists, purists such as Ficino denied that music had power over the soul; but the courtly Castiglione described music as 'a holy matter', and explained that 'most wise Philosophers [believed] that the worlde is made of musike, and the heavens in their moving make a melodie, and our soule is framed after the verie same sort and therefore lifteth up it selfe, and (as it were) reviveth the vertues and force of it selfe with Musicke' (*The Courtyer*, trans. Sir Thomas Hoby (1561), Book I).

Aeneas' response to her courtship is more powerful than the world's best music (that which is heard at Apollo's shrine at Delos), ravishing Dido's soul from her body and making it move in harmony ('unto the measures of delight') with the created world; the process is described in more detail by Crashaw in his account of the duel between the nightingale and the 'Lutes-master':

> thus doe they vary
> Each string his Note, as if they meant to carry
> Their Masters blest soul (snatcht out at his Eares
> By a strong Extasy) through all the sphaeares
> Of Musicks heaven; and seat it there on high
> In th'*Empyraeum* of pure Harmony.
>
> ('Musicks Duell')

The sceptic's retort would be that of Benedick in *Much Ado About Nothing*: 'Now, divine air! now is his soul ravished! | Is it not strange that sheeps' guts should hale souls out of men's bodies?' (II. iii. 60–1).

56 disdaine ... lap] Dido indulges a somewhat exaggerated metonymy which presents Disdain in the person of Aeneas while she herself represents Fancy.

61–3 Hold ... woo'd me] Dido is rehearsing the words and action of Jupiter in Act I, scene i.

Act IV, scene i

9 the divels revelling night] The storm might have been pretty in performance (see General Introduction), but the comments of Anna and Iarbus attempt to convey the terror of Virgil's description of the event—giving rise to Tucker Brooke's observation that it was 'A kind of Walpurgisnacht'.

11 *Apollos* Axeltree] Tucker Brooke responded to this allusion by citing other

references in Marlowe's works to the axis on which the sun was thought to rotate. The protagonist of 1 Tamburlaine speaks of '*Clymens* brain-sicke sonne, | That almost brent the Axeltree of heaven' (IV. ii. 49–50); in Part 2 of that play, Orcanes recalls the fury of battle 'As when the massy substance of the earth, | Quiver about the Axeltree of heaven' (I. i. 89–90); and in *Dr Faustus* Mephostophilis explains that 'the spheares [are] | Mutually folded in each others orbe, | And ... all iointly moue vpon one axletree' (A 667–9). Tucker Brooke also remarks on Shakespeare's (only) allusion to the notion in Ulysses' description of a bond which was as 'strong as the axletree | On which heaven rides' (*Troilus and Cressida*, I. iii. 66–7).

19 *Tiphous* den] Typhoeus, or Typhon, was a monster with a hundred dragon-like heads who was imprisoned under Mt Aetna. Tucker Brooke suggests that the Q spelling might incorporate a turned *n*—since 'Typhon' is the name used in Marlowe's other reference to this giant, in *1 Tamburlaine*, III. iii. 109 (where Bajazeth speaks of the 'brats ysprong from *Typhons* loins'). But the trisyllabic form here makes up a regular pentameter; and it is that used by Virgil when he speaks of the rock *imposta Typhoeo* (*Aeneid*, ix. 716).

25 whist] Most of *OED*'s examples of the use of this adjective ('quiet, still, hushed') suggest that as well as being '*arch.* and *dial.*', it was also 'poetic'; its *locus classicus* must be Ariel's song in *The Tempest*:

> Come unto these yellow sands,
>   And then take hands;
> Curtsied when you have and kiss'd
>   The wild waves whist.   (I. ii. 375–8)

27 *Aeolus*] In classical mythology, Aeolus was god of the winds.

34 stumbling blocke] Although the phrase 'to stumble at a block' (i.e. a tree stump) is of early date, the expression 'stumbling block' was first introduced by Tyndale in the sixteenth century (1 Cor. 1:23), and this line from *Dido, Queene of Carthage* is the earliest of the examples in *OED* to illustrate sense c: 'something repugnant to one's prejudices'.

Act IV, scene ii

1ff. *Aeneid*, iv. 198ff., tells how King Iarbas had erected temples and altars to Jupiter where sacrifice was continually offered: *templa Iovi centum latis immania regnis, | centum aras posuit vigilemque sacraverat ignem.*' When rumour of Dido's relationship with Aeneas reached him, Iarbas intensified his supplication.

2 that gloomie *Jove*] The adjective is strangely recurrent—it occurs in IV. i. 27, the present line, and line 6 of this scene. Slackness of writing seems to be indicated, rather than carelessness of printing. Virgil's Iarbas addresses Jupiter as god of thunder (*cum fulmina torques*).

3 emptie Altars] This seems to suggest that the worship of Jupiter has been neglected; but there is no evidence of this in either poem or play.

6–7 That ... themselves] Iarbus attributes to Jupiter the function which in *Troilus and Cressida* is credited to 'the glorious planet Sol'—that of correcting the planets when they 'In evil mixture to disorder wander' (I. iii. 89ff.). Planets are 'ayrie creatures' in the sense (*OED* 1) that they are 'Of, or belonging to, the air'.

9–10 Whose ... resound] In his misery, Iarbus echoes the words and the movement of the happy lover's song in Spenser's 'Epithalamion': 'So I unto my selfe alone will sing, | The woods shall to me answer, and my Eccho ring.' Dido's original name, by which she addresses herself in *Aeneid*, iv. 610, was 'Elissa', of which a variant spelling is 'Eliza' (the name frequently used by flattering poets to address Elizabeth I).

11–16 The ... rites] In these lines Marlowe is very close to his source in the *Aeneid*:

> femina, quae nostris errans in finibus urbem
> exiguam pretio posuit, cui litus arandum
> cuique loci leges dedimus, conubia nostra
> reppulit ac dominum Aenean in regna recepit.   (iv. 211–4)

13 a hide of ground] A 'hide' was an old measure of land, equal to 100 or 120 acres. Marlowe, however, is more likely to be referring to the legend that when Dido landed on the African shore, escaping from the cruelty of Pygmalion (who had murdered her husband, Sichaeus), she begged for as much land as could be covered by an oxhide; cutting the hide into thongs, she obtained enough ground to build the citadel and found the city of Carthage.

18 fled] See General Introduction.

20 ruth] Here the word is used in the *OED* sense 1 of 'pity'; whereas the same word in line 39 has the sense of 'grief' (*OED* 3).

37 fancie cannot start] Tucker Brooke and Oliver differ in their readings of this phrase. The former, glossing 'fancie' as 'affection' (as in III. ii. 58), explains 'start' as 'become loosened'—where the verb would have the sense of *OED* 2 ('move ... from a position of rest'), or even perhaps *OED* 7 ('desert'). Oliver interprets it as 'love cannot (begin to) flow', explaining that 'start is used as the antithesis of 'fix'd'.

44 delight ... pensivenes] The words can be paraphrased as 'luxuriating in this swooning self-pity'. Although this sense of *die* is not recorded in *OED*, the word is commonly used in the sixteenth and seventeenth centuries to denote the action of orgasmic swooning with excess of joy or love: cf. Gaveston's longing in *Edward II* (I. i. 14) to go to 'The king, upon whose bosome let me die'; and Benedick's declaration to Beatrice: 'I will live in thy heart, die in thy lap, and be buried in thy eyes' (*Much Ado About Nothing*, v. ii. 99–100).

Act IV, scene iii

3 Hermes ... in a dreame] Marlowe appears to have reversed the order of the god's manifestations. In the *Aeneid* Mercury is sent in person to Aeneas as a result of Iarbas's prayer (iv. 219ff.); later (554ff.), after the Trojans have embarked, the hero dreams that Mercury urges him forward in his destined voyage of discovery.

6 Phenissa] The reference in the *Aeneid* (i. 713) is to Dido's Phoenician origins.

18 reames] The Q reading, 'beames', can be nothing but a printer's error: 'reame' is a common form of 'realm', and in *The Jew of Malta* it permits Ithimore's pun: 'Give me a Reame of paper, we'll have a kingdome of gold for't' (IV. ii. 114–15).

28 thy ... lips] One of the possessive pronouns in Q's 'my bodie to my lips' must be changed; it would be perverse and meaningless to offer any other than Dyce's emendation, which has found general acceptance. This is the most striking example of the *m* | *th* confusion which is found in this text (see I. i. 144n.).

51 coll] The verb, meaning 'To throw one's arms around the neck of' is described as obsolete in *OED*.

Act IV, scene iv

10 silver whistles] Among *OED*'s early examples of the use of *whistle* are references to the mariner's whistle (used for signalling), including a quotation from *Act 24 Henry VIII* (1532–3): 'It shalbe lefull for ... maisters of the Shipps ... and maryners to weare whistells of Silver.'

11 *Circes* sent *Sicheus*] Circe ('Circes' is a common Elizabethan variant) was the enchantress who turned Ulysses' followers into swine; although she was celebrated for her knowledge of magic and venomous herbs, there seems to be no record of her having any special power over the winds, nor of any commerce between her and Dido's husband, Sichaeus.

15 were hoysing up] The intransitive use of *hoise* (a variant form of *hoist*) is paralleled by Golding in *Metamorphoses*, ii. 215–16, where Ovid tells how Phaeton tried to take his father's place but 'the Waine for want of weight it erst was wont to beare, | Did hoyse aloft'. According to *OED*, the verb was originally nautical, used transitively with the sense 'To raise aloft by means of a rope or pulley and tackle'.

29–30 Hath ... here?] These are puzzling lines, especially as the importance of the future of Ascanius has been so heavily emphasized. There are, I think, only two possible interpretations: Aeneas may indeed be speaking the truth when he tells Dido that he did not intend to sail away; or else, as Clifford Leech has suggested, 'Marlowe is implying that up to this point Aeneas has forgotten, or has been prepared to abandon, his son in his attempt to steal away' ('Marlowe's Humor', in *Essays on Shakespeare and Elizabethan Drama*, ed. Richard Hosley [London, 1963], 69–82).

50 Clowdes ... fleest] In an old-spelling edition there is no need to follow Dyce's emendation of 'fleest' to 'fledst'. G. L. Brook explains that in the second person singular preterite 'syncope of unaccented vowels often led to the creation of heavy groups of consonants which were difficult to pronounce. This difficulty was sometimes overcome by the omission of one consonant. Hence *likd'st* became *likst* and *lookd'st* became *look'st*' (p. 124).

The allusion itself is not clear. In Book V of the *Iliad* Homer tells how Phoebus wrapped a dark-blue cloud around Aeneas when both he and his mother had been wounded by Diomedes; and in Book I of the *Aeneid* the hero gains access to Carthage veiled in a cloud: *infert se saeptus nebula (mirabile dictu) per medios miscetque viris neque cernitur ulli* (i. 439–40). In Book V, Neptune, claiming to have watched constantly over Aeneas, reminds Venus that when her son seemed to be at a disadvantage against Achilles, the god snatched him to safety in a cloud: *nube cava rapui* (line 810).

66 Gennet] *OED* defines this as 'a small Spanish horse', but the definition may be too precise; Golding refers to the Sun's horses as 'Genets' (*Metamorphoses*, i. 211).

85 Doe ... way] To modern eyes, Q's punctuation might seem to admit a crude jest—that Dido should issue orders to Aeneas immediately after she has vowed to 'call [him] Lord'; but in the rhetorical punctuation of the Elizabethans the comma could indicate emphasis on the following word, as Dido turns to address her sister.

90 lives] Most editors accept Dyce's emendation, but Grosart decided to make sense of Q's reading in his edition of the play: 'Though preferring *lives*, I now feel disposed to retain *loves*: for it is sufficiently good sense if we understand him to say that he will do this for *love* of Troy, of Priam, and of his kinsmen slaughtered, as well as for the sake of the "thousand guiltless souls".' N. F. Blake has suggested to me that the 'kinsmens loves' could also be 'the beloved ones of their kinsmen'.

92 fire ... heads] As Tucker Brooke observed: 'The spectacle of a conflagration appealed as much to Marlowe's fancy as did that of the conqueror riding in triumph through the streets.' But there seems to be no good reason for the ·choice of Lacedaemon (also called Sparta) for the parallel to Troy in the act of vengeance against 'the hatefull Greekes'.

122–3 For ... kisse] Both Marlowe himself and Shakespeare seem to have had a proper respect for these lines. Shakespeare adapts the first of these lines of Marlowe's for Cleopatra's description of her love with Antony: 'Eternity was in our lips, and eyes' (i. iii. 35). Marlowe invests the second with ironic intensity when Dr Faustus, at the climax of his damnation, embraces Helen of Troy with the demand that she should 'make [him] immortall with a kisse' (A 1359).

127 Packt] *OED* lists two relevant senses of the verb *pack*: *v.*[1] includes the nautical expression (3b) 'To pack on all sail' (meaning 'to put on or hoist all possible sail for the sake of speed'). The more obvious sense is that of *v.*[2] 2: 'to be an accomplice or confederate in a plot'.

133 But ... still] Earlier, Dido dreams of hanging the sails in her bedchamber, so that the winds can 'conspire' with the sails to float her Carthage palace to Italy; that way, Aeneas will remain in Carthage, even though he sails to Italy.

134–5 And ... armes] Both the sentiment and the wording are echoed by the monarch in *Edward II*: 'Ere my sweete *Gaveston* shall part from me, | This Ile shall fleete upon the Ocean' (i. iv. 49–50).

154 and ... seas] The conjunction *and* could be used (*OED* 8) to introduce a consequence ('God said "Let there be light"; and there was light').

Act IV, scene v

5 Servises] Pears.

6 Dewberries] The name was given to a kind of blackberry, and also to goose-berries.

20 twigger] *OED* cites this as an example of the slang usage of a word orig-inally applied to a ewe who was 'a vigorous, prolific breeder'.

25–34 O what meane I ... sinewes drie] Virgil's description of Dido's broken speech (see III. iv. 12n.) could be applied to the Nurse's words here; and rationalizing punctuation is as inappropriate now as it would have been for Dido's passionate utterances.

28 your] Bowers objects to Q's reading, and accepts Deighton's conjectural 'our' on the grounds that it is more consistent with the familiar 'thy' which the Nurse uses to address herself in line 30. I believe that the inconsistency is itself appropriate, and that, furthermore, the change from the formal to the intimate mode of address might be accounted for by suggesting that in line 28 the Nurse speaks with a new-found self-respect, while in lines 29 and 30 she uses the accus-tomed, even reprehending, language of familiarity.

Act V, scene i

0.1 *platforme*] *OED* describes as obsolete its sense 2 of *platform*, meaning 'A plan or representation on the flat (of any structure, existing or projected)'.

6–10 And ... about] Aeneas' projects for a moated, walled city are comparable to Dr Faustus' plans to 'wall all *Iermany* with brasse, | And make swift *Rhine* circle faire *Wertenberge*' (A 120–1).

13 *Hybla*] A mountain (and town) in Sicily, famed for its honey.

38–9 Yet ... yeares] The prophecy was that Ascanius would found Alba Longa, and that he and his descendants (Iulus was the son of Ascanius, born in Lavinium) would rule the empire for centuries to come; cf. I. i. 95ff.

57 *Deucalion*] Deucalion and his wife, Pyrrha, are the Graeco-Roman equiva-lents of Noah and his wife—the only beings preserved from the flood that was divinely ordained to destroy mankind.

74 what thing so ere] The adverb *soever* was used (*OED* 2) 'with generalizing or emphatic force'.

89 the Rhode] *OED* 3 explains this as the 'roadstead, a sheltered stretch of water beyond the harbour but close to the land'.

110 Let me ... hence] McKerrow's suggested emendation, attributing the line to Dido and not Aeneas, shows the Queen's hurt amazement as she echoes her lover's words, both here and in line 124.

131 wey] A variant form of *weigh*, used in the sense (*OED* 13) of 'care for, regard'.

134 by our spousall rites] In the *Aeneid* Dido conjures Aeneas to remain with her *per conubia nostra, per inceptos hymenaeos* (iv. 316). Virgil's Aeneas is more harsh than Marlowe's in his rejection of this appeal, denying categorically that any such rites have been performed: *nec coniugis umquam | praetendi taedas aut haec in foedera veni* (iv. 338–9).

136–8 *Aeneid*, iv. 317–19: 'If I ever deserved well of thee, or if aught of mine

has ever been pleasant in thy sight, have pity on a falling house and, I pray you—
if there is still a place for prayers—abandon this plan of yours.'

139–40 *Aeneid*, iv. 360–1: 'Cease inflaming both yourself and me with these
laments; it is not of my own free will that I search out Italy.'

146–7 *Paris* ... *sackt*] Cf. *Dr Faustus*, A 1364–5: 'I will be *Paris*, and for love
of thee, | Insteede of *Troy* shal Wertenberge be sackt.'

156–9 Thy mother ... sucke] *Aeneid*, iv. 365–7:

> nec tibi diva parens, generis nec Dardanus auctors,
> perfide, sed duris gemuit to cautibus horrens
> Caucasus, Hyrcanaeque admorunt ubera tigres.

The Caucasus, a mountain range of exceptional ruggedness, provided a common
Elizabethan simile for hardness of heart; cf. *Edward II*, v. v. 52–4:

> And then thy heart, were it as *Gurneys* is,
> Or as *Matrevis*, hewne from the *Caucasus*,
> Yet will it melt, ere I have done my tale.

The Hyrcanian tiger, bred in the wilds of Persia, did the same for cruelty; cf.
Lucans First Booke, 327–30:

> A brood of barbarous *Tygars* having lapt
> The bloud of many a heard, whilst with their dams
> They kennel'd in *Hircania* evermore
> Will rage and pray.

165–6 Serpent ... bosome] According to *Brewer's Dictionary of Phrase and
Fable*, 1870 (revised by Ivor H. Evans, London, 1970), 'The Greeks say that a
husbandman found a frozen serpent, which he put into his bosom. The snake was
revived by the warmth, and stung its benefactor' (p. 1982). Marlowe's scholarship
may have given him access to the original story, but the expression, in any case,
was proverbial.

201 a Mermaides eye] The sense of the passage makes it clear that Anna is to
look upon Aeneas with the 'alluring eyes' that Iarbus deplored in iv. ii. 50. The
confusion of mermaid and siren is common.

202 *Aulis* gulfe] This was the assembly point for the Grecian ships preparing
for the attack on Troy.

221 too keene] Dido could mean that the Nurse is too eager to become a
traitor; *OED* also offers the meanings 'savage' (2c) and 'insolent' (2d).

243 like *Icarus*] Dido has found a useful purpose for the faulty wings that
caused Icarus' downfall; the image reappears with tragic irony in *Dr Faustus*,
where the protagonist's 'waxen wings did mount above his reach, | And melting
heavens conspirde his overthrow' (A 22–3).

247 *Tritons* neece] There is a confusion here of two Scyllas, one the sea-
monster who was related to Triton, the other the daughter of Nisus who swam
after her lover and clung to his boat (*Metamorphoses*, viii).

248 *Arion*] The musician Arion was thrown overboard by thieving sailors, but
was carried to shore by a dolphin who had been enchanted with his playing.

256 leefest] A variant form of *lief* ('beloved').

257–61 Now ... love] Tucker Brooke felt that these lines were so like lines 189–93 of this scene as to arouse suspicion that they were originally alternative versions of the same passage.

274 Not farre from hence] Marlowe approximates the Virgilian remote: in the poem Dido stresses the distance between her court and the temple of the Hesperides: *Oceani finem iuxta solemqe cadentem|ultimus Aethiopum locus est* (iv. 480–1). The wise women of the poem is not a 'Daughter' but a priestess of the temple where the Hesperides, themselves the daughters of Atlas and Hesperis, guarded the golden apples which Juno gave to Jupiter on their wedding day.

306 a Conquerour] i.e. Hannibal.

310–11 *Littora ... nepotes*] *Aeneid*, iv. 628–9: 'May shore clash with shore, waters against waters, arms against arms;|may they have war, they and their children's children.' This quotation may identify the Latin text that Marlowe used; most editions read *nepotesque*, but Oliver has discovered two, presented with a commentary by Willich in 1547 and 1586, which read *nepotes*. Identification of the edition is of academic interest only, since there are no substantive variants in the text, and Marlowe does not appear to have made use of the commentary.

313 *Sic ... umbras*] *Aeneid*, iv. 660: 'Thus, thus I go rejoicing into the darkness.'

317 tires] *OED* offers this as an example of sense 2c of the old verb *tire*, meaning 'To prey upon'.

319 prevaile] *OED* (4b) notes the use of *prevail* with the sense of 'to benefit'.

HERO AND LEANDER: Commentary

1 *Hellespont*] In *Heroides* XVIII (*Leander Heroni*) Leander reproaches the waters and recollects that *satis amissa locus hic infamis ab Helle est* (line 141). Helle, daughter of Athamas, King of Thebes, fled from her father's house to escape the cruelty of her stepmother, Ino. With her brother, Phryxus, she was carried through the air by a ram with a golden fleece; but she became giddy, fell, and was drowned. Phryxus continued his journey, and arrived at Colchis, where he sacrificed the ram but kept its fleece as treasure.

2 In view and opposit] T. W. Baldwin reads this as evidence that Marlowe was working from a Greek text of Musaeus, and not from a Latin translation. He quotes Musaeus and the parallel Latin text of Musorus (published in the Plantin edition of 1567):

> Σηστὸς ἔην καὶ ″Αβυδος ἐναντίον ἐγγύθι πόντου.
> γείτοές εἰσι πόληες.

> Sestos erat & Abydus è regione, propè mare
> Vicinae sunt urbes.

Baldwin explains that the key word is ἐναντίον, which Stephanus (1572) translates as *Adversus, Qui est in conspectu seu coram, Qui est erogione, Oppositus* ('Marlowe's Musaeus', *Journal of English and Germanic Philology*, liv (1955), 478–85).

3 Seaborderers] In his comic retelling of the story, Nashe explains that Hero

and Leander were 'either of them sea-borderers' (*Nashe's Lenten Stuffe* (1599); McKerrow, iii. 199).

6 *Apollo*] No known myth associates this god with Hero, but according to Ovid, Apollo was *crinibus insignis* (*Amores*, I. i. 11).

14 proud *Adonis*] In Lodge's poem *Scillaes Metamorphosis* (1589), Venus wears a 'stately roab . . . wherein with cullored silke, Her Nimphes had blaz'd the yong Adonis wrack' (stanza 86). The 'carelesse and disdainfull eies' (line 13) seem to be those of Shakespeare's Adonis, who 'smiles as in disdain' when Venus begins to woo him (*Venus and Adonis* (1593), line 241). Ovid's youth is more responsive (*Metamorphoses*, x).

17 a myrtle wreath] The myrtle was sacred to Venus, one of whose surnames was Myrtia. When the goddess Elegia visited the poet of the *Amores*, *in dextra myrtea virga fuit* (III. i. 34).

19–20 Her vaile . . . deceaves] Maclure comments: 'This description sets out the ideal so often expressed in Renaissance literature of the *trompe-l'oeil* in art.' Cf. *The Faerie Queene*, II. xii. 61, and the description of Arachne's web in *Metamorphoses*, v.

31 Buskins of shels] The notion is repeated in Thomas Edwards' *Narcissus* (1595): 'Her buskins all of shels ysilvered ore.'

33–6 Where . . . bils] Nashe's *Unfortunate Traveller* (1594) describes a Roman garden in which

One tree for his fruite bare nothing but inchained chirping birdes, whose throates beeing conduit pipt with squared narrowe shells, & charged syring wise with searching sweet water driven in by a litle wheele for the nonce . . . made a spirting sound, such as chirping is in bubbling upwards through the rough crannies of their closed bills.

(McKerrow, ii. 284)

The necessary hydraulic system was devised by Hero of Alexandria in the second century BC; he explained:

A vessel is taken, provided with several transverse partitions. In the chambers are placed siphons conducting into the chambers beneath, the streams through them being unequal. In the lower compartment is placed the pipe which produces the sound, and the stream of water falls into the upper compartment. It will be found that when the upper chamber is filled, water passes through the siphon placed there into the chamber below, until it has arrived at the lowest, and the vessel being air-tight, the air in this chamber is driven through the pipe and produces the sound.

(*Pneumatics*, ed. Marie Boas Hall (1971), no. 44, 'Notes produced from several Birds in succession, by a Stream of Water')

45 *Venus* Nun] Maclure points to the identical phrase in Stephen Gosson's *The Schoole of Abuse* (1587), when Gosson describes the London prostitutes: 'Other there are which . . . live a mile from the Cittie like Venus Nunnes in a Cloyster at Newington . . . where . . . they . . . spende their dayes in double devotion' (E7). There is no need, however, to suppose that Marlowe borrowed from

Gosson. The parallel text of Musaeus and Musorus has Κύπριδιτ ἦν ἱέρεια, and *Veneris erat sacerdos*, respectively. The regular Elizabethan translation for *sacerdos* was 'nun'.

49–50 Therefore ... blacke] The mythopoeia may well be Marlowe's own. Ovid offers a quite different explanation for the blackness of the 'Ethiopians' (*Metamorphoses*, ii); and Sir Thomas Browne makes no reference to Hero in his chapters on common fallacies concerning 'the Blackness of Negroes' (*Pseudodoxia Epidemica*, IV. x and xi).

52 divine *Musaeus*] Nashe picked up Marlowe's words, and added his own praise for his contemporary when he writes of 'Leander and Hero, of whom divine *Musaeus* sung, and a diviner Muse than him, *Kit Marlowe*' (*Nashe's Lenten Stuffe*; McKerrow, iii. 195).

57 the vent'rous youth of Greece] After the murder of Phryxus (see line 1n.), Jason led a party of Greeks to Colchis in search of the Golden Fleece.

59 *Cinthia*] Diana, goddess of the moon, was surnamed Cinthia after the mountain (Cinthos) on Delos where she was born. The notion of Leander's arms as the sphere of the moon could perhaps be compared to Donne's suggestion for the sun's orbit in 'The Sunne Rising': 'This bed thy center is, these walls, thy sphere.' Diana's love for the mortal Endymion is often cited as the cause of the moon's pallor.

61 *Circes* wand] The enchantress Circe ('Circes' is a common Elizabethan variant) struck with her wand to turn men—most notably the members of Ulysses' crew—into beasts (*Metamorphoses*, xiv; *Odyssey*, x).

62 *Jove* ... hand] Marlowe introduces the comparison of Leander and Ganymede which he develops later (lines 651ff.) when he describes Neptune's infatuation. Ganymede was Jove's cupbearer.

63–5 delicious meat ... shoulder] Pelops, son of Tantalus, was killed by his father who, visited by the gods and wanting to test their divinity, served his son's body for meat. The gods refused to eat—but Ceres absent-mindedly consumed one of the boy's shoulders. When Jupiter restored Pelops to life, he replaced the missing portion 'Betwene the throteboll and the arm' with a prosthesis made of ivory (*Metamorphoses*, vi).

70 blazon] *OED* (*v.* 1) cites Guillim's *Heraldry* (1610) for a definition: 'To blazon is to express what the shapes, kinds, and colours of things born in Armes are together with their apt significations.' Cf. *Romeo and Juliet*, II. vi. 24–6: 'if the measure of thy joy | Be heap'd like mine, and that thy skill be more | To blazon it.'

73–6 exceeding ... any] Ovid describes how Narcissus was enamoured of the 'white and red indifferently bepainted in his face', and strove to kiss his reflection in the water. Rejecting the love of the nymph Echo, he pined to death (*Metamorphoses*, iii). Shakespeare, however, shares Marlowe's version of the story, and tells how 'Narcissus so himself forsook, | And died to kiss his shadow in the brook' (*Venus and Adonis*, 161–2).

77 wilde Hippolitus] A son of Theseus, Hippolitus was famous for the virtue

with which he rejected the advances of his stepmother Phaedra (*Metamorphoses*, xv).

81 barbarous Thratian soldier] The Thratians were notoriously savage warriors: Horace speaks of *bello furiosa Thrace* (*Odes*, II. xvi. 5).

91–4 The men ... guest] For a few lines, Marlowe translates Musaeus:

Δὴ γὰρ Κυπριδίη πανδήμιος ἦλθεν ἑορτή,
Τῇ ἀνὰ Σηστὸν ἄγουσιν Ἀδρνιδι καὶ Κυθερεή.
πασσυδίη δ' ἔπευδον ἐς ἱερὸν ἦμαρ ἱκέσθαι   (42–4)

For lo, the public festival of the Cyprian goddess was come,
Which they celebrate in Sestos to Adonis and Cythereia,
And in full host they hastened to come to the sacred day.

Adonis, metamorphosed into an anemone after he had refused Venus' love, was a type of Osiris—a vegetation | fertility god.

95 To meet their loves] Musaeus remarks that the 'youths who loved maidens' (φιλοπάρ θενις) attend such festivals:

οὐ τόσον ἀθανάτων ἀγέμεν σπεύδουσι θυηλάς,
ὅσσον ἀλειρόμενοι διὰ κ̣ι αλλεα παρθενικάων.   (53–4)

('not so much to make sacrifice to the immortals,
As to foregather for the sake of the maidens' beauty'.)

95–6 such ... festivall] Cf. the first line of the '*Pervigilium Veneris*' (? fourth century AD): *Cras amet qui nunquam amavit quique amavit cras amet.*

97–9 For ... earth] Inviting the County Paris to his feast, Old Capulet promises that he shall 'behold this night | Earth-treading stars that make dark heaven light' (*Romeo and Juliet*, I. ii. 24–5).

99 melancholie earth] In the humoral theory (deriving from Hippocrates and Galen), 'each humour corresponded to an element, and possessed the same two primary qualities as its element possessed' (J. B. Bamborough, *The Little World of Man* (1952), 58). Melancholy corresponded to Earth: both were cold and dry.

101 *Phaeton*] Ovid tells how Phaeton, son of Phoebus Apollo, drove his father's chariot for one day. The horses of the sun proved unmanageable, and the Earth was forced to plead for Jupiter's intervention, warning him that 'If Sea and Land doe go to wrecke, and heaven it selfe doe burne | To olde confused Chaos then of force we must returne' (*Metamorphoses*, ii. 379–80).

105 Sea-nimphs] Sirens (often identified with mermaids) sang to lure sailors to their deaths off the coast of Sicily.

107 Not] Q's 'Nor' could easily have been the result of carelessly distributed type, since *t* and *r* in this fount are very similar. The emendation to 'Not' makes better sense, and forms a crisp introduction to the rhetorical figure *dirimens copulatio*, described by Henry Peacham as the scheme produced 'when we bring forth one sentence, with an exception before it, and immediately joyne another after it, that seemeth greater' (*The Garden of Eloquence* (1577), 171). Comparable in form (but more complex) is Milton's description of the Garden of Eden in *Paradise Lost*, iv. 268ff.: 'Not that fair field of Enna ....' It is doubtful whether

the reading of *Englands Parnassus* (1600) was a conscious attempt at emendation on the part of Robert Allot, who compiled this anthology of 'The choysest Flowers of our Moderne Poets', since the volume as a whole is remarkable for its printing errors.

107–11 that ... flood] Marlowe combines fact and fancy in his listing of the attributes of the moon. The moon is a planet, and planets were called 'wandering', or 'erring', stars to distinguish them from the 'fixed' stars of the firmament. Planets were said to have a 'double motion', expressed here by the rare 'thirling' (for which *OED* offers the synonyms 'darting' and 'whirling'); in *Dr Faustus* it is explained that the planets 'All joyntly move from East to West in 24. houres upon the poles of the world, but differ in their motion upon the poles of the Zodiake' (A 664ff.). The 'yawning dragons' seem to be original with Marlowe; Dr Faustus also, in his attempt 'to scale *Olympus* top', was 'seated in a chariot burning bright, | Drawne by the strength of yoky dragons neckes' (A 813–15). '*Latmus*' was the mountain where Diana, goddess of the moon, slept with Endymion, and the moon's pallor was sometimes attributed to lovesickness. The star is 'watrie' because of the relationship between the moon and the tides.

113 gawdie] The sense of the adjective here seems uncertain; it is perhaps an attributive use of *gaudy* (*OED sb.* 4), meaning 'rejoicing, merry-making'.

114 Wretched ... race] Ixion attempted to seduce Juno; at Jupiter's command he was punished in hell by being eternally bound to a wheel of fire. The result of his intercourse with a cloud in the form of Juno was the breed of centaurs, monsters with the head and shoulders of a man, and the four legs of a horse. They were notoriously savage and lecherous.

133 were] A common Elizabethan form of *where*.

135–56 So ... bee] In the description of Venus' temple, Marlowe enters into competition with the mythological displays of the Temple of the Sun (*Metamorphoses*, ii), Arachne's web (*Metamorphoses*, vi), and the House of Busyrane (*The Faerie Queene*, iii. xi. 28–46).

137 Proteus] A sea-deity, Proteus was noted for his ability to change his shape. Ovid refers to 'Unstable Protew chaunging aye his figure and his hue, | From shape to shape a thousand sithes as list him to renue' (*Metamorphoses*, vi. 13–14).

139 light headed *Bacchus*] One of the embroideries in Arachne's web showed 'how the faire Erygone by chaunce did suffer rape | By Bacchus who deceyved hir in likenesse of a grape' (*Metamorphoses*, vi. 156–7).

147–50 *Jove* ... cloud] As well as featuring largely in Arachne's web, Jupiter's metamorphoses are depicted on the tapestries of the House of Busyrane. Stanza 31 tells how

> into a golden showre
> Him selfe he chaung'd faire *Danaë* to vew,
> And through the roofe of her strong brasen towre
> Did raine into her lap an hony dew.

Spenser refers to 'gealous *Iuno*', but does not point out that she was Jupiter's sister as well as his wife. Stanza 34 describes the kidnapping of Ganymede from

Mt Ida; and the tapestry also shows Jupiter disguised 'like a Bull, *Europa* to pervert' (stanza 30).

150 And ... cloud] In his capacity as rain-god, Jupiter (surnamed Pluvius) would have legitimate reason to be hidden in the clouds with Iris, messenger to the gods, who was usually portrayed as a rainbow.

151–2 Blood-quaffing ... set] With the aid of the Cyclops, the one-eyed monsters who worked in his forge under Mt Aetna, Vulcan forged an iron net so as to trap his wife, Venus, with her lover, Mars, the god of war:

Now when that Venus and hir mate were met in bed togither
Hir husband by his newfound snare before convayed thither
Did snarle them both togither fast in middes of all theyr play
And setting ope the Ivorie doores, callde all the Gods streight way
To see them: they with shame inough fast lockt togither lay.

(Metamorphoses, iv. 220ff.)

153 Love ... Troy] Throughout his career as a writer, Marlowe was fascinated by '*Hellen*, whose beauty sommond *Greece* to armes, | And drew a thousand ships to *Tenedos*' (*2 Tamburlaine*, II. iv. 87–8). Dido is wishing that 'as faire *Troy* was, *Carthage* might be sackt' (*Dido Queene of Carthage*, v. i. 147); and in a famous apostrophe, Dr Faustus praises 'the face that lancht a thousand shippes | And burnt the toplesse Towres of *Ilium*' (*Dr Faustus*, A 1357–8).

154–5 *Sylvanus* ... tree] Silvanus was a wood-deity, usually depicted with a cypress in his hand: Virgil addresses *teneram ab radice ferens, Silvane, cupressum* (*Georgics*, i. 20). Cyparissus, 'the fayrest Wight that ever man did see' (*Metamorphoses*, x. 128) accidentally killed Apollo's favourite stag. He was greatly distressed, and Apollo could not comfort him:

But still the Lad did sygh and sob, and as his last request
Desyred God he myght thenceforth from moorning never rest.
Anon through weeping overmuch his blood was drayned quyght:
His limbes wext greene: his heare which hung upon his forehead whyght
Began to bee a bristled bush.

(141–5)

158 turtles blood] The turtle-dove was a type of constancy in love—poetically affirmed by Shakespeare in 'The Phoenix and the Turtle':

Love and constancy is dead,
Phoenix and the Turtle fled
In a mutual flame from hence.   (22–4)

159 Vaild] *OED* offers this as the only example of *vail*, *v*². 8: 'To bow or bend down to the ground in obeisance or salutation'. The derivation is from the old French *valer*, or aphetically from *avale*.

161 Loves arrow] Ovid explains the effects of Cupid's two arrows:

t'one causeth Love, the tother doth it slake.
That causeth love, is all of golde with point full sharp and bright,
That chaseth love is blunt, whose stele with leaden head is dight.

(Metamorphoses, i. 566–8)

167–70 It lies ... win] Marlowe's possible indebtedness to Hoby's translation (1561) of Castiglione's *Il Cortegiano* was pointed out by Sir Walter Ralegh in his edition of *The Courtyer* (Tudor Translations, 1900); he quotes the passage: 'And forsomuch as our mindes are very apte to love and to hate: as in the sights of combats and games ... it is seene that the lookers on many times beare affeccion without any manifest cause why, unto one of the two parties, with a gredy desire to have him get the victorie, and the other to have the overthrow' (p. 48). It should also be remarked that Marlowe appears to be denying the opinion of George Pettie, whose *Petite Palace of Pettie his Pleasure* (1576) is a source for several of the ideas in *Hero and Leander*. At the start of his story of 'Germanicus and Agrippina' Pettie affirms: 'I am ... settled into this sentence, that not the planets but our passions have the chief place in us, and that our own desires, not the destinies, drive us to all our doings' (*Petite Palace*, ed. I. Gollancz (1908), i. 71).

174 eies] The function of the eye as a channel for love—the means by which the soul apprehends beauty—was a commonplace notion, whose *locus classicus* is Plato's dialogue *Phaedrus*. Marlowe is following Musaeus when he inserts the comment at this point.

176 Who ... sight] The sentiment is endorsed by Phebe in *As You Like It*: 'Dead shepherd, now I find thy saw of might, | "Whoever lov'd that lov'd not at first sight?"' (III. v. 81–2).

183–5 He toucht ... hands] The encounter seems to anticipate the first contact—'palm to palm'—of Romeo and Juliet (Act I, scene v).

189 mystie *Acheron*] Acheron, the name of one of the four rivers in Hades, is sometimes used in synecdoche for Hades itself. As the marginal gloss points out, the figure here is *periphrasis*, otherwise known as *circumlocutio*—'when that which might be sayde with one word, or at the lest with very few, is declared and explicated with many' (Peacham, THE GARDEN OF ELOQUENCE (1577), Hiv). In *A Midsummer Night's Dream* Shakespeare seems to echo Marlowe when Oberon instructs Puck to 'overcast the night; | The starry welkin cover thou anon | With drooping fog as black as Acheron' (III. ii. 355–7).

197 Sophister] 'At Cambridge, a student in his second or third year'; *OED sb.* 3 quotes a source of 1577: 'The first degree is that of the generall sophisters, from whence ... they ascend higher unto the estate of batchelers of art.' Implicit in Marlow's usage is the sense of *sophist* 3: 'one who makes use of fallacious arguments; a specious reasoner'. In *Edward II* the elder Mortimer, suspicious of his nephew's argument, warns him not to 'play the sophister' (I. iv. 255).

198 accosted] '"... Accost" is front her, board her, woo her, assail her' (*Twelfth Night*, I. iii. 56).

199ff. Faire ...] Leander attacks Hero's ideal of virginity with an amalgam of arguments from Musaeus, Ovid, and Pettie.

203–4 mishapen ... ruffe] Cf. the musing of Pettie's Germanicus: 'Is it possible that bounty should not abide where beauty doth abound, and that courtesy should not accompany her comeliness?' (i. 77).

203 stuffe] The dismissive, generalizing noun is illustrated in *OED* (*sb*¹. III. 7c) with an example from *Love's Labour's Lost*: 'I never knew man hold vile stuff so dear' (IV. iii. 272).

207–8 My words . . . truth] Cf. Marlowe's translation of Ovid in Elegy i. iii. 5–6 and 13–14:

> Accept him that will serve thee all his youth,
> Accept him that will love with spotlesse truth
>
> .   .   .   .
>
> My spotlesse life which but to Gods gives place,
> Naked simplicitie and modest grace.

211 you exceed her farre] The platonic lover worshipped the beloved as a deity (cf. *Phaedrus*, 251). Odysseus approaches Nausicaa in this way (*Odyssey*, vi. 249), and Shakespeare parodies the manner when Demetrius hails Helena as 'goddess, nymph, perfect, divine' (*A Midsummer Night's Dream*, III. ii. 137). In the Greek of Musaeus, Leander properly addresses Hero as Κύπρι φίλη μετὰ Κύπριν, 'Αθη ναίη μετ'Αθήνην (line 135; 'Dear Cypris, next after Cypris'). Marlowe's Leander characteristically exaggerates.

231 *Vessels . . . shine*] Cf. the translation in Elegy i. viii. 51: 'Brass shines with use.'

247 faire jem, sweet in the losse alone] Q's additional comma turns 'sweet' into an endearment—and makes nonsense of the line.

255–7 One . . . bee] Leander's pseudo-academic argument plays lightly with some Aristotelian concepts that had become commonplaces by the sixteenth century. Professor Peter Nidditch has referred me to Aristotle's *Metaphysics*, Book N. 1088a6, for the formulation that 'one is not a number'; he explained that for Greek mathematicians and philosophers, *two* is the first number proper, since number was conceived as inherently related to plurality; and *one* was thought of as the 'principle', or 'source', of number—the basic constituent of numbers—and not itself a number.

Pettie's Germanicus, persuading Agrippina to relinquish the 'virginity which you so highly esteem of' speaks of women 'receiving their perfection from men, according to the opinion of Aristotle' (i. 82). Martin cites Aristotle, *Problemata*, iv. 10 (in a sixteenth-century Latin translation): *Nunc autem cum coniunguntur perfectum* [sc. the man] *imperficitur, et imperfectum* [sc. the woman] *perficitur*.

265 allow] *OED* sense I: 'To praise, commend, sanction, view or receive with approbation'; one of the examples is Sir Thomas More's explanation (1532) that 'Saint Mary Magdaleyn was more alowed of Christ for bestowing that costly oyntment upon his head . . . then if she had solde it'.

270 essence] In its early usage, *essence* is not restricted to spiritual or immaterial qualities, but refers (*OED* sense 2) to 'Something that *is*; an existence, entity'.

296 tralucent] A rare variant of *translucent*, from the Latin *tralucere*, to shine through.

298–9 Made . . . court] Implicit in the description is a comparison with the Milky Way—our galaxy—which classical legend held to be the pathway to the court of Jupiter.

299–310 Hee . . . demands] Musaeus (lines 141–7) afforded some slight suggestion for this passage. His Leander argues that παρθένον οὐκ ἐπέοικεν ὑποδρήσσειν ᾿Αφροδίτῃ, παρθενικαῖς οὐ Κύπρις ἰαίνεται. ('It is not fitting a virgin attend on Aphrodite. Cypris takes no pleasure in virgins.')

301 Dorick musicke] Milton's angelic host moved 'in perfect phalanx to the Dorian mood' (*Paradise Lost*, i. 550), but the usual sense of martial, or military, music seems inappropriate for the festivals of Venus. Marlowe perhaps remembered that the fabulous musician Orpheus was said to have performed in Dorian accents—like the 'swain' in *Lycidas* who 'touched the tender stops of various quills, | With eager thought warbling his Doric lay' (188–9).

303 holy Idiot] *OED* records a specific sense (1b) for *idiot* meaning 'A layman—one who is unlearned in the mysteries of religion.' An illustration is from the panegyric verses in *Coryat's Crudities* (1611): 'he would not | Take orders but remaine an Idiote.'

307 Dietie] *OED* records this as an 'obsolete form of *deity*'.

308 formall puritie] The collocation with 'formall' (*OED* 2c: 'That which is merely in outward form or appearance') suggests that Hero's 'puritie' has an element of the hypocrisy which the Elizabethans associated with religious puritanism. Baldock in *Edward II* is charged with puritanical conduct and dress, but explains that 'I hate such formall toies, | And use them but of meere hypocrisie' (II. i. 44–5).

321 Flint-brested *Pallas*] Pallas Athene (the Roman equivalent is Minerva) was dedicated to perpetual celibacy; the goddess of war as well as of wisdom, she was usually depicted in armour, sometimes bearing the image of the gorgon on her breastplate. The 'strife' with Venus may refer to the competition of the two goddesses, with Juno as a third contender, for the Apple of Discord, awarded on the judgement of Paris.

323–8 Love ... kept] In Musaeus' poem, Leander seeks to seduce his Hero by urging classical precedent; the rather utilitarian arguments used by Marlowe's Leander are influenced by Ovid's lover in the *Amores*. Cf. Marlowe's translations of Elegy I. viii. 53: 'Beauty not exercisde with age is spent,' and II. iii. 14: 'Unmeete is beauty without use to wither.'

331–2 *Heroes* ... jarre] Cf. Musaeus, lines 131–2: καὶ γὰρ ὅτ᾿ ἠιθέοισιν ἀπειλή σῶσι γυναῖκες, | Κυπριδίων ὀάρων αὐτάγγελοί εἰσιν ἀπειλαί. ('For so it is whenever women threaten youths, | Threatening its very self is herald of Love's converse.')

338 Who ... maid] Cf. Musaeus, line 175: τίς σε πυλυπλαγέων ἐπέων ἐδίδαξε κελεύθους; ('Who was it taught you the paths of devious utterance?')

349 golden *Morpheus*] There seems to be no classical precedent for the application of 'golden' to the god of sleep. Marlowe's usage perhaps inspired Dekker's familiar line: 'Art thou poor, yet hast thou golden slumbers' (*Patient Grissil*, c. 1600).

352 *Venus* swannes and sparrowes] Doves, swans, and sparrows were the birds commonly associated with Venus; they were used to draw her chariot through the air.

353 A dwarfish beldame] In the Greek, Hero's companion is simply a maid-

servant (ἀμφιπόλος), although she is clearly older than her mistress since Hero complains of the lack of friends of her own age (οὐδέ μοι ἐγγὺ ἔασιν ὁμήλικετ, lines 191–2). The writer of the nineteenth *Heroides* has a *nutrix* with whom she has a relationship comparable to that between Juliet and her Nurse: the *nutrix* is a confidante, and Hero tells Leander how they talk about him in his absence: *ego cum cara de te nutrice susurro* (line 19).

361 like a planet] The Ptolemaic (geocentric) system explained that the planets, each guided by its own intelligence, had a natural motion from west to east, but they were also moved diurnally from east to west by the force of the primum mobile, and compelled to other orbital irregularities by various other influences (such as the movement of the ninth sphere). Using the same image in 'Goodfriday, 1613. Riding Westward', John Donne elaborates:

> the other Spheares, by being growne
> Subject to forraigne motions, lose their owne,
> And being by others hurried every day,
> Scarce in a yeare their naturall forme obey.

370 above the emptie aire] Martin tried to explain this with the suggestion that 'The sense is probably "above the lower air" as contrasted with the upper air or ether'. But the explanation is unhistorical: the prevalent belief was that there were three, not two, divisions of the sphere of air (located between the spheres of earth and fire). In *1 Tamburlaine* Marlowe refers to 'the triple region of the aire' (IV. ii. 30). Dyce emended 'above' to 'about', which makes a rather more mundane sense of the phrase. I would suggest that Cupid flings the vows so far away that they pass right through the sphere of air.

371 sinowie] In Elegy I. i. 27 Cupid 'bent his sinewy bow upon his knee'. The present spelling is perhaps authorial, and may have given rise to the textual crux in *1 Tamburlaine*, II. i. 25, where early printed texts describe the hero's fingers as 'long and snowy' (O 1–3) or 'long and snowy-white' (O 4).

377–84 Then ... such] This section is a complicated tissue of mythology interwoven with Marlowe's own invention. Cupid's appeal to the Destinies has no counterpart in Musaeus' poem, and the entire episode of Mercury's passion for the 'countrie mayd' (line 388), with the unrequited love of the Fates and the restoration of Saturn, is without classical foundation. The personalities and their attributes, however, have the authenticity of tradition.

377 the Destinies] The three goddesses, also known as the *Parcae*, or the Fates, who ruled over the life of man from birth to death. They are traditionally depicted with spindle, distaff, and knife (or shears): Clotho and Lachesis spun the thread of human life, drawing it out until Atropos cut it short with her 'deadly fatall knife'.

382 Threatning ... glaunce] Marlowe plagiarizes his own *Dido Queene of Carthage*, where the invader Pyrrhus is described as 'Threatning a thousand deaths at every glaunce' (II. i. 231).

386 *Mercury*] The son of Jupiter and Maia, Mercury (Hermes is the Greek equivalent) was employed as messenger and ambassador of the gods. He wore winged sandals on his feet and a winged cap. The 'snakie rod' referred to in line 398 is the caduceus, his attribute as a herald, with which he conducted the souls

of the dead to the infernal regions, and which had certain sleep-inducing powers. Two serpents were entwined at one end of the rod, in the form of two equal semi circles. Mercury was patron of shepherds and travellers, the god of orators (celebrated for his 'smooth speech'), and protector of pickpockets and thieves.

388 *Argus*] Because Argus had one hundred eyes, only two of which were asleep at any one moment, he was ordered by Juno to keep watch on Io, one of Jupiter's loves who had been metamorphosed into a cow. Jupiter sent Mercury to charm all the hundred eyes to sleep, so that he could rescue Io.

402 her fancie to assay] Here 'fancie' seems to have the sense of 'Amorous inclination, love'(*OED* 8b); cf. the lyric 'Tell me where is fancy bred' (*The Merchant of Venice*, III. ii. 63), and the description of the 'imperial vot'ress . . . | In maiden meditation, fancy free' (*A Midsummer Night's Dream*, II. i. 163–4). *OED* defines *assay* in one usage (15b) as 'to assail . . . with love proposals', and cites an example from *The Merry Wives of Windsor*, where Mistress Page is indignant that Falstaff 'dares in this manner assay me' (II. i. 25).

410 Boasting his parentage] In *Metamorphoses*, ii. 880 ff., 'The Bearer of the charmed Rod, the suttle Mercurie' courts Cecrops' daughter, and tries to get admission to her room by claiming that 'My father is the mightie Jove'. Apollo, in his pursuit of Daphne, made the same boast: 'The king of Gods himselfe is knowne my father for to bee' (*Metamorphoses*, i. 630).

411 *Elisium*] The region of the underworld reserved for those specially favoured by the gods.

431 *Nectar*] The enormity of this demand—nectar is the drink of the gods—is made clear by Marston in his crude version of Marlowe's fable (*The Scourge of Villanie* (1598), Satyre II):

> Here *Ioues* lust pander, *Maias* iugling sonne,
> In clownes disguise, doth after milk-maides runne,
> And fore he'le loose his brutish lechery,
> The truls shall tast sweet Nectars surquedry.

43 *Hebe*] Daughter of Juno, Hebe was Ganymede's predecessor as cupbearer to the gods.

438 *Prometheus*] After Jupiter had removed all fire from the earth as a punishment of mankind, Prometheus climbed to the chariot of the sun, and restored fire to the earth. The angry Jupiter condemned Prometheus to be chained to a rock in the Caucasus, where vultures fed on his liver for 30,000 years.

444 Adamantine Destinies] The decrees of the *Parcae* were immutable: even the gods 'could not breake the strong decrees of destinye' (*Metamorphoses*, xv. 877). Marlowe appears to have in mind more than one tradition relating to the *Parcae*. The adjective 'Adamantine' seems to link them with the myth recounted in Plato's *Republic* (x. 616ff.), where the Fates are identified as the Daughters of Necessity. Although slightly different from the *lanificae* (spinning sisters) of the more familiar myth, they still twirl a spindle, which rests on the knees of Necessity and functions as the axis of the geocentric universe. According to Plato, the spindle of Necessity has a shaft of adamant. Milton (perhaps influenced by Marlowe) also seems to combine traditions in *Arcades* when he writes of

those that hold the vital shears,
And turn the adamantine spindle round,
On which the fate of gods and men is wound.   (65–7)

445ff. He wounds . . .] Marston also seized upon this part of Marlowe's fiction in *The Scourge of Villanie*, Satyre V:

Thou subtile *Hermes*, are the Destinies
Enamor'd on thee? then vp mount the skies.
Aduance, depose, doe euen what thou list,
So long as Fates doe grace thy iugling fist.

449 engins] *OED* 4: 'A mechanical contrivance, machine, implement, tool.' Following 'the deadly fatall knife', one would expect these to be the other properties associated with the Fates—the spindle and distaff.

450 Which . . . up-wayd] This is a remarkably difficult line. The home of the Fates was 'ougly *Chaos* den', as Spenser explains in *The Faerie Queene*:

Downe in the bottome of the deepe *Abysse*,
Where *Demogorgon* in dull darknesse pent,
Farre from the view of Gods and heauens blis,
The hideous *Chaos* keepes, their dreadfull dwelling is.   (IV. ii. 47)

Spenser also tells ('An Hymne in Honour of Love') how 'this worlds still mouing mightie masse, | Out of great *Chaos* vgly prison crept', but in his account it is Love who is responsible for the creation; and no 'engins' are referred to. The multiple possible sources and meanings of the line are discussed by A. R. Braunmuller, 'Marlowe's Amorous Fates in *Hero and Leander*', *RES*, NS 113 (February 1978) 56–61.

458 *Stigian* Emperie] The river Styx encircled the region of hell.

465–8 And . . . Ignoraunce] I cannot trace the movement of Marlowe's mind in these four lines. Perhaps, as Professor Peter Nidditch has suggested, Marlowe was vaguely remembering Roger Bacon's account of the procession of philosophy: first revealed to Adam by God, it was preserved after the Fall by Zoroaster, Prometheus, Atlas, Mercury, Apollo, and Aesculapius, until it was reborn in the days of King Solomon and grew to maturity with Aristotle (cf. Paolo Rossi, *Roger Bacon* (English trans., 1968), 69).

468 Ignoraunce] An initial capital seems justified here in view of the capitals of '*Learning*' and '*Povertie*' (lines 465 and 470), which to some small extent personify the abstract qualities.

470–8 That . . . farre] The author of the *Parnassus Plays* (ed. J. B. Leishman, 1949) appears to have been greatly impressed by these lines. In *The Pilgrimage to Parnassus* Consiliodorus dilates upon the subject of academic poverty for the benefit of his sons, vowing that

If I were younge, who nowe am waxen oulde,
Whose yontes youe see are dryde, benumd and coulde,
Though I foreknewe that gold runns to the boore,
Ile be a scholler, though I liue but poore.   (I. i. 61–4)

He has already told the boys to 'scorne each Mydas of this age' (lines 54), and goes on to remark that 'Learning and pouertie will euer kiss' (line 76).

475 *Midas* brood] A Phrygian king, Midas won the gods' favour, and they granted his request that everything he touched should be turned into gold; he regretted his avarice when even the food in his mouth was so changed. On another occasion Midas rashly judged the playing of Pan to be superior to the music of Apollo. He thus became the epitome of the rich philistine. In *The Pilgrimage to Parnassus* Madido appeals to 'anie leaden Mydas, anie mossie patron', promising that in return for 'some prettie sprinkling', he will 'dropp out suche an Encomiu[m] on him, that shall im[m]ortalize him as longe as there is euer a booke binder in England' (II. i. 167ff.). In *The First Part of the Return from Parnassus* Philomusus repeats Marlowe's observation: 'Yea, Midas' brood fore eare must honored be, | While Phoebus followers liue in miserie' (v. iii. 54–5).

477–8 fruitfull ... farre] *The First Part of the Return from Parnassus* provides an expansion of this couplet, and an explanation of the 'regions farre'. Disappointed of their expectations, the scholars Studioso and Philomusus resolve to desert their native land:

> *Studioso.* To Rome or Rhems Ile hye, led on by fate,
>   Where I will ende my dayes, or mend my state.
> *Philomusus.* And soe will I; heard hearted clyme farewell,
>   In regions farr Ile thy vnkindness tell.   (v. iii. 1560–3)

The *Parnassus Plays* seem to have been written for performance at St John's College Cambridge (perhaps during the Christmas festivities of 1598 and 1599). The anonymous author has turned Marlowe's careful vagueness into a threat: Rome and Rheims were asylums for expatriate English Catholics, and were particularly attractive to 'discontent' graduates of Oxford and Cambridge.

496 to traine] The sense is that of *OED* II. 4: 'To draw by art or inducement'. Now described as 'archaic', it is said to be the most frequent early use of the verb, influenced perhaps by *train sb.*[2], whose meanings include 'guile' and 'trickery'.

501 Graces] Marlowe is probably thinking of the three goddesses, otherwise known as the Charites, who were the beautiful daughters of Venus, and her constant attendants. Traditionally they are represented holding hands, as though in a dance.

504 pointed] An aphetic form of 'appointed': presumably the appointment was arranged in the letters.

510 affied] An obsolete form of 'affianced', but the implications are solemn: in *Measure for Measure* Mariana could accept Angelo into her bed because, although the marriage ceremonies had not been completed, she was 'affianc'd this man's wife, as strongly | As words could make up vows' (v. i. 227–8).

516 pais'd] A variant spelling of 'peised' ('weighed').

530 light *Salmacis*] The story is told in *Metamorphoses*, iv. 353ff., of the unrequited passion with which the nymph Salmacis loved Hermaphroditus. The climax is reached when the unsuspecting boy is bathing:

> The prize is won (cride Salmacis aloud) he is mine owne,
> And therewithall in all post haste she having lightly throwne
> Hir garments off, flew to the Poole and cast hir thereinto
> And caught him fast between hir armes, for ought that he could doe.

Shakespeare fused this narrative with the traditional story of Adonis in his *Venus and Adonis*.

535–70 Like ... ever] Occasional slight similarities of phrase or idea suggest that Marlowe is once again recollecting *A Petite Pallace of Pettie His Pleasure*.

Aesops cocke] The fable, attributed without foundation to Aesop, was a commonplace in the sixteenth century: scratching for corn in the farmyard, the cock uncovered a rich jewel—for which, of course, he had no use. The hero in Pettie's story of 'Alexius' wisely refuses to 'change for the worse', and give 'a precious stone for a barley-corn with Aesop's cock' (ii. 148).

536 as a brother with his sister] Salmacis at first asks nothing more from Hermaphroditus: 'the Nymph desirde most instantly but this, | As to his sister brotherly to give hir there a kisse' (*Metamorphoses*, iv. 410–11).

539 creatures wanting sence] Inanimate objects. The same belief is asserted in Donne's 'Nocturnall upon S. Lucies Day': 'Yea plants, yea stones detest, And love.'

540 appetence] *OED* gives 1610 as the date of its first quotation, where the noun is fairly synonymous with 'appetite, desire'. But the sense in Marlowe's poem is more wittily 'metaphysical' than *OED*'s synonyms would suggest, and the account of *appetency* (*sb.* 3) is more appropriate: 'Of things inanimate. Natural tendency, affinity.' This usage is illustrated by a nineteenth-century example: 'The spherical form of the planets has been ascribed by Copernicus to the gravity or mutuall appetency of their parts.'

559 the tree of *Tantalus*] Whenever the imprisoned Tantalus, confined in a pool of water in Hades, reached for the fruit that hung overhead, the tree retired beyond his grasp.

562 gemme] In Pettie's story of 'Sinorix and Camma', the heroine explains that chastity 'ought to be the joy, jewel, and gem of all gentlewomen' (i. 22).

571 Now ... steeds] It was the function of Aurora, goddess of the dawn, to precede the horse-drawn chariot of the sun-god through the skies; but no myth relates her as a lover to either Phoebus Apollo or his father, Hyperion.

589 *Cupids* myrtle] Leander wears the badge of the Ovidian lover: electing to write in the elegiac modes (i.e. to write love poetry), the poet implored (in Marlowe's translation): '*Elegian Muse*, that warblest amorous laies, Girt my shine browe with Sea-banke Mirtle praise' (I. i. 33–4).

597 incorporeall Fame] The nature and progress of Fame, in the sense (*OED* 1) of 'public report ... rumour' were commonplace: the *locus classicus* of poetic description is Virgil's *Aeneid*, iv. 173ff.

600 reeking] steaming (*OED* 2).

602 like ... sphere] The simile is unusual, but 'the reference is surely to the displacement of air from its proper "sphere" in the Ptolemaic cosmology' (Maclure).

604 *Alcides* like] Hercules (grandson of Alcaeus) was renowned for his strength; but no particular myth is referred to here.

607 in a Dyameter] directly (*OED* 4b).

613 an Index to a booke] The comparison of lover and book is worked out in great detail in *Romeo and Juliet*, I. iii. 81ff.

625 a hote prowd horse] The spirited horse as an image of violent sexual desire appears in *Venus and Adonis*:

> Imperiously he leaps, he neighs, he bounds,
> And now his woven girths he breaks assunder;
> The bearing earth with his hard hoof he wounds,
> Whose hollow womb resounds like heaven's thunder;
> The iron bit he crusheth 'tween his teeth,
> Controlling what he was controlled with.   (265–70)

628 Checkes] strikes, hits (*OED* 2).

639 the saphir visag'd god] Neptune, god of the sea and father of Triton; he is traditionally depicted with a trident (the 'triple mace' of line 656), whereas his son blows on a conch-shell (cf. *Dido Queene of Carthage*, I. i. 130: '*Triton* I know hath fild his trumpe with *Troy*').

641 *Ganimed*] Ganymede, described in *Dido Queene of Carthage* as 'that female wanton boy' (I. i. 511), was snatched up to Mount Olympus by Jupiter, and became the god's cupbearer.

663 *Helles*] Having fallen from the golden ram (see note to line 1), Helle was drowned in the straits that now bear her name.

671 threw] Dyce emended Q's reading to 'throw'; and Bowers, approving and accepting the emendation, suggested that 'threw' was either the result of a compositorial *e* | *o* confusion, or else 'a sophistication to bring the word into a false parallel structure with the verb "turnd" of the preceding line'. He pointed out that the structure 'goes back to "would he slide" of line [668]' with 'would' being understood before all the succeeding verbs (except 'turnd'). The argument is convincing; but I think it equally possible that Marlowe, influenced by 'turnd', could have momentarily forgotten or neglected his own structure.

679ff. Playd ...] Neptune's pastoral narrative recalls the entertainment planned by Gaveston in *Edward II* (I. i. 58ff.) which was to include 'men like Satyres grazing on the lawnes'.

679 so faire and kind] Q1–8; so lovely fair and kind, Q9, 10; so faire and so kind, Brydges, Bowers. As the collation shows, attempts have been made since 1629 (Q9) to regularize this line. The editor of Q9 certainly had no authority for his reading, but at least the 'lovely', by adding another iambic foot, gives rhythmic uniformity with the poem's pentameters. The monosyllabic 'so', which was introduced by Sir Egerton Brydges in his edition (1815), fails to perfect a pentameter, and, for the regular iambic rhythm, substitutes a dactyllic line which is uncomfortable to read either as three dactyls (stressing 'and'), or as two dactyls with one anapaest (where the emphasis falls on 'kind').

682 Least ... brinke] This was the supposed fate of Hylas, the beautiful boy who accompanied Hercules on the Argonauts' expedition (cf. Apollodorus, *The Library*, I. ix. 19: 'Hylas ... a minion of Hercules, had been sent to draw water

and was ravished away by nymphs on account of his beauty.') In *Edward II* the king measures his own grief for the loss of his favourite, Gaveston, by reference to this fable: 'Not *Hilas* was more mourned of *Hercules*, | Then thou hast beene of me since thy exile' (I. i. 144–5).

684 Fawnes] The fauni—rural deities who were half man, half goat—seem to have been identical with the Greek satyrs.

687 *Thetis* glassie bower] Marlowe has practised forms of this trope before. In *Dido Queene of Carthage* Aeneas cannot fulfil his destiny until 'he hath furrowed *Neptunes* glassie fieldes' (IV. iii. 11); and in *2 Tamburlaine* the hero prophesies that 'The Sun unable to sustaine the sight, | Shall hide his head in *Thetis* watery lap' (I. iii. 168–9). Thetis was a minor sea-goddess.

689 O ... wings] As Maclure points out, Marlowe seems to be recalling Leander's cry in *Heroides*, xviii. 49: *nunc daret audaces utinam mihi Daedalus alas* ('Now would that Daedalus would give me his daring wings').

699–702 The greefe ... hinds] Such a notion was popular in Neoplatonic thought; it is expressed by Spenser in his 'Hymne in Honour of Beautie':

> Therefore where ever that thou doest behold
> A comely corpse, with beautie faire endewed,
> Know this for certaine, that the same doth hold
> A beauteous soule, with faire conditions thewed,
> Fit to receive the seede of vertue strewed.
> For all that faire is, is by nature good;
> That is a signe to know the gentle blood.

709–10 'Tis ... failes] The sentiment is similar to that of the bawd Dipsas who tries (Elegy I. viii. 61–2) to persuade her mistress: 'Let *Homer* yeeld to such as presents bring, | (Trust me) to give, it is a witty thing.'

718 crooked Dolphin] The adjective was prompted by the stock epithet used by Leander (*Heroides*, xviii. 131) when he writes of the *curvi ... delphines*. It was thought that dolphins were charmed by the human voice: when the bard Arian was in danger of drowning, one of the dolphins who had been attracted by his singing bore him to land on its back.

739–40 like ... clay] There is a hidden allusion here to the Prometheus story. In the earliest mythology, Prometheus is a benefactor of mankind: in later versions, he is its creator. Ovid (*Metamorphoses*, i. 95ff.) seems to stand somewhere between the two, but Apollodorus gives a succinct account of the later myth: 'Prometheus moulded men out of water and earth and gave them also fire which, unknown to Zeus, he had hidden in a stalk of fennel' (*The Library*, I. vii. 1). The original 'fire from heaven fet' was necessary to give life to the clay. Shakespeare uses the same version of the myth in *Othello*, when, before murdering Desdemona, Othello meditates:

> Put out the light, and then put out the light:
> If I quench thee, thou flaming minister,
> I can again thy former light restore,
> Should I repent me; but once put out thy light,
> Thou cunning'st pattern of excelling nature,

I know not where is that Promethean heat
That can thy light relume.   (v. ii. 7–13)

742 drerie] *OED* 1: 'Gory, bloody'; or 2: 'Cruel'. The derivation is from the
Old English *dreori3*, and *OED* instances *The Faerie Queene*, 1. vi. 45: 'With their
drery wounds, and bloody gore'.

745 Like chast *Diana*] The virgin goddess Diana was bathing in a spring when
Actaeon, the famous hunter, caught sight of her. The story is recounted in *Metamorphoses*, iii; and the spectacle was part of Gaveston's projected entertainment
for the king: 'a lovelie boy in *Dians* shape ... | Shall bathe him in a spring, and
there hard by, | One like *Actaeon* peeping through the grove' (*Edward II*, 1. i.
61ff.).

754 the *Harpey*] The harpies were monstrous winged creatures with the faces
of women and the bodies of vultures who destroyed all that they preyed on. Maclure, praising the 'daring' of Marlowe's image, suggests *Aeneid*, iii. 225–8, as a
source for the notion: here the harpies plunder the banquet set for Aeneas and his
comrades. Maclure comments: 'Hero may be said to be withdrawing the banquet
of herself.' The harpies are described more horrifically by Apollodorus: 'These
were winged female creatures, and when a table was laid ... they flew down from
the sky and snatched up most of the victuals, and what little they left stank so that
nobody could touch it' (*The Library*, 1. ix. 21).

759–60 (a globe ... blis)] The geography of amatory exploration is worked out
more fully in Donne's elegy 'Love's Progress'.

761 with *Sysiphus*] The actual crime of Sisyphus is in some doubt, but he was
eternally punished in Hades by being condemned to roll a huge stone to the top of
a mountain; when the stone reached the summit, it immediately rolled down
again.

763–74 Wherein ... wing] Commonsense dictates that these lines should be
placed in the sequence first adopted by Tucker Brooke: in all early quartos they
are printed after the present line 784.

771–4 Love ... wing] A similar observation is made by a very different writer,
Samuel Richardson. In *The History of Clarissa Harlowe* (1753–4), Mr Lovelace
writes to his friend John Bedford, discussing the planned seduction of Clarissa:
'There may possibly be some *cruelty* necessary: but there may be *consent in struggle*: there may be *yielding in resistance* .... We begin, when boys, with birds; and
when grown up, so on to women; and both perhaps, in turn, experience our
sportive cruelty' (Vol. II, Letter XCIII).

775–6 (like that ... world)] In *Metamorphoses*, i, Ovid describes the original
Chaos, 'a huge rude heape' where

No kinde of thing had proper shape, but ech confounded other.
For in one selfesame bodie strove the hote and colde togither,
The moist with drie, the soft with hard, the light with things of weight.
This strife did God and Nature breake, and set in order streight.   (17–20)

781 Theban *Hercules*] Several heroes went by the name of 'Hercules', but the
'Theban' was the most famous; he was said to be the son of Jupiter and Alcmena,
wife to the King of Thebes.

782 The orchard of Th'*esperides*] The Hesperides (daughters of Hesperus) were appointed to guard the golden apples which Juno gave to Jupiter on their wedding-day. The apples (and the garden) were protected by a dragon that never slept; and it was one of the labours of Hercules to procure three of the apples.

789 like *Mars* and *Ericine*] Ovid tells how Mars and Venus (called 'Erycene' after her shrine on Mt Eryx) were discovered by Apollo—the sun—after a night of love, and exposed to the ridicule of the gods as they lay enmeshed in a net forged by Vulcan (see lines 151–2n.).

793 so charily she kept] In Pettie's 'Sinorix and Camma' the heroine muses on 'that chastity which I seek so charily to keep' (i. 31).

804 glympse] A form of *glimpse* (*OED v.* 1 *intr.*): 'To shine faintly or intermittently, to glimmer'. Cf. Elegy 1. v. 3–6:

> One window shut, the other open stood,
> Which gave such light, as twincles in a wood,
> Like twilight glimps at setting of the Sunne,
> Or night being past, and yet not day begunne.

810 *Dis*] Plutus, god of wealth; he is also god of the underworld, in the sense that the earth is the wealth-giver ($\pi\lambda\hat{o}\hat{v}\tau os$), and this permits the joke in *The Jew of Malta* when Ithamore refers to '*Dis* above' (IV. ii. 97).

811 *Appollos* golden harpe] Apollo was both sun-god and patron of music; he was often depicted with lyre in hand.

813 *Hesperus*] The planet Venus, the first heavenly body to be seen after sunset and variously known as 'Hesper' and 'Vesper'; it is also the morning-star, when it is properly called 'Phosphor' or 'Lucifer' (see my Note 'Hesper | Vesper—and Phosphor' in *Notes and Queries*, xxvii. 4 (August 1980), 318–19). At this point in his poem Marlowe seems to have returned to *Heroides* xviii: *Iamque fugatura Tithoni coniuge noctem | praevius Aurorae Lucifer ortus erat* (111–12).

818 Dang'd] An acceptable form of the past tense of *ding* (*OED* 4: 'To knock, dash, or violently drive'). The editorial emendation of Q2 is unnecessary.

her loathsome carriage] In Elegy 1. xiii. 38 the unwelcome dawn drives a 'hatefull carriage'.

ACCIDENTAL EMENDATIONS

II. x
    6 loveliest] love-liest   15 alone] a lone

II. xiv
    6 tormented.] ~,   29 *Colchis*] *Cholcis*

II. xv
    16 cleaves,] ~.   19 hit,] ~.

II. xviii
    14 deseignes,] ~.   26 harpe.] ~,   36 mid-alarmes] mid∧alarmes
39 incline] inclnie

II. xix
    11 hale] haole   17 shee,] ~∧   21 threshold] thre-shold

III. i
    1 stands] ~,   2 god head] good head   63 and] &

III. ii
    32 them.] ~∧   63 hang downe] ~-~   66 chariot-horses] ~∧~

III. iv
    38 beleeves,] ~.   45 friends thy] ~,~

III. v
    84 undetected.] ~:

III. vi
    25 night,] ~.   79 bloud] bould

II. viii
    3 *Elegia*] *Eliga*   52 unkeembd] unkeembe   53 kisses] ~,
55 departing,] ~∧   lov'd] ~,

III. ix
    10 their meate] there meate   14 broake.] ~∧

III. xii
    7 clouded,] ~∧   17 back.] ~∧   21 darts,] ~∧

III. xiv
    title *Venerem*] *venerem*   2 set,] ~∧   3 framde,] ~∧
4 defamde).] ~ ~∧   14 praise.] ~∧

Substantive Variants in the Elegies common to
BINDLEY, ISHAM, *and* MASON

Elegy	Line	Gill	Bindley	Isham	Mason
I. i	4	thy	the	—	—
	5	upreard	—	—	prepar'd
	5	meant	meane	meane	—
	8	tooke	take	take	—
	19	*Tempe*	—	—	*Temple*
	21	workes	worke	worke	—
	22	Love	I	I	—
	22	numbers	number	number	—
I. ii	1	is soft	~ so ~	—	—
	7	slender	tēder	—	—
	9	strugling	striving	striving	—
	12	shakt	—	—	slackt
	26	with thy hand	~ ^ ~	—	—
	28	triumph	triumphes	triumphes	—
	36	have	—	hath	—
	38	thine	thy	thy	—
	44	wounds	wordes	—	—
	45	thine	thy	thy	—
	51	bands	handes	—	—
I. iii	1	her	—	—	he
	2	may never hate	~ ^ ~	—	—
	3	aske	crave	—	—
	4	*Love*	love	Love	*Jove*
	6	love with	~ thee ~	—	—
	7	make me	cause me to be	—	—
	9	land	lands	lands	—
	13	gives	give	give	—
	18	ere	or	or	—
	18	shall	shalt	shalt	—
	22	Swanne	Bull	Bull	—
	22	*Jove*	love	Jove	—
I. v	10	tresses	trells	—	—
	12	wooers	lovers	lovers	—
	12	sped	spread	spread	—
	23	lik'd	pleasde	pleasde	—
	24	naked	faire white	fair white	—
	25	tirde	tyrde	tyrde	tride
I. xiii	1	ore	on	on	—
	14	And . . . fight.	[*line om.*]	—	—
	21	client hate	~ both do ~	~ both do ~	—

Elegy	Line	Gill	Bindley	Isham	Mason
	24	setst	seest	—	—
	25	All	This	This	—
	37	leavest	leav'st	leav'st	—
	39	heldst	hadst	hadst	—
	41	Doest punish	Punnish ye	Punnish ye	—
	43	with	and	—	—
	47	chid	chide	—	chide
I. xv	2	termst	tearmes	tearmes	—
	2	my	our	our	—
	2	dustie	—	—	rustie
	8	may	might	might	—
	10	into	to the	to the	—
	10	doth	shall	shall	—
	13–14	The . . . weake	[lines om.]	[lines om.]	—
	26	conquered	conquering	conquering	—
	32	shal nere decay	~ ∧ ~	—	—
	33	To verse let Kings give place	Let Kings give place to verse	Let Kings give place to verse	—
	34	And	To	To	—
	41	rakes	rocks	racks	—
II. iv	8	Am	And	And	—
	10	make	makes	makes	—
	12	glance	glas	glasse	—
	14	would	should	should	—
	14	nimble	quick	—	—
	14	shees	she is	—	—
	22	lie	be	—	—
	28	those hands	~ nimble ~	—	—
	29	her	she	she	—
	31	with all	withall	withall	—
	35	say	speak	speak	—
	37–40	I . . . fellowe.	[lines om.]	[lines om.]	—
	43	Amber	Yellow	Yellow	—
II. x	8	And this	This	This	—
	13	woods	—	—	wood
	14	vast deepe	deep vast	deep vast	—
	29	slayes	—	—	layes
	31	souldiours chase their	souldier chase his	souldier chase his	—
	32	their	his	his	—
	36	set	let	—	—
III. vi	3	lov'd not	lovede her not	—	—

Elegy	Line	Gill	Bindley	Isham	Mason
	8	Her armes farre whiter then	That were as white as is	That were as white as is	—
	11	sir	—	—	sire
	16	I	Io	Io	—
	18	When	Seeing	Seeing	—
	19	that	and	and	—
	26	we had	had we	had we	—
	30	And	Had	—	—
	31	make	—	makes	—
	37	adde	and	—	—
	38	vigour	rigor	—	—
	40	wore	—	—	more
	46	The	This	This	—
	47	receiv'd	restored	—	—
	47	in I get	and in I got	and in I got	—
	49	to refuse	and refusde	and refusde	—
	56	and	nor	nor	—
	58	loved	—	—	moved
	60	nor	ne	—	—
	61	eares	yeres	yeares	eare
	70	Seeing thou	~ now ~	~ now ~	—
	72	sore losse	great hurt	—	—
	76	droupt	dropt	—	—
	84	on	in	in	—
III. xiii	2	know	wit	—	—
	7	nights	night	night	—
	7	pranckes	sports	—	—
	8	And	Or	Or	—
	16	folke	people	—	—
	18	tricks	toyes	—	—
	22	yours ever mine	mine ever yours	mine ever yours	—
	38	thorough	through	through	—
	40	dead	dying	dying	—
	43	deed	deedes	—	—
	45	deny	yeeld not	yeeld not	—
	47	palme	garland	garland	—

* A straight dash indicates that the reading corresponds with Gill.

LUCANS FIRST BOOKE

3 launcht,] ~∧ Q   4 uprooted,] ~∧ Q   5 force] ~: Q
8 *Romans*] Romans Q   10 *Babilon*] Babilon Q   18 *Euxin*] Euxin Q
21 *Roome*] Roome Q   24 rear'd] reaer'd *L, F, H*; reafer'd *B*
44 Room] Room Q   50 chang'd;] ~, Q   55 *Roome*] Roome Q
beams;] beams∧ Q   72 *Roome*] Roome Q   82 strong] ~. Q
89 earth the] ~, ~ Q   ayre the] ~, ~ Q   95 *Roomes*] Roomes Q
106 *Roman*] Roman Q   109 *Roome*] Roome Q   117 down,] ~. Q
121 *Pompey*)... dim] ~∧ ... ~) Q   122 *France*] France Q
123 wracke.] ~∧ Q   149 gods,] ~∧Q   167 *Roomes*] Roomes Q
168 Ransackt] Ransanckt Q   188 *Roome*] Roome Q   190 Turret-
bearing] ~, ~ Q   193 *Romans*] Romans Q   198 *Roomes*] Roomes Q
201 *Roome*] Roome Q   205 *Roome*] Roome Q   *Roomes*] Roomes Q
226 *Italy* [Italy Q   246 *Roomes*] Roomes Q   250 *France*] France Q
258 *Roome*] Roome Q   269 *Roome*] Roome Q   276 will,] ~. Q
277 *France*] France Q   281 hence,] ~∧ Q   282 hurts] ~∧ Q
283 *France*] France Q   *Roome*] Roome Q   287 *Roome*] Roome Q
304 *Alpes*] Alpes Q   *Roome*] Roome Q   308 *France*] France Q
310 *Roome*] Roome Q   348 Spread] Spead Q   352 *Roome*] Roome Q
355 Room] Room Q   359 *Romaine*] Romaine Q   360 *Rooms*] Rooms Q
381 *Jove*; [~, Q   382 streames,] ~; Q   387 *Roome*] Roome Q
395 *France*] France Q   396 *Roome*] Roome Q   404 boats] bloats Q
407 wind,] ~; Q   416 deepe,)] ~∧∧ Q   419 assignes] ~, Q
425 *Rhene and Leuca*,] ~, ~ ~∧ Q   428 *Averni* too,] ~, ~∧ Q
themselves] ~; Q   477 purpose,] ~; Q   495 *Roome*] Roome Q
506 *Roome*] Roome Q   509 *Roome*] Roome Q   516 in] iu Q
517 *Roome*] Roome Q   519 fled.] ~, Q   543 unbarred] ~; Q
58 *Rome*] Rome Q   572 fiend] ~; Q   604 *Roome*] Roome Q
643 *Rome*] Rome Q   644 plague;] ~? Q   667 furious] firious Q
669 *Rome*] Rome Q   673 *Romans*] Romans Q   681 *Rome*] Rome Q
689 *Rome*] Rome Q   691 againe] ~; Q

DIDO QUEENE OF CARTHAGE

I. i
111 Stygian] stygian Q   132 *Cimodoce*] Cimodoae Q   210 Punick]
punick Q   248SD *Exeunt*] Exit Q

I. ii
SD Cloanthus] *Cloanthes* Q

II. i
77–8 *as one line* Q   239 *Neoptolemus.*] ~, Q   322 *Cithereas*]
Citheidas Q

III. iii
35, 40 (prefix) *Cupid*] *Asca* Q   62SD *manet*] *manent* Q

III. iv
52 Delian] delian Q

IV. i
  15 (prefix) Çupid] *Asca Q*

IV. iv
  67 Punicke] punicke *Q*   124 (prefix) [*Lord*]] *om. Q*   165SD *Exeunt*] *Exit Q*

V. i
  45 dandlest] danlest *Q*   109 farewell.] ~, *Q*   100 (prefix) *Dido*] *prefixing line* 111 *Q*   110 hence,] ~. *Q*   187 obdurate] abdurate *Q* 224SD *anticipated at line* 223 *Q*   274–5 *as one line Q*   320–1 *as one line Q*

HERO AND LEANDER

  57 allur'd] *Q3*; allu'rd *Q1–2*   72 eies,] ~ ∧ *Qq*   134 spye.] ~, *Qq* 169 stript,] ~ ∧ *Qq*   184 *dissembled*.] *Q4*; ~ ∧ *Q1–3*   186 stands.] *Q5*; ~ ∧ *Q1–4*   191 day.)] *Q8*; ~ ∧) *Q1–5*; ~,) *Q6–7*   222 Loves] *Q8*; loves *Q1–7*   320 done.] *Q8*; ~ ∧ *Q1–7*   329 arguments] *Q2*; argumsnts *Q1*   330 before.] ~, *Qq*   336 thought] *Q2*; rhought *Q1* 377 Destinies] *Q3*; destinies *Q1–2*   442 *Jove*] *Q2*; Jove *Q1*   452 *Jove*] *Q2*; Jove *Q1*   501 Graces] graces *Qq*   516 pais'd.)] ~ ∧) *Qq* 650 abode.] *Q4*; ~, *Q1–3*   652 *Jove*] *Q3*; Jove *Q1–2*   659 swim,] ~. *Q1–6*; ~: *Q7–10*   676 I.] *Q5*; ~, *Q1–4*   774 wing,] ~. *Qq* 782 Th'*esperides*,] Th'*esperides*. *Qq*   788 night,] *Q8*; ~. *Q1–7*